LAFAYETTE

His Extraordinary Life and Legacy

Samuel F.B. Morse: *Lafayette*, 1824-1925. City Hall, New York City

Lafayette

His Extraordinary Life and Legacy

Donald Miller

iUniverse®

LAFAYETTE: HIS EXTRAORDINARY LIFE AND LEGACY

iUniverse books may be ordered through booksellers or by contacting:

iUniverse
1663 Liberty Drive
Bloomington, IN 47403
www.iuniverse.com
1-800-Authors (1-800-288-4677)

ISBN: 978-1-4917-5847-2 (sc)
ISBN: 978-1-4917-5998-1 (hc)
ISBN: 978-1-4917-5997-4 (e)

Library of Congress Control Number: 2015903012

Print information available on the last page.

iUniverse rev. date: 7/31/2015

Front cover painting from: Samuel F. B. Morse: Lafayette, *1824-1825. City Hall, New York City, N.Y.*

Donald Miller
731 Provincetown Drive
Naples FL 34104-8746

Contents

Books by Donald Miller

Robert Vickrey's Nun Paintings: Creatures of the Spirit
Tiffany Desk Treasures: A Collector's Guide, with George A. Kemeny
Aaronel: The Art of Aaronel De Roy Gruber
The Architecture of Benno Janssen
Malcolm Parcell: Wizard of Moon Lorn
Organic Vision: The Architecture of Peter Berndtson, with Aaron Sheon

---

Men differ more than breeds of dogs.
— Michel de Montaigne

Acknowledgments

I am grateful to Jacques, Comte de Trentinian, historian and vice-president-general of the French branch of the National Society of the Sons of the American Revolution, who volunteered his expertise on the manuscript. I am also indebted to the *Fondation Josée et René de Chambrun,* which administers the Chateau de La Grange-Bléneau and its secretary I. Sophie Grivet. I have also been helped by Arnaud Meunier du Houssoy; Michel and Genevieve Aubert La Fayette, of Chateau de Vollore, Volloreville; William Kirchner, past president, the American Friends of Lafayette; Daniel Jouve, co-author of *Paris: Birthplace of the U.S.A.*; Boilly Philippe, Parc de St.-Cloud; and Chateau Musée Lafayette, Chavaniac-Lafayette.

My late friend Leon F. Miller winnowed hundreds of Internet references. Assistance came from historian Thomas Fleming; Diane Wyndham Shaw, director, Skillman Library, Lafayette College; Dr. Robert Rhodes Crout, Lafayette historian and past president, the American Friends of Lafayette; Jean-Pierre Collet, former honorary French consul; Ellen McCallister Clark, library director, and Emily L. Schulz, deputy director and curator, The Society of the Cincinnati; and Patrick B. Stevens, Carl A. Kroch Library, Cornell University;

George Lupone and staff, French-American Collections, Cleveland State University; the staff of Monticello; Hugh MacDougall of the James Fenimore Cooper Society; G. William Thomas, president, James Monroe Memorial Foundation, and member Robert Selle; Albert Knute Oberst, former vice president, the American Friends of Lafayette; historian Bob Arnebeck; Eric Pominville, National Park Service; Dr. Jean-Pierre Cap; and Michel and Suzanne Dagnaud. I am thankful to Wikipedia, rich in French 18th century articles, which saved me countless hours. I profoundly appreciate the patience and encouragement of my artist wife Bette W. Miller.

For Bette

Introduction

This is the most complete biography in English of an aristocrat who advanced personal freedoms for all. In many ways, Lafayette's long life in Europe after voluntary service in the American Revolution is more revealing than the heroism of a young father longing to shed blood for American independence. My interest in him is to provide more knowledge of Lafayette's life.

His American success helped Lafayette become the strongman of France in the years leading to the French Revolution. As founding commander general of the Paris National Guard, he sought no dictatorial power which he could have had while seeking unification of France under Louis XVI.

Becoming a politician was Lafayette's means of improving the life of every Frenchman, reaching its zenith in his writing *The Declaration of the Rights of Man and Citizen.* For the first time in European history the document enumerated the nature-given, not god-given, privileges to which all humans are entitled. This has become to the present day the standard to which oppressed people aspire. Like the founding fathers of the United States, Lafayette belongs to all nations, although his fame appears to have dimmed since his spirit was saluted at his grave in World War I.

One of the curiosities of Lafayette's long life is why on at least three occasions he avoided accepting France's highest office since he had long participated in public life. My theory is that, although he denounced aristocrisy, his mind was aristocratic from the days even before his huge family inheritances. Lafayette learned from public office that an elected politician is the public's servant. But he always wished to express his own thoughts and choose his own way.

Lafayette not only participated in three revolutions. After languishing in vile prisons for five years, he returned unbidden to France to find Napoleon Bonaparte, who had saved him from prison, misdirecting the First Republic. It was Lafayette who rose to deny the emperor's return after Waterloo yet counseled him on escaping to the United States. Lafayette then found cunning and subversive ways to deal with two kings he knew well from his youth at Versailles who restricted freedoms during the severely autocratic Bourbon Restoration. Elected four times to the Chamber of Deputies as a liberal, Lafayette agitated publicly and secretly during the repressive reigns of brothers Louis XVIII and Charles X. He sought to limit their powers while he supported independence for foreign freedom-fighters.

Meet Comte de Broglie-Ruffec, former member of Louis XV's secret spy system who was Lafayette's commandant at Metz. Broglie-Ruffec planned the purchase of the ship Lafayette first sailed to America on, filling the hold with cannons and chose the officers who helped win the colonists' freedom from Great Britain. Broglie-Ruffec wrote to his protégé Baron Jean de Kalb he dreamed of replacing Washington as commander of the Continental Army and then becoming king of the young republic. He thirsted to outshine his older royalist brother who, had he acted faster, might have prevented the attack on the Bastille.

Historians have said Lafayette was naive for wanting to attack Britain's Caribbean islands. But his cousin, Comte de Bouillé, governor of French holdings in the West Indies, welcomed Lafayette to the war. Later, Bouillé, denouncing Lafayette's desire for a constitutional monarchy, devised the plot for the royal family to flee France. On ordering the royals' return to Paris, Lafayette became their virtual captor. Later, while he headed the French Army of the North against invading Prussia and Austria, bloodthirsty Jacobins charged Lafayette with treason. On escaping into exile and imprisonment, Lafayette's ideas on individual freedom only deepened.

This book abounds in other vivid characters: Adrienne Lafayette, who loved her husband so much she and their two daughters joined him in prison; George Washington, whom Lafayette regarded as his wise adoptive father; Louis XVI, who loved the French Navy but never went to sea; Beaumarchais, who shipped supplies to the colonists while writing successful plays; Alexander Hamilton, brilliant but erratic, who died on the dueling field that had claimed his son; Thomas Jefferson, who as president chided Lafayette for refusing to become governor of the Louisiana Territory.

Here are Aaron Burr and his turncoat partner General James Wilkinson, who wanted to create a country from the Louisiana Territory and Mexico; Justus-Erich Bollmann, who failed to rescue Lafayette from prison and later became Burr's secret agent; President James Monroe, who, having helped the Lafayettes on several occasions, arranged with Congress for his triumphal tour of the United States; President John Quincy Adams, who admired Lafayette but hated his Masonic friends; and James Armistead Lafayette, Lafayette's black counterspy who helped defeat Lord Cornwallis.

Returning to the United States forty-one years after its independence as "the nation's guest," Lafayette was feted in twenty-four states over eleven months and eight days as no one has ever been. Americans in the mid-1820s wanted to meet "our Marquis" — Marie Joseph Paul Yves Roch Gilbert du Motier de Lafayette — last living major general and hero of the American War of Independence. Follow Lafayette's adventures on his triumphal tour that his press secretary recorded day by day. This book also reveals an irony that in 1935 Pierre Laval, later Nazi collaborationist premier of France, gave money to save the champion of liberty's beloved chateau from ruin.

The book concludes with events long after Lafayette's time: the discovery of his long-lost letters and documents walled up in his chateau and recent auctions setting world records for objects "the hero of two worlds" owned, now returned to his chateau. Completing the biography is a chart of American sites named for Lafayette or La Grange, his home, showing his continuing impact on America.

D.M.

PART ONE: Adventure

ONE: PROMISE OF FAME

The forest was dangerous. In the mountains of south central France, rumors fed fears of werewolves. Lafayette, a hearty boy of eight with gray-blue eyes and reddish brown hair, knew he descended from medieval knights. He would lead his young friends, pretending to fight the British with wooden swords, in slaying the beast of Gevaudon.

This large she-wolf had killed at least sixty-eight children, twenty-five women and six men. But before the boy with his father's musket could find it, a hunter slew the animal and sent it to Louis XV at Versailles, ending national fears. Englishman Horace Walpole saw the huge animal covered by a sheet in the queen's antechamber.

Life at Chateau de Chavaniac in the Province of Auvergne centered on our Lafayette: Marie Joseph Paul Yves Roch Gilbert du Motier de La Fayette. Aware early of being heir to Chavaniac, Gilbert, as he was called, loved his years there, thrilled by tales of his ancestors and his future as a French officer.

In a jacket, waistcoat, breeches, buckled shoes and tricorn hat, the boy loved seeing farmers and townfolk bow as his *grand-maman* Catherine de La Fayette and he rode in her carriage over the countryside, inspecting her sparse lands or visiting relatives and friends' chateaus. She earned peasants' gratitude by taking food from her fields for her family and giving the rest to them. Peasants plowed fields with their feet in rags. They could not afford shoes or own land but were heavily taxed while nobles paid none. Lafayette learned from Catherine: he would respect all people on merit and champion the oppressed.

The name Lafayette — or De La Fayette as it was before the general dropped the aristocratic *de* (although he, his son and grandson used it on official papers) — is of ancient origin. It came from an estate in Auvergne, where an abandoned Roman garrison was documented as *Villa Faya* about 1000 A.D. Today, the spelling *La Fayette* is his registered name in Europe while *Lafayette*, as Lafayette spelled it, using *LF* as a monogram, prevails in the United States. Motier, an original family name without literal meaning, became Motier de La Fayette.[1]

Young Lafayette's father — Michel Louis Christophe Roch Gilbert du Motier de La Fayette (Gilbert IV) — inherited the title from an older childless brother who died in war. Gilbert IV became Marquis de La Fayette, Baron de Vissac, Seigneur de Siaugues-Saint-Romain *et* Fix. Also a soldier, he pursued his intended wife Marie Louise Céleste Julie de La Rivière sight unseen until shortly before their arranged marriage in May 1754. De La Rivière influence at court helped Gilbert IV, twenty-two, quickly become a colonel and member of the esteemed Order of St. Louis.

At twenty, Julie, pretty and pale, had grown up in a convent. Her grandfather Charles Ives Thibault, Comte de La Rivière (1662-1771) — he lived to be 108 — was a highly decorated lieutenant in the French army. His son and Julie's father, Joseph Ives de La Rivière, called Comte de Corlay and Marquis de La Rivière (1695-1770), was a very rich agent for British nobility but was miserly and denied a dowry. The bridegroom, hoping his father-in-law's fortune would come to him, did not argue. Julie told her husband she would be content in Chavaniac but after three years there she returned to her family's gilded suite in Paris' Luxembourg Palace. When Louis XIV and his grandson Louis XV found Versailles to their taste, they had allowed noble families to occupy the Luxembourg. Julie knew Paris' distance from Chavaniac was then a two-week carriage ride on rough roads and found country life dull.

She gave birth there on September 6, 1757 to the fifth Gilbert. His father, traveling from Paris in 1758 to see his new family, had been born in the same turret room. The stone chateau, begun as a manor-fortress in the fourteenth century and burned in the seventeenth, brooded over southwestern Auvergne, a land of forests, ancient farms, dark mountains and volcanoes.[2] The chateau's façade of the early 1700's looks on a terrace to the north and a lake to the west. Made of dark boulders once covered in white stucco, the building rises between two cylindrical towers under slant-roofed cupolas. For Julie, the nearby hamlet of sixty dwellings was not only rustic but also the domain of a strong mother-in-law and her two daughters.[3]

North façade of Chateau de Chavaniac, Lafayette's birthplace.
Author photograph, 2002.

But the marquise saw a brilliant future for her son. He was christened in Saint Roch Church, down the hill in the village. "I was baptized like a Spaniard with the name of every conceivable saint who might offer me more protection in battle," he recalled.[4] When he was almost two, his father was killed in battle during the Seven Years War, the world's first global combat. Gilbert IV followed the family tradition. He married higher than his station, sired an heir and returned to the army where, for La Fayettes, early death was customary. It came at twenty-seven in the Battle of Minden near Hanover, Westphalia, claiming 13,000 soldiers.

Fighting the English on August 1, 1759, Gilbert IV rushed to replace a fallen comrade on an exposed hill and died in cannon fire.

Prussia and Austria's desire for Silesia grew into a coalition of France, Austria, Russia, Sweden and Saxony against Prussia's Frederick the Great and Britain.[5] With Austria's defeat, France and Russia quit the war, but Britain and France expanded their conflict, each wanting North America and India. Britain won both. The war is called the French and Indian War in America. Loss of Canada and territories filled Gallic hearts with a desire for revenge. Julie, spending winters with relatives in Paris and Versailles, was presented to Louis XV in 1762. Minden's news devastated her. She left young Lafayette with his loving grandmother and aunts and moved to Paris, seeking connections for her son.

"My mother was a woman of lively temperament," Lafayette wrote, "who once had a liking for the frivolous, but after her husband's death plunged into religion with all the strength of her character. Although she loved me devotedly, it would never have occurred to her to take me away from my grandmother for whom she had a deep reverence."[6]

His grandmother, Marie Catherine de Suat de Chavaniac de la Fayette, was the good and wise widow of Ēdouard du Motier de La Fayette, Gilbert IV's father. First in the second line to the title, he died in battle in 1740. Catherine, spartan compared to the La Rivières, had urged her son to marry Julie. La Fayette territory once extended almost 100 miles wide and two or more days north to Clermont-Ferrand, Auvergne's capital. *Auvergnats* traveled miles to seek Catherine's advice. Her daughters were: Marguerite Madeleine du Motier de La Fayette, a spinster, and Louise Charlotte de la Fayette de Guérin, Baronesse de Montialoux. When Gilbert was five, she came as a widow to live at the chateau.[7] Gilbert loved Charlotte's daughter, Marie, a year younger than he, like a sister. Later the wife of the Marquis d'Abos de Benanville, of Lozère, southern France, she died in childbirth at twenty during Lafayette's first American voyage.

TWO: INDEPENDENT SPIRIT

Catherine hired a Jesuit priest as her grandson's first tutor but he left when France suppressed the Society of Jesus for its excessive political power in 1761. Lafayette found a second tutor, Abbé Fayon, a village priest, prejudiced and "lacking in those qualities which a man who is destined to live in the great world should have," he would later write in his *Mémoires*. "But a child's real education, I think, comes from the feelings and attitudes of the family in which he grows up, and in this respect no one was ever more happily placed than I. It was but natural that I should hear much talk of war and glory among close relatives whose minds were ever filled with memories and regrets and a profound veneration for my father's memory."

Besides basic study, the abbé told of Vercingetorix, defender of Gaul and Auvergne against the Romans in 52 A.D. and a hero to the boy. "From the time I was eight," Lafayette wrote, "I longed for glory. I remember nothing of my childhood more than my fervor for tales of glory and my plans to travel the world in quest of fame."[1] His twenty-eight-year-old cousin, François Claude Amour, Marquis de Bouillé (1739-1800), lived in Chateau de Cluzel, St. Eble, Haute-Loire.[2] A distinguished general with battles to his credit, he wrote:

"I spent some days [at Chavaniac] and found the young La Fayette much grown and singularly well informed for his age, astonishingly advanced in reason and skilled in argument, remarkable for his thinking, his wisdom, his discretion, his self-control and his powers of judgment. Yet I discovered in the boy the seed of self-esteem and even of ambition. His tutor asked me what I thought of him. I replied that the child had the qualities of mind that are proper to great men, namely the power to think and judge, and that if a vigorous character were added to these, he would some day do very great things." Both cousins shared the family's long noses and back-slanting foreheads.

Lafayette's grandparents had sent his father at age eleven with a servant to Paris to make his way with the aristocracy. And so in 1768, Julie summoned her son there. He entered the Collège du Plessis, Sorbonne University's boarding school for high-born children. Living in an attic room until 1772, he visited his mother at the Luxembourg on Sundays and holidays. Mastering Latin, he enjoyed the Roman republican writers who valued independence and democratic thought. He never forgot them as he learned some history, geography and elementary mathematics. His teachers' main duty was to prepare noble sons to become courtiers or diplomats.

"I spent four years in the college," Lafayette recalled. "During that time I experienced two years of the most ardent religious devotion. My confessor told me… I was an object of envy to him. All my energy of character was concentrated on that one concern, and if I cannot really say how I became so pious, I should find it still more difficult to explain how I ceased to be." Latin would later help him communicate in prison but he regretted not being made to study Greek.

Military dress stirred Lafayette's adolescent blood:

> "I was all on fire to have a uniform. When I was thirteen I was made to enter the company of musketeers that my grandfather had commanded. I enjoyed the honor of being reviewed by the king and of riding to Versailles on horseback in full dress… I found it all very delightful, the more so since before I could take part in the review I had to learn [maneuvers] with my comrades.
>
> "I will venture to say that I was much liked in the Collège. I even acquired such an ascendancy over my

> fellow pupils that when I appeared in the schoolyard I was immediately surrounded by my young friends, many of them bigger than I, who were all eager to assume the appearance of disciples and would, had the occasion arisen, have fought fiercely in my defense.
>
> "Once I tried to stir up a revolt to prevent one of my comrades from being unjustly punished. I was not so well supported as I had hoped to be. I was never myself threatened with any disciplinary action. I was determined not to deserve it, and should, I think, have put up a pretty good resistance with my sword, for in accordance with the good usage of those days, all the boys wore swords when they were invited out to dine, and this matched well with their embroidered coats, their hair-bags (queue protectors), and their powdered and pomaded curls."

He had an independent spirit:

> "One of the subjects I was given for an essay was to describe a perfectly trained horse, which, at the mere sight of the rider's whip, became immediately obedient. I drew a picture of this perfect animal throwing his rider when the whip was shown to him. My professor of rhetoric, Monsieur Binet, a man of intelligence, laughed instead of scolding me. He has since then often reminded me of the incident."

Not leaving the lad's marriage prospects to chance, his great grandfather, Comte de La Rivière, approached an old friend, Jean Paul François de Noailles, Duc d'Ayen (1739-1824), elder of two sons of a *maréchal.*[3] D'Ayen was very wealthy with mansions in Paris and Versailles. He was a brigadier general and close to Louis XV. D'Ayen's famous family had originated in the southern province of Limousin in the eleventh century. Eldest sons took the name D'Ayen, after their chateau in the village of Ayen, waiting to inherit the De Noailles dukedom, while younger sons became Marquises de Noailles. Jean Paul d'Ayen had been a soldier but his passion was inquiry. Elected to the Academy of Sciences in 1777, he would become fifth duc de Noailles on his grandfather's death in 1793.

At twelve, Lafayette experienced two shocks in the spring of 1770. His mother died suddenly of influenza at thirty-four.[4] Her father also died that year and Lafayette's great-grandfather followed in 1771 at age 108, some said of grief. The orphaned marquis received a staggering double inheritance of many properties in Brittany, Auvergne and elsewhere — plus an annual income of 120,000 livres (a livre was worth about $100; meaning about $1,200,000 today).[5] As one of France's wealthiest men, Lafayette, an eligible bachelor, had the court's attention. D'Ayen proposed the second of his five daughters as a wife. Doll-like Marie Louise Adrienne Françoise de Noailles, ten, would bring her husband a dowry of 200,000 livres. Seeing the wisdom of the arrangement and knowing the Noailles' importance, the young marquis agreed.

D'Ayen was Lafayette's protector and first father figure. He invited the youth to live at the Noailles' home in Versailles' Rue de la Pompe. Although maturing in a grand noble's house, Lafayette saw Adrienne only occasionally. He soon bought riding horses for himself and friends. Comte de la Rivière until his retirement in 1766 had headed the Second Regiment guarding the king. D'Ayen had Lafayette made a second lieutenant in this elite corps, called the Black Musketeers, in April 1771. Although much admired, these youngsters had no combat experience but looked superb as the royal family's ceremonial protectors.

D'Ayen enrolled Lafayette, a thin fifteen with broad shoulders, in the Académie of Versailles. Here, as at a university, sons of royals and peers completed their formal education while mastering riding, dancing and court etiquette. Lafayette met the foremost families and for a time guarded Polish-born Queen Maria Leszczynska. As officer of the day, he would ride up to Louis XV on royal hunts. With his best military bearing, Lafayette would ask for orders only to see His Majesty wearily wave him away. After sixty years as king, empty ceremony totally bored Louis XV.

Lafayette was important in Chavaniac but in courtly company he was shy and awkward. At the royal stables he rode with Louis, Duc de Berry, the future Louis XVI, and his two younger brothers. Berry became dauphin (crown prince) when his father, Louis Ferdinand, died at thirty-six of tuberculosis.[6] Louis, born August 23, 1754, was three years Lafayette's senior, had a strong body and stood almost six feet, four inches.

His brothers were Comte de Provence, future Louis XVIII, almost two years older than Lafayette, and Comte d'Artois, later Charles X, a month younger. Lafayette's riding skills were second to Provence's. He disliked Louis' brothers' hauteur but respected the dauphin for his intelligence. Louis, who liked Lafayette, was a different person from unknowing or prejudiced writers' words.[7] He occasionally exhibited wit and besides loving to hunt made clocks, locks and collected books. Later, he composed instructions for Admiral La Pérouse's fateful discoveries in the Pacific Ocean in 1785-1788.

After seven years of marriage, Louis and his flighty queen had no heirs. It has often been written that when Louis XV learned from the royal surgeon the dauphin had a restricted foreskin, he ordered an immediate operation. But Louis hunted on the dates of the supposed procedure and an examination proved he had no restriction. It is thought the couple was sexually naïve. Louis' brother-in-law, Austrian Emperor Joseph, spoke with him about technique, and the couple soon enjoyed parenthood amid public celebration. In giving the dynasty four children, two dying in infancy, Marie Antoinette was joined to the throne. Lafayette believed Louis and his queen meant the best for France. But Louis lived under rules imposed by tradition. Lafayette was ready for change.

THREE: YOUNG LOVE

The tall wooden gates of the De Noailles' vast limestone palace in Paris opened from a gated courtyard on fashionable Rue du Faubourg Saint-Honoré near the historic Church of St. Roch.[1] The house was a virtual museum with paintings by Leonardo, Raphael, Rubens, Rembrandt, Van Dyck, Watteau, Fragonard and Boucher. This *hôtel particulier* was just north of the Louvre and Tuileries Palaces, although the royals were rarely there. The Tuileries completed the western side of the Louvre complex. Catherine de Medici began the huge building in 1565 on land bought from a tile company, hence its name.[2] André Le Notre, foremost creator of seventeenth-century gardens and landscapes who was born nearby, designed the gardens. Always open to the public, they extended to *Place de Louis XV*, with the king's bronze equestrian statue dominating the square.

Adrienne's mother, Duchesse d'Ayen, Henriette D'Aguesseau de Noailles, blonde, devout, clever, was orphaned by noble parents. She, like Adrienne, was taught in a convent. Smallpox had disfigured her face but spared her five daughters. At first she protested her husband's plan for Adrienne's marriage, viewing Lafayette's wealth and orphaned status as possibly troublesome. But she came to love him and admired his suave charm. Marie Adrienne Françoise de Noailles, twelve and deeply pious like her mother, had no say in the matter but was deeply attracted to Lafayette and he to her.

But Lafayette had, he wrote, "two romances dedicated to beauties who were then very celebrated, in which my head had a larger part than my heart. The first, scarcely begun, broke against the obstacles of jealousy with which I collided head-on. The other — in which I wanted at first to triumph less over the object herself than over a rival — I pursued, despite long interruptions, on every possible occasion. … It is more pleasant for me to speak of the tender and stable affection that I never cease to feel for the woman whom I had the good fortune to marry."

Lafayette was smitten with Ēlise-Aglãé Barbentane, Comtesse d'Hunolstein, doe-eyed and wanton. Ēlisabeth Vigée-LeBrun, Marie Antoinette's favorite portraitist, captured the countesse on canvas. She was the mistress of the Duc de Chartres (later Orléans) while also his wife's lady-in-waiting. Aglãé's husband was a cavalry colonel in the Regiment de Chartres, one of sixty brigades nobles had financed privately since feudal times. She refused Lafayette but accepted many others, gaining a scandalous reputation. Lafayette, believing his former room mate and friend, Louis-Philippe, Comte de Ségur, was her lover, challenged him to a duel. Ségur laughed at his pointless anger while the court chattered over his anguish. Later Aglãé, impressed by Lafayette's American success, became one of his conquests.

Versailles in Lafayette's youth was the apex of exquisite tedium. Louis XIV had set the style by suggesting nobles vie for his favor. He wanted them away from their domains and close by so he could keep his eye on them. To fill the time, court specialists devised frequent entertainments and intricate demands of etiquette. It could take, with servants as intermediaries, a day or more for a nobleman to meet a noblewoman. One never knocked — three knocks meaning a prostitute — but always scratched a door with a little finger. An army of obsequious servants waited hand and foot on courtiers — high-born, pious or libertine — for the palace was a warren of seduction. Bored men and women, occupying their time in gossip, took hours to dress in pastel satins for galas, plays and concerts in regal splendor. In fair weather, festivities culminated with fireworks amid playing fountains. At quieter times card games offered diversion.

Women of the court wore tall elaborate headdresses of artificial hair with corseted bodices and elliptical hoop skirts with side bustles called *panniers,* baskets. Marie Antoinette chose less formal styles, loose hair arrangements and softer dresses. Gentlemen took pride in wigs powdered with chalk. The custom began with Louis XIII, who was bald. Louis XIV added tall wigs and high heels to his shortness. Wigs — *perruques* — were popular in Europe and the colonies for 175 years. Gentlemen wore knee breeches tied with laces, elaborately ruffled shirts, frock coats and long hose. Silver buckles graced shoes which were identical right and left until the 1860s.

Louis XV had fine taste in the decorative arts but was an ineffectual ruler who blundered into costly wars. Defeat in the Seven Year's War plunged France into debt. Although an absolute ruler, Louis XV, unable to improve his country's problems, foresaw its collapse. He spent his time hunting, gambling, acquiring luxuries and penetrating women. He was called "the Well-Beloved" with a carnal snigger. A satyr, he had countless country girls brought to his bed. Two mistresses ruled over him: intelligent and decisive Madame de Pompadour; and after her death, Marie Jeanne, Comtesse du Barry, an officer's wife with a courtesan's past who was better in bed than at court.

The large rooms of the huge palace — the western façade is two thousand feet long — were embellished with acres of marble and elaborate gilding on doors and walls. In the Hall of Mirrors, 240 feet long, afternoon sunlight streamed in on courtiers, visitors and the splendidly patterned parquet. At night a thousand candles in crystal chandeliers and lamps in the shapes of gilt goddesses shed a glow on guests while on the ceiling painted figures celebrated Louis XIV, the Sun King. Wall mirrors reflecting everyone looked toward seventeen windows garnished with orange trees in silver cachepots.

Versailles housed 3,000 to 10,000 people in every conceivable space. D'Ayen, despite his nearby palace, had a suite there. Protocol prevailed. The less grand were assigned tight chambers under flat roofs where they froze or roasted. Waste moved in chamber pots. Bathing was almost unheard of and guards on duty voided in secluded corners. Courtiers lived for pettiness, intrigue and displays of pomp. Noblemen and women with lovely chateaus worried whether the king, his family, his ministers or mistresses had sufficiently acknowledged them. Louis XV's favorites gambled with him for high stakes in his apartments to help pass evenings. He often slipped away by a private staircase for dalliances.

Queen Maria Leszczynska, seven years his senior and daughter of Stanislaus I, deposed king of Poland, bore Louis XV ten children but found her solace in religion. One of Lafayette's female relatives was close to the king's favorite daughter Princesse Adélaïde, who, like her younger sister Victoire never married. Adélaïde hated the Austrian dauphine, her harsh accent and youthful ways. According to custom, the roughest peasant could see the royals dine. At the grand staircase, a visitor could rent a sword proclaiming him a gentleman for a few sous. One with smallpox may have hurried the king to his death.

Marie Antoinette, two years older than Lafayette, hearing how clumsy he was, invited him to dance. Nervous, he fell in front of her. Laughing at him she invited him to more parties. Silent amid the court's splendor, he was easily embarrassed and uncomfortable. On hearing gossip or prattle, he refused to speak. This was noted and some dismissed him as stupid or slow. He saw how artificial this society was from the natural, humanistic one he learned Voltaire and Rousseau advocated. Yet Lafayette met everyone with courtliness. It was said you could always tell someone who had grown up at Versailles.

Lafayette and Adrienne wed in the de Noailles' flower-filled chapel in Paris on April 11, 1774. He was sixteen, she fourteen. A feast followed as two great houses joined amid approving nobles and aristocrats. Louis XV, debauched widower of sixty-four, lay ill at Versailles but sent the dauphin and his brothers with a congratulatory message and signed the wedding contract with them.

Adrienne forgave her husband's indiscretions. She understood society expected men, in arranged marriages or not, to have mistresses. They had only to note Louis XV's flagrant concupiscence. While pursuing ladies, Lafayette did not forget his relatives in Chavaniac. Before marriage he spent Christmases there. Later his bride would write Charlotte in a girlish hand, "I trust, Madame, you will permit me to ask that you think kindly of the new little niece who dares to call you her aunt."

On May 20, the king expired, his once elegantly dressed body black with smallpox. The corpse was layered in quicklime and sealed in a lead casket. The cortege hurried his remains, with minimal obsequies, to predecessors entombed in the Basilica of Saint Denis, north of Paris. His twenty-year-old grandson became Louis XVI. Influenced by his aunts, he sent Du Barry to a convent for two years. Afterward she lived in two chateaus with successive lovers. The revolutionary tribunal judged her an enemy of the government and at fifty she was guillotined in 1793.

Lafayette's marriage joined him to the esteemed second branch of his new family. Its head, Philippe, Comte de Noailles (1715-1794) was a younger brother of the fourth duke, Louis de Noailles (1713-1793). He had inherited the Spanish title Duc de Mouchy and a chateau in Oise, north of Paris. Mouchy had fought at Minden and elsewhere. He was made a *maréchal* the same day as his brother. Under Louis XVI he was superintendant and governor of the Palace of Versailles, where he and his wife were longtime court favorites. His wife Anne was first lady of honor to Marie Antoinette, who called her "Madame Etiquette." Anne instructed the dauphine in formal French manners from the day she arrived. (For nearness to the crown the elder Mouchys were guillotined in 1794.)

Their first son, Philippe de Mouchy, Prince de Poix (1752-1819), was a short, capable and agreeable military officer who enjoyed theater and parties. Almost five years older than Lafayette, Poix, captain of the king's household guard, succeeded his father at Versailles. (He would be elected a noble deputy to the Estates-General in 1789.) The prince's younger brother, Louis-Marie, Vicomte de Noailles (1756-1804), a year older than Lafayette, attended the Académie with him.[3] Louis married Adrienne's older sister Louise, who was also his cousin, done to keep D'Ayen's line active, since he had five daughters but no sons. Louis the vicomte would father four children.

D'Ayen nearly negotiated a place at court for Lafayette in the Comte de Provence's service. But not wishing to be a courtier or surrender his independence, Lafayette insulted the king's brother. At a ball he recognized Provence in a mask boasting of his memory. "Everyone knows memory is a fool's substitute for wit," Lafayette retorted.[4] Provence refused to hire him, never forgot the slight but gave Lafayette his wish to leave. Irritated, D'Ayen sent Lafayette to the Metz garrison on France's quiet northeastern border where he became a captain in his grandfather-in-law's de Noailles Dragoons. Adrienne stayed close to her mother. The couple's home was the Hôtel de Noailles while Lafayette was in service.

FOUR: CALL OF AMERICA

Lafayette's regiment guarded the border. His officer was his cousin by marriage, Philippe de Noailles, eldest son of the Duc de Noailles, who used his Spanish title, Duc de Mouchy, to distinguish him from de Noailles cousins. Philippe was called Prince de Poix since his family held title to an old Norman principality by that name.[1] Poix's younger brother Louis the vicomte was a dragoon lieutenant. France was at peace and service time dragged. The garrison commander was super-ambitious Comte Charles François de Broglie, Marquis de Ruffec, who, aware of Lafayette's importance, became fatherly toward him.

Broglie-Ruffec had a covert past. He recently had prepared to sail to the Americans' aid. And twenty years earlier for Louis XV, Broglie had planned a secret invasion of the United Kingdom that was never done. Early in his reign, Louis XVI had ministers examine Broglie-Ruffec's plans and did not object to them, since they were the best devised for landing in England. But later, Louis, fearing the British would capture Broglie-Ruffec and his soldiers en route to America, aborted the venture. He made Broglie-Ruffec commandant at Metz, an important post for *maréchals* and generals. Broglie-Ruffec introduced Lafayette to an exceptional officer, Jean (Johann) de Kalb, fifty-five, a powerfully built, over six-foot-tall Bavarian native.[2] Probably the natural child of an aristocrat, Kalb was not a German nobleman and so could not be a

Prussian officer. France and Austria had similar prohibitions. Wily Broglie-Ruffec, having bought a marquisate, arranged one for Kalb,

Kalb, long Broglie-Ruffec's protege, had fought in the 1740s' War of the Austrian Succession and was an adjutant general in the Seven Years' War, involving European powers in North America, Caribbean, West Africa, India and Philippines. Inventing the title "Baron de Kalb," with Broglie-Ruffec's help Kalb purchased a feudal estate, Milon la Chapelle, and so became ennobled in 1769. Besides a wife and young children — he married at forty-three — Kalb had also been a spy.

In 1768, French foreign minister Ētienne, Duc de Choiseul had sent Kalb to America to determine if the colonists were ready to revolt. Finding no dissent, Kalb, who spoke English, asked a contact to report any change and returned to France. Reading Kalb's report on June 7, 1770, hawkish Choiseul would have promoted him to brigadier general had Choiseul not been dismissed later that year.[3]

Kalb showed his report to Broglie-Ruffec, who had convinced Choiseul in the first place to order Kalb's mission. But Broglie-Ruffec was disappointed with Kalb's findings, since he dreamed of leading the American troops to victory and much more. Short and prideful, he burned to surpass his less shrewd elder brother Victor François. Their great grandfather, of Piedmontese origin, having changed his name from Broglio, was Louis XV's commanding general in the Seven Years' War with his great grandsons as generals. Kalb and Lafayette admired Broglie-Ruffec. He was former ambassador to Poland and the most powerful member of Louis XV's unofficial spy operation, the "*Secrèt du Roi.*" One of Louis XVI's first acts was to end his grandfather's spy ring.

Broglie-Ruffec had led thousands in battle and knew with his considerable diplomatic experience he could be useful to a new nation like America. He was widely respected in Europe while Washington would only become a statesman after the revolution. But Broglie-Ruffec had not visited America, spoke no English and knew nothing of frontier warfare. But, he reasoned, if he were to lead American troops, unlike Washington who was slow and losing the war, his importance as a European commander would bring great attention and support to America. Broglie-Ruffec's scant knowledge of Washington convinced him he was the superior *généralissime.*

He probably did not know that Washington's great-great-great-grandfather, Nicolas Martinau, was a Charente-Maritime Huguenot born in coastal France in 1591. Arriving in Virginia in 1620, Martinau became a burgess, platted Yorktown and died there in 1657. But Broglie-Ruffec knew that in 1755 Washington, twenty-three and Major General Edward Braddock's aide-de-camp, failed to stop the French, Canadians and Indians from slaughtering 456 British officers and 1,400 troops in western Pennsylvania's wilderness.

French losses were few but Braddock, on his fifth horse, was fatally wounded. Washington, unscathed, had two horses shot from under him and bullets pierced his coat four times as he tried to control his terrified men.[4] Broglie was unaware Braddock rejected Washington's plea to fire from cover. By contrast, French commander Daniel de Beaujeu dressed and whooped like an Indian. The British "ran like sheep pursued by dogs," Washington wrote his revered mother Mary Ball Washington.[4]

On August 8, 1775, Broglie, eager for American news, gave a dinner at the governor's palace in Metz for George III's brother, Frederick Henry, Duke of Gloucester and Edinburgh, (1743-1805), touring Europe with his wife. Broglie's wife, extremely wealthy Louise de Montmorency de Broglie-Ruffec, was the only woman present. George III was peeved at his brother for marrying Horace Walpole's illegitimate niece.[5] Gloucester stormed that his government's reprisals against the colonists were disastrous for the empire. Lafayette, Poix and Kalb heard Gloucester deplored Britain's hiring Germans to fight the war since Britons were stretched thin guarding global territories. Lafayette often said — until he believed it — he immediately wanted to fight for the colonists. He likely did not decide until later, influenced by Broglie plans or opinions of 250 French officers who preceded Lafayette in America.

Writing of his adventures in two memoirs, Lafayette, or his son Georges — edited them to suit his aggrandizement. Historian Louis Gottschalk wrote this was not deliberate lying: Lafayette came to believe his versions as the truth.[6] In any case, the American Revolution was an opportunity he could join completely. Working for America's victory, Lafayette reasoned, would also gain him fame at home.

"When I first learned of that quarrel, my heart was enlisted, and I thought only of joining the colors. Some circumstances... had taught me to expect from my family only obstacles to the attainment of my goal. I therefore relied upon myself and dared to take for a device on my coat-of-arms the words *Cur Non?* [*Why not?*] which could serve me both as an encouragement and response."

The motto was that of a fifteenth century ancestor Lafayette found in an old family book. For as long as he could remember he had hated the British for killing his father and hoped to avenge it. Frederick the Great controlled the region where Lafayette's father died, but George III was Hanover's hereditary ruler, another reason for fighting him. Broglie at first opposed Lafayette's leaving for America, saying he had seen a cannonball destroy Lafayette's father and reminding him he was his family's last male and a father with another child on the way.

Lafayette returned to Paris to plan for America. Interested in new discoveries, particularly those regarding health, he was variolated, a procedure predating inoculation or vaccination. Infectious matter from a patient with mild smallpox was scratched into the skin. A lighter infection gave immunity but death was possible. Lafayette's mother-in-law, surviving the disease, accompanied him to a rented house in nearby Chaillot. With Adrienne attending him, Lafayette returned to health in several weeks. He then visited Chavaniac. Adrienne, after a miscarriage with a second pregnancy, remained at home.

Louis XVI had forbidden Broglie and Kalb from leaving Le Havre for America and possibly tumbling France into war. But in 1775, foreign minister Charles Gravier, Comte de Vergennes, had hired Julien Achard de Bonvouloir (1749-1783) for an unofficial secret mission to Benjamin Franklin in Philadelphia. Bonvouloir, who had been to America in 1770 but spoke no English, was to determine how prepared the Americans were to fight for independence. Helped by a French-speaking American friend working in Franklin's Library Company, Bonvouloir, posing as an Antwerp merchant, denied vehemently he had a connection to French diplomacy. Franklin and John Jay, meeting him in Carpenter's Hall, the library company's home, indicated the country was ready for war. Bonvouloir conveyed this to Vergennes in glowing terms. Vergennes' report to Louis XVI ignited royal decisions to rearm the French Navy, send a dozen infantry battalions to the West Indies and dispatch military engineers.

In early 1776, Vergennes devised a plan: French and Spanish governments would pay large sums and hide behind a clandestine operation, *Rodrigue Hortalez et Compagnie*, to supply the Continental Army with weapons and materiel. Pierre Augustin Caron de Beaumarchais, who while on a royal secret mission to London became a champion of the colonists, was chosen to run the operation. Clever and daring, Beaumarchais rose from being a clock-maker like his father to high status. After two marriages to wealthy women, Beaumarchais purchased state offices and gained status as advisor and special secretary to Louis XVI. Beaumarchais assembled shipments in the *Hôtel des Ambassadeurs Hollande* where he lived on Paris' Right Bank. America was to repay the loans but never fully did.[7]

In May 1776, two months before the *Declaration of Independence*, Beaumarchais' rented trading ships began deliveries. September 1776's shipment of "horticultural equipment" was: 200 bronze cannons, 30,000 light muskets, twenty-seven mortars, 100,000 cannonballs, 13,000 bombs, 3,000 tents, 30,000 blankets, 45,000 pounds of wool cloth and more. The ships returned with produce, mainly tobacco. By 1779, after Franklin's urging and with master chemist Antoine Lavoisier's improved processing, France had sent more than 800 tons of Europe's finest gunpowder.

"By Yorktown," historian Joe Jackson wrote, "British soldiers complained that they could not get close enough to shoot colonials before they themselves were blasted from their garters."[8] But Broglie-Ruffec, frustrated by Continental battle losses, now urged Kalb to sail with Lafayette to America — and to negotiate secretly on Broglie's behalf with Congress. Broglie expected Lafayette's presence in America would bring France more directly into war. But French secrecy was not so secret.

FIVE: Visit to George III

Adrienne's great-uncle Emmanuel, Marquis de Noailles, former envoy to the Netherlands, became French ambassador to the Court of St. James's, an extremely sensitive post, in 1776. London strongly suspected France wanted to help the Americans. The French knew British spies swarmed French ports and vice versa. British spies reported to David Murray, Lord Stormont, second Earl of Mansfield and ambassador to France. To enhance relations, Marie Antoinette and Louis gave the wily Scot, future laird of Scone Castle, Perthshire, a Louis XV writing table.[1] Unknown to Stormont, Louis XVI, violating the 1763 Paris peace treaty ending the Seven Years War, was sending Americans 500,000 livres ($50,000 today) quarterly, perhaps more than 100 million ($13 billion) total, from the royal treasury.

Lafayette and Poix sailed to London to visit their Great-Uncle Emmanuel. At nineteen, Lafayette observed firsthand the leaders and people he despised, an advantage Washington and his generals never had. The junket also veiled plans Lafayette knew D'Ayen and court leaders, at least nominally, would oppose.

Broglie-Ruffec had in his confidence his secretary's younger brother, François Augustin du Boismartin, thirty-five, of Barbezieux, Charente, who hoped to join Lafayette. He had left the navy for the Saint Domingue (later Haiti) legion, rising to first lieutenant. Because of his brother Guy du Boismartin's royal connections, François was an active member of Louis XV and XVI's spy cabinets and captain and knight of the Order of St. Louis. Broglie-Ruffec asked "*Petit* Dubois," as he called him, differentiating him from his brother, to purchase a ship for Lafayette in Bordeaux where there were fewer British spies. But Stormont reported the pending voyage and Louis XVI's displeasure with it to Lord Weymouth, British secretary of state. Stormont left France for higher government office in London in 1778.[2]

According to Broglie-Ruffec's long hidden papers, revealed in Bernard de Larquier's book, *La Fayette, Usurpateur du Vaisseau La Victoire*, Broglie not only sent all of the officers but one to the ship; he also devised a system in which they spied on each other and reported to him. Lafayette was in charge of the vessel, but Kalb, who wrote his wife he would prefer being with her and the children, was in fact chief officer, but discreetly so. Broglie ordered Petit Dubois to purchase the ship, watch Lafayette closely and report back. Another officer, Vicomte Charles Louis de Mauroy, was to keep tabs on Kalb, and so on down the line of intrigue.

De Larquier states money to purchase an old trading ship, *La Clary*, formerly *La Bonne Mere* (*The Good Mother*), came not from underage Lafayette, who claimed to have bought her, but from others. Possibly Broglie out of sums due him from Versailles, but he never says so, and from Petit Dubois and Pierre de Larquier, a Bordeaux harbor official and the author's ancestor. Lafayette was expected to repay them on coming to full inheritance at twenty-five but he did not explain this in his writings.[3] Petit Dubois baptized the tub with Lafayette's choice of name, assertive *La Victoire*. In her hold were not bolts of rich textiles, as his *Mémoires* say, but brass cannons and firearms. Broglie had bought not only the Chateau de Ruffec and its domain east of Bordeaux but also a munitions foundry. The cannons and arms *La Victoire* carried were probably worth three times the ship.[4]

Lafayette had written to Benjamin Franklin, learned American emissary in Paris, giving his case for serving in the Continental Army. Franklin, seventy-one, was extremely popular in France for defining the nature of electricity as well as for his wit and clothing. He played on French beliefs of American simplicity and Rousseauvian ideals. Women fashioned headdresses after Franklin's fur cap worn to emphasize rusticity. Lafayette did not visit Franklin at his house in the village of Passy, correctly suspecting British spies were watching it closely. The two did not meet until 1779.

Franklin and Silas Deane, the American agent in France who had willy-nilly recruited many unsuitable French officers for America, had helped to develop Beaumarchais' covert operation. Franklin and Deane encouraged Lafayette to visit London. Sailing from Calais, he had written to Adrienne, promising more on landing: "...Farewell, dear heart. Wherever I go I shall always love you very tenderly. I wish you could know how sincere that assurance is, and how important your love is to my happiness."

Ambassador De Noailles introduced his grandnephews to George III at court in early spring of 1777 and Lafayette stayed three weeks. His new cousin, Louis Philippe, a dandy, was nicknamed *"petit Poix,"* a pun on *petits pois,* little peas.[5] The young men observed King George in an embroidered satin suit emblazoned with a star medal. It was said he hated Frenchmen and Catholics but knew none. At a performance of *Israel in Egypt* by Handel, the king's favorite composer, Lafayette met General Sir Henry Clinton, back from defeating Washington on Long Island.[6] Lafayette would fight Clinton in New Jersey but now he danced at the home of Lord George Germaine, colonies minister opposed to independence, and met Lord Rawdon, another general returned from New York.

Thinking of his Atlantic voyage, Lafayette visited court only once but found its constitutional monarchy more attractive than France's absolutism. Knowing no English, Lafayette felt the warmth of his and Poix's hosts and new acquaintences who entertained them at parties and balls. The pair never missed a chance to defend the Americans and found Britons expected more war. Lafayette hoped to learn English from Kalb, the most experienced officer on the expedition. Receiving his message that the ship was ready, Lafayette feigned illness, to his uncle and the king's surprise, and sailed to France alone. On April 9 before leaving London, he wrote D'Ayen revealing his intention, hoping the Duc would not see it until after Lafayette was underway. He falsified traveling time:

You will be greatly astonished, my dear Papa, by what I am about to tell you. It pains me more than I can say not to have consulted you in this matter... I know that I am making tremendous sacrifices, and that no one will suffer more than I do at having to leave my family, my friends, and you, my dear Papa... But the voyage is not considerable, and many people every day make far longer ones solely for their pleasure. Besides, I hope when I return to be more worthy of those who may have been so kind as to regret my departure. Goodbye, my dear Papa: I hope to see you again soon. Think of me with feelings of kindliness. I am much desirous of deserving them, and do already deserve them by reason of what I feel and of the respect which I shall ever entertain for you...

He was seasick recrossing the Channel. Plans still incomplete, he hid for three days at Kalb's house in Chaillot, a village west of Paris, wanting to avoid his family, spies and the army even though cost-cutting had made him a reservist. He wanted everyone, especially D'Ayen, to think he was in London. Adrienne's closeness to her parents kept him from confiding in her. He knew they would take care of her, in her third pregnancy, and little Anastasie. His matrimonial roots were still meager and Adrienne little more than a child. He would send her a letter explaining everything. The greatest adventure of his life could easily go wrong. He and his comrades longed to distinguish themselves in battle and thought of little else. Lafayette asked the Duc to "present my respects" to Uncle Emmanuel in London.

Lafayette and Kalb had visited Silas Deane at his office on Rue Jacob. The Continental Congress was angry with Deane for approving too many French officers who demanded high salaries, spoke little English and scoffed at the untrained rebels. Congress paid sorely needed funds to return them to France or the Caribbean war. Deane, knowing Lafayette's title, wrote letters recommending both him and Kalb as major generals.

Broglie-Ruffec sent some of his finest officers to *La Victoire*. Lafayette knew some, Kalb more. Broglie- Ruffec sent Petit Dubois to purchase *La*

Victoire. The other officers were: Louis de Morel de la Colombe, twenty-two, Lafayette's Avergnat friend and the only officer Broglie did not send; Charles Louis de Mauroy, forty-three, an experienced officer and cousin (his grandmother was a De la Rivière); Charles de Bedaulx, twenty-five, of Neuchâtel, Switzerland, officer in the Versailles Swiss-Dutch guard; Jacques or Simon de Franval, birth date and place uncertain, probably born in Orbec, Normandy; Jean-Joseph de Gimat, thirty, of Gascony; Louis Cloquet de Vrigny, forty-two, regimental hussard; Jean-Pierre du Rousseau de Fayolle, thirty-one, son of Marquis Duquesne (c. 1770-1778), governor general of New France during the French and Indian War; Jean Thevet de Lessert, forty, knight of Saint Louis; Louis de Valfort, fifty, of Tarare, Rhône; Jean Capitaine, thirty-eight, of Ruffec; Charles François du Buysson, twenty-five, another of Lafayette's distant Avergnat cousins; and Edmund Brice, twenty-five, a Marylander.[7]

Lafayette took three servants; Du Boismartin, two; Kalb, one. Philippe Louis Candon, born at Versailles and who had the Mouchys as godparents, was also a servant. Capitaine, La Colombe, De Vrigny and Brice were Lafayette's aides-de-camp. Jean Capitaine was not Michel du Capitaine du Chesnoy (1746-1804), the mapmaker who would record Lafayette's battles and whom he called "a present from De Broglie." The ship roster identified all as Catholics, except Protestants Kalb and Bedaulx, and also gave their respective hair colors.[8]

Lafayette wrote Carmichael that he liked Brice, who acted as his secretary. A student of Charles Willson Peale, Brice was returning after studying painting in France. He helped Lafayette learn English. Du Buysson became Kalb's aide-de-camp. Du Boismartin, declining that post, would soon return to the French Army in Saint Domingue.

Most of the officers, all yearning to fight the British, had seen more military duty than Lafayette. There would have been two more, but D'Ayen pressured Louis de Noailles and Louis-Philippe, Comte de Ségur, not to go. Ségur, Lafayette's school roommate, married Adrienne's aunt — the Duchesse d'Ayen's younger half-sister — becoming Lafayette's uncle-by-marriage on April 30, 1777. Lacking wealth, both men obeyed D'Ayen but joined the war later: Louis, with D'Estaing, took part in storming Grenada and was in the attack on Savannah. He departed America as a Saintonge Regiment colonel in second with Comte de

Rochambeau, commander of French forces in America. Ségur arrived in 1782.

Franklin and Deane wrote to the American Committee of Secret Correspondence, which represented American interests in France, on May 25, 1777:

> *...The Marquis de Fayette (sic) a young nobleman of great family connections here, & great wealth, is gone to America in a ship of his own, accompanied by some officers of distinction, in order to serve in our Armies. He is exceedingly beloved, and everybody's good wishes attend him. We cannot but hope he may meet with such a reception as will make the country and his expedition agreeable to him. Those who censure it as imprudent in him do never the less applaud his spirit: and we are satisfy'd that the civilities and respect that may be shown him will be serviceable to our affairs here, as pleasing, not only to his powerful relations & to the Court, but to the whole French nation. He has left a beautiful young wife big with child: and for her sake particularly we hope that his bravery and ardent desire to distinguish himself will be a little restrain'd by the generals prudence; so as not to permit his being hazarded much but on some important occasion...*

Problems beset departure. Lafayette and Kalb left Paris on March 16, arriving in Bordeaux three days later. Their vessel weighed 268 tons and had two bad small cannons. She had sailed several times to America, traded with Saint Domingue, but "could not have escaped from the smallest privateer." With youthful bravado, Lafayette vowed to blow her up rather than surrender to the British. Captain Jean-Baptiste Le Boursier commanded a crew of forty-two. No ship description is known but one may perhaps compare her to the 200-ton *Mayflower* on which the Pilgrims sailed in 1620: ninety feet long and twenty-four feet wide. Hubert Robert and Gustave Alaux did imaginary paintings of *Victoire* with two or three masts and poop deck. Passengers lived midship behind crew's quarters toward the prow, under the top deck and over an eleven-foot-deep hold. Lafayette and Kalb probably had cubicles, the rest hammocks.

Lafayette wanted to avoid any incident between his king and the British. To cover his being in Bordeaux, he visited the Duc de Mouchy, his uncle-by-marriage, who was there. Uncle Immanuel the ambassador angrily thought Lafayette had duped him to gain an introduction to George III, possible grounds for recall. D'Ayen sent word that Lafayette should meet him and his somewhat eccentric sister Adrienne, Comtesse de Tessé, who loved Lafayette, in Marseille, start of a three-month tour of Italy and Sicily. D'Ayen had foreign minister Jean-Frédéric, Comte de Maurepas, send a letter forbidding *Victoire's* sailing. As Lafayette and Kalb boarded her, a royal messenger arrived to say the king was sending a restraining order. But they cast off for Los Pasajes, a small Spanish port south of the French border, to avoid British frigates. Stormont knew of it. On Lafayette's reaching Los Pasajes, a French government order told him to go at once to Marseille.

With the ship safe, he rode swiftly alone back to Bordeaux, wrote the royal ministers of his intention to sail and considered returning to Paris for D'Ayen's approval. The Bordeaux commandant urged him to go to Marseille. Kalb believed the order was too important to disobey and saw how serious it would be for France if the British captured *La Victoire*. London would have loved to display the French ambassador's great-nephew in chains. Kalb urged Lafayette to cancel the voyage and return the ship to the sellers with a default penalty of 20,000 livres. Kalb wrote his wife he expected Lafayette to quit and return to Paris.[9]

In Bordeaux, Lafayette found going to prison or joining his father-in-law equally repugnant. Mauroy, whom Deane had recommended as a major general in America, joined *La Victoire*, telling Lafayette D'Ayen had instigated the warrant but powers at Versailles disagreed, wanting him to go to America. In disguise, Lafayette eluded police and rushed back south. In Saint-Jean de Luz, an inn owner's daughter recognized him from his earlier visit. He signaled her and she misled the police. Crossing the Spanish border, Lafayette rejoined his impatient shipmates. Stopping briefly in the Basque port of San Sebastian, he bought muskets to defend the ship and lied to Adrienne in an April 19 letter:

> *"Ah, dear heart, they thought that fear would have more effect upon me than love. They have misunderstood me, and since they tear me away from you, since they compel me not to see you for a year, and since they wish only to humble my pride, without affecting my love, at least that cruel absence will be employed in a manner that is worthy of me... My voyage will be no longer, perhaps shorter, and you will have news of me even more often. A thousand ships will bring it to you constantly. I shall not expose myself, I shall take care of myself, I shall remember that you love me; you can set your mind at ease. It is more as a philosopher than as a soldier that I shall visit all of that country..."*

He had met obstacles and defied his king. He would not be deterred. Whatever lay ahead, he had made his decision.

SIX: Journey to the Unknown

On April 20, 1777, Lafayette breathed the tang of the open sea. The creaking ship sank low in a trough as the wind filled her sails and land disappeared. He found his cubicle and heard cries of the crew in the rigging. After weeks of seasickness, he adjusted to the rolling waves. Ahead lay seven weeks on the Atlantic. The food was tiresome — dried peas and meat, hard bisquit, watered wine — too much at the start, too little later. Confinement, aimless talk of America and the possibility of British or French frigates overtaking them filled the long hours. Lafayette suffered privation with the others but remained the most cheerful. Progressing slowly with English books and dictionary, he contained his impatience and wrote letters.

Captain Le Boursier, with proper papers, insisted on stopping in Saint Domingue. Lafayette dissuaded him, believing arrest warrants awaited them. He chose not to sail directly to Philadelphia but took a safer southerly route "less from choice than compulsion." He described the voyage in a May 30 letter to Adrienne:

> *On board La Victoire: I am writing to you from very far away, dear heart, and to this cruel separation is added the still more dreadful uncertainty of the time when I shall hear from you. I hope, however, that it will be soon...*

The sea is so dismal, and I believe we sadden each other, she and I. I should have landed by now, but the winds have cruelly opposed me, and I shall not see Charleston for eight or ten more days...

I was very ill during the first part of the voyage... I treated myself in my own way, and I recovered sooner than the others. Now I feel almost as if I were on land. Once I arrive, I am sure that I shall have acquired the hardiness that will assure me perfect health for a long time. Do not fancy, dear heart, that I shall run great risks in my service here. The post of general officer has always been regarded as a warrant for long life...

Receiving his letter in August, Adrienne later said she first heard of her husband's going to America from her mother who had learned it from her father and could not fault her husband. Adrienne loved him completely and awaited his return. She vowed not to add to her family's problems and never displayed her emotions despite her fears for Lafayette's safety. She oversaw little Henriette, prepared for another child and walked in the courtyard garden. She heard the ship had reached Boston. The royal court speculated but she kept silent.

On June 7, he wrote:

I am still on this dreary plain, dear heart, and it is so dismal that one cannot make any comparison with it. To console myself a little I think of you, and of my friends. I think with pleasure of meeting you again, my dear; what a delightful moment it will be when I arrive and suddenly embrace you, when you do not expect me. Perhaps you will be with our children. Even thinking of that happy moment gives me the greatest pleasure. Do not fancy that it will be a long time. It will surely seem long enough to me, but in fact it will not be as long as you may imagine. Without being able to set the day, or even the month, without seeing for myself the state of things, I can assure you that I am certainly not going to inflict a truly long one upon myself....

The rocking dark and becalmed periods on board were interminable. Thoughts of Adrienne warmed the hours before sleep; and the solo pleasures of men at sea. One hundred and twenty miles from Charleston, *Victoire* came upon a small ship. On seeing her, Le Boursier "turned pale," but she was an American man-of-war. Although he tried to keep up with her, she soon passed them. They saw her encounter two British frigates that, preoccupied, did not notice them. "And this is not the only time when the elements seemed bent on opposing Lafayette as if it were with the intention of saving him," he would remark in his *Mémoires,* written in the third person to avoid boastfulness.

Avoiding British frigates around Charleston, *La Victoire* sailed north along the coast, dropping anchor off North Island near Georgetown, sixty miles above Charleston. It was fifty-four days since leaving Spain, a long crossing, with winds becalming the ship for periods as well as prevailing in the opposite direction. They spent the night on board, feeling Low Country humidity. At 2 p.m. the next day, June 13, Lafayette, Kalb, Brice, Du Buysson and servants entered a longboat. Crewmen rowed them into an inlet with hope of finding a pilot to guide them to Charleston. They moved up the Waccamaw River in wilderness and saw no one.

Toward evening they surprised slaves in dugouts gathering oysters. The men belonged to Major Benjamin Huger (pronounced "*Hewjee*"), a rice planter, assemblyman and Huguenot descendant who would die defending Charleston in 1779. The oystermen led them upriver. The darkness' jungle sounds were so different from the ocean. At midnight they saw candlelight at Prospect Hill, Huger's plantation, and stepped onto land. Dogs barked and a loud voice demanded to know who they were.

Kalb shouted in English they were French officers arrived to join the army, their ship was at the inlet, they were hunting a pilot and needed a night's shelter.[1] Huger welcomed them to his summer home and a late supper. Lafayette patted the head of one of his sons, Francis, delighted with their good luck. That night he was pestered, he wrote Adrienne, by "gnats" — his first encounter with mosquitoes.

Lafayette told Jared Sparks, author of *The Life of George Washington,* that on this night he "retired to rest, rejoic[ing] that he had at last attained the haven of his wishes and was safely landed in America beyond the reach of his pursuers." The next morning he was enchanted with the novelty of everything around him: his room, the bed with mosquito curtains, the black servants who came to ask his needs, the beauty and strange appearance of the country seen from his window. The luxuriant verdure had a magical effect, touching him with "indescribable sensations."

A pilot steered *La Victoire,* its remaining officers and cargo to Charleston, the continent's fifth largest city. They anchored a few days later without incident. After two days with the Hugers, Lafayette and Kalb borrowed horses and rode to the city. Since Huger had no carriages there, the others walked to Charleston, arriving exhausted and bedraggled. But Lafayette met important townsmen and was, Du Buysson wrote, "shown all the honors due a marshal of France." Greeters included Governor John Rutledge, Congress' foremost orator, Generals William Moultrie and Robert Howe. Moultrie had commanded an American force in one of the war's first battles on June 28, 1776, preventing the city's capture. Howe led North Carolina troops defending Charleston. The fort, built of palmetto palm logs and sand packed sixteen inches apart, had stood firm, absorbing cannon balls that strengthened it. (The palm became central icon in the state seal.) Lafayette and Moultrie toured the fort named for him.

But Lafayette did not say much about why he and his comrades had come, best saved for Congress. He described to his wife the people he met to convince her of why he had joined them, and hoping to justify his action to anyone reading the letter. Adrienne showed it at court, setting it talking. She defended him against all critics, even her father. In describing America, Lafayette's words were larger than life.

> *A simplicity of manners, a desire to please, the love of country and of liberty and a pleasing equality are to be found everywhere among people. The richest man and the poorest are upon the same social level, and, although there are some great fortunes in this country, I defy anyone to discover the least difference in the bearing of one man to another...Everything recalls more or less*

> *the English customs, though there is more of simplicity here than in England. What delights me most is that all the citizens are brothers. There are no poor people in America, not even what may be called peasants. Every man has his own property and each has the same rights with the greatest landowner in country... I have just this moment returned from a grand dinner that lasted five hours, given by a gentleman of this city in my honor. Generals Howe and Moultrie were there and several of the officers of my caravan. We drank many healths and spoke very bad English, which language, by the way, I am beginning now to use a little...*

Charleston was first to ignite his fame. The city had known its share of French soldiers seeking work; they were pests. With celebrity, semi-rustic Lafayette vanished forever. To officials and gentry he was a pleasant young aristocrat with royal connections who, with his noble friends, appeared ready to help the war effort and liberty.

But in his haste to leave Bordeaux, Lafayette had signed the contract for *La Victoire* without reading it. Du Buysson, later becoming a major, wrote in his journal:

"...We had planned to leave on June 25, but an entirely unforeseen obstacle arose. The Marquis had a rich cargo on board his ship, all of which he had advertised for sale, and he had expected to make a three or four hundred percent profit on it. With such a large sum he hoped to be able to take care of all of us, and we expected to live comfortably [in America] for two or three years. Thus we were astounded when the captain of the ship brought the Marquis a note for 40,000 livres in favor of the company that had supplied the ship and signed for by Lafayette. The note stated that the vessel and its entire cargo should return to France to be sold, and from the proceeds the company would deduct the 40,000 livres due it, and thirty-five percent in addition — twenty-five percent for insurance and ten percent for commission. At Bordeaux the Marquis had signed without examination every paper placed before him by the man who offered to aid him in his pursuit of glory."[2]

This long accepted account is markedly different from those in

Broglie-Ruffec's papers that De Larquier published in 1987 and Bernard Vincent, Université d'Orléans, published online in 2004. Du Buysson's silence on this or what was in the ship's hold may have been in deference to his former commander who was extremely secretive by nature.

As Le Boursier crossed Charleston harbor under sail for France on August 14, *La Victoire* struck a submerged rock and sank. The *Gazette of the State of South Carolina* reported a month later she was loaded with "rice for the French market."[3] Lafayette in his *Mémoires* wrote she went down with an uninsured cargo worth 200,000 livres. But the ship had been insured, in France and America. That month Lafayette's Paris business manager, Gérard, had word from the seller, Recules, de Boismarein & Compagnie, that *La Victoire* was in Charleston and returning with an important cargo. It offered to advance insurance money rather than risk loss at sea. André Maurois, author of *Adrienne,* wrote with D'Ayen in Sicily, his wife and Adrienne agreed to pay for the insurance before the ship sank. Since the owners had insured the cargo in three cities, it was some time before the books were cleared, with little expense to the family.[4]

Lafayette's attention was on getting to Philadelphia. Equipping his comrades for the expedition as promised, he secured a loan of $7,000 in Charleston with much difficulty and bought horses, conveyances and necessities for the journey. They left Charleston June 26 with hopes high, but the experience was brutal. They suffered from the heat. Capitaine became ill and stayed behind for a while in North Carolina. Du Buysson wrote:

"The aide-de-camp of the Marquis [Brice] undertook to be our guide, although he had no possible idea of the country. This was our marching order as we came out of Charleston. The procession was headed by one of the Marquis' servants dressed as a hussar. The Marquis' carriage was like an uncovered settee on four springs with a forecarriage. Beside it one of his servants on horseback acted as his squire. Kalb sat in the same carriage. Lafayette's counselors followed in a two-wheeled shay. The third vehicle held aides-de-camp and the fourth, luggage. A black man on horseback brought up the rear.

"Four days later," he wrote, "some of our carriages were reduced to splinters; several of the horses, old and unsteady, were either worn-out or lame, and we were obliged to buy others along the road. This outlay took all our money. We had to leave behind us a part of our luggage and part was stolen. We traveled a great part of the way on foot, often sleeping in the woods, almost dead with hunger, exhausted by the heat, several of us suffering from fever and dysentery. At last, after thirty-two days of marching, we arrived at Philadelphia in a more pitiable condition than on entering Charleston..."[5]

On July 27, the weary but still enthusiastic men reached Philadelphia, America's largest and most important city. They had traveled almost 900 miles through the Carolinas, Virginia, Maryland, Delaware and Pennsylvania in a month and a day. On terrible roads they had passed many forests, rivers, farms and towns. Philadelphia's Georgian red brick and white buildings were severely unlike Versailles' grandeur. Yet the city on the Delaware possessed a serious intent, aimed at a king and Parliament in London. Congress was fighting a war with little money or gunpowder and no trained army. Its navy would be a few converted trading ships, far outnumbered by armed privateers. About 1,000 colonial ships traded with British dominions.[6] Lafayette knew the City of Brotherly Love was the home of Franklin, widely respected for his discoveries and trying to win French aid through adroit diplomacy. How would Congress win the colonies from Britain when its sadly outclassed troops lacked materiel?

As soon as they found rooms and bathed, Lafayette and Kalb reported with their official papers. The welcome was not what they expected. Congress wanted no more French officers. When hired, the foreigners sometimes fell short of claimed skills. Many had come from the the war in the French West Indies. Exasperated, Washington had condemned them to Congress. Equally irritated, Congress rejected many who had arrived without invitation. Yet some were in camp with Americans. Pierre Charles L'Enfant, three years older than Lafayette, was a Paris-trained architect and civil engineer who had served in French colonial service and a month earlier had joined the army engineers as a volunteer. When Washington later asked him to design the Federal City, L'Enfant set the Capitol and president's house in similar relationship to the Palace of Versailles and Grand Trianon.

Just before Lafayette arrived, Congress had dealt with a liar, Philippe Tronson du Coudray, a French engineer.

"...I believe he has done us the most damage," Du Buysson wrote, "since he has disgusted the whole Congress. He arrived here with the airs of a lord, and let on he was one as well as a brigadier general in France, adviser to the royal ministers and friend of all the princes and dukes, from whom he carried some letters. He presented to Congress an agreement signed by Mr. Deane, by which he was to have the rank of major general and commander in chief of the artillery, the engineers and all the forts, including those not yet built, with the power to create positions, appoint and dismiss men, etc., with accountability only to the general and the Congress, with a salary of 36,000 livres [$360,000 today] and a promise of 300,000 [$3 million] more after the war. He even had the impudence to say and write to Congress all the aid sent from France was the result of his ardent and pressing solicitations.

"Congress did not dare either to grant his enormous demands or to refuse them outright, but when the four engineers sent by Mr. Franklin arrived, M. Du Coudray was confronted with them at a session of Congress. He was unmasked, and it was proven that he had deceived the Congress about everything, even his status, because he was the chief of an artillery brigade, and not a brigadier general, and the son of a wine merchant of [Rheims]."[7]

A month later, Du Coudray rode his horse onto a crowded Schuylkill ferry. It bolted into the river. Unable to free himself, he drowned. [7] Congress recalled Deane for his selections. Arthur Lee, of Virginia, an envoy to Paris, like Franklin, opposed Deane and accused him of profiteering. (Congress would recall Lee too.) Deane, a Groton, Connecticut, lawyer and congressman before going to Paris, could not clear himself. Writing letters critical of the government, he was called a traitor and died a recluse in 1789. Congress later found the charges were "a gross injustice" and voted $37,000 to his heirs in 1842.[8]

Despite his youth and inexperience, Lafayette was unlike the other French officers, Congress learned. His wealth and connections were too valuable to ignore. Angry at his treatment, Lafayette wrote to John Hancock, president of Congress, with a three-dot pyramidal symbol of his Masonic lodge: "After the sacrifices I have made in this cause, I have the right to exact two favours: one is to serve at my own expense — the other is to serve at first as a volunteer." He indicated he did not expect to stay long, but long enough to find glory.[9]

In a July 31 resolution, Congress commissioned him a major general without assignment, an honorary rank. In two flowery sentences it mentioned his being "anxious to risque his life in our cause." A commission for Kalb, angered by the delay and ready to return to France, came on September 15. It read: "Resolved, that another major general be appointed in the army of the United States; the ballots being taken, the Baron de Kalb was elected."[10]

Seeing the sad situations of Congress and the army, Kalb gave up hope of his mentor becoming American generalissimo. In a secret unsigned letter to Kalb on December 11, 1776, Broglie-Ruffec expected, after winning the revolution, to become king of the young republic. He died at sixty-two in 1781, two years before the war ended.[11]

SEVEN: Joining a Revolution

Lafayette's dream came true on July 31, 1777. As an army officer, he was invited to a Philadelphia party honoring Washington. The tavern meeting proved momentous for both. Washington, forty-five, reserved and six feet tall, looked like a supreme commander.[1] As a young self-employed surveyor, he had slept in barns under horse blankets, awakening to insect bites. In 1753, a British major at 21, Washington presented Virginia Governor Robert Dinwiddie's demand that the French vacate the region Dinwiddie mistakenly claimed on the Pennsylvania-Ohio frontier. Washington failed in this mission, but the French commander treated him and guide Christopher Gist to a savory supper. Returning south, the pair confronted an ice floe in the Allegheny River at future Pittsburgh on December 29. Gist saved Washington when ice knocked him off the raft.[2]

After sleeping on an island, Washington walked seventeen days to Williamsburg and wrote a successful book about the trip. The following July, Washington lost Fort Necessity, failing to prevent Braddock's defeat but fought with valor. Elected to the Virginia's House of Burgesses in 1758, he was a delegate to the First and Second Continental Congresses.

Washington's father died when he was eleven. From battle George addressed his mother as "Honored Madam." Eldest of four children, he revered her. Lafayette later visited her in Fredericksburg and in

1784 viewed her grave, noting its lack of a suitable memorial.[3] Through inheritance, marriage and purchase Washington owned several Virginia plantations. In 1770, he purchased 234 acres in Fayette County, Pennsylvania, containing Fort Necessity, site of his defeat. He loved his wife, Martha, a wealthy widow with a son and daughter. They added to Mount Vernon, inherited from Washington's beloved half-brother Lawrence, until there were twenty rooms. With orchards, paddocks, gardens and slave cabins, the estate was baronial. From its rear piazza the mansion offered a splendid Potomac vista. The river gave Mount Vernon its chief product, shad and herring, caught in nets and sold in barrels. With paid overseers directing the plantation and slaves, Washington left in 1775 to lead the revolution. He rarely visited over seven years but often wrote to his wife and managers.

Fighting as a loyal Briton, Washington objected to Parliament's tax acts in which colonists had no say. In Philadelphia on June 15, 1775, during the second Continental Congress, canny John Adams, of Quincy, Massachusetts, sought with other delegates to unite Southern and Northern colonies against Britain. They chose Washington, who offered military suggestions, wore a uniform to Congress and came from the strongest Southern state, to lead the war. Americans had fought numerous battles against the British before the *Declaration of Independence* was signed in 1776.

Since Britain could invade through the Hudson valley, Americans made several disastrous incursions into Canada. In one of the few successful attacks, at Fort Ticonderoga on Lake Champlain, Major Benedict Arnold and his troops forced General John Burgoyne's army from the former French bastion. But on October 11, 1776, at Valcour Bay on the lake, Arnold and his scruffy soldiers, forcing enemy ships into a straight too narrow to maneuver, still failed to entrap them. Yet this strategy delayed British invasion a year and led to Burgoyne's defeat at Saratoga, New York. Americans had lost far more battles than they had won. Almost everyone believed Washington was losing the war.

When he met the ebullient Lafayette more than fifty battles and skirmishes had already occurred. Washington fumed to Congressman Benjamin Harrison (father of President William Henry Harrison) on August 19, "The Marquis de Le Fiatte *(sic)* does not conceive his

Commission is merely honorary; but given with a view to command a division of this Army. True, he has said that he is young and inexperienced, but at the same time has always accompanied it with a hint that so soon as *I* shall think *him* fit for the command of a division…" he has actually applied to me (by direction, he says, from Mr. Hancock) for commissions for his two aides-de-camps..."

Harrison answered he and Congress regarded the commission as merely honorary and recalled Lafayette had said in a letter to Congress "his chief motive for going into our service was to be near you, to see service and to give him an eclat at home where he expected he would soon return. These you may depend on it were the reasons that induced Congress to comply with his request, and that he could not have obtained the commission [of major general] on any other terms. The other day he surprised everybody by his letter requesting commissions for his officers, insinuating he should expect a command as soon as you think him fit for one. Congress never meant he should have one, nor will it countenance him in his applications…"

Daunted, Lafayette wrote Henry Laurens, of South Carolina, president of Congress,

> *The moment I heard of America I loved her; the moment I knew she was fighting for freedom I burnt with a desire of bleeding for her; and the moment I shall be able to serve her, at any time, or in any part of the world, will be the happiest of my life.*

With growing English fluency, he would write many thousands of letters in French and English, depending on the recipient, often intending to change minds while remaining consistant in his own beliefs. He linked his French position with his personal enthusiasm while claiming no personal gain, a form of diplomacy he never lost. These were not just words or show, although he was adept at both. He expected to prove his good intentions.

Lafayette joined Washington at his temporary headquarters (August 10 to 23), a stone house the late John Moland, prominent Bucks County lawyer, had built in rural Scots-Irish Warwick Township. On Little

Neshaminy Creek, it was a day's ride — ninety miles — north of Philadelphia. Washington awaited the enemy's next move as his ragged troops bivouacked on twelve acres. Time moved slowly. Washington wrote letters, officers drilled soldiers and staff kept busy with paperwork. Lafayette was billeted in a house near the Presbyterian Church. Washington told him experienced men were holding all officer posts and refused him an assignment.

But the young man's admiration, verging on idolatry, won over his commander. Lafayette reminded his hero of his own commitment to liberty. He spoke of his court connections but few knew how tenuous they were. He had never seen a battle much less been in one. But he was prepared for duty. Freemasonry helped forge their bond. Lafayette later told Americans in Delaware he was inducted into Masonry at Valley Forge with Washington presiding, but there is no proof of this. But being a Mason profoundly influenced Lafayette, who enjoyed its rituals and camaraderie. Freemasonry, an international society beginning in sixteenth-century Scotland, employed stonemasons' terms and instruments in rites said to have begun, at least metaphorically, with Solomon's temple. Masons professed love of liberty, good character as well as intellectual and spiritual values. Charitable deeds and brotherliness helped members succeed in business and politics, but their quasi-secret meetings caused widespread distrust. Yet Masonry greatly advanced Lafayette in America.

He and Washington shared moral values and belief in brotherliness. "It is somewhat embarrassing to us to show ourselves to an officer who has just come from the army of France," Washington said. Lafayette replied adroitly, "I am here to learn and not to teach." He did not have long to wait.

On August 20, Polish nobleman Casimir Pulaski arrived at camp and presented Washington with a letter from Benjamin Franklin urging his admission to the army. Pulaski had fought against Russian domination of Poland and Lithuania. He delivered a letter from Adrienne. The next day Washington and Lafayette wrote letters introducing Pulaski to Congress. Several weeks later he was appointed first general of the cavalry and served valiantly. (Pulaski died at thirty-four from his wounds six days after the Battle of Savannah on October 15, 1779.)

Lafayette with his personal servants must have seemed an exotic peacock to battle-hardened officers. The army had had its greatest success the previous Christmas in Trenton where it captured 1,300 Hessians and slew their commander. Lafayette's link with other French officers was their native tongue. His closest friend was brilliant bilingual Lieutenant Colonel Alexander Hamilton. Two years older than Lafayette, Hamilton was one of two brothers born out of wedlock to the fourth son of a Scottish laird on Nevis, British West Indies.[4] On St. Croix, he learned French and honed his mathematics as a clerk in an import-export business. His mother, of English-Huguenot stock, died when he was twelve. His admiring employer and others sent him to King's College (Columbia University) in New York. Hamilton left college at nineteen to organize a regiment of sixty artillerymen who fought at White Plains and Trenton. He quickly became Washington's aide-de-camp, secretary and in all but name chief of staff. Lafayette and Hamilton's friendships included Lieutenant Colonel John Laurens,[5] son of Henry Laurens, wealthy planter, slave dealer and president of Congress. They were compared to the Three Musketeers.[6]

Lafayette wrote to Hamilton from Paramus, New Jersey, "...Before this campaign I was your friend and your very intimate friend agreeable to the ideas of the world — since my second voyage my sentiment has increased, to such a point the world knows nothing about that. Both from want and from scorn of expressions, I shall only tell you."[7] Lafayette urged Washington to make Hamilton adjutant general.[8]

In Canada meanwhile, General Burgoyne decided to invade New York near Lake Champlain and descend the Hudson valley to New York City. At the time, American Major General Horatio Gates was massing troops in upstate New York. But General William Howe in New York City was not told of Burgoyne's invasion. Had he known, Howe could have met Burgoyne to cut Northern and Southern states apart. Howe, illegitimate descendant of George I, had won the Battle of Bunker Hill over ill-prepared Bostonian patriots and, without a shot, took Manhattan as Washington retreated.

Howe's advantage was almost 30,000 soldiers hired from six petty German princes. Shortly after Lafayette and his comrades had reached Philadelphia, Howe and his Hessians arrived at Long Island on August

22, 1777. The Hessians were not true mercenaries. Their princes paid wages with little or nothing for overseas service while the British paid the princes well. The most notorious of them was Frederick II of Hesse-Cassel. His first wife was George II's daughter. Frederick, egoistic namesake of Frederick the Great, sent the most of more than 16,000 Germans to America. The British, distrusting his avarice, paid his men with theirs. Frederick, dazzled by Versailles, spent his income on castles and the *Oktagon,* a huge mountainside cascade that is still a wonder.[9]

Through hearsay, Washington thought well of these foreigners: "One thing I must remark in favor of the Hessians ... our people who have been prisoners generally agree they received much kinder treatment from them than from the British officers and soldiers." Many Americans hated that Hessians worked for George III. Mostly farm boys seeking adventure, they came from 300 principalities and drilled with Prussian discipline. Elite marksmen wore green jackets, early camouflage, beneath tall helmets. Most Hessians were honest but some were rascals and plunderers. Finding nearly 200,000 Germans living in America; 5,000 Hessians remained after the war.

Forcing Washington's retreat through Brooklyn and to the south, Howe, with the Hessians, began a campaign. Setting sail from Staten Island and Sandy Hook with his elder brother, Admiral Richard Howe, the general set out in an armada: 17,000 troops in ten ships of the line, twenty frigates and nearly 300 transports carrying provisions, weapons and horses. Washington, perplexed at this action, found it more difficult than necessary. Still, Howe had beaten Washington in four important battles in fourteen months.

Hiding in the low New Jersey hills, Washington and scouts watched the fleet sail by. Admiral Howe led *H.M.S. Eagle*, a third-rate ship of the line carrying sixty-four or more cannons on three decks. While she was berthed at Staten Island, a lone American operator of *Turtle*, the first submarine — a clam-shaped contraption on which Franklin had offered ideas — failed to attach a bomb to *Eagle's* hull. Was Howe headed to Charleston and a Southern campaign? That was not his intention. The convoy experienced six weeks of Atlantic storms, hundreds of seasick men and many dead horses. Finally, the ships rode up Chesapeake Bay, mud trapping many in shallow Elk River, and troops disembarked at

Head of Elk, Maryland.[10] Howe may have wanted to avoid rebel forts on the Delaware but his cannons could have leveled them. Washington finally saw Howe's objective was to take Philadelphia.

Howe expected that many eastern Maryland loyalists would help him but they shunned both redcoats and rebels. If Howe and his weary men had navigated the Delaware River, it would have taken them to the capital. Instead, his troops, towing artillery and provisions, had to slog fifty miles overland. Rains turned roads into ponds, ruining black gunpowder wrapped in paper for both armies. Ninety miles from New York City, Philadelphia could have been reached overland in five or six days. Instead, Howe created a disaster.

Washington had an easier time. To boost morale in a war he was losing, he ordered his ragtag army, sporting green sprigs on their hats, to parade through Philadelphia to cheering crowds. Even patriot-critic Adams found them "extremely well armed, pretty well cloathed and tolerably disciplined." Thirty-nine lashes lay in store for anyone braking ranks. The rebels reached Wilmington, Delaware, as Howe landed at Head of Elk. Washington and 11,000 men marched northwest to rural Chadds Ford, Pennsylvania, hoping to block Howe's 15,000 soldiers. Washington chose high ground above the eastern bank of Brandywine Creek. The enemy had to cross it to reach Philadelphia. But Howe and Hessians under Lieutenant General Wilhelm von Knyphausen marched to Kennett Square, six miles farther northwest. Both armies met on the foggy morning of September 11, 1777. The battle, massed on ten acres, raged four to five hours.

Washington thought Howe would approach from the south along the Great Road leading to Chadds Ford.[11] But this was only one of the south-flowing run's eight crossing points amid valleys and wooded hills. Acting on that idea, Howe ordered Knyphausen's 8,000 men with their army's provision wagons to spread out on the road for miles in a column while filing back and forth, making a din and raising dust. This ploy and several false field messages fueled Washington's incorrect conclusions. From his headquarters east of the creek in the house of Benjamin Ring, a patriotic Quaker, Washington with a telescope saw the dust clouds. Before dawn that hot day, Howe had ordered Major General Lord Charles Cornwallis, who had helped drive the Americans from Long Island, to cross the stream farther north at Jeffrie's Ford. Commanding the best British troops, Cornwallis marched to the east through the woods in a pincer movement and fell on the rebels from behind.

Considered the war's finest British general, Cornwallis had a distinguished history. An earl's son born in Suffolk in 1738, he attended Eton and Cambridge. He enjoyed Eton where a hockey blow misaligned his right eye. Since Britain had no military universities then, he briefly studied soldiering in Turin, Italy. He joined the Seven Years War and had fought at Minden. Six years younger than Washington, Cornwallis, like many American revolutionary generals, had served in the French and Indian War. Elected to Parliament as a liberal, Cornwallis, bucking the tide, voted against repressing colonists. But after Lexington, as a personal friend of George III, he supported Britain. Later inheriting the title of second earl and the estate of Brome Hall, he became a marquess. His wife Jamima died during his return from America in 1779. Grief-stricken, he rededicated himself to winning the war. In battle, Cornwallis moved quickly, rare for a British general. He resented Howe's slowness and had favored Clinton as strategist.

Washington, who chose to make the British cross the Brandywine, liked his plan of a six-mile-long line of 1,800 men. But they faced 2,200 elite Britons and Hessians. American Generals Sullivan, Stephens and Sterling hoped to block them east of the creek. Washington too late reacted to Cornwallis' outflanking action. As Knyphausen's troops advanced with booming cannonades, they nearly overwhelmed the Continentals. From a line on the upper battlefield, Cornwallis' brigades and grenadiers swung around the rebels. Americans, almost surrounded, caught British crossfire at Sandy Hollow.

Lafayette now begged to join the battle. Too harried to argue, Washington consented. Lafayette charged on his horse into battle, Gimat and La Colombe beside him. The Americans were confused. He urged them repeatedly to fire on the enemy for as long as they could and not lose the field. He rode back and forth among them, pushing them on. But their long rifles took more than a minute to reload.

Dashing through rifle and cannon fire, he saw all around wounded men groaning and screaming in pain. The Continentals fell back and again Lafayette surged forward. Gimat saw blood dripping from Lafayette's boot. A musket ball had passed through his left calf. In the heat of action he had not felt a thing. He had said he would give his life for America. Now he was thrilled to shed blood for her!

As Americans neared exhaustion, Count Pulaski, with Washington's permission, gathered horsemen and charged the surprised enemy. In the battle was Captain James Monroe, a farm lad from Fredericksburg, Virginia, seven months Lafayette's junior. As an advance guard in Washington's first major victory the previous Christmas at Trenton, Monroe was shot in the shoulder by a musketball he would carry for life. The surprise attack on crossing the Delaware led to 1,000 Hessians' capture and their commander's death. A new friend, Monroe and others helped Lafayette to a field hospital.

A fifth British advance pushed the patriots into the forest two miles farther east. But Lafayette's action kept the siege from being an American rout. The talley: nearly 400 killed, 600 wounded and 400 of the enemy captured. The British suffered eighty-nine dead, 488 wounded and six missing. With both sides exhausted, Howe halted immediate pursuit. He had won again but knew his adversary's power.

General Nathanael Greene, a Rhode Island Quaker, directed the army's retreating rear guard. Lafayette was now moved east to Chester. Washington ordered his doctor, John Cochran, soon surgeon general, "Look after him as though he were my son." His request reverberated in Lafayette, who afterward thought of himself as Washington's adoptive son. This unofficial status furthered Lafayette's aura and he would name his own son Georges Washington Lafayette. Washington became his godfather. Washington saw similarities and dissimilarities in their lives and characters, caring deeply for "my dear Marquis," as he addressed him in letters.

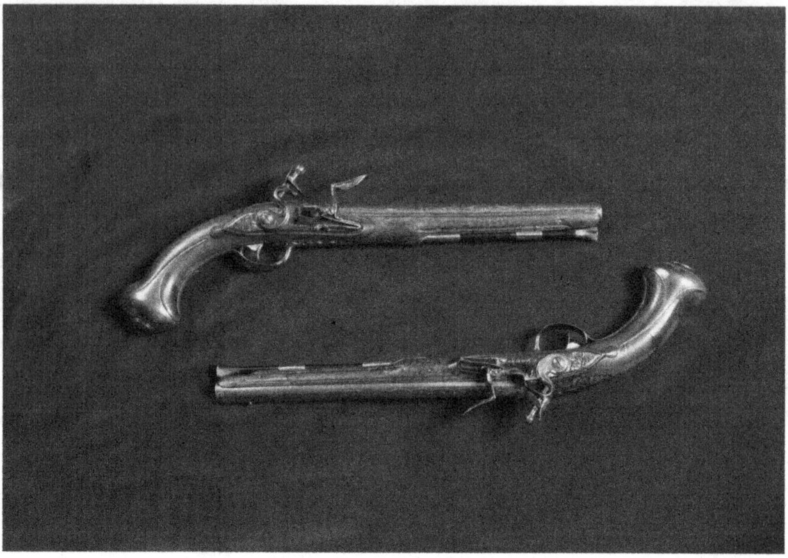

Lafayette gave these fine saddle pistols to George Washington in 1777.
Courtesy Fort Ligonier Museum, Ligonier, Pa.

They gave each other many gifts. Among the most important were exquisite steel and walnut saddle pistols Lafayette presented to the commander in the winter of 1778.[12] Lafayette later asked Thomas Paine to deliver to Washington the main iron key to the Bastille, symbol of despotism's overthrow, with a small painting of its being razed. They remain where Washington hung them by Mount Vernon's staircase. The men also gave each other their portraits by Peale.[13]

Charles W. Peale: *Marquis de Lafayette in Continental Uniform, 1778-1780.*
Courtesy Independence National Historic Park, Philadelphia, Pa.

After midnight in Chester, Washington coolly wrote to Hancock, "Notwithstanding the misfortune of the day, I am happy to find the troops in good spirits; and I hope another time we shall compensate for the losses now sustained." As Howe moved toward Philadelphia, Burgoyne's redcoats, after a sizable defeat at Bennington, New York, marched down to Albany. Meanwhile General Gates drove north with some 8,000 American troops. Although he had fought in the French and Indian War, Gates' military bearing was off the mark and he was said to resemble an old woman. A senior officer at forty-nine and four years older than Washington, Gates was still ambitious.

The patriots fought at Freeman's Farm, New York, on September 19 and met the enemy again on October 7 at Bemis Heights near the town of Stillwater, nine miles south of Saratoga on the upper Hudson. Gates sent word of victory to Congress but not to Washington. Saratoga, after two and a half years of war, was such a stunning American victory that France openly declared its support, although Foreign Minister Vergennes had had this in mind for some time. Charleville cannons,

French black-powder flintlock muskets, lighter and more maneuverable than Brown Besses, won Saratoga and more victories to come.

Brigadier General Thomas Conway, forty-four, an Irish adventurer and former colonel in France, had joined the Americans on May 13, 1777, a few months before Lafayette. That October, currying favor, Conway wrote in a letter to Gates, "Heaven has been determined to save your country; or a weak General and bad counsellors would have ruined it."

Colonel James Wilkinson, who carried news of Saratoga to Congress, gave that part of the letter to an aide of Brigadier General Lord Stirling, one of the commander's trusted officers.[14] Forwarding this insubordinate remark, Stirling wrote Washington, "Such wicked duplicity of conduct I shall always think it my duty to detect." Washington showed the note to a few officers, including Lafayette, who had learned of it from Conway. Most of the camp knew of it. On November 5, Washington sent Conway a brief message saying he had received the comment, repeated it and signed his name.

Conway answered immediately, hemming and hawing on his wordage. If "weak General" had slipped from his pen, he wrote, it indicated Washington allowed others to trouble him. Conway did not offer an apology and implied he would write the French government on the Continental Army's losing Philadelphia, although it would not contain anything he would not say to Washington directly. But it indicated, Thomas Fleming writes in *Washington's Secret War*, "Washington was to be treated with disrespect and even with contempt by Gates, Mifflin, Conway, their circle and by Congress. What they hoped to accomplish was carefully concealed from everyone but those who could be trusted to deny the dirty game they were playing" to oust Washington.[15]

Gates wrote Washington he hoped the commander would help him find the man who had "stealingly copied" his private letter. Although Gates had no idea who it was, he said he was sending the letter to Congress because a crime of "such magnitude" should be punished. Washington, biding his time, moved to more pressing matters.

Lafayette in his broken but courtly English explained to Washington how he was duped. Conway deferred to him because he wanted Lafayette to speak well of him at the French court and to his protector, Marquis

Charles de Castries, commandant of the elite cavalry (gendarmerie), governor of Flanders and Hainault (later naval secretary, royal conservative adviser, *maréchal*) and Lafayette's close friend. Lafayette added that Conway, a dangerous man, tried to change Lafayette's opinion of Washington and wanted Lafayette to quit America.

Washington, genial with his young friend, replied the next day: "...We must not, in so great a contest, expect to meet with nothing but Sunshine. I have no doubt but that everything happens for the best; that we shall triumph over all our misfortunes, and shall, in the end, be ultimately happy..."

But Howe, en route to Philadelphia, again defeated Washington and his troops at the romantically named Battle of the Clouds in Chester County. Heavy rains once more ruined American munitions.

PART TWO: SUCCESS AND FAILURE

EIGHT: RECOVERY AND DUPLICITY

Lafayette was carried on a litter into Philadelphia's Indian Queen Hotel, where members of Congress visited him. The commander-in-chief's protégé had proved his loyalty to the cause by what he called "my *vound* of Brandywine."[1] With Philadelphia's capture near, Lafayette left for Bethlehem, Pennsylvania, in the carriage of Henry Laurens, who was leaving at the last minute for Lancaster, capital for a day. Congress then retreated southwest to safer York, Pennsylvania.

Here Henry Laurens was elected president of Congress. With few members there, an embarrassing twenty-two or so, Congress met in a second floor room of the county courthouse until returning to Philadelphia in June 1778, finding the British had left the capital looted and fetid. Moravians nursed Lafayette. He stayed with the Boeckel family out of danger. Peter Francisco, a young giant six feet five tall who had impressed Washington with his fighting skill was also recovering and a companion. Lafayette's nurse was young Lisa Boeckel, comely and vivacious. He wrote Adrienne charming lies.

> *...To put the best face on it, I could tell you that mature reflection had induced me to remain in my bed for several weeks, sheltered from all danger. But I must admit that I was invited to stay there because of a very*

slight wound in the leg. I do not know how I received it; in truth, I did not expose myself to enemy fire. It was my first battle, so you see how rare battles are... The ball passed through the flesh and touched neither bone nor nerve.

The surgeons are astonished by the rate at which it heals; they are in ecstasy every time they dress it, and maintain that it is the most beautiful thing in the world. I myself find it very foul, very tedious, and rather painful; there is no accounting for tastes. But, finally, if a man wished to be wounded just for his amusement, he should come and see my wound and have one just like it...

He recovered in six weeks but was lame for some time. Now twenty, he rejoined Washington on October 16 at the Methachton Hill camp.[2] While he was away, the Continentals were defeated at Germantown, near Philadelphia, and at Forts Mifflin and Mercer. The marquis enjoyed high status as the commander's friend who had spilled blood for America. Some older officers were jealous but Lafayette had a further power: troops assumed he had close connections to the French government and believed it was only a matter of time until more support arrived.[3] This incorrect expectation probably stirred Lafayette to seek help at court just as Broglie's actions stirred his wanting to fight for America.

Pondering how to hurt the British, Lafayette as early as October 24, 1777 wrote from Whitemarsh Camp to Vergennes asking to lead an attack on Britain's West Indian islands.[4] He would have called on Valley Forge companions. This was not whimsy, as has been written. Lafayette's cousin, François de Bouillé, was not only a general and governor in the French West Indies — variously Guadeloupe, Martinique, Saint Lucia — but also regularly fought the British for other islands. The link between the American Revolution and the Caribbean was so close that American independence was gained there as much as at Yorktown. Saint Lucia, for instance, changed ownership fourteen times through conquest but only once during the Seven Years' War. Europeans were far more interested in Caribbean riches — sugar, rum, weapons, gunpowder trade — than the North American wilderness. Pressed by his own war, Washington declined. But the Franco-American Treaty of 1778 gave Americans the so-called "right" to take Canada and Bermuda, while former owner France renounced further claims.

Impressed with Lafayette's courage and leadership at Brandywine, Washington twice asked Congress to permit him to lead a division. Lafayette, pleased with his part at Brandywine but impatient, knew how inactive troops would become in the Northeastern winter. Should he return to France as so many others had? Reality cooled his former zeal. The Americans were so untrained. But they, buoyed by a near-win at Germantown, believed they could defeat a great army. At least they had spirit.

In late November, Washington sent Greene and 400 men to harass Cornwallis, settled in Gloucester, New Jersey, for winter. Lafayette, concealing his men, several of whom were French, went out alone to a point projecting into the Delaware River. Howe's frigates patrolled it as Cornwallis' barges ferried forage and provisions to Philadelphia. Lafayette spied Hessians on an earthen redoubt and his troops saw him show himself to them. Lafayette believed he was never in trouble when comrades and Americans saw his bravery. Their calls of safety drew him back. At twilight he led an attack on a Hessian outpost, chasing them a half-mile. The rebels, firing at the Hessians' cross-belted backs, killed twenty, wounding and capturing as many more. These actions won Lafayette the command of a division.

Homesick in camp, Lafayette compared his good treatment in Bethelem with the motley soldiers. They barely stood at attention and off duty mostly played cards. They were kind to him but were so unlike Parisians, who prized gentility. War could be confusing. On October 6, for instance, the British under Sir Henry Clinton defeated rebels under Major General George Clinton, capturing Fort Clinton on New York's Hudson River.

Lafayette was pleased to speak French with his servants and officers. But, although writing often to his wife, he heard nothing from her.

"When I was in Europe," he confessed to Washington, "I thought here almost every man was a lover of liberty and [would] rather die free than live slave. You can conceive my stonishment." He found as many Americans devoted to the king as believed in a new republic. He spoke of returning to France, but on December 1 Washington, with Congress' approval, offered Lafayette one of several army divisions needing officers. He chose fighters in Washington's Virginia.

On December 19, as the army marched with bare and bloody feet to Valley Forge, Lafayette received a letter from the old ambassador, *Maréchal* de Noailles, announcing the July birth of Anastasie, his second daughter. Lafayette sent letters to Adrienne and family with John Adams, on his way to replace Deane. It was probably at Valley Forge Lafayette met Pierre Charles L'Enfant, who had joined the army also as a volunteer in 1776. He had attended Paris' Royal Academy of Painting and Sculpture. At Valley Forge, although serving as an army engineer, he drew officers' portraits, including Washington's, which led to further assignments.[5]

Lafayette was thrilled about his new daughter. "I have never been as happy in my life as the moment when the news arrived," he hurriedly wrote Adrienne. "I love you with unspeakable tenderness, I love you more than ever, and I hope we shall be happy the rest of our lives together." Thinking of her father's desire for grandsons, he added, "What pleasure it will give me to embrace my two poor little girls. You do not believe me so hard-hearted, and at the same time so ridiculous as to suppose that the sex of our new infant can have diminished in any way my joy at its birth.... I kiss each of our daughters a thousand times; tell them their father loves them madly, as he loves their wonderful mother. Believe me. I shall not lose a moment rejoining you as soon as I can. Adieu, adieu, I kiss you ten million times." First-born Henriette had died two months earlier. He would not know of it for some time.

Washington chose Valley Forge as winter camp for its supposed advantages. The forge was in bountiful farming country and near enough to spy on Philadelphia, twenty-five miles away. The Continentals were themselves constantly spied on. Records show the winter of 1777 was no worse than usual, but privations made life miserable. Troops without clothes and shoes cut logs and made crude huts sixteen feet long, each sheltering twelve men. Not until March were there enough to house them all. They split wood for roof shingles, which leaked, and chinked and daubed walls with mud to stop the wind. Many men lacked britches and marched with bare feet in the snow, turning it crimson.

Everyone, even Washington and Martha on her visits, subsisted on the most basic food, when they could get it.

Many men contracted smallpox and other diseases. Lafayette persuaded Washington to variolate the troops, the largest effort then to control smallpox in America. Washington was already immune. Visiting Barbados with his tubercular half-brother Lawrence, Washington, nineteen, survived the pox that may have left him sterile. Lafayette's French doctor — perhaps Félix Brunot — oversaw the procedure. Redcoats were already immunized, but smallpox killed a son of George III and more than 200 Hessian soldiers in America.

Loyal to the crown, Quaker farmers refused almost worthless Continental dollars and sold produce in Philadelphia for British gold. Congress, with virtually no income, printed money without sufficient backing. States could raise taxes but refused to relinquish their power to Congress even in the face of possible defeat. Army quartermasters stole money, food and uniforms in an extensive black market. Lafayette had guards make warm capes from old blankets. He found Quakers' religious practices curious and their British loyalty traitorous.

Knowing how French officers had angered Congress and Washington, Lafayette avoided Du Coudray but was impressed by Conway, whose protruding eyes glowed as he told of his battles with astonishing verbiage.[6] Events were going so poorly several congressmen wanted to replace Washington. They included Dr. Benjamin Rush, of Philadelphia, who later regretted his opposition; James Lovell, of Boston, and a few officers, most notably General Horatio Gates, hero of Saratoga; General Thomas Mifflin, a weak-willed quartermaster; and Conway. All found Washington incompetent. As the so-called "Conway Cabal," they intended to replace him with Gates.

As part of the plan, Congress asked Lafayette to lead an invasion of Canada. Since it had a large French-speaking population, it was said he had the best chance of urging them to join America, as though these Catholics would want a Protestant British-style government. This deception was designed to remove the marquis from Washington, supposedly leaving him more vulnerable to criticism and dismissal, meanwhile making Lafayette look ridiculous.

Washington complained to Congress of thievery he saw in supplying troops with clothing and provisions. He asked that trusted General Philip Schuyler be made the army's inspector general. But Congress wanted Conway, then in Albany, for that. Washington knew invading Canada would be disastrous. But he did not stop Lafayette, who believed taking Canada would earn him glory in France. Riding to York, he agreed to join Conway but cannily asked to remain under Washington's command. The marquis found that incompetent congressmen were legislating as well as attempting to run the war while inexpert committee members often made poor decisions.

With Congress' assurance of support, Lafayette rode fast to Albany's wintry outskirts to muster invaders. He found Conway and 1,200 half-naked boys and old men, a fraction of troops promised. There were few firearms, provisions or officers and estimates of enemy strength were highly inaccurate. Lafayette vented his disgust at Congress. But he trained his men into a fighting force while keeping Conway busy with administration. By March, Congress, seeing invasion as hopeless, canceled it. Lafayette for this venture spent $12,000 of his own money for clothing and supplies.[7]

There was one gain from Albany: at Schuyler's suggestion, Lafayette built an alliance with the Northeastern Indians. Former French allies, they had gone over to the British but still admired their leaders in the French and Indian War. Traveling in sleighs, Lafayette, Schuyler and other commissioners attended a council of the Six Nations — Cayugas, Mohawks, Oneidas, Onondagas, Senecas and Tuscaroras — winning them to the American side. The Indians, impressed by Lafayette's splendid uniform, knew of his lineage. They called him *Kayewla,* after a legendary chief. Lafayette, like others who found fault with civilized society, accepted Rousseau's "noble savage" theory, regardless of its incorrect assumptions. The Indians enjoyed Lafayette's graciousness and the *louis d'ors* he gave them as tokens of his esteem. He overshadowed the American negotiators but the result was an alliance treaty. Lafayette wrote Congress to dislodge Conway, who was sent to a minor post in Peekskill. Congress, apologizing to Lafayette for its mistake, ordered him and Kalb to rejoin Washington at Valley Forge.

NINE: THE EFFECTIVE BARON

Relief was at hand. Washington urged Congress in March 1778 to appoint Prussian Baron Friedrich Wilhelm Augustus Steuben acting inspector general. Steuben (1730-1794) had served with distinction in the Seven Years' War. He claimed to have been an aide-de-camp to Frederick the Great, his hero. Steuben's father had falsified the title of baron and his son rose no higher than lieutenant colonel. But Beaumarchais and Deane introduced him as a lieutenant general in the Prussian Army. For twenty years Steuben was chief minister at the Hohenzollern-Hechingen court. This small German state was ruled by Frederick's spendthrift relative who paid Steuben $400 a year. Through a friend, he was elevated to a knighthood and the Order of Fidelity with its flashy star. He also served in Baden-Durlach, another state with a small army. In 1776, Steuben was allegedly dismissed for fondling boys.[1]

Needing a job, Steuben hurried to Paris where French war minister Saint-Germain and Beaumarchais, urging him to try America, paid for his travel. Franklin, author of many hoaxes as a newspaper publisher, suggested Steuben embroider his past to succeed in America. Historian Thomas Fleming called Steuben's story the greatest deception concocted for a good cause.[2] Borrowing money from John Hancock and Robert Morris, Steuben appeared at York with his American secretary-translator John North, a Russian wolfhound and wearing a Fidelity star on his chest. After impressing the congressmen, Steuben received a hearty welcome at Valley Forge.

As Franklin advised, Steuben volunteered his services, asking compensation only if America won the war. He taught soldiers precise maneuvers and trained his best students to improve the others. Unlike the British, he required officers to take a personal interest in their men's military needs. While demanding and cursing on the drilling field, Steuben showed much sensitivity elsewhere. He compiled military marching formations in a handbook used even after the war. Later, lobbying Congress for back pay, Steuben won a $2,500-a-year pension and 16,000 acres near Utica, New York. He also accepted friends' handouts. In later years his male coterie included Charles Adams, the second president's second son. A homosexual and alcoholic father, Adams witnessed Steuben's will.

Pleased with Steuben but fearing rumors might turn the baron against Washington, Lafayette wrote Steuben from Albany on March 12, giving him his opinion of the commander. Lafayette returned to Valley Forge late that month, wiser but fearing he had made a fool of himself. A relieved Washington assured him he would not be widely criticized and urged him not to give up and return to France. Lafayette had previously sworn to French friends that when France entered the American war he would report to the French Army. Despite words of duty to America, he felt honor-bound to fight for his homeland.[3]

To elude the British, he planned to return via the French West Indies. Twenty French infantry battalions had been dispatched to the Caribbean in November 1775, two years before Lafayette had dreamed of America.[4] He wrote to Bouillé in Martinique and also to Premier Maurepas urging government support for what Gottschalk called Lafayette's scheme of joining French attacks on British islands. After some delay, Bouillé greeted the idea favorably but not until Britain declared war on France on February 6, 1788 for aiding the Americans. Lafayette's uncle-in-law, the ambassador in London, delivered France's war declaration to the British court on June 17. Washington applauded this event, but, lacking a fleet, looked askance at any American invasion of the Caribbean. None occurred.

Congress hastily ratified the alliance treaty with France on May

6. To mark the occasion Washington invited the army to a religious service where all heard the good news. During a troop parade cannons fired thirteen salutes to the American states. Each man fired his musket and at a signal all shouted, "Long live the king of France! Long live the friendly European states!" Then they hailed, "To the American States!" Stirling commanded on the right and Lafayette, wearing a new white scarf, led on the left with French officers around him. It was a day of high hopes. Thanks to Steuben's instructions, the soldiers performed brilliantly.[5]

Washington learned the British and Hessians would leave Philadelphia because of the French threat to Britain's West Indian sugar islands. He put Lafayette in charge of 2,200 troops to observe whether the enemy would attack Valley Forge. On May 18, Lafayette and the Americans with fifty Oneida marched ten miles east to camp at Barren Hill, a high point flanking the Schuylkill ten miles from Philadelphia. Spies informed Howe, being recalled to London, of the reconnaissance. General Henry Clinton was replacing Howe as commander-in-chief. To mark the exchange, Philadelphia Tories celebrated that night with a *mischianza,* Italian for a variety of events: parties, barge regatta, a medieval-style tournament and fireworks.

Festivities joining 750 people in their finest silks lasted from 4 p.m. to early morning. Event planners included popular Captain John André, born to Huguenots in London, who lived in Franklin's house. Senior officers found such folderol in wartime appalling. But during the diversions Americans under Captain Allan McLane penetrated enemy lines north of the city and set fire to enemy abates, pointed logs jutting from barricades and meant to impale attackers.

Howe, confident he could trap "the boy," as his officers referred to Lafayette, decided on his pincer action, with Clinton heading his four most experienced generals. On May 19, the British and Hessians sent 4,000 of their best troops northwest in a twenty-mile arc to prevent Lafayette's return to Valley Forge. Another 4,000 soldiers under Clinton marched along Germantown Pike past the town of Roxborough to halt Lafayette's right and frontal positions. Confident of capturing the marquis, Howe planned a party the next night to show off his prize to the ladies in Philadelphia.

When the Americans knew they were surrounded, rather than panic they followed Lafayette and kept moving. For an unknown reason, Lafayette assembled several hundred men in St. Peter's Lutheran churchyard, in hindsight a mistake. The stone sanctuary was empty and surrounded by a stone wall strong enough to take musketfire. A man running in his sleeping gown alerted them of the approaching danger. Lafayette ordered a hundred men to march quickly to the rear, as if heading a much larger army.

Seeing this, British General James Grant halted his advance and took time to assess the seeming counterattack. This delay was exactly what Lafayette, cool and in charge, needed. Rapidly pulling troops back from this feint, he and his troops followed experienced American Generals Enoch Poor and James Varnum down a hidden path toward the town of Conshohocken, across the Schuylkill at Matson's Ford and to high ground on the opposite bank. The Oneida were the last to leave and ford the river. Continental reports said their war whoops frightened the redcoats. But the Oneida were terrified too; they had never seen so many redcoats.[6]

The men waded across the river holding onto each other "like corks in a net," in a British view. Meanwhile, Generals Grant and Grey, thinking they had Lafayette trapped, arrived to find an empty churchyard. Their 8,000 men had been outfoxed. Deflated, they all marched back to Philadelphia. This was the first test of Continental maneuverability, with only a few lives lost to enemy fire. Although nothing was won, Washington was pleased with the action's efficiency, called one of the most spectacular escapes in military history. It gave the Continentals a sense of accomplishment and the British never attacked Valley Forge.

Howe, after taking New York City, was criticized in Parliament for not handling the war more aggressively. Clinton in his memoirs did not mention the humiliation of Barren Hill, later renamed Lafayette Hill. For Lafayette there were new assignments. After nine months of occupation, 15,000 British left Philadelphia on June 18. Americans reclaimed it the next day. On June 20, 1778, Washington led his army from Valley Forge northward to New Jersey and the enemy. Congress left York four days later, resetting the floundering government in Philadelphia. Washington made war hero Benedict Arnold the city's military commander.

Arnold had wintered at Valley Forge, recovering from a leg wound acquired at Saratoga. On crutches with his left leg two inches shorter than his right, he fumed about Gates not sharing Saratoga's victory with him who had helped achieve it. A brilliant militarist, Arnold also resented not being promoted from major general to brigadier general. He knew Congress preferred giving that rank to those closer to Congress; and it also refused to reimburse his expenses for his troops. As a Connecticut lad, Arnold had fought in the French and Indian War in Canada, losing to French General Montcalm. The French, promising amnesty after the battle of Quebec, which they won against the British, had not stopped their Indian allies from scalping many Britons.

So Arnold opposed an American alliance with France. Ironically, this occurred after Louis XVI learned of the American victory at Saratoga. In Philadelphia, Arnold bought a fine carriage and entertained lavishly beyond his means. Thirty-eight and a recent widower with three sons, he wed Margaret Shippen, eighteen, spirited loyalist daughter of a Philadelphia judge, in March 1779. André, her friend, had introduced them. Before quitting the city André stole books, instruments and a portrait of Franklin from the inventor's house.[7] Arnold requested and received in June 1780 prestigious command of the fort being built at West Point, key to control of the Hudson valley and New England.

Troops under Washington, sniping at the British and Hessians as they crossed New Jersey, had suddenly, on June 28, 1778, met Clinton's army in the bloody Battle of Monmouth Courthouse, a hazardous region cut by three ravines. As great a problem was Washington's second in command, General Charles Lee. Born in Cheshire, England, the same month and year as Washington, Lee was considerably worse than Conway.

Lee, a British soldier like Washington, Horatio Gates and Thomas Gage, had served under Braddock in the French and Indian War. He became a Virginia planter and married a Mohawk chief's daughter. Returning to Europe as a colonel under British General John Burgoyne, Lee served in Portugal and Poland where he was King Stanislaus II's aide-de-camp and major general. In America, Lee offered his services to Congress. He had fought longer than Washington and was disappointed when not named commander-in-chief. His slipshod nature was the opposite of Washington's and, having forfeited his English properties, he wanted to be paid. As an American major general, Lee was considered second to Washington. Serving six months in the Southern department or theater, Lee was called to the main army and became a problem. In 1776, he and his men were slow in retreating from Forts Washington and Lee. (The last fort, on New Jersey's Hudson shore across from Fort Washington in New York, was named after him.)

Lee started a letter campaign to congressmen urging Washington's replacement, spurring the "cabal." Washington accidentally opened a Lee letter condemning him for army problems but did not immediately react. Lee was also late reaching the army's 1776 winter bivouac in Morristown. He stopped first at White's Tavern in Basking Ridge, three miles from his soldiers. The next morning a British patrol captured him in his dressing gown writing letters. Lee spent fifteen months in jail until Americans exchanged British General Richard Prescott for him. During his imprisonment Lee secretly reverted to British loyalty.

Washington knew Lee was duplicitous but rode four miles from Valley Forge to welcome him "as if he had been his brother," wrote Elias Boudinot, commissioner of prisoner exchange. Soldiers hailed Lee on his way to camp and a dinner was held in his honor. Washington invited Lee to stay with him and Martha in a back bedroom holding his belongings in their small stone farmhouse. Lee opened his bedroom door to a camp follower, a British sergeant's wife, who joined him that night. Washington was annoyed when Lee, disheveled and soiled, appeared late the next morning.

Two years later, Washington held a war council with his generals near Monmouth, New Jersey.[8] Several, including Lee, wanted to retreat instead of chasing the enemy across Jersey. Washington, aware the public wanted a victory, countermanded them. He increased the assault force by 1,500 men, adding 5,000 more from the 11,800-man army later that day. Washington wanted Lafayette to lead well-trained troops against the British rear guard of 11,000 men who were slowly driving a heavy wagon train through rains, mud and intense heat to Sandy Hook, a spit of land pointing to New York. Admiral Howe's frigates would transport them from New Jersey. But Washington, only guessing Clinton's plan, deferred to Lee, offering him the troop's leadership. Lee refused. But realizing how many men Lafayette would lead, Lee changed his mind, writing him a whiny letter: "It is my fortune and my honor that I place in your hands. You are too generous to cause the loss of either."[9] Although unimpressed by Lee, Lafayette complied since it was Washington's idea.

The marquis took another regiment and with General Anthony Wayne hurried on horseback into the woods to hector the enemy. Over-eager, Lafayette pushed too hard into the British force. Responding, Clinton suddenly ordered his rear guard to wheel around and pursue the Americans. Wayne prevented Lafayette's entrapment. When other American generals, seeing their men panicking, asked Lee what to do, he said he had no plan. He was startled to see British troops pouring toward him in full pursuit. Ordering a full retreat, Lee fell into Washington's advancing army. The commander was furious at Lee's disobedience, having no reason to ignore the order to advance. Washington swore, rare for him, at Lee, who countered "with inappropriate words." Washington had Lee arrested. With Lord Stirling presiding, Lee expected vindication but was court-martialed.

Washington took command of Lee's men and rallied them. Despite British fusillades bursting around him, Washington dashed about on a white horse he had just been given and was visible to the enemy. If he had fallen, Greene would have taken over. But because of his luck so far, Washington believed he was destined to survive, a hint of suppressed egotism.[10] The warfare continued until Lafayette with Wayne and their 4,000 men arrived from skirmishes along another route and helped to stop the British attack. In crossing New Jersey, the enemy had savaged the countryside: burning buildings, shooting cattle, carving steaks from carcasses, felling cherry trees instead of climbing for fruit. Battle- and heat-exhausted, both sides lost men to sunstroke.[11]

That night Washington spread his cloak for Lafayette to join him on the ground where they discussed Lee's behavior. Washington needed a confidant. Lafayette never forgot the honor. During the night, Clinton ordered his troops to march away quietly. The next day the Americans found many enemy dead and wounded. Admiral Howe ferried his troops to safely barricaded New York. Washington saw the situation repeating two years earlier. But Steuben's professional drills gave the Americans an advantage. They reasoned Clinton had not beaten them but simply retreated from Monmouth. Washington's ignorance of Clinton's plan may explain the American general's behavior at Monmouth. Offering a command to Lee suggests Washington may have wanted to force Lee's compliance; dangerous, considering Lee's vehemence. But this brought Lee's insubordination to a head, which Washington may have also sought.

The carnage: sixty-nine Americans dead, 161 wounded, 130 missing; the British count: sixty-five killed, 160 wounded, sixty-four missing. Continentals found hundreds of unburied and uncounted enemy bodies. Four hundred Hessians, seeking friendship among German immigrants, deserted. Despite each army's claims, Monmouth brought no real victory to either. Americans suffered slightly fewer losses, averted a tactical disaster and their prowess won the public's renewed patriotism.

Monmouth, the revolution's longest battle, was not only the last major encounter in the North but also the largest before Yorktown. Nothing was decided at Monmouth. Washington was buoyed by its outcome, but this time Lafayette was not mentioned in accolades for superior service in Hamilton's report or the commander's citation to Congress. Lee accurately estimated the British had outnumbered him almost two-to-one — 10,000 to 5,440 — which to some justified retreat. His obduracy was another matter. Found guilty of disobeying orders and being disrespectful to the commander, Lee was removed from service for a year but never returned to duty. He continued writing strident attacks on Washington and lost believability before the army dismissed him. John Laurens, aide to Washington, identified the commander's honor with his own. In a duel defending the leader's honor, Laurens wounded Lee slightly in his side. Lafayette and Laurens decided Lee was a traitor.[12]

In 1782, four years after his court-martial, Lee died of apparent fever in Philadelphia where he was buried. He might have been tried as a British deserter since he did not resign his lieutenant colonelcy for several days after joining the Continental Army. Also while General William Howe held him prisoner in 1777, Lee wrote a war plan against the Americans — found in Howe family archives in 1857.

Thomas Conway, seeking to reverse his fallen status, wrote about resigning from the army. His letter was forwarded to Congress and quickly accepted. He challenged General Cadwalader to a duel for calling him a coward for hiding in a barn during the battle of Germantown. Conway misfired but Cadwalader shot him through the mouth, "putting a stop to the rascal's lies," he said. With no friends in Congress, Conway returned to France to fight in French India. He may have been accused unfairly of plotting a cabal. But with him and Lee gone, Washington's war with Congress ended.

TEN: DEPENDING ON D'ESTAING

With the enemy in New York, Washington, Lafayette and their troops crossed the Hudson at White Plains. Lafayette's attachment to France became important in July when twelve ships of the line commanded by Vice-Admiral D'Estaing arrived off the Delaware Capes.[1] Jean-Baptiste d'Estaing, a distant Lafayette *Avergnat* relative, had sailed under orders from Toulon. Washington, delighted, wanted him to invade New York but that was not possible. The British had laid a bar across the harbor entrance, removed beacons and there was no trustworthy pilot. The two then chose to attack the British island garrison at Newport, Rhode Island, with Washington calling 10,000 soldiers to join the battle. On August 5, the French fleet appeared in the Sekonnet Passage, panicking the British, who destroyed their ships while Admiral Howe's fleet was sailing from New York to protect them.

Lafayette saw himself the logical liaison between the French and Americans. But for Rhode Island, Washington, having to deal with Generals John Sullivan and Nathanael Greene, divided troop reinforcements between Lafayette and Greene, offending neither, and left Sullivan in charge of the region. D'Estaing found mooring difficult: his crew had scurvy and enemy warships were in the passage near shore. Lafayette cleared the air with D'Estaing about the king's displeasure with him over joining America and learned his father-in-law had warmed to his successes. Lafayette joined D'Estaing in planning his attack on the British. The admiral was appalled Sullivan had not sufficiently prepared for battle. Lafayette saw his plans for further glory vanish when Sullivan and Greene urged delay. He fumed about how this inaction was disappointing French troops come to fight the enemy. His own faith in the Americans wavered. He thought the French would question the Americans' ability. Laurens wrote his father Lafayette's "private views withdrew his attention wholly from the general interest."[2]

The allies agreed to a joint attack on August 9, 1778. But Sullivan, seeing the British were leaving part of their island territory, sent his troops in first without telling D'Estaing. The infuriated French saw Sullivan as trying to steal credit but continued to prepare for attack. Through fog the next morning, D'Estaing spied Howe's fleet bearing down in a strong wind. As he prepared to fire, the storm became a gale, greatly damaging both fleets. Howe's ships limped back to New York. D'Estaing, sailing to Boston for repairs, offered to rescue any American troops caught without his backup but nothing more. Sullivan, angry at the admiral's departure, made matters worse. The Americans, he wrote in his August 24 orders, would seize what "their allies refused them assistance in obtaining." But American desertions followed D'Estaing's pullout. The land battle continued for a month, with thirty Americans and thirty-eight Britons killed.[3]

Lafayette, furious with Sullivan, was said to be thinking of challenging him to a duel. Sullivan backed off his remarks but Lafayette still felt betrayed. He resisted protesting against his American friends but again considered rejoining France when she declared war on Britain. Washington, reassuring him the alliance was necessary, chided Sullivan. He in turn asked Lafayette to tell D'Estaing that maintaining the alliance was as important as knowing what the admiral's plans were. The marquis rode quickly to Boston, where John Hancock, offering his goodwill, gave D'Estaing a portrait of Washington encircled with laurel. Lafayette rode back to Rhode Island to report. He was too late for a fierce battle in which Americans fought well but suffered from lack of French support. But Sullivan was pleased with Lafayette's help in smoothing things out in Boston. Even Congress, eager to please the French, complimented him.

But London was still angling for an American compromise. Tory statesman Lord Carlisle, leading the commissioners seeking an answer, criticized the colonists' "preposterous connection" with France, enemy "to all civil and religious liberty." Lafayette challenged the peer to a duel for the slur and thought of joining D'Estaing in the Caribbean campaign. Washington gently dissuaded him from both ideas, knowing Carlisle's talk would offend the French. Carlisle, demurring, wrote Lafayette that the two fleets could best handle the matter. After all, everyone knew a duel was fought for personal, not political, reasons.

But the French, soon to hail Lafayette as "the hero of two worlds," regarded his challenge to Carlisle with joy since it touched their national pride. Lafayette now eagerly sought the glory he saw denied. With the French envoy to America concurring, he asked for an indefinite leave from the American Army in the name of "patriotic love." D'Estaing then sailed back to the islands, leaving the alliance in tatters. Congress, making the most of Lafayette's departure, on October 21 sent a letter urging him to ask Franklin for more help from the king and to discuss with the good doctor sage ways of getting it. Congress invited Lafayette to sail in the new thirty-nine-gun frigate *Alliance* and to return as an American major general whenever he chose. Congress wrote to Louis XVI extolling Lafayette's abilities in the war and ordered Franklin to have an elegant sword made for him in Paris.

While in Boston, D'Estaing, with Lafayette assisting, had been busy trying to talk French Canadians into making Canada "the fourteenth state." Dashing from Boston to Philadelphia without leave, and feted at parties where he overindulged, Lafayette came down with a severe fever at the Brinkerhoff mansion in Fishkill, New York. Again Washington sent his doctor to Lafayette's bed where he could easily have died. Fretting that his fever was a terrible anticlimax to recent events, the marquis recovered after several weeks.

Washington visited Lafayette in Fishkill, and without telling him wrote to Congress to discourage any Canadian action, still believing it would be more difficult and require far more troops than anyone anticipated. The commander also considered: if the French helped take Quebec what would prevent them from wanting Canada back?

While awaiting *Alliance*'s readiness, Lafayette wrote a blizzard of letters to Washington and Congress urging the Canadian invasion and promotions for Gimat, La Colombe and Capitaine du Chesnoy. Brice had advanced to brevet lieutenant colonel (an honor without right of command). Lafayette, expecting his comrades would return with him to France, wished them to be honored as much as possible.

Sailing from Boston on January 11, 1779, *Alliance* nearly foundered in a storm off Newfoundland. The warship lost its main topmast, topyards, sails and tender. The crew repaired the damage with calmer days. Diverting Lafayette from seasickness, thirty-eight sailors, Irishmen and Britons hired in Boston, attempted mutiny. Captain Pierre Landais, a former French officer, dreamed of being the Continental Navy's Lafayette. But his erratic insubordinate behavior was more like Charles Lee's than the marquis. The would-be mutineers hoped to seize the ship, murder almost everyone and sail to England. They could expect the king to reward them for the vessel with Lafayette as a second prize. But an American crewman with an Irish accent from years in Ireland learned of the plot and told his officers. Lafayette, sword in hand, led them in clapping the rebels in irons. Landais wanted to hang them. Lafayette intervened and they were later exchanged for American captives. Reaching Brest in Brittany — the crossing was just twenty-three days — Lafayette would remain in France thirteen months. He sought not only more American aid but to lead an expedition.

Instead of going to his family, he hurried to Versailles to report to Maurepas, acting as Louis XVI's principal adviser. Unannounced, Lafayette entered the house of his cousin, the Prince de Poix, his London companion of nearly two years before, and a splendid ball at 2 a.m. and met with Maurepas the next day. Word quickly spread: the war hero had returned and was much changed. No longer awkward or a captain on reserve, he was a manly battle-seasoned officer with thinning hair. Because he was still in official disfavor, Lafayette was confined to a brocaded prison, the Noailles' Paris mansion, and told to see no one except his family for a week. Adrienne was overjoyed.

Lafayette wrote a self-excusing letter to Louis: "Love of my country, a fervent desire to see the humiliation of her enemies, a political instinct which the recent treaty would seem to justify, those, Sire, are the reasons which decided the role I played in aiding the American cause." The king chided him gently but invited him to his *levée* and a hunt. At court the marquis was deferred to and lionized as never before. On February 15, 1779, the queen interviewed him at the Noailles.' [4] Ladies' welcoming kisses soon stopped but he remained in the cabinet's good graces. Promiscuous beauty D'Hunolstein, impressed with his accomplishments, saw him often and he was the star of many dinner parties. But his fame did not erase his irritation with Congress' negativity on Canada.

Franklin's gout prevented his traveling from Passy to Versailles. Lafayette and he did not meet about winning more French support for weeks. Jacques Necker, finance minister since 1776, opposed more money for America, saying she had already been given too much. He wanted new spending cutbacks to prevent the treasury's collapse. Lafayette became fired by ideas perhaps learned in Brest from friends of American Captain John Paul Jones about a plan to invade England. Not yet knowing the French government was planning to send troops to America, Lafayette wrote secret letters to royal ministers and Jones: Lafayette wanted 1,500 to 2,000 men to burn English cities on the Irish Sea to frighten them and dilute recent British victories in South Carolina and Georgia. The plan appealed to Franklin, who first had the idea, as well as the experienced new French foreign minister Charles Gravier, Comte de Vergennes, ingenious planner of the future French presence in America, and Antoine de Sartine, naval secretary of state.[5]

The problem was finding the money. Lafayette tried to get the Swedes to lend warships but they wanted indemnity for losses. He sought to bring the Irish, festering against England, into his plan. French journals had stories of his preparing to lead a large force to America. This threw everyone off the actual strategy which was a secret armada, an expeditionary force, to be sent to the Caribbean. Lafayette later wrote in his memoirs — his "golden legend," as historian Jacques de Trentinian describes it — claiming points that Vergennes and court ministers originated, such as providing America with more money.[6] Lafayette did not know that these ministers, with Spain and its Bourbon monarch Charles III, Louis XVI's cousin, were thinking of invading England on a much larger scale. Lafayette wrote the dumbfounded Jones their plan had been rejected and informed the king.

Vergennes wrote, "Why, my dear Marquis, you blame yourself for confiding in me about your concerns! I can assure you that nobody cares more than I do…I guess you enjoy the recent developments in America [that is, arrival of D'Estaing's fleet and, not then known to Vergennes, its loss of two Newport battles and Savannah]… Let us hope the Comte d'Estaing will not stop half-way… I don't know yet what we can plan for the future with regards to America; unilateralism no longer effective, we need to cooperate with our allies; it is clear enough that we must send troops to keep control of the situation, but that is not enough…I wish your American friends would push a bit harder. They made some noise in Stony Point [satirizing the July 1779 stalemate there]; hopefully they are not content with it…"[7]

ELEVEN: SECOND RETURN TO WAR

Marie Antoinette in a rare show of appreciation proposed Lafayette's promotion to lieutenant commander of the King's Dragoons and Louis agreed. Lafayette willingly paid 80,000 livres ($800,000) for the prestigious post. For a man of twenty-two to have this honor was unheard of, but he was a national hero. The position activated his military service. The dragoons were based in Saintes, a medieval southwestern town near La Rochelle, more than a week away from Versailles, where for his plans Lafayette needed to be. He expected to emulate his father-in-law who seldom saw his dragoons in Metz. The honor was premature for one eager to return to America, but such offers were rare.

Details for this post were completed in April 1779. That month France and Spain signed a treaty to invade Britain. The "agreement" was a disaster from the start. France was to fight until Gibralter was returned to Spain (it never occurred); and Spain, worried about Americans in its Florida territories, was not compelled to recognize the United States or fight beside Americans. Lafayette was called to standby service against Britain in June. But the whole plan, very close to Broglie's old written one, was dropped in November. The Spanish fleet's late arrival and French epidemics on frigates made the effort impractical.

Vergennes resumed what Lafayette wanted, a large military force to help the Americans. Vergennes asked him to return, resume his rank and inform Washington France would send 6,000 men led by Comte de Rochambeau, a veteran of the Seven Years' War. The force, 2,000 more troops than Lafayette had hoped for, included eleven warships: seven ships of the line, two frigates, a cutter and a ship of the line made into a hospital. As Lafayette urged, Washington would be the expedition's supreme commander.[1]

Disappointed at not being named the French leader, Lafayette saw his youth as an obstacle. But after months of meeting and writing letters to French ministers, Washington, Americans and Irish contacts, he was thrilled that his mission in France was not in vain. Because the French disapproved, he admonished Americans to stop squabbling with each other. He was far from the liberal he would become. He had not yet probed both countries' social ills. His call for unanimity was typically French. Insisting on this quality in her own revolution would keep France from compromise, a meeting of minds, because, unlike in Britain, there was no such precedent.[2]

Two other events brightened Lafayette's visit. In August Franklin sent his grandson, William Temple Franklin, to present the beautiful gold-handled sword Congress had ordered for the marquis. Engraving depicted his American battles. Franklin wrote: "By the help of the exquisite artists France affords I find it easy to express everything but the sense we have of your worth and our obligations to you. For this, figures and even words are found insufficient."[3] Franklin made sure the gift received maximum press attention. Lafayette had hoped to carry the sword "into the heart of England" but that was not to be.

Lafayette asked Adrienne to oversee his accounts, a continuing role since he had no head for sums. For his war use he urged his loyal business manager, Jacques Philippe Grattepain-Morizot, to raise large amounts of money. Morizot frantically extracted rents from debtor tenants and made sure a 600-livres pension awarded for Gilbert IV's death was current.[4] Lafayette's first American stay had cost 140,000 livres; the second 610,000, a total of 750,000 (about $7.5 million today).[5]

He was delighted on December 24, 1779 when Adrienne bore Georges Washington Lafayette, who grew up to stand by his father. Lafayette was permitted to return to Paris and sent orders to his dragoons. When not writing, he devised military strategies for Rhode Island and Virginia. Certain of his importance to both allies, he saw himself as an intermediary. Before returning, he met with Franklin on shipping clothing. He ordered 4,000 American uniforms that never arrived in America. John Adams, returned to France, wrote introductory letters for him. Lafayette emphasized to Rochambeau that Americans needed everything and to be sure to transport a printing press, mortars, flints, flour, biscuits, wool, cloth, leather, tenting, tools and bricks.[6]

As the king's secret emissary, Lafayette sailed to America with Gimat, Capitaine du Chesnoy, a secretary and five servants on the 145-foot frigate *Hermione* from Rochefort on March 20, 1780. (In Greek mythology Helen abandoned her daughter, Hermione, to join Paris, her lover.) Louis XIV had made Rochefort, a coastal town near Bordeaux, a shipbuilding center to avoid enemy detection. The king ordered Captain Latouche to admit no other passengers. *Hermione,* one of a trio, carried approximately thirty-two cannons and for speed her lower sides were sheathed in copper. They encountered a British cutter and exchanged fire but otherwise the voyage was uneventful. Lafayette was again ill on a rough ocean. *Hermione* stopped at Marblehead, which hailed his return, and on April 28 reached Boston. Lafayette received a hero's welcome with ringing church bells and marching band. On this twenty-month visit he would increase his laurels.

Little had changed. An outnumbered Franco-American force failed to take Savannah from the British. D'Estaing, wounded, sailed directly to France while Admiral Comte Piquet de La Motte's squadron sailed to Fort Royal, Martinique, and De Grasse's fleet to Le Cap, Saint Domingue. Overprinting had made the Continental dollar worthless and Congress still had no law to levy a tax for desperately needed cash. The army had spent the winter in Morristown, nearly as severe as Valley Forge the year before. Lafayette wrote Washington from Boston and he replied, "… I most sincerely congratulate you on your safe arrival in America, and shall embrace you with all the warmth of an affectionate friend when you come to headquarters where a bed is prepared for you. Adieu till we meet."[7] Lafayette hurried to inform him a grand expedition was coming as a gift from the king, the best news the commander had heard in a long time. Together they planned for the French to attack New York, where the enemy had reduced its presence.

But hope for victory was poor. The British had beaten the Continental Army at Charleston, its worst defeat in the war. American troops in Connecticut had rebelled over army conditions but the protest ended peacefully. In Pennsylvania, two mutinous leaders were hanged. Lafayette, soon frustrated by Washington and Rochambeau's inaction as they waited for French support, was impatient for glorious involvement.

Short and crusty, Jean-Baptiste Donatien de Vimeur, Comte de Rochambeau, fifty-four, was scarred from war wounds and limped with arthritis. He was the American army's only lieutenant general, outranking the marquis, who annoyed him with importuning letters. Writing as "old Papa Rochambeau, speaking to his dear son Lafayette, whom he loves," he offered advice on his forty years' experience: "There are no troops more easily beaten than when they have lost confidence in their commander, and they lose it immediately when exposed to danger through private and personal ambition." Lafayette accepted the criticism.

Given command of a crack Continental division, he gave each section a military flag, donated swords to officers and chose a black and red feather for soldiers' hats. None saw battle. Washington was embarrassed by his undermanned and poorly supplied army and Rochambeau was reluctant to fight without greater naval backup. With the British blockading France's second naval division at Brest, more men and ships could not be expected until autumn. Townspeople gave Lafayette a magnificent white horse. In his immaculately tailored Continental uniform, he looked like an officer despite few battles just then. Rochambeau and his soldiers would spend almost a year at Newport awaiting backup.

On August 16, 1780, Gates and the Southern army suffered a humiliating defeat from Cornwallis' troops in Camden, South Carolina. Kalb, fighting with the strength of ten, died heroically in battle. Without support, the Americans beat a hasty retreat into the forest. Of 3,500 in the battle 700 reached Hillsborough, 180 miles from Camden in North Carolina's central Piedmont. Gates disgraced himself by galloping ahead of his men all the way to Hillsborough.[8] The victorious redcoats advanced on North Carolina.

TWELVE: A TERRIBLE TREASON

Washington, anticipating the British would try to seize control of the Hudson, ordered General Arnold to gather scattered Northern troops at West Point. As Rochambeau had requested repeatedly, Washington met him at Wethersfield, south of Hartford, and with Lafayette as translator, secretary and liaison, stayed at Silas Deane's house.[1] Leaving to plan with Rochambeau a joint land and sea attack on New York City, they learned British Admiral George Rodney had arrived with more ships to defend the city, thus making a French attack there implausible.

With Rochambeau's divisions marking time in Newport and Roxbury, Massachusetts, Washington saw the horrendous amount of money the French government was spending. While Rochambeau refused to move, his soldiers made the most of their time. They charmed citizens with purchases of food and supplies and exhibited exemplary behavior. The French were also pleased by Washington's quiet yet friendly demeanor. With both commanders agreeing on their need for French troops, ships and money, Rochambeau dispatched his son, Donatien, Vicomte de Rochambeau, colonel in the Bourbonnais Regiment, to deliver these requests to Versailles. Lafayette asked him to take letters to Franklin, Adrienne and his family. Memorizing the dispatches in case of capture, the young vicomte sailed on *Amazone*, a swift frigate captained by Jean-François de La Pérouse, who later gained renoun as a

Pacific explorer. Rochambeau accepted Washington's plan of attack on New York that Lafayette urged. Both leaders agreed if New York proved too difficult a Southern strategy was possible.

Lafayette found among the French officers his brother-in-law, Louis de Noailles, as well as an older cousin, Chevalier de Chastellux, who would write an account of his experiences. A handsome Swedish friend, Count Axel von Fersen, Marie Antoinette's companion, was one of Rochambeau's six aides-de-camp. In their royal white and gold uniforms the superbly trained Frenchmen contrasted vividly with the Continentals. But the French were impressed by Washington's sense of command and calmness yet he believed his control over them was "upon a very limited basis."[2]

The Continentals finally began to have successes in the South but Washington still expected the next major battle should logically be in New York. Rochambeau had detected the British were weakening, weary of Greene leading them to pointless battles in the Carolina backwoods. He suggested the next confrontation should be in Virginia. Washington, seeing the wisdom of this, still left the decision open. British General Clinton also thought the Continentals would storm New York and sought more troops. Surprised that the Americans did not attack, Clinton reluctantly turned toward Cornwallis and his own troops' remaining prowess. Unknown at the time, the Northeastern war was, in effect, over. The British now believed victory lay in the South where Washington depended on Greene.

While returning to headquarters after leaving Rochambeau, Washington on a whim decided to show Lafayette the site of fortifications French officers Louis Lebègue Duportail and Jean-Baptiste Gouvion were to build at West Point. Duportail, the Continental Army's superb chief engineer, planned fortifications from Boston to Charleston. He also helped devise the defense strategy that wore down the British and directed allied construction of siege works at Yorktown.

Washington was shocked. Arnold was not at his command and fortifications were far from what Arnold had led him to believe. Washington and his officers waited for Arnold at his comfortable house, confiscated from a loyalist on the eastern side of the Hudson south of the fort. They were late for an expected breakfast. Washington and Lafayette regarded Arnold as a friend, and younger officers always enjoyed seeing his pretty wife. Washington awaited an explanation that came quickly.

Alexander Hamilton, who had breakfasted with the Arnolds, rushing back horrified from the fort, handed the commander damning papers: Major John André, thirty, a British adjutant-general, had been arrested wearing civilian clothes in nearby Tappan, New York. Hidden in his boot were West Point's defense plans. Arnold had written two of them. Washington ordered Arnold's immediate arrest, but the traitor had escaped to the British warship *H.M.S. Vulture* on which André had arrived. Continentals had fired on her earlier and she had moved three miles downriver, leaving André stranded. Arnold's treachery, which would have split the country geographically, was discovered the day he was to turn the fort over to the British for about $10,000.

The former hero was in debt from high living, gambling and spending his own money on troops for which Congress had not reimbursed him. Bored by the stalemated war, feeling unappreciated and passed over for promotion, Arnold betrayed his country for gold. His wife, a loyalist who feigned ignorance of the plan, became hysterical, fainted and was almost convincing. Writing from *Vulture*, Arnold asked for her pardon and his hastily abandoned clothes and received both. His wife and child returned to her father in Philadelphia. Arnold swore no one else was involved in his defection. Reaching London, he became a brigadier general there but was shunned by officers and society. Washington ordered André's court-martial in Tappan and Lafayette was one of fourteen officers empanelled.

The verdict was death by hanging, as the British had done to patriot Nathan Hale. Clinton asked that André be treated as a prisoner of war. Washington said he would be if Clinton returned Arnold but he refused. André asked to face a firing squad, a more dignified military death, saying, "I am reconciled to my fate, but not to the mode." Washington refused clemency. André was a model prisoner. Lafayette and Hamilton liked him when they talked to him in his cell but Lafayette avoided his execution.[3] Officers pitied André, who downplayed his death as "a momentary pang." With the rope secured to a gallows, he placed the noose on his neck, setting the knot behind his right ear, covering his eyes with a white handkerchief. The wagon pulled away and his body swayed lifeless. Buried in a coffin at the site, André's remains were placed in Westminster Abbey in 1821 under a sculpture of *Britannia* weeping, which the Arnolds visited.

The Continentals detested Arnold. His troops burned tobacco warehouses in Richmond and in early September 1781 he attacked the seaport of New London, Connecticut. Returning to London, Arnold later lived in Canada before returning to the British capital where he failed in business. Leaving five children by Peggy and three by his first wife, Arnold died at fifty-nine, ill and remorseful. He was buried in his Continental uniform in London in 1801. Peggy, after paying his debts, died of cancer three years later.

Lafayette had another surprise from the two Americans he respected most. As he and Hamilton were talking on the stairs — Hamilton probably saying he wanted active service again — Washington summoned him to his office. Hamilton continued speaking to the marquis before joining the commander who reproved him for being ten minutes late. Hamilton abruptly asked to be transferred and Washington quickly agreed, but the two soon resumed their friendship out of mutual admiration. Hamilton would play a pivotal role in Cornwallis' defeat, later becoming the first and most influential secretary of the Treasury. Each man knew the other's value to the country and himself. Lafayette remained close to both.

Another foreign soldier came to help West Point. Thaddeus Kosciuszko (1746-1817), a Polish major general in the Continental Army, fought at Bemis Point, Saratoga, and wintered at Valley Forge. He strengthened West Point's redoubts above the river so well the British never fired on the fort. Kosciuszko designed an iron chain across the Hudson that could be raised to halt enemy ships. Kosciuszko, a quiet engineer, at first deplored Lafayette and French officers for their self-promoting ways. But Lafayette thought highly of him and they became friends whose ideas on freedom and America ran parallel. Both would support Polish independence but did not live to see it. General Greene, with whom Kosciuszko worked in the war's Southern department, said of him, "His modesty equals his merits, [making] him a very agreeable man." Jefferson wrote, "He is as pure a son of liberty as I have ever known."

Kosciuszko suggested to Washington that West Point, called "the American Gibralter," should become a military academy. Kosciuszko returned to Poland with scant funds or prospects. In 1784 he returned to Philadelphia. The Russians imprisoned him in the unsuccessful 1794 Polish uprising for independence. In his 1798 will, Kosciuszko made Jefferson his executor and instructed him to sell the general's American land to purchase slaves. He or others were to "giv[e] them liberty in my name" and see them educated in trades. Jefferson dealt with this until age forced him to make other arrangements; $50,000 went to Kosciuszko's granddaughters.[4]

The war's last winter headquarters was in New Windsor, near Newburgh in the Hudson Highlands. Soldiers, displaced men, women and children occupied a city of 700 log huts. Here Washington established the Badge of Merit, later the Purple Heart medal. With the war concentrated in the South, Washington ordered Lafayette and 1,200 troops to "act against the corps of the enemy now in Virginia." Since Lafayette did not know the land with its mountains and rivers, why was he sent there? Washington saw in the marquis the qualities of a chessboard knight, bounding from place to place — tactics to keep Cornwallis on the run, wearing down his army. Lafayette's men were not equipped or numerous enough to defeat the British there.

Washington expected Lafayette with his flood of letters to keep him abreast of activities. The commander understood there are few humans more powerful than single-minded youths with the will to succeed. He told Lafayette to communicate with Steuben, already in Virginia. At Washington's order the baron gathered a militia ready to join Lafayette's men and probably wondered if this favored Frenchman would usurp his command which seemed inevitable. Washington wished Lafayette "a successful issue to the enterprise and all the glory which I am persuaded you will deserve." If he caught Arnold, Washington advised, he was to punish him "in the most summary way."[5]

THIRTEEN: THE VIRGINIA CAMPAIGN

Lafayette took command of Continental detachments in Virginia on February 20, 1781. The commonwealth, having sent troops to the North and South, was vulnerable. After asking Washington for more military aid, Jefferson, who was Virginia's second governor, had moved some government records from Richmond, the second capital after Williamsburg, the year before. Lafayette campaigned widely and vigorously, exposing himself to great danger. His management of troops was also difficult. He marched them from New Windsor to Annapolis and expected to board French ships that had not arrived. As Washington had urged Rochambeau on their second meeting, Captain Destouches succeeded the leader of the French expedition's first armada, Admiral De Ternay, who had died.

Destouches sailed from Newport to support Lafayette and his troops, mostly men from New England and New Jersey. But the British in New York, having sent a fleet under Admiral Marriott Arbuthnot, arrived first. French and British fleets encountered each other in the First Battle of the Capes fought in Chesapeake Bay, 200 miles long and thirty miles across at its widest point.

Rear Admiral Destouches had seven ships of the line, one frigate and some transports; Arbuthnot, eight ships of the line. Destouches damaged three British warships, but their blockade kept him from entering the Chesapeake. On March 26, he returned to Newport. Of the two sea fighters, Destouches, firing at enemy masts and sails, was the more advanced. Veteran Arbuthnot, in touch with Arnold on land, fired at French cannons. Destouches was unable to deliver 1,120 soldiers to Lafayette. But, it is argued, had he persisted he could have entered the bay.

Versailles criticized his actions. London, also displeased, recalled Arbuthnot. This complete disaster and loss of lives greatly distressed Washington.[1] Lafayette, not knowing about the French fleet's departure, left his men and took an open barge with a few officers down to Yorktown "and very luckly escaped the dangers that were in the way."[2]

He joined Steuben in Williamsburg on March 14, 1781 and formed a larger force with the baron's militia which had also suffered desertions. Lafayette avoided taking command over Steuben and learned why the French ships had not arrived. Upset by Destouches' retreat, Lafayette started for Annapolis. Detouring to Fredericksburg, he met Mary Ball Washington, who is said to have offered him gingerbread.

Curiosity drove Lafayette to Mount Vernon. Washington had not been there since the war began and Martha was with him in New Windsor. There is no record of Lafayette meeting family members or staff. But he acknowledged his brief visit in a gushing April 8 letter to the commander, who was to return there soon. Lafayette told Washington his nephew, Lund Washington, had saved the estate from damage by offering the British provisions. Washington knew this and said he never would have done so, criticizing his nephew.

Riding to Alexandria, Lafayette re-entered Maryland and rejoined his detachment at Head of Elk on April 3, expecting to lead it back to Washington. But a message from the commander ordered him to return south under Greene's command. Washington and Lafayette sometimes communicated in secret code because the commander knew British spies read all of his messages. As Jefferson had warned, Lafayette found it was not easy to recruit soldiers in Virginia. He also met Northerners who refused to fight in the South.

Nineteen men from Massachusetts and nine from Rhode Island

deserted, saying the region was not worth the risks, fevers or diseases. Again Lafayette found Americans were not united in seeking freedom. Conditions were extremely difficult. "… We have neither money, nor clothes, nor shoes, nor shirts and in a few days shall be reduced to [eating] green peaches," he wrote Chevalier La Luzerne, French ambassador to the colonies, "…Our feet are torn for want of shoes and our hands itchy for want of linen… all that will not prevent us from marching… and tomorrow we shall set out to execute the orders of the general who believes that course necessary."[3] His soldiers, looking much like the bedraggled redcoats, captured several spies and traders who mistook them for British.

As Lafayette's soldiers and baggage crossed the Susquehanna River, one of the captured men was tried and hanged after three days. While waiting at the ferry, Lafayette received a fateful message from Washington: the New York engagement was again postponed. "The Susquehanna was my Rubicon," he wrote, comparing it to Julius Caesar's fateful decision. Lafayette expected this news would mean that instead of returning to New Windsor headquarters he would spend the rest of his fighting in Maryland and Virginia. He lamented to Greene, "While the French are coming I am going…If I go to exile, come and partake it with me."[4]

The next day in Baltimore, he raised about 2,000 pounds on his bond. He bought "a few hats, some shoes, some blankets, and a pair of linen overall and a shirt to each man."[5] On a coastal sail down to Williamsburg with his men, he tumbled into the water while reboarding. Since he did not swim, he nearly drowned.

Rejoining the army's Southern department, Lafayette still could not impress Virginians into service. In frustration he had 200 oxen seized; at least there would be beef. He wrote Jefferson he was determined to "conquer or die in our noble contest. It is with the greatest reluctance that I sign any impressing warrants, but I hope my delicacy in the matter will be such as to render me worthy of the approbation of the state." Leaning on charm, he always sought official approval if available. From North Carolina, Greene ordered him not to allow any British in Virginia to join Cornwallis in the Carolinas. But the English lord had entered Virginia and was eager to capture Lafayette. But Cornwallis felt pressure dealing with Arnold.

Now a British general, Arnold led 1,600 mostly loyalist troops in ravaging eastern Virginia. He occupied Portsmouth in January 1781 as British warships controlled the Chesapeake Capes. Fighting along the James River, Arnold joined General William Phillips' troops. Superior to Arnold, Phillips was the British commander at Minden the day Lafayette's father was killed. (Cornwallis, then a lieutenant, was also there.) Lafayette's artillery fired on Phillips' commandeered house but he had already died of typhoid fever. Lafayette later claimed he had avenged his father's death by killing Phillips and came to believe it.

While the marquis skirmished with Arnold, Cornwallis reached Petersburg, twenty miles south of Richmond, on May 20. Meanwhile in Pennsylvania, General Wayne had dealt with mutiny when his troops, paid in paper, revolted. Twelve leaders were sentenced to death. Six were shot. When the seventh did not fall to squadron fire he was bayoneted. Five others were hanged. Wayne finally reached Lafayette with a regiment of 800 Continentals on June 7, with much needed men and materiel. (Wayne was nicknamed "Mad Anthony." A wastrel who spied for Wayne had irritated him and Wayne had him beaten. "Mad he is," the man shouted, "Mad Anthony Wayne!" It stuck.)

The day before Wayne arrived, Lafayette attacked Cornwallis near Green Spring, a few miles from Williamsburg. As the British crossed the James near Jamestown, Cornwallis tricked Lafayette into thinking the army's main body had passed but most of it remained on the north shore to attack him. He lost the encounter but saved himself and most of his men. But knowing the colonials' need for victories, Lafayette swore he won the combat since Cornwallis had not made a stand but kept marching south.[6] Describing the engagement, Cornwallis wrote Clinton that after "smart action" for some minutes "the enemy gave way, & abandoned their cannon" to be used against the allies at Yorktown.[7] Cornwallis and his troops reached Williamsburg on June 25, heading to Yorktown on July 4. The general occupied the home of the president of the College of William and Mary. Later in July, Williamsburg became headquarters of American and French forces until they too moved to Yorktown. After this battle, Washington and then Rochambeau returned to Williamsburg. They stayed in respected Congressman George Wythe's house where Lafayette also probably had rooms.

Disappointed that Southerners did not join him as he expected, Cornwallis combined his troops with Arnold's, totaling 7,200 soldiers. But the earl detested the turncoat and moved away when Clinton ordered him to dispatch six of his regiments to New York. Cornwallis led them to embark at Portsmouth but he needed them himself. His remaining soldiers began to fortify Yorktown, Williamsburg's port, and the hamlet of Gloucester Point on the York River's eastern bank. Cornwallis took his engineers' advice to make Yorktown his base. From there he could march north or south, relay troops elsewhere or escape on warships. He ignored Arnold's warning not to become ensnared there. Lafayette, not sure of Cornwallis' intentions until he settled in, thought the earl might go to Baltimore.

As Arnold's troops swept the James burning storehouses and other structures, Jefferson found only 200 volunteers to defend Richmond. Most of the others had served elsewhere and did not feel obligated. Arnold boldly informed Jefferson he would leave the city undisturbed if his men could move tobacco, wine and other stores to British ships. Jefferson refused and Arnold's troops plundered and burned everything they found. A changing wind set fire to many buildings. Jefferson and Lafayette considered attacking Arnold, but thirty-two British ships and 2,000 troops spoke otherwise. Jefferson fled to Monticello.

John "Jack" Jouett, a Virginia militiaman known later as the "Paul Revere of the South," rode forty-four miles there to warn the governor he had spied Colonel Banastre Tarleton gathering seventy-eight mounted infantrymen and 180 dragoons. Jouett guessed they wanted Jefferson. Cornwallis had ordered Tarleton, his cruel subaltern at Camden, to capture the governor. Tarleton was called "Bloody Ban" for slaughtering 100 Americans at Waxhaw, North Carolina. Jefferson, slow to leave his estate, barely escaped as Tarleton and company rode to Monticello. Thwarted by Jefferson's absence, they consumed his wines. Cornwallis ordered the mansion and furniture spared. In nearby Charlottesville, Tarleton's soldiers seized seven assemblymen whom Jefferson had urged to escape from Richmond. The British also destroyed military supplies in the town.

Jefferson, thirty-eight, fled through the woods to Poplar Forest, the fine retreat he designed near Lynchburg. On ending his term on June

4, he turned the governorship over to Yorktown's Thomas Nelson Jr., elected on June 12. A brigadier general, Nelson commanded the Virginia militia in the Yorktown siege. Jefferson, who was called a coward for fleeing, later overcame this charge being used against him politically. Governor Nelson and the assembly barely escaped to Staunton, the temporary capital thirty-two miles west, while Arnold's men took slaves, burned and looted properties and slaughtered horses and cattle wherever they went.

Arnold wrote to Lafayette, who refused to reply, saying he would be pleased to hear from any other British officer. Arnold returned to Portsmouth. Lafayette, wanting to spy on British operations there, crossed the James to the camp of General Peter Muhlenberg near Suffolk, south of Portsmouth. As with Steuben, Lafayette did not assume command. Moving north on warships to New London, Connecticut, Arnold and his men bayoneted eighty-five American soldiers and wounded sixty. They also destroyed 151 buildings, ruined the town's shipping industry and stole trade goods.[8]

Like the Americans, British officers suffered dissention. Clinton cursed Howe's ponderous orders. Cornwallis, who would become Clinton's second in command, lost his trust by reporting his outburst to Howe.[9] The two barely communicated when, with Clinton in New York and Cornwallis in Virginia, they most needed to. Defending his Virginia actions, Cornwallis wrote Clinton he was "most firmly persuaded that until Virginia was reduced," their troops "could not hold the more southern provinces, but afterwards [they] would fall without much resistance."[10]

British warships forwarded Cornwallis' six regiments to New York. Clinton was sure Washington would attack the city. But in Virginia, Lafayette and his men fought their far larger enemy at Hanover, Fredericksburg, Charlottesville and Richmond up and down the James. Washington, who had stayed at Wilton, undoubtedly told Lafayette of this 2,000-acre tobacco plantation that *Declaration* signer William Randolph III had built on the James in 1753. Lafayette and 900 troops bivouacked on its lawns May 10-20, 1781, with his letters beginning "Camp Wilton on the James." But skirmishes did not win wars. Lafayette must have been surprised to receive this message on July 7, 1781:

Sir: A number of your prisoners have arrived from Charlestown agreeable to the Artcl settled for the Southern department. Part of them have already been landed, and the officers in whose charge they came have directions to deliver the remainder to persons appointed by you to receive them for receipts, upon an assurance from you that an equal number of our prisoners shall be sent with as much dispatch as possible to James City Island [Jamestown] where the flag vessels will remain to receive them. And trusting that your prisoners will remain in a state of inactivity until a reasonable interval elapses from the delivery of ours to enable us to put our prisoners in military duty. I have the honour to be, Sir,

Your most obedient & most humble servant.

Cornwallis[11]

The exchange apparently occurred. Even war can have honesty when enemies gain from mutual decisions. Lafayette, consistently avoiding capture while building his forces, said in letters he was afraid of Britain's best general. But there is no record Cornwallis ever wrote, "The boy cannot escape me."[12] Weary of the chase, Cornwallis followed Clinton's order in building a garrison for New York's defense at Yorktown. The village, twelve miles south of Williamsburg on fifty acres, nestled on a bluff above the river. It seemed like a fine place to dig in.

FOURTEEN: VICTORY AT YORKTOWN

The Yorktown region is an undulating tableland. The eastern escarpment looks down on the wide York River near the Chesapeake Bay's eighteen-mile-wide union with the Atlantic Ocean. Above the waterfront, wealthy merchants' houses lined Main Street with shops and taverns. Grace Church, of 1697, was a meeting place amid more than 200 village buildings. Some plantation owners, exhausting the land with tobacco, had moved west, leaving a population of 1,800. Nelson owned an impressive house built by his grandfather in 1730.[1]

Cornwallis moved his troops there in early August, making Nelson's house his headquarters while continuing to fortify the York River but not yet near the town. He followed Clinton's orders but nothing more; distant fortifications lagged. He did not anticipate what would occur. And Clinton, until he knew Cornwallis had been tricked, thought he was safe there. Suddenly on August 30, Comte de Grasse, quitting hurricanes in the Caribbean, sailed into sight of Yorktown with twenty-six frigates from Saint Domingue and a chest of 1,000 livres for Continental field needs.[2] De Grasse had contacted Rochambeau, whose troops left Rhode Island and Massachusetts in twenty-eight ships of the line and four frigates in June and were then in the New York suburbs. Rochambeau alerted Washington: De Grasse would help them by blockading Chesapeake Bay just south of Yorktown.

The admiral wanted to return to the Caribbean in late October, so there was no time to waste. Delighted by the news, Washington decided his troops and the French would fight in the South, ending his and Lafayette's hope of attacking New York. The marquis again pushed to invade Canada. Washington dismissed that idea but yearned to drive Clinton from Manhattan. This would prove unnecessary but no one knew that. De Grasse's blockade cornered Cornwallis, proving Washington's belief that an army could not be successful without a navy. France's naval force, which Louis XVI saw as the best challenge to the enemy, was second only to Britain's.

On August 19, 1781, Washington ordered Major General William Heath to make 3,500 soldiers still in Peekskill visible to the British, hoping Clinton would think they were the entire Northern Continental Army. Washington with 2,000 men asked Rochambeau to join them with 4,500 French troops and artillery. The armies set out on three routes for the 400-mile march south. They passed through Philadelphia a day apart. The Americans took time to petition Congress for their pay. Washington's Peekskill ruse fooled Clinton for eleven days. It was not until September 2 that he wrote Cornwallis about the allies' movements, saying he was sending a fleet to protect him and his men. Washington ordered Major General Henry Knox in Philadelphia to send Continental artillery south. The commander also wrote Lafayette to keep Cornwallis pinned down on the bluff.

Lafayette enlisted the spy services of a slave, James Armistead (1748-1830). His master, William Armistead, of New Kent County, Virginia, was a Continental commissary who loaned James to the army. As Lafayette's counterspy, James foraged for Cornwallis' army while reporting its plans and troop movements, aiding Lafayette's tactics. Cornwallis, invited to dinner at the marquis' house after the surrender, was surprised to find James there. Lafayette in his 1784 visit to Richmond wrote to the Virginia Legislature commending James Armistead, then a farmer, for his war duties. Two years after James asked for his freedom, the Legislature granted it plus a service pension. He also changed his name to James Armistead Lafayette.

As troop commander, Lafayette strove to provide necessities for his men. He became meticulous in handling accounts. In a barrage of letters about the poor way his troops were supplied, Lafayette challenged those he called "the impoverished, incompetent and lethargic commissary agents of Virginia and Maryland." He kept the letters out of his *Mémoirs* but they are in the states' archives. Not publishing them showed his public relations genius, Gottschalk wrote.[3]

Lafayette contracted yellow fever and was pleased to turn the campaign over to Washington and Rochambeau. The French commandant's formidable train, led by Major Louis Alexandre Berthier, totaled 1,500 horses, 800 oxen and 220 wagons. The marquis was too ill to join Washington and Rochambeau on September 17 as they visited De Grasse on the 106-gun flagship *Ville de Paris* off Cape Henry. The admiral had awaited Rochambeau's soldiers and artillery, expecting them to arrive from Newport on Admiral Louis de Barras' ships. When Lafayette recuperated, thin and wan, he met with De Grasse on his bark. He had De Grasse's promise that during Yorktown's land battle the admiral would attack the British at Wilmington, North Carolina, or Charleston. That never occurred.

Adding to the marquis' irritations was the rumor Clinton would fight in Virginia. No one knew for sure. Lafayette had learned someone in Paris had written an unflattering ditty about him and D'Hunolstein. He urged Louis Noailles to defend him against French officers who might be laughing at him and "a person whom I love."[4] Lafayette fumed: the tune had traveled 3,000 miles, making the lady "the victim of some wicked fiction." Since it emanated from high society, he suspected Chartres (later Duc d'Orléans/Philippe Ēgalité), "or perhaps even the king's brother, the Comte de Provence." It was the latter.[4]

Washington and Rochambeau, joining their respective divisions of 2,500 and 4,900 men (fewer than 8,000 in all), departed from New York and took transports at Head of Elk, Baltimore and Annapolis.[6] Reaching Lafayette's camp in Williamsburg on September 14 in under five weeks, they were buoyed to learn Spain's governor of Louisiana Bernardo de Galvez had not only recognized the Republic of the United States but also had defeated British General John Campbell at Pensacola, Florida, although the Spanish king and government had not authorized it. De

Galvez also retook western Florida from the British, who had defaulted on its defense.

The marquis was thrilled to welcome both armies, knowing, with Washington leading, they would pursue the enemy he had harassed. Lafayette's supreme moment in Virginia was joining this force. In Williamsburg, Lafayette, Washington, Rochambeau and Marquis Henri de Saint-Simon — who with Barras had conducted 3,300 infantry from Newport and would lead French troops in battle — viewed their first full-dress parade. Continental officers mingled with French counterparts at a fine supper in Saint-Simon's house. Two days later generals and divisions marched to their Yorktown encampments: Americans south and east of the target, French on the west.

The next day, September 29, Cornwallis, with 8,885 soldiers, pulled back from all but one of his outer defenses protecting Yorktown. Clinton had sent word Admiral Samuel Graves, leaving New York on October 5 with warships and 4,000 soldiers, was coming to his aid. But Graves, insisting on repairing ships damaged on September 5's Battle of the Virginia Capes with De Grasse, did not embark until October 19 — day of surrender. The war's greatest naval engagement allowed Barras to enter the bay with siege cannons. British warships arrived off Cape Charles near the bay's northern entrance. There they found De Grasse's fleet and followed it south to Cape Henry at the bay's southern tip. Ordered to maintain a straight battle line, a customary end-to-end formation, the British could not attack the French fleet's open areas, giving it time to fight. French ships of the line plus two frigates fought twenty British ships of the line and six frigates, firing at each other until dark. Five more days of bombardment ended when the British sailed to New York. Two days later, their damaged *H.M.S. Thunderer* sank with seventy-four guns. Barras had earlier captured *H.M.S. Iris* and *Richmond*. Masters of the bay, the French completely blockaded Cornwallis' army.[5]

Feeling trapped and deserted, Cornwallis stationed men in ten redoubts with scant protection from cannon and mortar fire. Allied forces took a week to erect and equip their camps. On October 6 they set their first siege line northwest and parallel to the British garrison and three days later began bombardment. When the British became almost unable to fire back, abandoning their siege line, the allies made it their second front line on October 11 and pulled up their combined artillery. Working at night to avoid attack, allied troops dug a trench almost 1,100 feet long, only 657 to 875 yards from the enemy. This trench led directly to Redoubts 9 and 10 south of Yorktown: on the bluff and within the British inner defense line. On the night of October 14, Americans and French took both redoubts in less than thirty minutes.

Eye-witness Captain Stephen Olney wrote: "Our regiment of light infantry, commanded by Colonel Gimat, a bold Frenchman, was selected for the assault and paraded just after daylight in front of our works. General Washington made a short address or harangue, admonishing us to act the part of firm and brave soldiers, showing the necessity of accomplishing the object, as the attack on both redoubts depended on our success. I thought then that his Excellency's knees rather shook, but I have since doubted whether [they were] not mine."[6]

Storming the rampart, Olney was bayoneted in the belly and pushed his intestines in with both hands. Taken to Williamsburg, he returned to service in "about three weeks." On meeting him after the battle, Lafayette clasped him in his arms and shed emotional tears.

Lafayette commanded the American assault with Hamilton, Gimat and Laurens under him while Comte Christian de Deux-Ponts, under Baron de Viomenil, headed the French advance. Colonel Hamilton claimed seniority over Gimat. He and Lafayette gave way and Hamilton fearlessly led the Redoubt 10 assault, scaling the earthen berm and overwhelming a British major and troops. On October 16, some 350 British soldiers under Lieutenant Colonel Robert Abercromby attacked the French along the allied trench at two positions. But the French forced them back to their line. A storm that night kept Cornwallis from ferrying his troops to freedom at Gloucester Point. The allies completed a new battle line, at point-blank range, on the morning of October 17.

Suddenly at 10 a.m. in the cannons' crescendo, a British boy arose on a rampart and drummed a tattoo calling for a meeting. A British officer waving a white handkerchief stepped onto the battlefield. The allies halted and the man was blindfolded and escorted to Washington. Cornwallis, after nine days of constant bombardment, sent a note requesting a ceasefire. Washington answered that only surrender was acceptable. The next day, Laurens and Noailles were with both sides drafting terms of capitulation. Cornwallis's headquarters were in Governor Nelson's house in the village, but surrender terms were written in the white clapboard Augustine Moore house perched on the bluff, the river behind the American first parallel line.[7] Washington had the document prepared and returned to Cornwallis to sign. Typifying the age's formality and respectfulness, Lafayette and Washington in writing always referred to him as General or Lord Cornwallis.

Two days later, October 19, 1781, the British marched out at 2 p.m. to the surrender field, about a mile and a half from their garrison. The Americans were arrayed on the right of the plain, the French on the left. The British tootled airs on their fifes and drums — but not *The World Turned Upside Down,* written later. They had kept their flags cased and after presenting arms lay their weapons on the ground. This action recalled how they had commanded Major General Benjamin Lincoln to do the same following the Continental defeat in Charleston. The sullen redcoats avoided eye contact with the ragged but victorious Americans, looking toward the French in resplendent uniforms. Noting the slight, Lafayette ordered musicians to strike up *Yankee Doodle,* an anti-American British ditty the colonies had adopted.

The victors looked for Cornwallis. Humiliated and claiming he had a cold, his lordship did not appear. Instead Brigadier General Charles O'Hara, his second, presented his sword in defeat. He offered the weapon to Rochambeau, who directed him to Washington. Because the apologizing O'Hara was not commander, Washington asked Lincoln to accept the sword. He obliged and returned it to O'Hara, as customary. The last major battle of the war was over but there would be many more and deaths on both sides. Washington, astride his horse, quietly took pleasure in his first dictated surrender but he still expected to attack New York. That never occurred but the war would continue for two more years. A total of 8,700 Americans, 36,000 French and 8,081 British, plus 25 deserters and loyalists, fought at Yorktown.[8] The toll was about 156 British killed, 356 wounded. American and French losses were eighty-five dead, 199 wounded.[9]

De Grasse on his flagship welcomed Washington, Rochambeau and Lafayette after the battle. Washington soon left but the marquis spent a night and day trying to persuade De Grasse to attack British-held Charleston or Wilmington. The admiral agreed to transport 2,000 American troops. But a British fleet was spotted and he feared a permanent south wind might force him to sail directly to the West Indies, embarrassing these troops. This forced Major General Arthur St. Clair to march his men to North Carolina while De Grasse sailed with his fleet and a few captured British frigates to the sugar islands.

Lafayette asked Washington's permission to return to France. The commander decided the marquis could do more there than in an American winter. Lafayette applied for leave of absence in Philadelphia. Congress sent him off with a glowing resolution on his contributions. Washington, who had briefly entertained Rochambeau at Mount Vernon before they reached Yorktown, returned home for the winter. The French expedition of six regiments spent that time near Williamsburg while Lauzun's Legion went to Charlotte Court House near the North Carolina border. They with Axel von Fersen rejoiced sometime later on learning a dauphin, Louis Joseph Xavier François de France, had been born three days after the Yorktown battle. Four French divisions left Virginia in July 1782. Some officers visited Mount Vernon. About sixty Frenchmen lay in a collective grave near their Yorktown campsite.[10]

French troops left Boston for the West Indies in December 1782 to prepare a new campaign against Jamaica, a remaining British possession. Rochambeau, traveling separately and turning command over to the Duc de Lauzun, met Washington in Philadelphia. The king made Rochambeau on his return governor of Picardy. In December 1791, Rochambeau and General Nicolas Lückner were named the *ancien regime*'s last marshals. Thrown into the Conciergerie while ill, Rochambeau survived the Terror. Napoleon pensioned him and he died at his Vendome chateau in 1807.[11] De Lauzun was guillotined in 1793 and D'Estaing in 1794.

FIFTEEN: WAR IN THE CARIBBEAN AND ELSEWHERE

Americans in their war were scarcely aware that the British were also fighting France and Spain in the Caribbean, India, the Mediterranean and Philippines. For Europe the sugar-rich West Indies and the other regions they were engaged were far more important than all of North America, regardless of how remote these places were to Americans. Britain needed to disengage troops from America and deploy them against the French and Spanish in Jamaica and elsewhere around the world. Cornwallis' surrender did not end the war for the great powers. General Clinton, recalled to London, was blamed for the Yorktown defeat. In his memoirs he attacked Cornwallis, who responded and fared better, becoming envoy to Frederick the Great's court and governor-general of India in 1786. Eleven years later, as governor-general of Ireland he defeated a French-fomented uprising there. Back in India as governor-general, Cornwallis, feeling his sixty-six years, died there in 1805.

Lafayette, still wanting to invade Canada, Newfoundland, Bermuda and the Caribbean islands, was thrilled to learn in November 1781 his cousin Bouillé had recaptured tiny St. Eustatius, the most important port for American war supplies east of Puerto Rico. The British had retaken it only that February.

In fall of 1781, feeling close to the Continentals but eager to return home, Lafayette asked Washington, and then Congress in Philadelphia, for a furlough. They agreed he was more valuable at Versailles than in a stagnant war. They gave him letters of commendation and again commissioned him to secure as much money as possible for the war and to meet Rochambeau's naval needs. Lafayette saw himself as the best man for the job. Washington wrote, "It follows…as certain as that night succeeds the day that without a decisive naval force we can do nothing definitive, and with it every thing honourable and glorious. A constant naval superiority would terminate the war speedily; without it, I do not know that it will ever be terminated honourably."[1]

Although Lafayette enjoyed military life (especially with personal servants), the diplomatic arts also fascinated him. He consulted with American superintendent of finances Robert Morris and secretary of foreign affairs Robert Livingston on what he needed to know when pleading at court. Congress ordered Livingston to inform Franklin, John Adams and John Jay they were to confer with Lafayette on what he knew of conditions in the United States. Franklin was to consult with the marquis and employ his assistance in speeding supplies from Louis XVI. Morris and Livingston were to keep Lafayette informed of American news so he could be of greatest service. The letters took time to write. Lafayette and his companions left for Boston before the letters were ready but received them there.

Government meetings stimulated Lafayette's interest in national and international strategies. The funeral of Washington's stepson, John Parke Custis, his civilian aide-de-camp at Yorktown who had died of camp fever at twenty-six, delayed the general's seeing Lafayette in Philadelphia. But Washington and his grieving wife arrived in time to say farewell. Robert Morris entertained them at his home. The marquis was also appointed to preside at his second court-martial. Two young Continental soldiers, Lawrence Marr Jr. and John Moody, stole Congress' secret journals. Some accounts claim Benedict Arnold devised this Tory plot. Thomas Edison, a clerk for the secretary of Congress, pretended to take the books to the British but turned in the culprits. Moody, twenty-three, in a note leaving his soul to God, was hanged. Marr was imprisoned almost two years when his parents paid for his release and promise of good behavior.[2]

Lafayette spent an estimated 700,000 livres for his and troop expenses. He lived on money borrowed from French banker Leray de Chaumont through his agent, John Holker, in Philadelphia. Holker converted the total debt of almost 166,000 pounds in Continental paper to 1,273 pounds sterling. Accepting some of Lafayette's chattel, Holker further reduced the debt to 1,190 pounds.[3] This done, Lafayette reached Boston with his comrades on December 10. Congress asked Morris to arrange "a suitable conveyance" but it took more than two weeks before *U.S.S. Alliance* could sail.

The marquis had time to meet friends: General Hancock, Samuel Cooper, eloquent preacher and speaker on the revolution, and French consul Joseph de Létombe. Army officers of the Massachusetts line entertained him, Boston councilmen visited him and Samuel Adams addressed him. Developing his public speaking skills, Lafayette returned the honor. He also wrote many farewell letters, giving unsolicited advice on the war's "next campaign."[4]

But Lafayette politely rejected visiting John Paul Jones, in Portsmouth, New Hampshire; expecting to sail, he stayed on board.[5] Vowing to help the American cause in Europe, he assured all he would return soon. He embarked with Noailles, Duportail, Gouvion, La Colombe and thirty-two other French officers on December 23. Captain John Barry, an Irishman and future father of the United States Navy, avoided a British ship during the uneventful crossing. Barry, with 218 crewmen, wished to be on attack, not transporting French soldiers home. But such were the hopes and prestige riding with them.

"However happy I am to be in France and to enjoy the sight of my friends," Lafayette wrote Washington on January 18, 1782, "I anticipate the pleasure to find myself again in a few months on the American shore, and to feel that unspeakable satisfaction I ever experienced when, after an absence, I could once more arrive at headquarters." He asked a Washington relative to have copies made of his letters to the commander as well as bound versions of both their orderly books "to read when I grow old." This early romantic carried a small folded American flag in his breast pocket.

Alliance reached Lorient, Brittany, in twenty-five days. News of Yorktown and Lafayette's role in it had burst on France. Lafayette, now twenty-four, was hailed throughout the country as "the hero of two worlds." Fame could hardly be more intoxicating. The future looked well for the Americans but the war was far from over. He expected to return to more battles. No one knew how much diplomacy lay ahead. It would be more than a year and a half before a peace treaty could be signed in Paris. He would be the pivot on which history turned.

Honors came to French officers who fought in America and several would further distinguish themselves. Gimat became the last French governor of St. Lucia. Berthier, aide-de-camp to Rochambeau, who spirited Louis XVI's elderly aunts to Italy early in the French Revolution, became Napoleon's field marshal and most brilliant battle planner. Turning on the fallen emperor, Berthier escorted Louis XVIII into Paris. Three soldiers of the Saint-Simon family served at Yorktown.[6] One of them, Claude Henri, Comte de Saint-Simon, was wounded there and on *Ville de Paris*. Thought dead, he was cast overboard. The British rescued him. Much later he became internationally known as a *philosophe* advancing Christian socialism — those who work should be rewarded, the poorest first — ideas Karl Marx would adapt to communism. Like Lafayette, Saint-Simon had a profound impact on liberalism's evolution in Europe.

Of 312 deputies elected from the nobility to the Estates-General, 256 were army officers or former officers.[7] A minority of thirty percent of Frenchmen who fought in America later voted with revolutionary partisans. Sixty-four percent defended the monarchy; six percent remained undecided.[8]

SIXTEEN: CHARGED WITH A PURPOSE

After three days spent riding carriages to Paris, Lafayette found no one at home that afternoon at the Hôtel de Noailles. But townswomen, somehow learning of his return, came with laurel for the hero. Adrienne was with the royal family at the hôtel de ville — the French Renaissance city hall — two miles away where the queen presented the new dauphin to the citizenry.[1] Adrienne was told her husband had returned. Marie Antoinette, assuming more power since Maurepas's death, insisted on taking Adrienne home in the royal coach. On seeing Lafayette in the courtyard, Adrienne fainted in his arms. Reacquaintance was sweet. She found pleasure looking at him and endured his amatory adventures without comment. According to custom, he knew many women but remained faithful, in his fashion. She accepted this with loving resignation.

Lafayette was cheered wherever he went. At the opera when he tried to conceal himself in the Noailles box, he was called to receive a victor's wreath. A seemingly endless round of parties celebrated his return and the Yorktown victory. At a ball, the queen dressed as "la belle Gabrielle," Henri IV's mistress and wife. She danced with the hero whose haggard appearance was once again noticed.

But Lafayettet was now charged with a purpose. He saw Vergennes and anyone who could offer Americans more help. The day after his arrival he visited Louis XVI at his hunting lodge, Chateau de La Muette, near the Bois de Boulogne. The king quizzed him about Washington, who fascinated him, and the marquis' adventures. Louis was keenly interested in geographic exploration. His most extraordinary acts were financing the American Revolution and sending La Pérouse on his journeys of discovery after James Cooke's voyages.

Louis believed international peace depended on a strong navy, although he never traveled farther than Cherbourg harbor. Lafayette accompanied him for a harbor-building ceremony in June 1786.[2] To Louis, the Navy was his realm of dreams, a French historian has written. Louis XVI made decisions carefully but sometimes allowed others to act in ways he disliked and let good men leave the government.[3]

Louis, at first called Duc de Berry, was the third son of Louis XV's last surviving heir, Louis Ferdinand (1729-1765). When that dauphin's first wife died following the birth of a daughter who died, he married Princess Marie-Josephe of Saxony. She bore a daughter and two sons who died young, then blue-eyed Louis and his two younger brothers. Their father died of tuberculosis at thirty-six. Lafayette was taught riding skills with the three sons at the Académie in Versailles. Louis' grandmother, father, aunts and mother were pious and he was dutifully religious. He spoke fluent Italian and English and enjoyed Latin, history, geography and astronomy. On his grandfather's death in 1774, Louis, nineteen, banished Du Barry from Versailles. In August, facing the nation's debt and on conservative Maurepas' advice, he appointed Anne Robert Turgot finance minister, politely ordering him to correct France's fiscal problems.

Turgot began strict tax reforms but angered the unbending nobles who overrode him. Louis made wealthy Swiss-born French banker Jacques Necker director-general of finances in 1776. Being Protestant, Necker was not made finance minister. He established a stronger economy and fairer taxation, but the nation's huge debt overwhelmed him. He fled to Brussels and was called back. Lafayette was a friend of Necker's libertarian daughter, Germaine de Staël, a bluestocking and novelist (*Delphine*). Trapped in a loveless marriage with a Swedish ambassador, she shared many of Lafayette's political views.

Louis XVI was aware of the theories of the Enlightenment along with his religious beliefs. He had been tutored in higher mathematics, valued free enterprise and knew the value of diplomacy. His decisions were not absolute being always made with his cabinet of advisers, a traditional Bourbon practice. Secretive and taciturn, he said shortly before his death, "I would rather let people interpret my silence than my words."[4] He did not enjoy kingship, had little interest in the visual arts and kept council meetings from interfering with his hunts.[5] Fluent in English and Italian, he read Milton and owned 586 English books, twice that of Voltaire.[6]

Louis was impressed with Lafayette's American success and appointed him *maréchal de camp*, equivalent of brigadier general. Officers of lesser rank with longer service complained jealously and Lafayette threatened to resign. But the Marquis de Ségur, minister of war and his comrade's father, urged him to refrain.[7] So Lafayette accepted his new status. His closeness to Washington also invoked envy. He was welcomed to the Order of St. Louis, which offered claim to a pension. Lafayette knew his sovereign's weaknesses but respected him and the queen. They represented the head and heart of France and he would give his life to defend them.

Moved by American ideals, Lafayette became moderately liberal. He and Adrienne read and absorbed the ideas of Enlightenment *philosophe* Abbé Thomas Raynal. Study of European colonial and commercial expansion led to Raynal's attacks on slavery and support for national and popular sovereignty. Lafayette also greatly enjoyed being a valued commentator on the scene for the great Dr. Franklin, who, though wracked with gout, greeted him joyfully. Since Lafayette was now a French general, he ended his obligations to the Noailles Dragoons. He sold the regiment to Louis de Noailles, for 60,000 livres, 20,000 fewer than he had paid, but kept it in the family. Lafayette came into his full inheritance, including lands in Brittany and holdings in Paris. With his vast income and Adrienne's help, he increased his wealth while keeping his trusted manager. On September 17, 1782, Adrienne presented her husband with a second daughter, Virginie, named for Washington's commonwealth.

In November 1782, before leaving for Cadiz, Lafayette purchased a stone mansion with courtyard for 200,000 livres, of which 50,000 livres went for paintings, mirrors and decorations by architect Adrien Mouton. The Left Bank house (razed in the early twentieth century) was at 119 Rue de Bourbon (now Rue de Lille), near the Palais Bourbon, future home of the National Assembly. The Lafayettes bought fine French and American furniture and decorated in American style. They offered Franklin, Adams, Jefferson, William Pitt and many others American cuisine such as corn on the cob and Martha Washington's Virginia-cured hams. Aged Franklin heard young Virginie and Georges sing American songs. Lafayette framed and hung *The Declaration of Independence* in his office beside an empty frame awaiting, he said, France's declaration of citizens' rights.

Jefferson came to Paris in 1784 as an American trade negotiator with his daughter Patsy. Knowing little about American products, Europeans paid him scant attention. Jefferson succeeded Franklin, seventy-nine, as ambassador. He corrected Vergennes for saying he was "replacing" Franklin, since, as Jefferson observed, no one could do that. Jefferson's townhouse with courtyard and garden formerly stood on the north side of what is now the Champs Ēlysées at Rue de Berri. As he and Lafayette grew closer, Jefferson wrote to Washington of the marquis:

His zeal is unbounded and his weight with those in power great. His education having been merely military, commerce was an unknown field to him. But his good sense enabling him to comprehend perfectly whatever is explained to him, his agency has been very efficacious. He has a great deal of sound genius, is well remarked by the king and is rising in popularity. He has nothing against him but a suspicion of republican principles. I think he will one day be of the ministry. His foible is a canine appetite for popularity and fame; but he will get over this.

Jefferson, who stayed in France five years, misread Lafayette on his last point: he would always crave attention and never received too much. Both men helped each other as their friendship deepened. Lafayette found a use for American whale oil in Paris' street lamps and gained large sales for Virginia tobacco. Washington lauded him: "...Your successful endeavors, my Dr. Marqs., to promote the interest of your two countries (as you justly call them) must give you the most unadulterated satisfaction: be assured the measures which have lately been taken with regard to the two articles of oil and tobacco have tended very much to endear you to your fellow citizens on this side of the Atlantic..."[8]

Such praise pleased Lafayette. But all was not well. Aglăé d'Hunolstein, tired of the growing gossip and her mother's anger, pleaded to end their affair. He protested, declaring his love for her then and forever. She urged him to reconsider. So, back in France only a week, he and Adrienne set off for Chavaniac. He had not been there in ten years and it was her first visit. The natives admired Adrienne and her piety in church. Early in 1783, Lafayette purchased Langeac, a marquisate near Chavaniac, for 188,000 livres; possibly, it was rumored, to receive a dukedom. But his investiture as seigneur at twenty-eight was bumbling. Delays and drummers drowning out speakers taxed his love of ceremony. But as absentee lord, he could tax peasants using his mill, oven, wine press or breeding stock.[9]

His grandmother, maiden aunt and cousin had died. But Aunt Charlotte, living with a few servants, welcomed him with happy cries and invited in his old friends. Poor weather and a bad harvest had left peasants starving. When his bailiff suggested raising the price of wheat, Lafayette replied, "No, it is a good time to give it away." After consulting with officials, he donated hundreds of bushels to the poor and was moved when they brought rustic gifts and knelt before him. It is said he told a relative, "Wait three or four years and things will not be the same!" He planned changes within the government.

In Paris, Lafayette reluctantly gave up his lover and under family pressure she ended her days in a convent.[10] There would be other liaisons. Lafayette enjoyed the favors and counsel of Diane de Damas d'Antigny, Comtesse de Simiane. Wife of a homosexual courtier who served in America with Rochambeau, she became Lafayette's mistress in the 1780s and also sat to Madame Vigée Le Brun.[11] He was also an intimate friend of Princesse Adélaïde d'Hénin, lady-in-waiting to the queen in 1777 and wife of Artois' captain of guards.[12] The two lovely women occupied his attention for many years. Adrienne, small, plain, super-devout and proud, knew them and their roles in his life as he often mentioned them. She welcomed them as friends and asked Simiane's children to call her aunt. Adrienne excelled at details her husband avoided. But after he easily dropped the "*de*" in his name, she still signed hers "Noailles de Lafayette."

Working harder than ever for the Americans, Lafayette in his first week back from Auvergne saw how eager Vergennes and other court ministers were to help. He argued for loans "with greater weight than I could possibly do," Franklin wrote Robert Morris. But Vergennes was disappointed that Americans were not doing more to help themselves. Lafayette told Franklin he thought the next loan would not be large and to "act as if none were to be expected."[13] But he urged Castries, minister of the marine who was modernizing the Navy, to send food supplies in good ships and advised American agents to request the best supplies and munitions.

Lafayette gave money to the arts and the poor in America. He forwarded 500 livres to his elderly friend Henry Laurens. The British had captured him on the high seas on his way to borrow from the Dutch. Ailing in the Tower of London, Laurens was exchanged for Cornwallis and arrived in Paris two days before the signing of the peace treaty. At Vergennes' request, Lafayette submitted a list of topics to be covered in their conversations on America's need for ten or twelve million livres as well as more French troops needed to attack New York and Charleston. Vergennes, upset at being left out of American peace talks with the British, nevertheless, just over a month later, offered Franklin six million livres to be repaid quarterly.

Congress now insisted that John Jay, emissary to the Spanish court, ask Lafayette's help in convincing Spain to recognize American independence. Spain had been France's ally for three years, but her leaders were reluctant to openly support America's Protestant majority. Though he had his doubts, Lafayette wrote Jay the Spanish, rulers of the Netherlands in the sixteenth century through royal inheritance, would not let the Dutch, with whom John Adams was negotiating, recognize the United States first.[14] The French were exasperated by Spanish foot-dragging because, Lafayette learned from his king and ministers, it interfered with France's war efforts. A French and Spanish operation led by France's Duc de Crillon captured a British-held port on the Spanish island of Minorca, raising hope they might break Britain's hold on Gibraltar.

With Lord Frederick North, opponent of American independence, stepping down from twelve years as prime minister, the British had warmed to a peace treaty but wanted France at a separate conference. Seeking joint talks, Vergennes stormed, "France would never treat without her allies." Lafayette, writing American emissary Robert Livingston, called attempts to win the United States from France "insidious proposals." He learned Adams at The Hague, when questioned on an Anglo-American treaty, had replied, "Independence is the first step, and nothing could be done but in concert with France." Not so. Of American negotiators, Franklin most favored France. Adams secretly questioned her motives and in his diary criticized Lafayette for wanting to make America French. The opposite was true. Jay disliked the "papists," mostly the Spanish but also the French. Yet he relished the Lafayettes, who welcomed the Jays to their home. Adrienne, who spoke some English, was also very friendly with Abigail Adams. If Lafayette knew Adams sniped at him, he overlooked it.

The British asked to meet with a French representative in London. Lafayette wanted to be that man. But plans moved slowly. Rodney's defeat and capture of De Grasse in the Caribbean had Britons thinking they could negotiate with France from a position of strength — even avoiding the humiliation of recognizing American independence. Vergennes told Lafayette that France insisted on bargaining along with her American ally: there could be no such meeting in London. Disappointed, the marquis told Franklin of the impasse. The old wizard hobbled to court and was permitted to examine the letter from chief negotiator Lord William Grenville not mentioning France's allies. Franklin deduced the reason was De Grasse's capture. Vergennes assured Franklin that Louis XVI would never agree to negotiations impugning France's dignity. But De Grasse's defeat ended Vergennes' desire to send more troops to America. French cities, provinces and Freemasons, filled with patriotism, offered to pay for the ships De Grasse lost to replenish the French Navy.

When Grenville asked Lafayette when he was returning to America, the marquis, already tardy, snapped, "I see that the expectation of peace is a joke and that you only amuse us without any real intention of treating." Expecting to leave in six days, he became involved with the exchange in Paris of Cornwallis for Laurens. Since Lafayette was a general to whom Cornwallis had surrendered, he participated in the negotiations. He was saddened by John Laurens' death in August 1782 during an indecisive skirmish with the British in South Carolina, leaving his English widow and unseen daughter in London. Peace plans stagnated, partly because British leaders both favored and opposed American independence. Lafayette meanwhile wrote letters to America and to officer friends going there to fight. With peace stalemated, he saw the conflict as "dull as a European war."

SEVENTEEN: THE ELUSIVE PEACE

Curious about new discoveries, Lafayette attended séances in Paris and became a somewhat skeptical supporter of Dr. Franz Anton Mesmer. Medical doctors had forced Mesmer, born in Swabia, Germany, out of Vienna six years before. He "cured" Parisians' pains with "animal magnetism" that he said responded like metal to magnets. He and aides took metal rods from magnetized water tubs and pointed them at subjects' ailments. The rods seemed to draw off fluid, easing pain. The practice led to sensual behavior and orgies. Mesmer talked to his subjects, never touching them. Responding to complaints, in 1784 Louis XVI appointed a committee — Franklin, chemist Antoine Lavoisier, astronomer Jean-Sylvain Bailly and Dr. Joseph Ignace Guillotin — to determine if such a magnetic fluid existed. In double-blind tests, which were first invented for these experiments, subjects failed to respond to the rods. Mesmer, exposed and ordered from France, died in Switzerland at eighty-one in 1815. His power was autosuggestion.[1]

Lafayette also funded turbaned charlatan Comte de Cagliostro, later found to be Giuseppe Balsamo, Sicilian thief and confidence man. In Paris in 1785, he used techniques similar to Mesmer's. Cagliostro initiated Lafayette into the Egyptian Rite and was a delegate at two important Masonic conventions in Germany and Paris.

Cagliostro was acquitted in the scandalous affair of the diamond necklace. Rich but foolish Cardinal de Rohan, smitten with Marie Antoinette, was duped into ordering the elaborate jewelry in a plot devised by his lover, impoverished prostitute Comtesse de la Motte. The queen was shocked when the jeweler billed her for the necklace about which she knew nothing. But the incident further blackened her spendthrift reputation. La Motte for her duplicity was beaten and jailed with whores. Escaping to London, she published her memoirs, keeping to her story. Cagliastro, fleeing to Italy, died in a Roman prison in 1795.

Lafayette, while attending Masonic, Rosicrucian and pro-American gatherings, met the firebrand Jacques-Pierre Brissot de Warville. A journalist from Chartres, Brissot toured the United States in 1788 to learn how to start a revolution in France, or, if unsuccessful, to emigrate. He formed the Society of Friends of the Blacks in Paris that year, influencing Lafayette and others wanting to free slaves in the French colonies.

While awaiting a peace treaty, Lafayette learned more about the age's philosophical ideas. Previously he had done little substantive reading. His new ideas besides that of freeing people of color included religious tolerance, particularly for Protestants and Jews. Louis XIV had outlawed Protestantism in 1685, forcing believers to go underground or emigrate. Favoring bureaucratic controls limiting royal powers, Lafayette reasoned, was not being disloyal to the king but secured his place. As much as Lafayette disliked the British nation, he favored its government — king, lords and commons — dreaming of them for France.

In diplomacy, he wrote Washington, he always thought first of how his father would want him to act. There was no better model of strength, forbearance and moderation. But Lafayette was more precipitate and less focused on the larger picture (some have said muddle-headed) and not nearly as shrewd. Even worse, France had no experience with government based on equal rights and compromised differences. Lafayette determined he would help his country achieve these values. His philanthropy also blossomed. He attempted to alter a law at Versailles: the government and he, with Adrienne's help, would support teaching shepherds' wives at Chavaniac to weave and sell wool for income. This took years to establish because of bureaucracy.

As the peace treaty process dragged on, Grenville, who favored American independence, succeeded Pitt the Younger as prime minister.

Scottish merchant Richard Oswald replaced Grenville as negotiator. Oswald had lived three years in America and opposed colonial leniency unlike his superior, the Earl of Shelburne, one of several British secretaries of state. Shelburne — Dublin-born William Petty FitzMaurice, who had served at Minden — was Pitt's political heir. A Whig favoring free trade with America, Shelburne offended the king with his pro-American views. Briefly prime minister as the revolution ended, he was removed by elevation. Made first marquess of Lansdowne, he left politics.[2] David Hartley, son of the philosopher, was also a Parliament member sympathetic to Americans but no friend of Shelburne. Hartley replaced Oswald in April 1783, probably because Oswald was a friend of Franklin.

Although Lafayette urged Vergennes to send Americans more help, Adams and Jay began to suspect Vergennes and even questioned Lafayette's efforts. Adams wrote of Lafayette in his diary, "This unlimited ambition will obstruct his rise; he grasps at all, civil, political, and military, and will be the *unum necessarium* in every thing; he has had so much real merit, such family supports and so much favor at court that he need not recur to artifice." Vergennes joked to Lafayette he would strip Versailles clean to help furnish America. Adams admitted Lafayette was the first to seek more money from Vergennes.[3] But the minister himself had helped spend France into debt. The American negotiators learned that Vergennes, ignoring Lafayette, had sent his seasoned secretary, Joseph Gérard de Rayneval, to London on a secret mission regarding Gibraltar's fate and its effect on Europe. Jay feared Rayneval would work against America's western boundary and fishing rights.

Lafayette urged Jay to see Vergennes to learn the ministry's position but he refused. Without discussing the matter with France, Oswald convinced Jay that Britain was ready to conclude the war separately with the Americans. Oswald showed Jay an intercepted letter of March 1782 in which emissary La Luzerne's secretary, Barbé-Marbois in Philadelphia, was hostile to American fishing claims off Newfoundland. Jay feared Rayneval would not only ruin concessions Jay had reached with Oswald but also try to divide American western lands between Britain, France and Spain and settle fishing rights between Britain and France.[4]

They delved into fishing rights, repatriating American Tories to Canada and agreed to mutual traffic on the Mississippi. George III refused to yield an inch but a royal council overrode him in November 1782. Vergennes, delayed by Spain's stubbornness on Gibraltar, was not invited to Anglo-American negotiations. Jay's fears at least in part were not merited. The French government lived up to the Franco-American alliance: Louis XVI renounced forever claims to any part of North America belonging to Britain or the future United States. But France and Britain hungered for land beyond America's western borders.

Vergennes accepted each nation's negotiating peace on its own with London, provided they all agreed on terms. He had hoped to negotiate French claims to the Ohio and Mississippi valleys but none were made. Betraying Spain, he told London Britain might retain Gibraltar if Spain could keep Minorca and east and west Florida. This suggestion pushed the Americans to seek peace without France. On September 11, Jay told Benjamin Vaughan, Lord Shelborne's second delegate, the American delegation was ready to make a separate peace and was prepared to abandon its 1778 treaty of alliance with France. Adams arrived in Paris from the Netherlands on October 25 and approved of Jay's tactics. Franklin's kidney stones and his seventy-six years kept him from a strong negotiating role. (He died at eighty-four in 1790.)

After four years of siege, Spain and France had failed to take Gibraltar. Marquis de Castries, navy minister, surveying losses from the battle of the *Saintes,* had France replace lost warships within a year. In June 1782, on learning of De Grasse's failure, Vergennes and Castries urged France and Spain to send an armada against the British West Indies on the theory its victory would win bargaining power to force Britain's acceptance of American independence. Louis XVI agreed. Command was given to Admiral D'Estaing on September 29; he requested Lafayette as his second in command. D'Estaing left Versailles on November 2 to confer with Spain's Charles III, who accepted him as commander-in-chief of the armada's armies and navies. Louis XVI confirmed the plan through Montmorin, his ambassador to Spain. The fleet would consist of 24,000 men (13,598 French soldiers) and sixty-six ships of the line. It would be almost as large as Spain's Philip II's armada sent against England in 1588.

Lafayette and French warships rushed from Brest on December 8, 1782. Lafayette, aboard ship of the line *Richmond*, reached Cadiz on

December 23, six days after D'Estaing. Montmorin wrote them the American peace was approaching. On January 2, 1783, Spanish minister Floridablanca urged the armada to sail as soon as possible, confirmed around January 28. The plan was to seize the island of Jamaica and then attack New York. Lafayette, as land commander, would then lead 4,000 troops against Canada.[5] Besides the two kings and Montmorin, only D'Estaing and Lafayette knew the plan, yet realized the American war could end abruptly.[6]

As quartermaster general, Lafayette oversaw materiel. He was surprised Americans in Cadiz considered the war to be over. [7] The peace treaty's first papers were signed in Paris on January 20, 1783. Twelve days later, D'Estaing was officially informed the expedition was dead. Cancellation recalled how in 1779 France and Spain had aborted an invasion of England. Spanish delays and disease among 40,000 French soldiers, waiting on the continent for sixty-five warships to clear the way for 400 transport ships, halted that operation. Nevertheless Britons, frightened by this threat, had stationed troops and warships along their coasts.

Lafayette had been in Le Havre, one of two starting points for the expedition in mid-July 1779, when Vergennes asked for his ideas on the new armada. Lafayette inserted his dream of Canadian conquest but saw it dashed again. While disassembling the fleet in 1783 Cadiz, D'Estaing sent the aptly named corvette *Triomphe* speeding word of peace to America. This first news of victory reached Philadelphia thirty-six days later. On board were Lafayette's letters to Washington and other friends promising his return that June. He secretly informed Washington and D'Estaing he wished Congress would send him to London to ratify the peace treaty, "an honorary commission that would require the attendance of a few weeks." Washington and D'Estaing agreed — "if," Washington wrote, "consistent with our national honor." As Adams saw it, the marquis was too ready to be where glory could occur. No invitation was sent.

Hartley, Adams and Jay signed their peace treaty, with wording obsequious to George III, on September 3, 1783 in Paris' Hôtel d'York, Rue Jacob. France, Spain and Great Britain penned their own agreement later that day at Versailles, the delegates banqueting together afterward.

EIGHTEEN: DEALING WITH MADRID

Lafayette in his long "gazettes" to America now suggested that if the United States were to be free of danger from Britain and Europe, a new constitution must replace the Articles of Confederation. "There ought to be delegates from each state, and perhaps some officers among them, one of whom I would be happy to be, who towards next fall would meet together and under the presidence of Gen. Washington, may devise upon amendments to be proposed in the Articles of Confederation, units of states, etc., etc."[1] He asked Robert Livingston to make this paragraph known to the president of Congress.

Six years after Lafayette's proposal, the United States adopted its Constitution in 1787. The government began work under it on March 4, 1789. Lafayette was pleased to see his suggestions flourish. He also wrote Livingston about Spain's holding east and west Florida. Called "the Floridas," they included large parts of Louisiana, Mississippi, Alabama, Florida and territories west of the Mississippi.[2] Lafayette presumed Lord Shelborne wanted to see the United States and Spain fight over them. "A day will come, I hope," he predicted, "when Europeans will have little to do on the Northern Continent, and God grant it may even be for the happiness of mankind and the propagation of liberty."[3] James Monroe would make this hope manifest in 1823 in what would later be called the Monroe Doctrine.

Still working for the Americans, Lafayette reached Madrid on February 15, 1783 after the British garrison had prevented his visit to Gibraltar. Despite Lafayette's "rebel title and uniform," Charles III received him graciously at the Pardo Palace. Regarded as the best of Spain's Bourbon kings, Charles was an enlightened despot of sixty-seven. Long a widower, he had seven surviving children of thirteen. Although Spain had not recognized the United States, for several years Charles' ministers had secretly given less than five percent of French expenditures and materiel to Beaumarchais for the Continental Army.[4] When D'Estaing suggested Lafayette might become governor of Jamaica, the king exploded, "No, never! He would turn it into a republic!"

By not acknowledging the colonists, Spain had avoided British attacks on its New World ports and vessels plying the Atlantic. But Spain and Cuba had protected American ships in their harbors and even paid for repairs. If he knew this, Lafayette still found the grandees at court petty, "especially when on their knees" before their monarch. The Spanish were apprehensive of America. But Lafayette had promised Congress he would use persuasion "in forwarding any plans that may want either mercantile connections or the protection of the French government." He met with the powerful Spanish foreign minister, Conde de Floridablanca, who somewhat reluctantly agreed to open trade with the United States. In helping America, Lafayette learned the diplomatic intricacies of foreign trade and economics.

Still distrusting the Spanish, he was disappointed that, under the Paris treaty, Britain gave Florida back to Spain, a direct threat to the Americans. (In the Seven Years' War peace treaty of 1763, Spain, which never ran Florida cohesively, lost it to Britain, which also mishandled it.) Lafayette believed Spain would not be content controlling only the west side of the Mississippi. Spain, fearful of intruding Americans, tried to limit their river traffic. But under the 1783 Paris treaty, Britain and the United States agreed to equal river access: Americans could not be kept away from the Mississippi. Floridablanca declared Spain wanted harmony with the United States. Lafayette, pushing the point since he was leaving Madrid in a few days, asked for a treaty between Spain and the United States.

Floridablanca saw no problem. While resisting opening the Mississippi or discussing some commercial matters, he said he still hoped to satisfy the Americans. But when Lafayette hinted Spain might also like to lend Americans money, Floridablanca brushed that idea aside.[5] Lafayette wrote down the treaty points and submitted them. The first American Lafayette had met in Paris, *chargé d'affaires* William Carmichael, whom the Spanish had previously refused to recognize, was invited the next day to court and an ambassadorial dinner. Lafayette had another purpose for his list of points: he would show it to Congress. Spain's formal recognition of the United States came quickly in 1783, thanks to Lafayette. But Spanish-American border disputes continued for many years.

Traveling north by way of Bordeaux, Lafayette reached Paris on March 12. The American war presumably over, he received his promised rank of non-commissioned *maréchal de camp* (major general) in the army. The merchants of Bayonne begged him to have the government dredge their harbor to receive American traders. Lafayette extended his interest to allow the ports of Lorient, Dunkerque and Marseille to handle goods freely from America (he did not win Marseille). This led to his championing lower tariffs before the finance and foreign ministers. "In trading with the United States," he wrote Finance Minister Jean François Joly de Fleury, "we shall derive a great advantage from the war, our expenditures and the Revolution… It is up to us to get almost all the American trade. … By our shackles upon commerce we are in imminent danger of losing the largest share of it… I am unhappy to think that in repelling [French] trade rather than attracting it, we shall help the English much more than they can help themselves."

This was prophetic: French trade with America never matched Britain's and even shrank after the war. France, profiting little from its generosity in the billions of livres, kept only the tiny islands of St. Pierre and Miquelon, off Nova Scotia (which it still holds), and fishing rights off Newfoundland, a large issue at the time. As the French mob saw it — but not the king or his government — France had vengefully stripped an old enemy of its American colonies just as Britain had taken Canada from

France. The war's burden on the staggering French economy, however, was disastrous, forcing new taxes on those least able to pay. France spent more than it had on the Seven Years' War: 1.3 billion livres, equivalent of $13 billion today.

Lafayette, enjoying fame and the headiness of being a wealthy war hero, did not know how serious the situation was. Why else would he have pressed so fervently for American loans? Few knew the truth. He said nothing about this or the American treaty negotiators' seeming ingratitude toward France, which had assured their independence. It would have been unpolitic.

Lafayette became more liberal in seeking free trade. He wanted to improve conditions where he saw solutions. Often the real problem was French bureaucratic slowness. But his previous successes buoyed his optimism. He saw issues broadly and sometimes without clear definition. As his actions gained him more national esteem, his mind teemed with new ideas.

He proposed in a 1783 letter to Washington that they become partners in an unprecedented experiment. They would buy a plantation where American slaves could earn their freedom working in the fields. Washington, owner of 200 slaves by purchase, marital acquisition and inheritance, said he favored the idea. But, aware of what his involvement would mean as a Southerner and national leader, he did not pursue it. Yet it is likely Lafayette's position influenced Washington, for in his will he freed his slaves. Martha willed hers to heirs at her death in 1802.

Undaunted, Lafayette in 1786 wrote Washington, now president, he had bought a plantation, *La Gabrielle*, for 125,000 livres in the torrid colony of Cayenne (French Guiana), where he had 120 blacks working with crops and bountiful trees to earn their freedom. Washington, wondering how slavery in the United States could ever be overcome, saluted him. *La Gabrielle* ironically was named for a popular runaway slave, Gabriel, who around 1707 had raised an army but was captured and executed. A creek, river and mountain were named after him.[6] Jesuits had earlier built a monastery in this Roura region that grew cocoa and sugar cane. Adrienne Lafayette sent donations for the farm and local priests informed her of operations. She also oversaw workers' religious instruction, but neither Lafayette ever visited.[7]

The experiment ended abruptly in 1792 when the revolutionary tribunal in Paris closed the farm and sold the workers who said they would claim their freedom if Gabrielle were confiscated, or stay if it were not. Lafayette protested their return to slavery. He sought abolition by degrees, foreseeing problems if it occurred all at once. The colony of Cayenne, unlike Haiti, never revolted against France. Lafayette would later support two similar freedom attempts for blacks in the United States.

NINETEEN: Heartfelt Visit

Arriving in New York on August 4, 1784 for his third American visit of four months and seventeen days, Lafayette's main purpose was to see his adoptive father at Mount Vernon where his second floor bedroom would henceforth be known as the Lafayette Room. He had corresponded with Jefferson since the war. But Congress had appointed him to negotiate commercial treaties and he was en route to France as Lafayette sailed to America. In his first visit to Manhattan, Lafayette was greeted as a hero with parades, receptions, dinners and ringing church bells wherever he went. On his way south, he first stopped in Trenton and, on August 12 in Philadelphia where he spoke about Mesmer to the American Philosophical Society. Minutes of this special appointment with twenty-two members reported Lafayette:

> *"...Entertained with a particular relation of the wonderful effects of a certain invisible power, in nature, called 'animal magnetism' lately discovered by Mr. Mesmer, a German philosopher, and explained by him to a number of gentlemen in Paris of which members the Marquis was himself one. By this relation it appears that persons may be so impregnated with this power (by a process which the Marquis does not think himself at liberty yet to explain)*

as to exhibit many phenomena similar to those of metallic magnetism."[1]

Mesmer is said to have commissioned one of twelve-year-old Wolfgang Amadeus Mozart's first operas, *Bastien und Bastienne*, in 1768.[2] During séances, Mesmer played an eerily-sounding glass armonica, rubbing glass bowls' wet edges, an invention Franklin had improved. Although Mesmer had 600 imitators in Paris alone, his luck failed. France banished him the same year Lafayette spoke before America's most learned group.

Lafayette achieved his desired meetings and two visits with Washington, whose plan to visit his lands in western Pennsylvania interrupted their visit at a tavern in Alexandria, Virginia. They later met in Richmond and traveled in Washington's carriage to Mount Vernon where Lafayette spent eleven days in August. They discussed the war and European problems that could affect the young country. Washington insisted the United States had to stay clear of foreign entanglements and Lafayette told what he knew of them in Europe.

Riding out at dawn to study the general's lands, they met his overseers with the day's orders. They inspected planted fields, orchards, a greenhouse, slaves and animals. Mount Vernon and Monticello both whetted Lafayette's interest in farming and husbandry. He much enjoyed Washington's extended family and their bountiful meals together, enhanced by Martha's cured hams, fresh vegetables and peach brandy. Many guests dropped in, often unannounced, and left after eating. Martha sat at the head of the table with George at her side. Lafayette absorbed their daily life, writing to Adrienne that Washington's small adopted grandchildren first wanted to see whether he looked like "the man in the family portrait" the Lafayettes had sent:

> *...The general loved reading your letter and that of Anastasie, and I've been charged with sending you the most loving regards of the entire family, and Mrs. Washington told me today that, with both of them so old, you must not deprive them of the joy of receiving you*

and our little family; I made a solemn vow, sweetheart, to bring you with me on the next trip...[3]

Besides the group portrait, Lafayette over the years gave the Washingtons a marble fireplace and clock, horses, "a Jack and two she-asses," Briards (shaggy Brie shepherd dogs) and stag hounds.Washington crossbred the latter into ancestors of today's American fox hounds. In 1786, Lafayette sent a partridge and seven other birds, including a pair of golden pheasants — Louis XVI's gift from the royal aviary.[4] He requested mockingbirds, unknown in Europe, from Washington and sent him nightingales. He later shipped two Briards to Jefferson, who had them in the President's House and sent Lafayette a dozen Merino sheep in 1807. Lafayette later in his American tour presented John Quincy Adams with a young alligator that stayed in a bathtub in the East Room.[5]

Lafayette's stay deeply touched Washington. Believing his service to the nation to be done — "I have had my day," he wrote — he wished to live "under the shadow of my own vine and my own fig tree."[6] But five years later the nation would call on him again.

While Lafayette was in Philadelphia, Congress asked his help in preventing war between the six Northeastern Indian tribes. British in Canada were goading them to rebel against American settlers moving through their lands to the Ohio Territory. The Indians respected Lafayette, their *Kayewla*. He and they recalled how Oneidas had served at Barren Hill. Lafayette, an honorary Iroquois, negotiated a settlement reserving Indian lands, except for two forts, in upper New York. At Fort Stanwix, near Rome, New York, the tribes agreed to allow farmers to settle between Lake Erie and the Ohio River. James Madison, in Lafayette's entourage, hoped to gain more western lands and to open the Mississippi River. Lafayette eclipsed government negotiators, Madison wrote Jefferson, and also accepted an Onondaga family's request to rear their twelve-year-old son, *Kayenlaha*, with his children. The youth was a sensation at Parisian balls dancing in a breechclout.

At Niskayuna, a celibate community near Albany, Lafayette saw Shakers heal the ill by the "laying on of hands," a form of autosuggestion. He was impressed as Melville, Hawthorne and Emerson were later. On this trip, Lafayette wore a gummed taffeta raincloak that had been wrapped in newspapers. People could read the *Journal de Paris*, *Courier de l'Europe* and other newsprint adhering to it, reported a friend, François Barbe′-Marbois, who later negotiated Napoleon's sale of the Louisiana Territory.[6]

Lafayette corresponded with the Shakers during his life. It was said his spirit bade them farewell weeks before news of his death reached the United States.[7] On September 26, he and his young assistant, Chevalier de Caraman, met with James Madison and two other French nobles.[8] Lafayette liked traveling with companions. They sailed down to New York for four days of eating and drinking. Lafayette and Madison had met during the war. Both were interested in politics and economics and liked each other. Lafayette then traveled in New England and Madison returned to Philadelphia. Cities jubilantly hailed the hero, among them Albany, Hartford, Boston, Providence, Baltimore and Richmond. In Boston, Governor John Hancock held a banquet in his honor and merchants sponsored a dinner for 500 guests in Faneuil Hall. Massachusetts made him an honorary citizen. Speaking in Latin, he accepted a degree from Harvard College.[9]

On the French frigate *Nymphe,* Lafayette, Caraman and the Indian lad sailed to Virginia. The marquis, reviving memories of victory, paraded in tiny Yorktown on the battle's third anniversary. He met Washington in Richmond, which, in celebrating them, exploded with receptions, balls, fireworks. Lafayette's party and Washington reached Mount Vernon on November 22. Again Lafayette admired the children, the table and ambience before tearful farewells four days later. The men rode in separate carriages to a fork outside Annapolis where Washington turned back. At fifty-two, he was losing teeth and foresaw a short life like those of his ancestors. The two men wrote each other departing letters, Washington correctly assuming it would be their last meeting, Lafayette disallowing the possibility.

In future years Washington gleaned what he could of the marquis' adventures, sometimes offering advice. Washington could not bring himself to visit Paris, saying he was too old to learn French. He was unanimously elected president on April 30, 1789 and served a second term from 1792 to 1796. On a cold December day in 1799, Washington, sixty-seven, contracted pleurisy after inspecting trees and reading while in damp clothes. Mustard poultices were applied to his chest but pneumonia and over-zealous bloodletting proved fatal. Studying his current accounts, he murmured, "'Tis well," and joined eternity seventeen days before the century ended.

Lafayette rode northeast to Trenton and addressed the Congress of the Confederation there on December 11, 1784 on his hopes for the United States:

> *"... May this immense temple of freedom ever stand a lesson to oppressors, an example to the oppressed, a sanctuary for the rights of mankind! And may these happy United States attain that complete splendor and prosperity that will illustrate the blessing of their government, and for ages to come rejoice the departed souls of its founders."*[10]

He enjoyed Congress' applause and the company of president of Congress Richard Henry Lee, Monroe, Hamilton and many others. In New York, he met with Nathanael Greene, Henry Knox and again Hamilton. Lafayette asked them to send him their sons to be educated for several years and he would do the same with Georges, whom he wanted to go to Harvard College. At the generals' suggestion Lafayette accepted John Edward Caldwell, fourteen, orphan of an admired army chaplain. Lafayette and his wards sailed to France on December 21, 1784. Problems in finding Caldwell a non-Catholic education in Paris led to Lafayette's work on restoring rights to Protestants and Jews.[11] No one could foresee, in Thomas Carlyle's word, the maelstrom coming.

TWENTY: QUARRELSOME ESTATES

Returning to Rue de Bourbon, Lafayette was delighted to become the first foreign member of the Society of the Cincinnati. America's oldest military hereditary society, General Henry Knox's idea, was formed in 1783 and named for a legendary farmer: Lucius Quintus Cincinnatus. In the fifth century B.C., as a consul and general, he led Rome to victory and then returned to his fields. Later, as temporary dictator, Cincinnatus served fifteen days and, seeking no further power, again retired. The tale echoed Washington's life. The society was to provide fellowship for Continental officers and descendants, charity for original members' families and help securing military pensions. Franklin, Adams and others saw members as a potential aristocracy but the Society honored its purposes.[1]

Steuben conducted its first meetings in 1783 at Mount Gulian, former homestead of the Verplanck family and his headquarters as inspector general, in Fishkill. Leaving service in 1784, he moved to New York City, then to a log cabin north of Utica, New York. He kept the *de* appended to his name as he had for many years, not *von*, a nineteenth-century Prussian invention: both his will and gravestone read *De Steuben*. Washington was the Society's first president for sixteen years until his death when Hamilton succeeded him.[2] With Rochambeau and D'Estaing, representing French officers of the Royal Army and Navy respectively, Lafayette co-founded the Society's French branch. D'Estaing was its first president until his death in 1794. Lafayette represented French officers of the Continental Army. He unwittingly unleashed a flood of potential joiners, including Thomas Conway, who pressured with a mini-cabal. Not wishing to be vengeful but to curb him, Lafayette persuaded the Society to accept him.[3] L'Enfant, who presented to Louis XVI Washington's request for French officers to accept joining this foreign order, did not have enough to pay the Paris goldsmiths Duval and Francastel to cast his design of the Society's first golden eagle medals in 1784. Lafayette advanced him $3,014 to lessen his embarrassment.[4]

With his new popularity, Lafayette received invitations, opportunities and gave many dinners at home. Speaking constantly of American liberty, he had a profound impact on Europeans who felt stultified by monarchic despotisms. Loyalists claimed he infected Europe with democracy. He and Louis Noailles were called "*Americains.*" Rochambeau, Saint-Simon, Lauzun, D'Estaing and Ségur also caught the fever.[5] Even ardent despots — Frederick the Great, Catherine the Great and Joseph II of Austria — prided themselves on their enlightenment. Marie Antoinette, suspicious of Lafayette's liberalism, did not trust him and came to despise him. Feeling restless, Lafayette toured Europe, spoke on the American war of liberty and learned about European militarism. He saw field maneuvers of Frederick's machine-like 100,000-man army. At Sans Souci Palace, Potsdam, he found himself at a three-hour dinner seated beside Cornwallis, now British emissary to Prussia, and Von Knyphausen.

Sly, unclean, arthritic, Frederick shot questions at Lafayette, hoping to create an argument. But Lafayette expressed only his gushing praise of Washington, irritating Cornwallis. During the summer, Lafayette visited various princes and viewed vast numbers of goose-stepping soldiers on parade in Berlin, Breslau, Brunswick, Kassel, Prague and Vienna. Returning to Potsdam and Berlin, he conferred for hours alone with Frederick, developing his own ideas for a militia for America and perhaps France. Catherine of Russia asked him for Native American words to add to her commissioned dictionary and invited him to visit her in Crimea in the fall of 1785. He mailed her request to Washington instead. Fifteen months later, just before Christmas, he learned Versailles had announced a startling new plan for the nation and returned home to learn more.

On February 22, 1787, Louis XVI summoned an Assembly of Notables, the most illustrious men from the three traditional estates — clergy, nobility and everyone else. The First Estate had 100,000 Catholic priests representing the church that owned five to ten percent of France tax-free. The nobility, or Second Estate, represented 400,000 people who were freed of taxes by feudal precedent. Making up the Third Estate were about twenty-five million people: bourgeosie, commoners and the poor. The tax burden fell on the peasants, paying 20 percent of their income. Although France's population was larger than Britain's — twenty-six million to around eight million — British taxes were divided more evenly. Complicating matters: 75 percent of France was illiterate. Assembly delegates were to discuss how the nation's financial woes might be reformed. The uneducated, poor or destitute were not represented.[6]

Duc d'Orléans, joining the Assembly, disagreed with conservative royals. Lafayette saw the Assembly's purpose was "to have the government make money somehow or other to put receipts on a level with expenses." But the delegates were incapable of this. He punned to Washington about "the not ables." In spirit, Lafayette was not one of them, and besides, Virginia, Maryland, Connecticut and Massachusetts had given him honorary citizenship for his service.[7]

Having inherited his great-grandfather's holdings in Brittany, Lafayette was invited to join its provincial assembly in Rennes protesting new tax laws. Marie Antoinette asked by what right was he, a seigneur of Auvergne, involved with Brittany. "I am," he said, "in the same situation as Your Majesty. You are the queen of France and also a member of the House of Austria." She found him insolent. He lost his army commission the next day. Lafayette decided being a notable would allow him to promote his plans for popular provincial assemblies, removing trade obstacles and restoring religious civil rights. But his republican ideas kept him off the first list of invitees. Pulling strings with his friends Castries and Breteuil for a seat, he denounced the entire tax system.[8]

Delegates met in the large Doric-columned *Salle des Menus Plaisirs,* Hall of Small Pleasures, in the deer park half a mile from the throne. The royal entertainments were managed here. Clergy and nobles' robes and rich garments dominated the head of the candle-lit procession opening the convocation. Members set out from the Cathedral of St. Louis, built by Louis XIV, through the town to the hall. Lafayette wore a long cloth-of-gold coat, plumed hat and sword. He was embarrassed to walk with the nobles; his feelings were with the Third Estate. Its members, according to tradition, dressed in black. The king wore the state robe of blue velvet trimmed in ermine and embroidered with gold fleurs-de-lis. His new crown held a 141-carat diamond.[9] As tall as Washington, stout and near-sighted, Louis could only distinquish faces three or four feet away. Unknown to everyone, this evening marked the beginning of the end of the old order and the rise of the *bourgeosie* — upper middle class lawyers, merchants, bankers, writers and other professionals. Slowly the monarchy would lose power over the next six years.

Lafayette was pleased with Louis' low-keyed, almost muffled speech, reluctantly requesting delegates to reform France's social, economic and political systems. The king read from a gold throne. Below him sat the queen, with seven princes of the realm, including his brothers, arranged around them, nobles and clergy on either side. They faced a sea of seated attendees. Among them were observers Thomas Jefferson and Gouverneur Morris. No relative of Robert Morris yet once joining him in a business venture, Gouverneur Morris was a wealthy New York statesman and co-author of the *United States Constitution.* Morris saw Lafayette's growing importance and wrote in his diary, "He will have the opportunity of making the experiment… He means ill to no one, but "if the sea runs high, he will be unable to hold the helm." Morris followed Jefferson as minister to France in 1792.[10]

Outlining the fiscal dilemma was Charles Alexandre de Calonne, Metz lawyer and financial expert whom Vergennes had suggested as controller-general. In office three months, Calonne wanted to cut governmental spending, revive free trade, sell church property, equalize salt and tobacco taxes and establish a general land tax. He also suggested a stamp tax on documents. His idea was to call the Assembly to help obtain cash for the treasury, still gushing large sums to royal favorites. He wanted to tax the rich at what to them was shocking: two to five percent of their lands' value. That would relieve the king of asking provincial parlements to vote general taxes and set fair levies.

The delegates, meeting in three groups, were told their conclusions would be given to the king as suggestions. Not knowing how to proceed, they became deadlocked. Lafayette, in the Second Estate headed by Artois, only knew the rich avoided the *taille* (poll tax) while the poor had to pay *la gabelle* (a salt tax collected since the Middle Ages). Clergy and nobles declined to join the Third Estate even though more than 100 curés favored it. Lafayette was one of forty-seven nobles who wanted to commit to the Third Estate, which, in the British style, was informally called "the Commons" (*communes*).

For five weeks they met daily but there were no resolutions. Meanwhile, clergy and nobles dithered over whether the Commons would even recognize their decisions. No one knew. After a two-week stalemate, Louis invited the groups to meet in conference to resolve differences. There, Bishop La Luzerne of Langres proposed clergy and nobles should meet as one, Commons as another; in effect Houses of Lords and Commons. Lafayette dreamed of France becoming a constitutional monarchy.

On June 10, 1787, the Third Estate sent a final invitation to the higher orders to join with it, or it would declare itself the Estates-General of France. Both sides wanted reform. But reactionary nobles insisted on returning to feudal rights that permitted them, since they were traditionally trained in government and administration, to run the country. They said they would accept responsibility for dependents' welfare, expecting the people to trust their acting in the country's best interests. But the Third Estate found these positions were already ineffective and demanded an elected government, a written constitution and taxation only with public consent. There could be no compromise. Neither side could accept the other.

Lafayette declared the tax-gathering syndicate profited from dishonest rules and methods and he revealed names, places and dates. Louis notified the Assembly through Artois: anyone making charges must sign them. Possibly facing imprisonment, Lafayette called for the minutes, signed his speech and sent it to the king. In a postscript he urged Louis to appoint a commission of honest men with the courage to investigate administrative accounts, as the farmers-general controlled produce fees and courtiers' pensions. His request was ignored but he was too popular to imprison. Because of the parliaments' powers, these problems were beyond Louis and his advisors' ability to resolve.[11]

Six years before, in 1781, Necker had found a loan to float the government. He deliberately underestimated the national deficit in a glowing and widely published *Account Rendered to the King*. Insisting the treasury was increasing, he asked authority to borrow 80 million more. Notables now asked to see expense records to learn what had gone wrong. The queen had Necker banished that year, not over his false account but for thwarting the ambassador to London, Duc de Guines, whom she wished to benefit. Although he proved Necker had lied to hide the national deficit, Calonne was forbidden to restrict court expenditures. Stunned notables condemned him for revealing these problems and accused him of speculating with public money, of paying off his debts and mistresses. But they could not ignore that the nation's finances were seriously mismanaged. Lafayette regarded Calonne as a friend but the king and court disliked him. Louis dismissed Calonne in fewer than four months and sent him to a post in Lorraine.[12]

The queen, becoming more powerful, agreed with the king and ministers Montmorin and Lamoignon's choice of Calonne's successor: Ētienne de Loménie de Brienne, outspoken archbishop of Toulouse who had attacked Calonne's policies. The notables had confidence in Brienne, but inexpertise and the national debt overwhelmed him as court notables blocked any major changes to the old order. Studying the growing problems, some courtiers suggested Louis should summon the Estates-General to handle the crisis. This deliberative body could meet only at the king's order and had not been summoned since 1614. A resolution was introduced on July 13; the royal princes and the most powerful nobles opposed it.

Lafayette argued the Third Estate should have double the combined vote of the nobility and clergy since Commons represented more than nine-tenths of the population. His proposal did not pass. But the

Parlement of Paris revived it and Louis, despite his absolute veto, agreed out of desperation to 1,155 delegates: 266 from the church, 291 nobles and 598 commoners.

In Auvergne Lafayette ran for election as a nobleman, at his family's urging, but he wanted to join the Third Estate. The queen sent friends to speak against him, but he squeaked through with a three-vote majority of 393. The king's rules required him to vote only the nobility's position. This distressed him but he was allowed to speak in favor of Third Estate proposals. In time the rules were set aside and delegates voted as they wished.

Between elections employment dropped. A poor harvest made a four-pound loaf of bread difficult to buy at fourteen sous. A worker's daily bread took 97 percent of his income. Food riots were common, particularly in July before the harvest. Jean-Baptiste Réveillon, a wallpaper manufacturer, who was elected a liberal deputy to the Estates-General over Orléans' candidate, was rumored to have claimed that a workman could live on fifteen sous a day. A mob wrecked his house and factory and attacked armed troops with more than 200 people killed. Lafayette and Charles Maurice Talleyrand-Périgord, impious bishop of Autun, believed Orléans had fomented the riot.[13]

TWENTY-ONE: TIME FOR EXPERTISE

Autun, a town in Burgundy southwest of Dijon, had a remarkable Romanesque Cathedral of St.-Lazare. But observers saw Talleyrand, whose club foot had kept him from the army, as a shrewd politician happiest near earthly power. He would serve as a clever diplomat through several eras.

Orléans, a collateral descendant of Louis XIII, thirsted for the throne. Fabulously wealthy, lecherous and duplicitous, he hated the royal family and opposed the king whenever he could. The royal family detested him. But Marie Antoinette loved Orléans' birthplace, the lavish Chateau de Saint-Cloud in its huge park near Paris. She had Louis buy it from Orléans' father and doted on it.[1]

At forty, Louis Philippe d'Orléans was more interested in the grand baroque Palais Royal he had inherited in the heart of Paris. Cardinal Richelieu, for whom it was built, bequeathed it to Louis XIII. After his death, the regent queen mother and five-year-old Louis XIV lived there until 1661 when Louis XIV moved to the Louvre. Enlarging the complex to replenish his rental income, the duc added colonnaded arcades, fine shops, restaurants and theaters with apartments above.[2] He lived there when not at Villers-Cotterêts, his estate fifty miles northeast of Paris in

Aisne. His liberal-mindedness may have derived from English friends of the Prince of Wales, later George IV. Orléans had an enormously rich wife and gave money to the poor, opened the Palais Royal garden to the public and plotted for the throne. With its large courtyard, the Palais Royal drew lawful citizens as well as thieves, sharpsters and prostitutes. Intrigue swirled around the elegant, affable yet debauched duc. As grand master of the Masonic Orient Rite, he tried to win over Lafayette, as he had many others. Seeing through him, Lafayette never trusted him.

Rising in the Assembly in favor of the Estates-General, Lafayette had an idea. After the government's money-lenders had completed their contracts within five years, "It seems to me," he said, "that we should beg His Majesty to fix that period as one in which accounts of all these operations should be rendered to him, and to consolidate the happy result by convocation of a National Assembly." In controlling state business, an Assembly, superseding the parlements, could meet crises and curb kingly powers. His proposal struck delegates like an explosion and increasing Louis' doubts about him. The notables recommended provincial assemblies should be created and, by royal edict, they were established that year. The king or his ministers chose each member of the three estates and Louis had to approve their every act. Brienne viewed the notables as an obstacle. At his insistence, the king dissolved the Assembly on May 25, 1787, leaving delegates unsure of the future. As a stopgap, Brienne imposed an extremely unpopular stamp tax on receipts, legal papers, drafts, bills, newspapers and posters.

The Paris Parlement at first refused to register the edict, then did so but annuled it next day. Although it had done so for centuries, Parlement informed the king only the Estates-General could register new taxes. Louis found this an act of defiance. With Brienne urging him to crush opposition, he banished Parlement to the northeastern town of Troyes. Four days later Louis ordered Parisian political clubs, now centers of intrigue, closed.

Lafayette was exasperated by public indifference to needed reforms. "The people in this country are so apathetic that I almost need bleeding to save me from the consequences of my own vexation," he complained to Washington. On May 23, 1788 he wrote: "To die for liberty is not the cry on this side of the Atlantic. As all classes are more or less interdependent;

as the rich love their peace while the poor are enervated by poverty and ignorance, we have only one recourse, which is to inspire in the nation, by reasoning, a kind of passive discontent or non-obedience, which may weary the government and defeat its plans." This brilliant concept would flower in the twentieth century.[3]

To the public, the banished parlementarians became first-time heroes. Brienne said he would rescind the stamp tax if Parlement would register a decree increasing the income tax "without any distinction or exception whatever." Parlement agreed and was readmitted to Paris. But its refusal to register an edict raising a loan of 120 million livres ended with Parlement's consenting to abolish itself in favor of the Estates-General.

Brienne, unable to raise another sou, declared the government bankrupt. Louis dismissed him but not before the archbishop helped himself to half the treasury of 200,000 livres.[4] On November 19, the king, expecting to be defeated, refused to allow a vote on new loans. For his vocal opposition next day, Orléans was banished to his estate temporarily and two magistrates were imprisoned. In December, Louis promised to call the Estates-General within five years but, under severe financial pressure, summoned it only seventeen months later in May 1789. Helpless, he recalled Necker, still very popular with the public. While denouncing Calonne, Necker adopted some of his ideas.

On the strength of his name, Necker secured a loan of 25 million livres to pay civil servants, soldiers and seamen. Millions still went to the queen and her friends. The king recalled the notables in November 1788 to formulate new rules. He doubled the Third Estate despite nobles and clerics' protests. Clergy now had 291 members, nobles 270 (ninety of them liberals) and Third Estate 578, including 200 lawyers, three priests and eleven nobles. Holding supreme power, Louis gave each estate an equal vote despite Commons' having more members than the other orders combined. There was a stalemate. Necker, with so many problems, took too long to intervene. When Louis finally gave in, granting Commons greater power, it seemed like a weak but inevitable concession.

TWENTY-TWO: TENNIS COURT OATH

Lafayette added to his trade knowledge from the physiocrats, early French economists. Before industrialism they thought agriculture created a nation's wealth and farm surpluses generated goods and services. Lafayette sought the liberals' advice. They included political scientist Nicolas de Condorcet; lawyer and press minister Crétien Guillaume de Malesherbes (later Louis' defense lawyer and great-grandfather of historian Alexis de Tocqueville; (Lafayette wrote introductory letters for his cousin Tocqueville's American travels); François, Duc de la Rochefoucauld (a social reformer close to Lafayette) and writer/economist Pierre Samuel du Pont de Nemours. They followed Dr. François Quesnay, physician to the late Madame de Pompadour, and founder of the science of political economy and modern liberalism. He coined the term *laissez-faire* for unrestricted trade. Lafayette was eager to deregulate the farm market and reduce taxes on agriculture so that France, like Britain, could prosper with fewer restrictions. In turn, the physiocrats enjoyed the hero's support.[1]

Conferring with them, Lafayette proposed lowering the national debt. He urged cutting royal household expenses, particularly the queen's excesses. He insisted on closing rarely used royal game preserves to keep Louis' favorites from exploiting them. He insisted their fraudulent transfers should be publicly reported. Enraged, Artois reported the proposals to his brother. On May 23, 1787, Lafayette made a motion asking the king to restore Protestant rights. Bishop La Luzerne, brother of the royal minister in Philadelphia, seconded the move, saying he preferred Protestant "temples" to secret meetings.[2]

Lafayette saw no trouble ahead. He wrote Washington that France was inching toward better days "without a great convulsion to an independent representation and consequently to a diminution of the royal authority. But it is a matter of time, and will proceed the more slowly [since] the interests of powerful men will clog the wheels."[3]

Millions of French thought the same. Washington was not so sure:

> . . .The bold demands of the parliamentarians and the decisive tone of the king shew that but little more irritation would be necessary to blow up the spark of discontent into a flame that might not easily be quenched. If I were to advise, I would say that great moderation should be used on both sides... The king, though, I think from everything I have been able to learn, is really a good-hearted tho' warm-spirited man, [and] if thwarted injudiciously in the execution of prerogatives that belong to the Crown & in plans which he conceives calculated to promote the national good, may disclose qualities he has been little thought to possess...[4]

The Third Estate, with some members of the two other orders, turned itself into the National Assembly. This occurred without pomp in the king's crowded indoor tennis court at Versailles where the game was originally played with the palms of the hands. The delegates, led by mild-mannered Jean Sylvain Bailly, declared forcefully: "We swear never to separate ourselves from the National Assembly, and to reassemble wherever circumstances require until the constitution of the realm is drawn up and fixed upon solid foundations."

The June 20 oath occurred on the same day Necker had advised the king to call a meeting to reconcile differences with the Estates-General

— but delegates were not informed. Finding their chamber locked and guarded, they feared being caught in a royal coup d'etat and reassembled in the nearby *jeu de paume,* the royal indoor tennis court. Having vowed to continue drafting the constitution the king had forbidden until it was completed and assured, two days later they found themselves locked out of the tennis court. With a majority of the clergy, they returned to the Cathedral of St. Louis where the notables began their first procession.

On June 27, Louis accepted the validity of the National Assembly and ordered clergy and nobles to join the Third Estate. On July 9, 1789 this body renamed itself the National Constituent Assembly, implying the king's subsumed role.[5] On July 11 he dismissed Necker, who was unable to stop the growing debt and bread scarcity, and reassigned royal ministers. Lafayette scornfully said few worn-out machines could run for a shorter time than Necker; and southern delegate Mirabeau called him "the clock that always loses." But because of articles written by those who had enjoyed Madame Necker's soirees and believed what they heard there, the public was convinced he could do no wrong.[6] The stock exchange suspended operation and securities fell severely. Despite his legerdemain, Necker failed for wanting Louis to begin reforms and adopt more liberal positions. Court advisors, refusing any change, forced him out.

Fearing an aftershock, they asked Louis to activate troops in his German and Swiss regiments and provinces, less likely to revolt or join the Parisians. That day, Mirabeau, misreading Lafayette's cooperation in the Assembly, asked him to join in making Orléans lieutenant general, a role he and Lafayette would somehow share. Mirabeau claimed Lafayette was already on the royal removal list because he was the only Frenchman who could lead an army in revolt. Mirabeau hoped to make Orléans de facto ruler of France. But Lafayette wished to establish liberty for all, not replace the king. He brushed the idea aside and Mirabeau never mentioned it again.[7]

The court, tiring of Louis Comte de Puységur, war minister for seven months, called upon *Maréchal* Victor François, Second Duke de Broglie, seventy-one, the comte's brother, for his decades of military service and made him war minister. Broglie stationed 35,000 troops to guard roads and bridges between Versailles, Paris, Sèvres and Saint

Denis, then added 20,000 more. Avoiding unsafe Paris himself, he placed royal troops at the Champ de Mars. Parisians were angered by these postings and the king and National Assembly's indifference or inability to deal with their pressing needs. Assembymen of upper and middle classes were unaccustomed to considering the impoverished. As the royal government deteriorated, Broglie, war minister for just one hundred hours, left France unnoticed in a hackney to become an émigré commander in Austria, dying in Germany in 1804. He was succeeded by Comte Jean Frédéric de la Tour du Pin-Gouvernet, who lasted a year and five months. He later defended the king in court and followed him to the scaffold.

PART THREE: TRIALS AND DISAPPOINTMENTS

TWENTY-THREE: DECLARING CITIZENS' RIGHTS

It was the evening of Saturday, July 11, 1789. Lafayette had absorbed American delegate George Mason's *Virginia Declaration of Rights of 1776* proclaming the inherent rights of man. Standing before the National Assembly, Lafayette read his masterpiece: *The Declaration of the Rights of Man and of the Citizen.* First drafted in January, it was his contemplated companion to *The Declaration of Independence.* He had conferred with Jefferson, who made some changes, pro-royal Morris, who softened the call for liberty, and Talleyrand, a liberal First Estate member. Lafayette, though not a prose stylist, called his proclamation the "decalogue of the free man."

"While my instructions still deprive me [as a noble delegate] of the power of voting among you," he told the delegates, "I believe it nevertheless to be my duty to offer you the tribute of my thoughts," then he proclaimed:

Nature has made men free and equal; the distinctions between them are founded upon general utility.

Every man is born with inalienable rights; such are the right of property, the protection of his honor and his life, the entire disposition of his person, of his industry, of all his faculties, the pursuit of well-being and the resistance to opposition.

The exercise of natural rights has no limits except those which assure the enjoyment of the same rights to the other members of society.

No man can be persecuted for his religious views, nor for his opinions, nor for communicating his ideas through speech, writing or printing, unless by calumny and libel he disturbs the peace of the citizens.

No man can be subjected to laws unless they have been accepted by him or his representatives, announced previously and legally enforced.

The principle that all sovereignty resides in the nation.

The sole object of any government is the common good; legislative, executive and judiciary powers must be separated and distinctly defined; as no organization nor any individual can exercise an authority which does not expressly emanate from the nation.

The legislative power should be essentially exercised by deputies chosen in every district through the means of free, regular and frequent elections.

The executive power is to be exercised by the king, whose person is sacred, and by all individual or collective agents who shall be accountable to the nation no matter what other authorization they may have received.

The judiciary power must be limited to the application of the laws; legal procedure must be public and the administration of justice easy and impartial.

The laws must be clear, precise and uniform for all citizens.

Subsidies must be freely agreed upon and distributed proportionally.

And as the growth of enlightenment, the introduction of abuses and the rights of succeeding generations necessitate the revision of all human institutions, constitutional provisions must be made to assure in certain cases an extraordinary convocation of representatives of the people for the sole object of examining and modifying, if necessary, the form of the government.

The *Declaration* bore Lafayette's lofty tone, curious syntax and somewhat ambiguous meanings, but it established his view that every lawful person has a right to live unfettered by an unresponsive or tyrannical government. Its intent is unmistakable in calling for personal freedoms and just treatment. The word "citizen" in the title speaks more eloquently in liberal terms than "subject." The odd "general utility" refers to productive roles in society.

It is significant Lafayette chose to attribute freedom and equality to nature, not God, as Jefferson did in the *Declaration of Independence.* Lafayette saw human rights as more primary than religion; and birth alone, not a supreme entity, should convey these rights. His use of "inalienable rights" meant they could not be taken away, not even by fighting or accepting social or political opposition. Jefferson's "unalienable rights" of life, liberty and the pursuit of happiness, since they were God-given, also could also not be sold, taken or given away. Lafayette's fair-mindedness proclaimed equal rights for all, providing they caused no abuse of others. He placed the king in a special "above equal" position that, while ambiguous, was consistent with monarchy then. Lafayette restated his opinion on religious freedom and insisted general discourse should be limited only when false or potentially harmful.

Lafayette's sense of order is expressed in the credo that all citizens should obey legitimate laws their representatives favored. He believed national power rests with the people. The declaration allowed the king and other leaders to use this power provided they were accountable for their actions. Lafayette's statement that the king's body was "sacred" recalled ancient custom. It reflected Lafayette's loyalty to the traditional significance of the king as head of state, even though he knew Louis XVI's weaknesses. Lafayette presented mankind with an escape from tyranny by openly insisting government could be challenged and changed, effectively denying divine right. This was the battle he and fellow delegates were fighting. As he would throughout his life, Lafayette wanted to save the best aspects of the past while building what he always believed would be a better future.

The king had his own mixed but prophetic reaction. He wrote Bailly: "I do not quite understand the Declaration of the Rights of Man: It contains very good maxims for guiding your labors. But it contains some principles that require explanations, and are even liable to different interpretations, which cannot be fully appreciated until the time when their true meaning will be fixed by the laws to which the Declaration will serve as the basis."[1]

That would come. Delegates debated, then lightly edited and finally adopted the *Declaration* on August 26, 1789. It would become the introduction to the first French Constitution of the liberalized monarchy which until then had operated solely on tradition. The king signed the Constitution on July 14, 1790, the first of some fifteen versions and adaptations over the following centuries.[2]

The royal government had announced Necker's removal on July 12, 1789. Expressing regret for his dismissal, the Assembly remained in permanent session despite the hot weather. While it debated the *Declaration's* wording, a mood of forboding enshrouded the hall late into the night. Mirabeau thundered Necker's loss "will plunge the country into an abyss of misfortune."

In the face of public rebellion, Louis on July 16, 1789 was compelled to recall Necker from Coppet, his estate near Geneva. He was cheered in each town he passed en route to Versailles. As finance minister, Necker was certain he could save the country. But refusing to work with Lafayette or Mirabeau, his efforts proved valueless; completely discredited, he resigned in September 1790, returning to Coppet to write books of no influence.

Parisians were constantly supplied with information about the court. Rumors flowed from the town of Versailles and its new Breton Club, where left-wing Jacobins met as they sought power in the National Assembly. Daily reports of court activities went to the Palais Royal. It had become Paris' open-air meeting hall. Rumors also disturbed Versailles: courtiers trembled to hear prematurely that 100,000 Parisians were marching on them. Assembly delegates, favoring the king, rallied around him, hoping to ward off outside attack. Mirabeau insisted he wanted delegates to contribute "to the maintenance of order, to the public tranquility, to the authority of the laws and their ministers." He even said the king meant well, and if Louis had done anything wrong it was because he was deceived and poorly advised. On July 8 the Assembly asked Mirabeau to present an obsequious petition to the king to withdraw troops from the city. But most of the time the delegates did little but talk, hoping the king would side with the propertied classes rather than the people. They presented the petition only a few days before July 14.[3]

However, the queen and princes were secretly planning to dissolve the Assembly and send royal troops to crush Paris if it rebelled. It was said they would arrest and kill not only the principal rebels and Orléans but also Assembly delegates who wanted the king to become a constitutional monarch. Lafayette learned later this story predicted his and twelve others' deaths. Four days before the Bastille fell, Artois hurriedly pushed Baron Louis de Breteuil, a retired former ambassador in the queen's favor, to replace Necker as chief minister. He and Victor de Broglie were leaders of an unrealized royal counter-revolution.

"If it is necessary to burn Paris, Paris will be burned," Breteuil forecast. But he also said, "We are rushing like madmen to our destruction." Avoiding that, he fled France a few days after the Bastille fell with a blank sheet of paper signed by the king (literally *carte blanche*) to negotiate anything anywhere to help Louis. Broglie also wrote the Prince de Condé, grandmaster of the king's household, that a whiff of grapeshot would soon "disperse these argufiers and restore the absolute power which is going out, in place of the republican spirit which is coming in." He was as mistaken as Breteuil, the *ancien régime*'s last premier.[4]

On July 13, two days after Lafayette presented his *Declaration,* he was elected vice president of the National Assembly. No one else possessed the charisma of "the hero of two worlds." Since the weather was very warm, his election relieved the Assembly's elderly president, the archbishop of Vienne. Exhausted by the heat and building political pressure, Lafayette slept that night and the next on his bench in the Hall of Small Pleasures, where the Assembly had been readmitted. That evening there was a giddy *fête* at Versailles, with dancing in the Orangerie as the royals anticipated their coup d'etat against the Assembly and Parisians. Broglie's plan: the king was to go to Metz and amass an army to recapture Paris and disband the Assembly. Courtiers believed this would re-establish absolute rule.

Partying courtiers that evening presented royal soldiers with gifts to strengthen their allegiance to the crown. The Assembly found Louis' general behavior consistent but perplexing. First, he would resist change and then, when his resistance was expected, he would yield. On the other hand, Marie Antoinette would resist, agree and change her mind.

Still, the couple felt the frightening forces around them. Louis urged his brother, Artois, to flee. The queen bade a tearful farewell to her beautiful friend, Gabrielle, Princesse de Polignac. Marie Antoinette had not only made Polignac the royal governess but had also greatly enriched her. In return she became a much disliked ultra-monarchist. Polignac fled to Switzerland, dying of cancer in 1793.[5] Necker's removal was announced in Paris the next day. Expressing regret for his dismissal, the Assembly decided to remain in permanent session despite the hot weather.

TWENTY-FOUR: FALL OF THE BASTILLE

In Paris, Camille Desmoulins, a young disheveled lawyer, pampheteer and Freemason from Picardy, leaped on a table at the Café de Foy in the Palais Royal's garden. Frowning to control his stutter, holding a chestnut leaf as a symbol of resistance and waving a pistol for emphasis, he shouted Necker's dismissal was part of a conservative coup against the public. It was Sunday with people out strolling. Crowds formed throughout the city. Soon 10,000 people milled around Desmoulins. "This very night," he shouted, "all the Swiss and German battalions will leave the Champ de Mars to massacre us all. One resource is left, to take up arms!"

At the Tuileries a few blocks south, royal German cavalry regiment guards charged the crowd, knocking down one old man. Citizens, waiting until Jefferson in his carriage crossed Place Louis XV, pelted Swiss guards with stones. Others marched happily among the people with busts of Necker and Orléans taken from a wax museum, presaging future beheadings.[1] With Desmoulins' words in their ears, men in the city's sixty faubourgs forged 50,000 pikes in thirty-six hours. About 1,000 armed and furious citizens filled the streets as they marched many city blocks to the moated keep looking southward to the river. The

Bastille fired one cannon shot and surrendered, lowering its drawbridge. There were only seven prisoners.

Shocked by the insurrection, Louis de Noailles sped on horseback the 10.2 miles from Paris to Versailles to inform the Assembly. The derelict fortress — its name means "small bastion" — was meant for the king's prisoners. It held four forgers, two madmen and Comte Hubert de Solages, whose family had committed him for incest. All were freed.

Mad Marquis de Sade, a liberal notable imprisoned for pornography, had been removed twelve days before after causing a near-riot by screaming from his cell window, "They are killing prisoners here!"[2] Grisly stories colored the Bastille's history: tales of torture, prisoners buried in its earthen floor and secret dungeons where prisoners were literally forgotten. The insurgents stole 28,000 rifles from the Invalides' armory and marched on the fortress-prison for gunpowder, said to be stored there. Located in rowdy Faubourg Saint-Antoine, the Bastille had long been a popular symbol of despotic France. Many believed it had held the fabled man in the iron (or velvet) mask, thought to have been Louis XIV's brother. The Sun King's actual brother, youth-chasing Philippe de France, had founded the Orléans family's junior line.

The four and a half story stone prison was an eight-towered remnant of the fourteenth century's One Hundred Years War. When the Marquis de Launay, Bastille governor and garrison commander, attempted to address the angry crowd armed with pitchforks, pikes and firearms, he was beaten and dragged to the hôtel de ville. After kicking a baker in the groin, Launay urged the crowd to kill him and was stabbed repeatedly. His head was sawn off, mounted with his blood dripping on a pike and paraded through the city. The rabble decided Jacques de Flesselles, *prévost des marchands*, equivalent of mayor, was in league with the king and they shot him outside city hall. Four days later, Desmoulins, in the pay of Orléans, published a pamphlet calling for a republic, insisting violence was justified. A week after these murders, the mob found Joseph-François Foullon, a longtime royal administer thought to have become rich on public money. He was widely believed to have said in 1775, "If the public is hungry let them eat grass."[3]

As the demanding chief of the king's household, Foullon had no friends there or in Paris. He followed Necker as controller-general but his days were numbered. Foullon, seventy-four, tried to fake his own death exploiting a servant's funeral. He was caught hiding in a village near Paris. The mob forced him to walk to the city barefoot with a bale of hay on his back. He was strung up on a lamp post near the hôtel de ville three times before finally being hanged. After his decapitation hay was stuffed in his mouth. His son-in-law, Berthier de Sauvigny, also a royal administrator, received the same fate that day. The howling crowds lifted their heads on pikes through the streets. Suddenly, the city was papered with pamphlets making foul and scatological charges against the king and especially the queen who was said to have had sex with men, women, her son and animal pets. The sewers rose with odious drawings filled with obscenities directed at the royals, nobles and state.

Lafayette tried to calm the crowd to prevent the two murders. His entreaties were working when Foullon applauded his words. The mob immediately assumed he was being protected and took the matter into its own hands. The butchery disgusted Lafayette. Several times a day he quieted rebellions seeming to break out everywhere. Favor-seekers followed him to his house where he was often absent for days at a time. Adrienne feared and prayed for him. But her hero had a charmed life. People wanted to be with him, to cheer him, touch his hand, stroke Jean Leblanc.

He resigned as commanding general of the National Guard the day after Foullon and Sauvigny's murders. "The people have not listened to my advice," he wrote Bailly, "and the day in which the confidence they promised is gone. I must, as I said in advance, quit a post in which I can no longer be useful."[4] But he returned when an elector threw himself at Lafayette's feet and the Commune swore to obey him. He was the virtual dictator of France, a role he could never accept and still be true to Washington. But he *had* become the pawn of the public.

On the evening after the Bastille fell, the fearful Assembly, still obsequious to Louis, urged him to recall his ministers and remove troops from the streets. Reeling from news of the insurrection, courtiers realized for the first time nothing would be the same again. Many Assemblymen shivered as the tide of power slowly slipped from the monarch to the upper middle class. Politicians always fear sudden change. How would they survive the turmoil? Lafayette's cousin, Duc de

Liancourt, grandmaster of the wardrobe, informed the king the Bastille attack was not a riot, as the king supposed, but a revolution. With only his brothers, Louis walked to the Hall of Small Pleasures. The princes, having advised Louis on each misstep, would hasten abroad before long to negotiate his and his family's rescue. Provence fled to Westphalia (Germany) and later to Verona, while Calonne became Artois' lawyer in Turin. They would be among the first in a tide of loyalist émigrés yearning to recapture their past.

Lafayette conducted Louis to the Assembly delegates and asked them to remain silent because of the grave moment. The king's impromptu appearance astonished them. He asked them "to find means of restoring peace and order." He said he knew some people "had dared to say your persons [are not safe]: Is it necessary to reassure you concerning such criminal rumors, refuted in advance by your knowledge of my character? Well, then, it is I, who am one with my nation. It is I who trust in you! Help me in these circumstances to assure the salvation of the state! I expect this from the National Assembly, from the zeal of the representatives of my people." It was the first time he had called the Assembly by its name.

As he finished, Louis announced he had ordered the troops withdrawn from Paris. With that problem met, the delegates cheered him. They and the large crowd outside shouted, "Long live the king!" They smothered him with hugs as he walked slowly to the palace, powerless in the crowd, sweating under the searing sun. With Lafayette leading them, eighty-eight representatives sped in their carriages to Paris and announced the news at the Tuileries. Their way was lined with cheering citizens armed with pikes and every other weapon. The new city militia lined up between them and the carriages as they rolled on to the hôtel de ville. Before it in the large open Place de Grève (*Place de l'Hôtel de Ville*), delegates alighted amid another huge throng hailing them with relief and hope.

Reaching the meeting hall inside, Lafayette read the king's pullback speech, interrupted by cries of "*Vive le roi!*" Important citizens took the king's plea for peace as reason for calling themselves assembly electors. But they had no more authority than wanting to secure the peace, to find a leader for a new Paris militia loyal to the city, not only the king.

The militia had a diverse membership: policemen, soldiers, army officers and jobless citizens willing to serve for pay. The electors created a new government, the Commune, to run Paris. With soldiers and police deserting royal forces, Commune members feverishly debated in loud meetings who could protect the city.

Parlement lawyer Médéric Moreau de Saint-Méry, the electors' president, grandly gestured to Houdon's white marble bust of Lafayette on a mantel in the great hall, Virginia's gift of thanks to France.[5] Members quickly voted Lafayette commandant of the new Paris National Guard. To applause, he extended his sword and pledged his life to preserve "the precious liberty" they had entrusted to him.[6]

Lafayette in his Paris National Guard Uniform,
1790, after J.B. Weyler portrait.
Courtesy Marquis de Lafayette Collection, Lafayette College.

In an effort to quiet the insurrection, Louis XVI later in July visited the hôtel de ville, giving Lafayette barely a day to secure his protection with a militia of 200,000 men raised from the city's sixty quarters. They had no uniforms but each man held a weapon, usually a rifle, and wore a cockade, a circular device with tightly shirred folds of blue and red, the city's colors, on his hat. To protect the king and his retinue they formed double lines on either side of the streets.

Lafayette on Jean Leblanc met the king, pale and uncomfortable-looking, in his carriage at Point du Jour southwest of Paris to present his orders. Following the king were his royal guard and thousands of citizens, including untidy women waving branches and beribboned wreaths as well as weary Assembly deputies. They had walked from Versailles behind the king's troops and did not arrive until four in the afternoon. As a peaceful gesture the king had his guards remain outside the city. Thousands of spectators, craning at windows, rooftops and in the street, were relatively quiet.

No one cheered the king as they would have earlier. Reassuring Louis of his safety, Lafayette led the way along narrow Rue du Faubourg St. Honoré, past the D'Ayen mansion, and several more blocks to the hôtel de ville. There Mayor Bailly presented the king with the keys to the city and later a large cockade. Louis, seeking harmony, pinned the badge to his wide hat and appeared on a balcony to the crowd in the square. It cheered lustily when it saw the cockade. Inside, the monarch declared his allegiance to the new order.

Leaving the hall, the king told Lafayette he had looked for him to say he approved of his appointment as general commandant, but it seemed almost no longer to matter. Thousands in the square cheered, "*Vive Lafayette!*" The king returned to Versailles and the electors went to Notre Dame Cathedral for a *Te Deum* blessing the new unity. But the moment's headiness concealed great uneasiness. Rioting broke out again the next morning. Lafayette presented his son, Georges, now nine, to the crowds to calm them, and allowed the boy's tutor, Abbé Fréstel, to escape them.[7]

Many times that day the general commandant rescued individuals from the mob, milling in front of the hôtel de ville. One of Lafayette's first tasks was to oversee razing the hated prison within days of the attack. But first he sent electors and trumpeters to officially announce this decision. He seemed to possess superhuman ability, dispersing many thousands in the square from time to time with a wave of his hand.

TWENTY-FIVE: THE GREAT FEAR

Lafayette wrote to Diane de Simiane that night: "But this furious drunken people will not listen to me always. At this moment, while I write, 80,000 persons surround the hôtel de ville and say they are being deceived, that the troops are not withdrawing, that the king must come. They will not recognize anything that I do not sign… I reign in Paris, and over a people in fury, pushed by adominable cabals; on the other hand, a thousand infamies have been heaped upon them of which they have reason to complain. In this very moment they are raising terrible cries. If I appear, they will calm down; but others will come. Adieu."[1]

The Great Fear gripped France from July 20 to August 5, 1789. Anxieties brought on by the new government, social changes, poverty and inflation — no one had known such upheaval — triggered violent reactions. Peasants thinking nobles were denying them justice on rents attacked and burned their chateaus. Madame Ēlisabeth, the king's sister, told a friend she learned seventy were destroyed. The wealthy moved to safer cities or fled to foreign lands while their servants hunted for work at home.[2] City people believed rising prices were meant to starve them since they could not pay for bread, vegetables or wine. Suddenly, crowds of angry fishwives and shouting men at the Palais

Royal demanded the king return permanently to Paris where he could be watched.

Lafayette found time in his new office to approve proposals, hold daily audiences and oversee deteriorating conditions. For the National Guard, made up of six divisions of sixty battalions, he designed a snappy well-cut uniform with a blue tunic, red padded chest protector, white breeches, piping and silver epaulettes. For the first time, the belt buckle displayed the liberty cap. It became the revolution's symbol.[3] Knowing blue and red were Paris' and Orléans' colors and also royal, Lafayette created the *tricolore,* the national cockade, placing white, long associated with France, between the two others. White was not meant to represent the Bourbons as sometimes written, or it would have been removed in 1792. The three colors became France's new flag. It was no coincidence the banner and the uniform resembled those of his second country. But not identical: the new flag's blue was darker than *Old Glory*'s.

Lafayette presented to the Commune his aide-de-camp Mathieu Dumas' plans for running the militia.[4] Waving his blue, white and red symbol before members, he exclaimed, "I bring you a cockade that will go around the world, and an institution, at once civic and military, that must triumph over the tactics of Europe and reduce the arbitary governments to the alternative of being beaten if they do not imitate it, and of being overthrown if they dare to [ignore it]." He foresaw more constitutional monarchies. When a man seeking a favor from him said he had a title, Lafayette replied, "Monsieur, that is no obstacle." He regretted being too busy to join the Assembly in Versailles but he conferred with his political friends on pending legislation and influenced many decrees. On August 4, Louis de Noailles led the fight his brother-in-law championed, ending centuries of hereditary titles. The abolition infuriated Antoine Barnave, now a royal sympathizer, and he forced Noailles to a duel.

On August 9, Lafayette appeared in his new uniform. He and Adrienne attended a benediction of the flags in the Church of Saint-Nicolas-des-Champs. Promoting public relations, he asked the Commune to issue good conduct certificates and medals of esteem to the National Guards. But officers and gentlemen looked down on those not of their training or class. Lafayette found it difficult to persuade his men to adopt the American ideal of equality. The summer was filled with difficulties and disruptions. He had to appease the tailors making the uniforms — they struck on the Louvre's grounds — to get them to their tables. He cajoled workmen cutting down Montmartre's butte to end their strike.

And he constantly strove to restore peace in Faubourg Saint-Antoine, where the Bastille under his orders was being razed. Riots there broke out daily, which he had not anticipated. The peaceful transition he had predicted vanished as Paris descended into greater unrest and mayhem. France's curse was, unlike Great Britain, citizens had no experience with government led by the governed. Instead to most citizens it appeared everything they knew was being turned upside down. Lafayette even had to placate Bailly, who, always sensitive to procedural slights, was to be paid less than he.

Overcoming Bailly's ire, Lafayette, like Washington, worked without pay. On seeing poverty, he often donated his own money, considerably reducing his fortune. Many courtiers believed he would try a coup d'etat. But that, while possible, did not interest him. His causes were freedom for the people in the broadest sense, righting wrongs and protecting the royal family. He never sought national leadership, which some have seen as weakness or timidity but he was always much more interested in celebrity than power. Lafayette did not have a mind for governmental minutiae and already possessed many privileges of power. The burden of leadership, he learned, is to be called on for solutions. His weakness was a thirst for glory but none for power.

Being born an aristocrat, Lafayette was interested in his own wishes, seeing others' freedoms in the abstract, and had sympathy but not a deep understanding of the poor though he wished to make their lives better. He enjoyed his perquisites and, most of all, the freedom and means to do as he wished. He insisted on being his own person and to offer his own ideas when he had them. That was no more possible for the head of the National Guard than for the prime minister of France. He was not an analytical observer like Washington and was often at a loss for answers, though not words. Too often in this turbulent time he asked advice of others and found it difficult to make decisions, a fatal flaw when a leader must always be his own best counsel. Even though Lafayette seemed an ideal leader, his record in France, unlike that in America, shows he was not. This explains why in France he does not hold the same esteem of his countrymen that he does in the United States.

TWENTY-SIX: A SECOND REVOLUTION

Working hard at Versailles, the National Assembly wrote and passed the far-reaching August decrees of 1789, mainly to quell the Great Fear's widespread damage. Delegates abolished the feudal system and the serfdom of 300,000 peasants, although Louis XVI had abolished this practice for royal domains as early as August 8, 1779. The Assembly outlawed special hunting lands and rights (but allowed royal hunts) and suppressed municipal courts. It ended church tithes, expecting money for worship to be found elsewhere. It forbade fixed land rents and selling judicial and municipal offices. It declared taxes would be collected from all. It ended special privileges for certain regions and cities and made all male citizens eligible for civil and military service. The Assembly also decided it and the king could weigh all pensions and reduce them if undeserved.

The decrees were relatively far-reaching. The second article, for instance, abolished exclusive rights for bird-grazing and dovecotes: pigeons could now be seized if off their owner's land. Lafayette's thinking permeated decrees although he was rarely present. The Assembly adopted the *Declaration of the Rights of Man* on August 26. In a similar advance, Bailly succeeded in restoring citizenship for Jews. The king, however, bridled at Assembly restrictions on the clergy, lest his support of religion be misjudged. But on that subject it was only the beginning.

In early September, the Assembly granted the king a suspensive veto: he could delay signing a bill but could not veto it permanently. He was not permitted to have any of his representatives seated in the Assembly. On October 5 and 6, delegates approved the liberal monarchial constitution. That night crowds at the Palais Royal listened to four men: large bellowing lawyer Georges Jacques Danton, small Swiss-French doctor Jean Paul Marat (who sometimes treated Orléans' bodyguards) and shaggy pamphleteer Desmoulins. Deploring the lack of food, they excited to outrage a mob of mostly women, harridans, fishwives and suspicious men. The last, dressed in women's clothing but having dark cheeks and heavy shoes, were Orléans' lackeys. Mathieu Jouve Jourdan, a butcher called "Jourdan Coupe-tête," literally "cut-head," was in the vanguard. His custom was to sever victims' heads, wiping his face with their blood and thrusting their craniums on pikes. Fittingly, after a trial he went to the guillotine in May 1794.

About 150 of these people rushed to the hôtel de ville and, after smashing its doors, climbed to the second floor meeting hall to confront the mayor and electors. The mob stole rifles and two cannons from the hall's armory. Lafayette, aroused from his bed in the dark, reached the building to find the culprits gone. Guards showed him stones rioters had thrown at them. The mob, joined by others, and shouting that Lafayette and Bailly were traitors and should hang from the square's lamp posts, marched to Place Louis XV, Champ de Mars and on to Versailles. Stanislas Maillard, twenty-six, a National Guardsman and recent Bastille protester, at first urged caution on the women marchers at the hôtel de ville. But they, feeling the need for protection, adopted him as leader en route, and he voiced their demands before the General Assembly. Later before the Commune, he described his return to Paris with the women. He was sent to the Tuileries to help prepare it for the royal family.[1]

That morning Lafayette, finding Santerre, Orléanist commander of a National Guard battalion, had invited Bailly to Orléans' country house, summoned the perturbed mayor to help ease the tension. Lafayette then called up guard reinforcements and sent couriers to Versailles to report the latest disturbances to the king and Assembly. That afternoon, he looked from a window to the square and saw guards intermixing with a roiling sea of humanity. Thousands of people, their faces distorted with rage, clutched weapons from pistols and pikes to scythes and pitchforks.

The crowd no longer cried for bread but shouted, "On to Versailles!" He went down and quieted them, appealing to their loyalty to the king he sensed they still possessed. The crowd dispersed but another wave began bellowing for bread, rising to a roar. Several times those in the crowd removed the top of a street lamp to hang him, the hero they had cheered. Pistols were pointed directly at him several times but, recalling Washington, he remained calm, refusing to become excited. There could be no flinching or he would be lost. Soon this second mob began moving toward Versailles in a cold pouring rain.

TWENTY-SEVEN: BREAD, BLOOD AND TEARS

Lafayette was accustomed to commanding trained soldiers. Now he and his guards trailed an angry shouting hord of 8,000, many from the capitol's sewers and squalor, trudging through the muddy road in the dark. Finally reaching the palace, he ordered his men in soaked uniforms splashed with mud to pledge fidelity to the king, then rode to the Hall of Small Pleasures. The Assembly with a few delegates was barely in session. In the dim candlelight many who marched to Versailles besported themselves, weeping in their wet clothes or sleeping on members' benches. Prostitutes made fun of the Assembly speaker, mocking him with caresses. They also shrieked curses at the queen and shouted, "*Vive le Duc d'Orléans!*" Lafayette was sure he had incited the rebellion. Disgusted and exhausted, Lafayette rode to the palace where thousands of the king's subjects shouted in the three-sided Court of Honor below the royal balcony, defying the Swiss guards.

Lafayette and two Assemblymen entered the grand chateau and climbed the wide staircase to the *Oeil-de-Boeuf*, the waiting salon named for its large circular marble relief of the Sun King. Courtiers criticized him, one calling out, "There goes Cromwell!" He answered, "Cromwell would not have entered alone."

Royal guards admitted him to the king in his study. Lafayette said, "Sire, I thought it better to come here and die at the feet of Your Majesty than to perish uselessly in the Place de Grève." When he requested the king's orders, Louis asked, "What do the people want?" Lafayette replied, "Bread." Louis said, "Very well. Let them take it." They decided the king's Swiss sentinals around the palace and 400 mounted bodyguards standing by at the Trianon in the park would remain under his orders.

Louis told Lafayette he had agreed to ratify the August decrees and had adopted *The Declariation of the Rights of Man.* Momentarily pleased, Lafayette learned the mob was marching on the royal bodyguards' barracks intent on killing them because, as loyalists, they had trampled on the tricolor. As coolly as Washington, Lafayette had some troublemakers given a few coins and they vanished. He saw most of his Guards bedded down for the night. Royal troops were stationed outside their quarters and in the town. The battalion stationed at the Trianon vanished in the night, probably riding twenty miles to Rambouillet, a chateau Louis XVI had bought in 1783 from a wealthy cousin in order to hunt in its game-filled forest. Because of the queen's new interest in the simple life, he secretly built for her there a brick dairy with Sèvres milk pails mimicking wood.[1]

Lafayette reached the king's door at 2 a.m. but he and the queen had retired. Not having eaten or slept in twenty hours, Lafayette was nearly exhausted. After talking with Vergennes' successor, foreign minister Comte de Montmorin, an *Avergnat*, in his house near the soldiers' quarters, Lafayette crept at dawn into the Noailles mansion where his staff slept. A servant gave him bread and wine. He was about to lie down when an officer of his Guards rushed to report the mob had begun more trouble at the palace, pushing through the *Cour Royale*, across the *Cour des Princes* and into the chateau's marble staircase. Louis had ordered his guards not to fire on the people. Obeying him to the end, they were instantly murdered.

The corpse of the guard Deshuttes was dragged into the *Cour des Ministres,* where on the rain-slick cobblestones Jourdan Coupe-tête severed his head and covered his own face and beard in blood gushing from the neck. The crowd, screaming, did the same, dancing around the corpse. Then, crying for the heart of "the Austrian woman," they clattered up the royal staircase, shouting, "Where is the fucking *coquine*? (Wretch.) We will make cockades of her guts!"

The attackers reached the bodyguards' hall, where they smashed large double doors of two large anterooms to the queen's apartments. As the gilt doors splintered and crashed to the floor, her bodyguards, facing the attackers, braced their bodies against the assault. Guard François de Varicourt met Deshuttes' fate. Both heads were jammed on pikes as the murderers met more guards at the next doors. Guard Miromandre de Sainte-Marie ran to the queen's antechamber, calling for women inside to protect her as he and two other guards drew swords at that door. Victor de La Tour-Maubourg, a Guards subaltern, had previously entered the royal chamber. He spirited Marie Antoinette through a secret passage to the Oeil-de-boeuf and then to the king's apartments.

The mob, breaking through the second set of the queen's doors, entered to find her gone and, furious, rushed back to the Oeil-de-boeuf. Lafayette, responding to an alarm on his way back to the palace, rescued several of his men and officers from the mob, as one in the crowd called out, "Kill Lafayette!" He and his men hurried up the palace staircase to assist the royal guards. Outside, the mob still raged in the Court of Honor. But those in the palace, seeing Lafayette and his superior force, quickly became docile and were swept like rubbish down the stairs and outside.[2]

With the mob still roaring in the courtyard, Louis XVI attempted to hold a council of state in his quarters, but Montmorin and La Luzerne's agitation made them indecisive while Necker sobbed. Asked to join them, Lafayette declined. It was up to the king to decide to leave Versailles. Then Louis, stepping gingerly onto the narrow iron balcony, announced to the crowd below he would go to the Tuileries. In his memoirs Lafayette told what occurred next. But no one else recorded it and he described the drama to his advantage. That has not stopped many writers from repeating it. Lafayette said he asked the terrified queen, deathly pale and still in her yellow-striped wrapper, what she planned.

She stared at him, both knowing she hated him. "I know what fate awaits me," she said, "but my duty is to die at the feet of the king and in the arms of my children." He saw a new resolve and invited her to help quiet the tumult. As she fearfully stepped onto the balcony, the crowd's roar swelled. Moving suddenly beside her, Lafayette doffed his hat and bowed to the queen. Kneeling on one leg, he lifted her hand to his lips. The crowd that only minutes before had demanded her heart now shouted, *"Vive la reine!"* Then the cry arose, *"Vive Lafayette!"* When the king asked what Lafayette could do to honor the royal guards' bravery, he removed his cockade and pinned it on a tall guard's hat. Then embracing him, Lafayette kissed both of his cheeks to more cheers.

At noon carriages with the saddened royal family, including the king's sister, Madame Ēlisabeth, and his great aunts, began a seven-hour journey over muddy roads to the capital. Lafayette on Jean Leblanc moved amid the mob also heading back to Paris. To protect the royals he mostly stayed on one side of the carriages, Admiral D'Estaing, attached to the National Guard at Versailles, on the other. Several National Guard battalions rode behind the mob, keeping it in check. The slightly mollified crowd punctuated the procession with lifted pichforks and pikes. Many wagons in the transport hauled bread and bags of grain for Parisians. When Lafayette moved away from the royal carriages, ruffians hurled insults at the king and queen who would never see Versailles again.[3]

National Guardsmen were the official escorts since the king had turned his bodyguards over to Lafayette's command. It galled the royal family to pass the Duc d'Orléans, his lover Madame Genlis and his young son Louis-Philippe D'Orléans. They visited the mansion of the duc's friend Boulainvilliers in Passy to witness the cortege passing by, impatient at its length until seeing the royal coach. Judging by their wait, there may have been as many as 7,000 people in the entourage. The Duc on his friend's terrace delighted in the procession and the mob's cries: "We bring you the baker, the baker's wife and their assistant!" — the dauphin. Brigands, spotting Orléans, who tried to hide behind the others on the terrace, cheered him several times, tripling his pleasure.[4]

Protocol demanded that Louis present himself at the hôtel de ville. Tired from the day's events, Marie Antoinette asked to be taken to the Tuileries, but the president of the Paris electors requested she accompany her husband. Again Lafayette led the royal parade along crowded Rue du Faubourg Saint-Honoré. It was dark when the exhausted king addressed the electors in a voice so weak Bailly repeated his words, expressing Louis' "joy and confidence" in coming to his "good city of Paris."

The royals finally reached the 1,000-foot-long French Renaissance palace at 9:30 p.m. to begin their constricted lives west of the Louvre. A king had not lived there regularly in more than 100 years. During that day, many hundreds of army retirees, penniless nobles and old widows, living there rent-free, were ejected into the street. The royal couple slept on cots in adjoining chambers that night in a seemingly endless and dreary maze of rooms. A huge retinue of servants followed them to the city, but many months passed before the barracks-like building again resembled a showplace. Its condition reflected the royals' position. In every way but form the monarchy was finished. Lafayette was in charge. He had championed the Assembly, saved Versailles from the mob, put down rebellions and returned the monarch to the people. He was greatly relieved the day had not gone worse.

Putting clues together the next day, Lafayette confronted the march's chief plotter. Orléans, forty-two, natty in his English clothes and sportive air, denied everything. Lafayette ordered him to leave the country. After several meetings with false promises, Orléans agreed to visit the Prince of Wales, taking along Madame de Buffon, his mistress and the famed naturalist's daughter-in-law. Lafayette expected riots would lessen if the duc were in England. Few believed his visit to the prince was the real reason for the trip which was exile. Mirabeau, Lafayette's only rival as national leader, was furious with him about the departure.

At the same time the king, now a virtual prisoner, became less involved with his declining status in a sham court, exasperating his wife and others close to them. Louis asked Lafayette what he should do. Lafayette wrote a long letter, concluding he would end his time in politics at the end of the revolution. The king put the letter in his iron storage box as he had many others and ignored it. But France's problems could not be so easily set aside.

The National Assembly expressed new strengths. Talleyrand was a member of the committee drafting a national constitution on August 4, 1789, in a session Mirabeau called an *orgie* of abolished privileges. The near-apostate bishop and three other clergy proposed that the state seize church properties. Talleyrand's reasoning was that France had entrusted these properties to the church in the first place, to ensure its charity and social services. He argued France, on recovering these possessions, should assure those services by mortgaging properties to repay the state and selling any remaining one to state creditors. But he did not anticipate the extent to which Mirabeau took the issue — total confiscation of church property.

On November 9, a week after the Assembly nationalized and appropriated all church property, and also restricted Pope Pius VI's powers to doctrinal matters, delegates moved from Versailles to the archbishop's vacated palace in Paris. But that was just until the *Manège*, the old royal indoor riding school in the Tuileries Garden, at the rear of the Noailles' formal garden, was fitted with rows of green-upholstered benches. The Assembly president's high dais at one end faced the speaker's platform, or tribune, at the other.[5]

In December, the bankrupt Assembly authorized, over Talleyrand's objections, the printing of *assignats,* paper money backed by the value of church properties and lands seized from the crown and émigrés.[6] Joined with regular money, *assignats* sped hyperinflation and mass financial confusion. Only the wealthy profited from the taking of lands. The Assembly divided the population into *active* citizens (with property) and *inactive* (without property). Only the actives were allowed to vote, a further concession to the wealthy.

In January 1790, the deputies replaced the former provinces with administrative departments, and in February suppressed religious orders and monastic vows. Pius VI condemned these super-liberal acts, including the *Declaration of the Rights of Man and the Citizen.* France would later win this earthly contest in 1798 when, under Napoleon, General Berthier captured undefended Rome, ending papal rule over all church states except Vatican City. Pius, eighty-one, was taken by force to Valence in Dauphiné and died there six months later. Ironically, no pope has reigned longer than his twenty-four years. In May the Assembly rhetorically outlawed wars of conquest and, more substantively, abolished the nobility. These acts were followed on July 12 by the Civil Constitution of the Clergy. It required priests to swear loyalty to France, dividing them into those taking the oath or refusing to. This was called juring and non-juring, meaning oath-taking or not. Those not juring suffered harsh reprisals. Hundreds of men and women of the cloth were executed during the Reign of Terror (September 5, 1793-July 28, 1797).

TWENTY-EIGHT: THE GREAT FESTIVAL

Draping the mantle of patriotism over a year of unresolved turmoil, Lafayette guided and starred in the *Fête de la Fédération* on July 14, 1790. The huge celebration and feast honored the anniversary of the Bastille's fall and the public's rise over despotism.[1] An unprecedented and faultless occasion, the spectacle in the Champ de Mars was the commandant-general's greatest dramatic effort, and for a moment uniting disparate elements of government, rebellion and church. Its grandeur was designed to elicit French sentiments of brotherhood and loyalty to state and king.

A subtler purpose was to hurry the fractious General Assembly's completion of the constitution, not occurring until that November. Lafayette wanted both a commitment and moral reawakening, similar to what he had asked of Guardsmen at Versailles and what Washington had evoked at Valley Forge. A Commune committee invited everyone from all walks of life in France and elsewhere — "Swedes, Spaniards, Poles, Turks, Chaldeans, Greeks and dwellers in Mesopotamia," the *Journal de Paris* reported — to join in celebrating the creation of a constitutional monarchy. It would last ten months.

The Champ de Mars was a marching field several city blocks

long and a block or so wide just south of the Seine.[2] For this largely improvised celebration, the largest of several in France, enthusiastic citizens filled wheelbarrows with earth from the site and mounded it into two stepped rows on either side of the field.[3] Lafayette joined the workers for a few hours each week, shoveling in what were called "the days of the wheelbarrows." He urged National Guard units from France's eighty-three departments to send about 150 men each to the spectacle. Some 14,000 citizen soldiers assembled under eighty-three departmental flags. After marching through the streets of Saint Antoine, Saint Denis and Saint Honoré, the procession crossed the river on a temporary boat bridge in a pouring rain lasting all day.

Three hundred drummers and 1,200 wind musicians joined cannons mounted on the mounded steps, sounding a message of unity and loyalty across the ensemble — and metaphorically France. Soldiers, police and foreign dignitaries marched with their flags and banners under a splendid three-portal arch while other officers observed proceedings from its roof. To cheers, John Paul Jones, leading an American delegation with Thomas Paine at his side, displayed the *Stars and Stripes* for the first time abroad. To Lafayette the powerful spectacle was a thematic joining of France and the United States' democratic ideals. In his bishop's vestments Charles Maurice de Talleyrand-Perigord climbed to a high altar with smoking urns near the field's center. With 200 priests in tricolor sashes, he sang a Mass he did not believe. An audience of 160,000 sat on either side of the raised field with that many more people standing.

The royal family arrived late. Louis XVI and his family were invited to sit in a high-stepped scarlet-draped tribune, or tent, of rectangular form erected in front of the Ēcole Militaire, the cadet officers' school at the south end of the field.[4]

Constituent Assembly and Paris Commune deputies also sat mesmerized there. The event's pyrotechnics dazzled and temporarily silenced Lafayette's enemies. The celebration, splendid though diaphanous, was the highmark of his success as a national leader. Mirabeau, present in the tribune, was beside himself with frustration. He knew Lafayette had no follow-up plan or claim to further power, as Mirabeau had. To him it was the height of naivete. Lafayette, who preferred adulation to power, had no intention of filling a dictatorial vacuum.

At the appropriate moment Lafayette rode into the arena on Jean Leblanc. As he mounted the altar stairs amid pomp and blaring trumpets, cynical Talleyrand whispered to him, "Don't do anything to make me laugh." It would be his last act as bishop before Pius VI excommunicated him. Addressing the spectators, the man of the hour exclaimed:

"We swear forever to be faithful to the nation, to the law and to the king, to uphold with all our might the constitution as decided by the National Assembly and accepted by the king, and to protect, according to the laws, the safety of people and properties, transit of grains and food within the kingdom, the public contributions under whatever forms they might exist and to stay united with all French people by the indestructible bonds of brotherhood." The audience responded thunderously: *"We swear!"*

Louis XVI also made an oath, *"I, king of the French, swear to use the power given to me by the constitutional law of the state, to maintain the constitution, as decided by the National Assembly and accepted by myself, and to enforce the laws."* His notable concession was to call himself "king of the French," not absolute monarch of France. The National Assembly had suggested his response. Annoyed at not being seated beside her husband, Marie Antoinette also spoke. Displaying five-year-old Louis Charles, she exclaimed, "This is my son who, like me, joins in the same sentiments." That was all.

The royals were cheered but it was Lafayette who was embraced by Guardsmen as he descended the altar. He, his boots, saddle and even his attention-loving steed were kissed for "ending" the revolution. At that moment he was France's strongest man, determined to have the government work, protect the king and preserve the peace. One officer noted, "Mounted on his white horse...he seemed to be in command of all France." Another proclaimed, "You are watching Monsieur de la Fayette galloping into the centuries yet to come."

TWENTY-NINE: DEALING WITH MIRABEAU

Mirabeau, continuing to woo Lafayette, welcomed him and Bailly to the Assembly's new home. Later Mirabeau wrote Lafayette: "Whatever comes, I will be yours to the end because your great qualities have strongly attracted me, and because it is impossible for me to cease to take a very lively interest in a destiny so beautiful and so closely bound to the revolution that is leading the nation to liberty." Though Lafayette detested Mirabeau, he felt compelled to invite him to dinner and regretted it. Mirabeau was money-hungry while Lafayette took wealth as his due.[1] Mirabeau also wanted to be Assembly president, or at least a government minister or ambassador.

Lafayette was touched by a letter, the first in some time, from his American father, now president of the United States, comparing their similar roles. Lafayette asked Thomas Paine to deliver to Washington the main key to the Bastille and a painting of the prison being demolished. "How often, my well-beloved General," he wrote, "have I longed for your wise counsels and your friendly support..." Becoming discouraged with unanticipated changes in France, Lafayette must have wished he had Washington's wisdom. When Montmorin suggested Mirabeau be made envoy to London or The Hague, the cunning deputy suggested

Lafayette should become prime minister and a marshal of France. Lafayette agreed. But Mirabeau had recently refused a duel with an angry Saint Domingue deputy. Gouverneur Morris told Lafayette that Talleyrand believed Mirabeau's refusal cost him the Assembly's respect.

Lafayette also had critics. His friend, the liberal philosopher, mathematician and statesman Marquis de Condorcet observed, "I saw him painfully from the first months of 1790, being directed by schemes of all kinds, wishing to be at the top in negotiating with everyone, leading twenty different projects at once, and by this conduct ruining his reputation for integrity."[2] Again it was glory he sought, not power. This extremely hectic pace would end in a year and eight months. Mirabeau, dominating the Assembly and wanting the king's favor as well as his money, proposed royal ministers attend sessions, take part in discussions and be permitted to become royal ministers. But a Bordeaux deputy urged the Assembly to forbid members being government ministers. The line between liberals and conservatives was drawn.

Mirabeau and Lafayette, the government's most powerful men, consulted daily, with Mirabeau applying various forms of pressure to the commandant. Lafayette saw himself outmaneuvered. Friends were deserting him. Alexandre, Comte de Lameth, opposed to ordering Orléans to London and, with riots spreading across France, did not approve of Lafayette's methods of halting riots with force. Some deputies, wanting the revolution to be over, disagreed with Lafayette's seeking a constitutional government. Lameth joined deputies Barnave and Adrien Duport. As "the triumvirate," they controlled about forty liberal votes.

Deputies distrusted the perfidious Mirabeau. Yet he had sized up Lafayette and wrote him: "Ah, at what time have I failed to warn you that your dizzy position and the fatality of your personal indecision were blinding you to the impossibility of rendering permanent a state of things that success alone could justify? When, in paying homage to your qualities, have I not declared that your taste for mediocre men and your feebleness for your own views would cause the most beautiful career to miscarry, and, in ruining you, compromise the public good?"[3] Deeply offended, perhaps by the accuracy, Lafayette fell silent. But, on learning Orléans intended to return, he sent an aide-de-camp to London reinforcing the ban.

He returned to the disorderly Assembly, torn by violent debate, and argued for strict martial law. There he proclaimed prematurely, "The revolution having been accomplished, nothing remains but to establish its constitution. For the revolution, disorders were necessary, the old order was nothing but servitude; and in that case insurrection is the most sacred of duties. But for the constitution it is necessary for the new order to assert itself, that ... individuals be ... secure. We must cause the new constitution to be loved. The public power must exercise force and energy." His claim, "Insurrection is the most sacred of duties," would be used against him evermore.[4]

Lafayette was saddened that his loyalist cousin Bouillé, head of the Metz garrison after his Caribbean service, denounced all of Lafayette's plans. More unnerving was the startling exposure of an abortive royalist Christmas Eve plot to assassinate him, Bailly and Necker. For this crime the Marquis de Favras, betrayed by army friends, was arrested, sent to the old Châtelet prison on the Right Bank, tried and hanged in the Place de Grève. The public learned in this rare case that justice could be found for nobles as well as commoners.

A pamphlet on December 23, 1789 revealed that Favras, former first lieutenant in Provence's Swiss Guards, planned to have 30,000 troops surround Paris and starve rebels into restoring the king's powers. Evidence was insufficient and Favras remained silent. But when Lafayette prevented royalists from rescuing Favras, his "guilt" seemed obvious. Victor de Broglie later had the same intention before the Bastille fell. In a speech to the Commune and a letter to the Constituent Assembly, Provence denied knowledge of the affair. But years later as king he gave Favras' widow a pension.

THIRTY: DAY OF THE DAGGERS

Fascinating characters in a wide spectrum argued before more than 1,500 delegates to the Estates-General. The most forceful at first was Honoré Gabriel Riqueti, Comte de Mirabeau, a liberal propagandist who had denounced royal policies in his pamphlets and represented the Third Estate in southern Aix-en-Provence. His erotic excesses, driven in part by a constant need for money, sent him to prison for a time, weakening him physically. He was obese and horribly scarred by smallpox, yet his powers were alluring to women. Despite his tawdry past, Mirabeau's thundering oratory, laced with historical and philosophical allusions, upheld the public and won him great popular respect. As a brilliant politician favoring a constitutional monarchy, Mirabeau was the major challenger of Lafayette, whose popularity came from heroism, not his cool lordly speeches.

Mirabeau was too duplicitous for Lafayette, and he too naïve for Mirabeau. But the marquis' American ideals galvanized many citizens wanting the freedoms he espoused. When on June 23, 1789, the king, exasperated by delegates' disagreements, ordered his major domo, Marquis de Dreux-Brézé, to lock them out of the hall at the end of the day, Mirabeau exclaimed, "We shall not leave except with the force of bayonets!" Still in session, delegates adopted his motion, declaring their right not to be disturbed. Louis' limp response: "They don't want to leave? Very well, let them stay."

Although Lafayette and Mirabeau disliked each other, they held similar political views and were early members of the liberal Jacobin political club, one of several groups debating politics in Paris and the provinces. The club met in a former Dominican friars' hall. (In France, Dominicans were called Jacobins.) A majority of Jacobins, sitting on the Third Estate's raised backbenches, were called "the mountain" or "*montagnards*" (mountaineers). Much larger numbers of deputies seated below were "the plain." Jacobins loudly rejected the monarchy, favoring a republic. Lafayette, offended by their cries, held to his belief in a guided monarchy. Delegates varied greatly:

The mild-mannered writer and astronomer Jean-Sylvain Bailly, born in the Louvre and son of a court painter, had been elected chairman of the convention and first mayor of Paris. (A provost of the merchants had headed the city but was shot in the attack on the Bastille.) Bailly was unnerved by the stormy revolutionary government and public criticism of him.

Abbé Emmanuel de Sieyès, a respected delegate and cleric, wrote a pamphlet, *What Is the Third Estate?* Expressing the new age of reason, it condemned king, nobility and church and convinced many of the republican view. A decade later, writing a new constitution, Sieyès opposed the Jacobins' return. Although by then a member of the ruling but weak five-man Directory, he helped Napoleon Bonaparte to power and saw him usurp the new constitution.

In 1789, Talleyrand, sitting with the clergy at the convocation, called for the church's overthrow. Later escaping to London, he worked in a bank in the United States but returned to become a foreign secretary for Napoleon.

The minor nobleman Pierre Samuel du Pont was a respected economist and an inspector general of commerce under Louis XVI. He originated the idea that became the Louisiana Purchase to keep Napoleon out of the Mississippi valley. From Nemours, south of Paris, he took the town's name to distinguish himself from other Du Ponts in the Assembly.

One of the oddest convention delegates was Marquis Donatien Alphonse François de Sade, liberal noble, poet, critic and pornographic novelist. Mostly written during thirty-two years of imprisonment, the novels made him synonymous with cruel and aberrant sexuality. (Evading the scaffold, Sade lived in Picpus' "House of Health and Detention." The wealthy could escape the Terror there until their money ran out. Then, taken to the Conciergerie, they were tried and beheaded.

Mirabeau, like Lafayette, wanted a constitutional kingdom: where he could scheme to become premier. Secretly, he had been the king and queen's paid adviser since May 1790. With 50,000 livres to start and 6,000 a month, he lived as he loved, prodigiously. But the royals, believing in their divine right, ignored his advice. While seeking Mirabeau's favor, Marie Antoinette distrusted his liberalism. She often acted now for her husband who had become frustrated with overwhelming conditions. Had the couple acted to amend the tottering government, as Lafayette and Mirabeau hoped, they and the nation might have been spared disaster and instead hailed for their wisdom. Lafayette saluted the revolt of the tenant farmers in November 1788. Fired by the Assembly's discussion of ending noble titles, they refused to pay their landowners in the Dauphiné (its capital is Grenoble), as direct resistance.

Outbursts also occurred in France's eastern provinces. Lafayette of course wanted liberal friends to vote out "noxious" titles, except for royal magistrates. But, Mirabeau thundered, "The partisans of reform must fight their battle in the bosom of the nobility itself." This plan was adopted. It put Lafayette and his rival at odds but placed Mirabeau in the forefront of a growing democracy.

With soaring influence, Mirabeau was elected president of the National Assembly on January 30, 1791. Manorial concessions, however, eased provincial problems. Lafayette found himself traveling outside Paris to put down rebellions and stop destruction. On February 28, he sent out a battalion under Capitain Antoine Joseph Santerre, a former Faubourg Saint-Antoine brewer who had stormed the Bastille. Coming upon them, Lafayette stopped about sixty men, including Santerre, bent on destroying another symbol of oppression: the dungeon of the Chateau de Vincennes, an old royal palace east of Paris.[2] Rumors claimed the king was headed there for safety, even though he had not visited in years. Lafayette arrested the attackers, sent them to the Conciergerie and saw the damage under repair.

Returning to Paris, he was halted by closed city gates at Faubourg

Saint-Antoine and threatened to blow them open with cannons. A few shots were the only resistance. But while he crossed Rue Saint-Antoine in the dark, brigands grabbed at his horse. A grenadier drove them off with his bayonet. Lafayette was unhurt but a rumor quickly spread he had been killed. Rushing to the Tuileries just after the story reached there, he learned two or three hundred men, including knights of St. Louis, had entered the palace supposedly to protect the king and urge him to return his aunts to France. But the pious ladies, besides seeking safety away from a country now difficult for royals and aristocrats, abhorred mass-saying priests swearing fealty to the government over the pope. Lafayette, muddied and sweat-soaked, rode to the palace so hard that when he dismounted his horse collapsed.[3]

The king was startled to see these strange defenders enter his bedchamber. Fifty or sixty were dressed in court attire but most had a "gallows look," an eye-witness said. Lafayette was angered at the intrusion. But Louis said he did not know them, had not invited them and asked them to lay down their arms. His calmness quieted his chief protector who saw the invasion as defiance of his authority. Louis said, "They are too zealous servants who mistakenly believed I was in danger. Do everything you can to ensure they come to no harm," and asked that nothing be said of it. In his *Mémoires,* Lafayette recounts how his guards were drunk, loud and merry, inappropriate palace conduct, and broke what weapons they found in the courtyard — one hunting knife, it was said, and pistols. Guards gathered the "defenders," who had been issued passes by the two masters of the bedchamber, and roughly expelled them.[3]

Gouverneur Morris wrote in his journal on March 2 he had asked the commandant general about the affair. Lafayette replied his men were drunk and he was rude to the cavaliers, but Villequier, master of the king's bedchamber, had erred in letting them in. It was not learned who caused the incidents. Could it have just been the result of rumors affecting the public? Loyalists blamed Orléans, who had returned to France in October 1790, and the fiery republican Jacobins. Both thirsted for power but mutual hatred had kept them apart.[4]

Neither event helped Lafayette. The *Journal de Paris* published an account of both incidents the next day. The king, wondering who had prompted this, immediately wrote Lafayette to disavow it. He informed Louis the article had caused him "great indignation, for I believed that I could detect in it deliberate malice." He then wrote to the *Journal* defending his actions and said the first gentlemen of the chamber had "honored him with a personal correspondence" but he shed no light on the matter. Marie Antoinette turned pale on hearing Lafayette still being cheered in the streets. But "the day of the daggers," as it was called, set the public hero on a downward path.[5]

In the Assembly, Mirabeau's power continued to grow until April 1791 when he shocked France by dying from chronic physical abuse and overwork. Enormously popular and just forty-two, he was the first revolutionary to be buried with great pomp and honors in the Panthéon. The large and nearly new neoclassic limestone church was originally built to honor Paris' Saint Genevieve. But the new order needed a shrine. French immortals, among them Voltaire and Rousseau, would be entombed in its underground vaults. But when Mirabeau's duplicitous connection to the royal family surfaced, his remains were removed unceremoniously in 1794.

THIRTY-ONE: THE KING'S BETRAYAL

Lafayette was suddenly bombarded with rumors the royal family was planning to escape. When the king and queen had wished to spend Easter at Saint-Cloud in 1791, he ordered the National Guard to remove an angry crowd blocking the royal carriages in the Place du Carrousel before the Tuileries. But the royal family returned to the palace, not telling Lafayette they had changed plans. He informed them the road was open but they were firm. The queen said, "Now you know we are your prisoners."

Opponents called him the policeman of the Tuileries, but he insisted the royal family could travel anywhere in the country. That was technically true but he was their overseer and gatekeeper, and to the royals, their jailer. The king, promising Lafayette he would not flee, had planned for several months the best escape with loyal subjects. Courtiers and hundreds of servants were suspicious and spoke to others while revolutionary sheets like Marat's predicted the escape and urged its prevention, or an invading army attempting to put the king back on his throne would slaughter them.

On June 20, Lafayette spoke with Louis XVI and left after seeing him in bed at 11 p.m. Shortly afterward the king, disguised as a valet, with his sister, Ēlisabeth, and his two children left the palace by an unguarded door, hurrying in a forgotten passage toward a street along the Seine. The queen, dressed as a governess, joined them a half-hour later. Axel von Fersen, dressed as a coachman with his carriage, took them northeast across town to a large specially built and conspicuous berlin drawn by six horses at the Saint Martin gate. The king told Fersen for his own safety not to join them.[1]

At 7 a.m., a white-faced deputy, Antoine d'André, of Aix, awakened Lafayette in his bed. He dressed and rushed in his carriage to the palace while hearing churchbells and firing cannons trumpeting the escape. Lafayette conferred with General Gouvion, who had fought beside him in America and was greatly embarrassed by what had occurred during his command. Acting on his own after conferring with Alexandre de Beauharnais, Assembly president, Lafayette ordered guards to follow all roads to the frontiers.[2] Lafayette's cousin, François de Bouillé, not only favored the monarchy and rejected the liberal constitution but also detested Lafayette for supporting it. Principal plotter of the escape, Bouillé had conferred with the king for months in coded letters he memorized before destroying.

The plan was not, as often stated, to have the royals flee to Austria, where Marie Antionette's brother, Leopold II, was emperor. Instead Louis and Bouillé would summon loyal French troops to the eastern front where Austrian and Prussian soldiers would help rally more Frenchmen to Louis' side. They would then vanquish the rebels — guillotining Lafayette and others — and restore the monarchy with a new government. Bouillé, fifty-two, general commander of the army in northeastern France, was hated for harshly suppressing insurrections in Metz and Nancy. In *La Marseillaise* he was called a despot and tiger.[3] Lafayette had hoped earlier to convert his cousin. When that became impossible both would face dark times. Bouillé said perceptively of Lafayette: "He was more occupied in covering himself against the royalists, who were powerless, than in crushing the Jacobins, his real and more formidable enemies."[4]

The royal flight was disastrous. The heavy and ungainly carriage had an accident requiring repairs on the spot, ruining a precise timetable. The royals, three hours late, missed their first cavalry escort, a detachment of forty loyal men. This escort, after waiting seven hours and facing frowns of villagers who thought they were up to no good, finally rode away. Their leader, Duc de Choiseul, rather than have an aide ride back to the carriage, mistakenly sent a messenger ahead to say "the delivery" was not coming. After 8 p.m. the royals, traveling with false identities and passports, reached the relay station in tiny Sainte Menehould. Stable owner Jean Baptiste Drouet had seen the king and queen several times before. He recognized Louis as the face on a fifty-franc bill with which the king paid him. Drouet, a rebel, said nothing to the escapees but took a shortcut to Varennes and alerted authorities there before the carriage arrived.[5]

After many questions, Louis amiably admitted who he was. He and his party were held in local lodgings. They expected Bouillé to appear but barricaded roads prevented it. Learning the escape had failed, he fled to Russia.[6] The next morning, Lafayette rushed his order and an Assembly resolution to Varennes, but that did not end confusion there. Lafayette, deliberately avoided the word "escape." That would gain the constitutionalists nothing and he wanted to put the king in the best light.

He said enemies of the revolution had abducted the king. But surprised locals had seen no abductors. The Assembly, temporarily suspending royal authority, claimed supremacy for itself and demanded Louis' return. As Lafayette said, what was France without its king? National Guards flanked the royal train as it slowly rumbled back to Paris in the extreme summer heat. Crowds watching the procession swelled into many thousands. As the royal family neared Paris more and more angry threats were hurled at them.

The Assembly sent three commissioners to meet the royals halfway on their return at Ēpernay: Jérôme Pétion de Villeneuve, former Assembly president and head of Paris' criminal tribunal; Lafayette's friend Colonel Victor de Latour-Maubourg; and deputy Antoine Barnave. Maubourg refused to ride in the crowded berlin and was allowed a horse. The thirty-five-year-old queen dazzled Barnave, thirty, who stopped often to provide her with refreshment and support. The disheartened royals reached the Tuileries on June 25; the return had taken four days. Hungry and tired of country food, Louis ordered a large dinner. Court life resumed as though nothing had occurred. That evening Lafayette, according to custom, asked for his orders. Louis replied, "It seems you are not at my orders but I am at yours." Yet in secret letters he and the queen pled more fervently for foreign intervention.

Lafayette, weakened politically by the king's flight, still retained some power. He overlooked Louis' lying to him, believing the country could not stay together without its king. The people were too uneducated, too easily misled, Lafayette believed, to elect the best leaders for a republic. He knew his rejection of the aristocracy made him a traitor to them. His hope of calmly restructuring the nation under the king was too moderate for Jacobins fanning the revolution. Having isolated himself, he considered leaving his post. Keeping the peace was growing more difficult as Jacobin agitation, incendiary pamphleteering and public disruptions grew worse daily. Danton verbally attacked Lafayette, who visited the Jacobin Club the evening after the king's escape. Lafayette knew the fiery young deputy was secretly in Louis' pay and had even warned him earlier that Louis was about to flee.

"You swore the king would not go way!" Danton roared. "You said you would protect him or lose your own head. Why have you not paid your debt?" As when Mirabeau had challenged his rhetoric, Lafayette made no reply.

THIRTY-TWO: CHAMP DE MARS HORROR

The Assembly was interested in the king's perjury before his attempted escape and his repudiation of recent agreements. Maximilien Robespierre, a short and owlish thirty-year-old Third Estate lawyer from the northern town of Arras, wanted a national convention to decide the matter. Condorcet, Lafayette's liberal friend, called for deposing the lying king and founding a republic. His speech ended his ties to the constitutionalists. Lafayette never spoke to him again.[1] When Assembly moderates Pierre Samuel du Pont de Nemours and Louis Alexandre de La Rochefoucauld d'Enville, Lafayette's friends, asked the same question, he stood and said, "If you dethrone the king, I and the National Guard will declare his son king the next day."[2]

Loyalist Barnave argued the king had not tried to escape but wanted some time in Malmedy, a northeastern border town, to clear his mind of mounting political pressures. Barnave predicted if the king were removed and commoners allowed the vote, private lands would be confiscated. Lafayette supported him. Louis was reinstated on July 15, 1791, twenty-two days after his return. The Assembly declared those advancing revolution were criminals. This pleased those who honored the king and saw no reason to meddle with tradition. But

Parisians and others across the country were infuriated by this vote. Passions soared.

The younger Jacobins, wanting Orléans to be king, and the slightly less radical Cordeliers Club led by Danton invited angry citizens everywhere to a mass meeting in the Champ de Mars on Sunday, July 17, to protest the vote. They were asked to sign a petition demanding dethronement, placed for the day on the national altar.

Early that morning, a jobless wig-maker and his friend with a wooden leg, both army veterans, crawled under the altar with a wine cask. They brought a gimlet, a small handscrew, and bored a hole through a step to peep up women's dresses as they neared the petition. The pair was discovered when the gimlet pierced a woman's shoe. The crowd, already angry and singing Ça Ira (*It Will Come,* a rebel chant), dragged the culprits out and thought their cask held gunpowder to blow up the altar of the fatherland. Their explanations were ignored. In a fury both were hanged, their heads hacked off and paraded on pikes. Proclaiming martial law, Bailly raised a red warning flag over the hôtel de ville.

By the time Lafayette arrived with a detachment of guards the crowd of 15,000 had turned ugly and Orléans' henchmen had made overturned carts into barriers. As Lafayette ordered the crowd to leave, a man shot at him but the bullet misfired. A known cut-throat working for the duc, Fournier l'Américain, from Martinique, fired at close range, just missing Lafayette's head. Guards would have shot Fournier on the spot but Lafayette ordered him freed, prompting mob comments Lafayette had set up the incident and the shooter was an *agent provacateur.* Jacobins promised there would be no more disturbances. Accepting that, Lafayette posted guards and went home. Later that day, he was informed the mob was preparing to attack the National Assembly and Tuileries.

Gathering a large force of guards, Lafayette returned with Bailly to the Champ de Mars. They were met with boos and pelted with stones. Lafayette ordered the rioters to leave. Guards fired warning shots in the air. The volley was ignored but heckling and stone-throwing grew. Reloading, the guards fired with deadly intent into the mob too quickly for Lafayette to stop them. Jacobins claimed he ordered the fusillade as did Marat in his newpaper. But like the king, Lafayette was horrified by mass bloodshed. He is said to have stood before a cannon to silence it.

About fifty people were killed, including a child, and many more wounded. Rumors exaggerated numbers into many thousands. The deaths stained Lafayette's reputation as the people's defender and his popularity plummeted. After the gunfire the rioters ran away. But a group marched to Lafayette's house and threatened to decapitate Adrienne and take her head on a pike to her husband. She and the servants bravely resisted the attackers who scaled the mansion's garden walls. By chance, Guardsmen arriving on the scene frightened them off. Lafayette knew nothing of it until returning home.

Since Jacobins had called the meeting and largely fomented the riot, they expected to be arrested, even executed, and assumed Lafayette would use the attack for a coup d'etat. Hearing the news, Jacobins fled the Assembly, many jumping from windows. Danton escaped to London. Robespierre disappeared into his secret rooms in Paris. Desmoulins, Fréron and Brissot also vanished and Marat hid in a cellar. He wrote, "The patriots dare not show themselves and the enemies of liberty fill the Senate galleries and are seen everywhere."[3]

THIRTY-THREE: A NEW POLITICAL CLUB

With the king returned and order restored, Lafayette quit the Jacobins because they wanted Louis deposed. He formed the Feuillant Club, pro-royal, pro-constitutional, anti-revolutionary, with friends in the summer of 1791. It soon dominated Paris' politics. The club's formal name was the Society of the Friends of the Constitution. It included Alexandre de Lameth, who had served with two brothers in America; Louis Noailles; Adrien Duport, a magistrate and constitutional monarchist; and the recently defrocked Talleyrand. They met in the former Paris convent of the Feuillants, a strict order of Cistercian monks.[1] Their spokesman was Barnave, since Mirabeau's death the Assembly's greatest orator. But by spring of 1792, with Lafayette often absent, the Feuillants lost strength.

But the Girondists, *Girondins* in French, another Assembly group of moderate rightists, were to be reckoned with. Their name, a convenience, was derived from a few leaders who came from the Gironde region in southwestern France and Bordeaux, its wealthy capital. At first the impoverished journalist Brissot de Warville, a native of Chartres, had led them inside the Jacobin Club. Girondists believed in provincial rights over Paris, private wealth and property, universal sufferage, the constitution and governance by "the better people." They voted with the Feuillants, supported the revolution and opposed foreign intervention. But the liberal Jacobins, gaining more power than the other groups, denounced "the royalists, the federalists, the Brissotins, the *Girondins* and all the enemies of democracy."[2]

Robespierre was at first a quiet Jacobin. But he propelled the rebel faction with his eloquent speeches denouncing the king and aristocrats. His extreme ideas on justice and religion spurred the Terror (1793-1797) when trials of an hour or less often ended at the guillotine. Robespierre had humble rooms above a shop on Rue du Faubourg Saint-Honoré, some blocks away from the Assembly. Banishing oppressive tradition, he ordered a new national calendar. He supplanted Catholicism with worship of a Supreme Being in its temple, Notre Dame. "Reason," symbolized by a goddess, replaced Christianity, so great was public hatred of the church's usurpations.

Lafayette's enemies called him a lackey of the bourgeosie and loyalists. Brissot, who had often dined at Lafayette's table, turned viciously on him. The monarchists, losing influence with Louis' escape, hoped a foreign invasion would re-empower the old regime. Three million Frenchmen were deprived of the vote. A king who could not be trusted could still delay legislation four years with his suspensive veto. Inflated money prevented higher wages. The feudal dues Louis Noailles fought to end were still in effect. In the new Assembly, the Jacobins, often ill-trained or ignorant of government, knew what they wanted: democracy, the end of active and passive rules for citizens, more equitable redistribution of nobles' lands and a revised constitution.[3]

Leopold II of Austria, the last Habsburg Holy Roman emperor, hoped to help Louis XVI, his brother-in-law. Leopold met with Prussia's Frederick William II in Pilnitz, near Dresden, the Saxon capital, in August 1791. They declared they would intervene should Louis be threatened — but only if all European powers agreed. This declaration was meant to appease French émigrés who were calling for foreign intervention. Leopold knew Britain's prime minister, William Pitt the Younger, opposed invading France, and it was doubtful any other nation would accept it. But the French National Assembly, misreading the declaration, thought Leopold was about to declare war. The French were furious at the idea of foreign intervention. Fiery leaders insisted France should carry its revolution to other kingdoms.

In September, Louis, addressing the Assembly, approved the year-old constitution. He said, "To extinguish all hatreds let us all consent to forget the past."[4] He was reinstated as head of state, and the Constituent Assembly dissolved itself on the last day of September. All members resigned to clear the way for new deputies. Days later, a newly elected, more radical Legislative Assembly convened. Many returned with the new body, particularly the Jacobins and Robespierre, their most outspoken member. Diehard loyalists were conspicuously fewer, their power all but evaporated.

French émigrés who had been invited to stay in Koblenz, north of Cologne, Germany, were horrified when Louis and Marie Antoinette accepted the constitution and agreed to be subservient to the state.[5] They were further disturbed in November 1791 when the Legislative Assembly ordered all émigrés, about 20,000, to return under threat of death and confiscation of possessions, but Louis vetoed the bill.

Lafayette, although seeing the tide turning, believed like many others the revolution was over, its goals met. He lost his command when the Assembly divided the National Guard leadership between four officers, each in charge a month at a time. One of the successors was brilliant Lazare Carnot, engineer, statesman, tactician, who devised victories for the French revolutionary army.[6] Lafayette resigned on October 8. Adrienne saw him for the moment safe and away from danger.

In his Assembly farewell, Lafayette said the revolution had "given place to an organized government, and to liberty and prosperity which it guarantees." He claimed France's enemies abroad should see, "in view of the public happiness," how absurd was "any menacing combination against the rights of the people... Liberty and equality, once established in two hemispheres, will never retrograde."[7]

The family left next day for Chavaniac. Lafayette was moved by great outpourings of praise wherever they stopped. The provinces still admired him. With Washington and Jefferson as models, he intended to become a gentleman farmer. But he knew little of agriculture and was bored with country life and politics.

In Paris, Bailly, butt of many accusations and with no Lafayette to lean on, resigned. Friends entered Lafayette's name as candidate for mayor, but Pétion easily won with Jacobin support and the queen's opposition.

Reacting to the Pillnitz Declaration and welcoming the possibility of war, the Assembly created three armies of 50,000 men each to defend the eastern frontier against Austria and Prussia. Most deputies favored war for different reasons, but Robespierre feared defeat would end revolutionary gains. If France won, he saw a dictator emerging, possibly the hero of two worlds.

Two months after leaving Paris, Lafayette, began calling himself "general" and, rejecting his marquisate, accepted command of the Army of the North. His co-commandants were *Maréchals* Comtes Jean Baptiste Rochambeau and Nicolas Lückner. An eastern Bavarian, Lückner had joined the French Army in 1763. Rochambeau urged Lafayette for the top post. Louis XVI, the queen and court meanwhile were secretly doing all they could to support the émigrés. But on December 14, 1791, the king informed the applauding National Assembly he had sent an ultimatum to the Elector of Trèves in the Koblenz region.[8] He ordered all noble émigrés expelled before January 15, 1792 to return or France would intervene. Artois retorted by denouncing the Pillnitz Declaration, often called his Koblenz Manifesto.

This angered Louis XVI, exposed him to patriotic revenge and virtually sealed his fate.[9] But tiny semi-autonomous Trèves could not defy France without Austrian or Prussian support. Louis, underestimating the public's rage and mood, quickly wrote a secret message to Leopold II urging his help. Louis halted French weapon and munitions production and gave orders weakening the eastern borders. He wrote to other sovereigns suggesting "a congress of European powers, supported by an armed force, as the best means of putting a check on the factious persons here." Prussia's Frederick William said he would do anything to help, if paid. Louis replied the royal treasury would compensate him.

Lafayette now at the front saw the Tuileries loyalists had set up his so-called army to fail: it was an undisciplined, ill-trained mob without weapons, supplies or horses. The Jacobins, wanting to run the army without him, infiltrated ranks with volunteer followers. They spread distrust of officers who, they claimed, hoped to lead them into a trap and surrender to the foreign invaders.

Leopold, wanting to avoid war, believed negotiations could avert it. He ordered the Koblenz elector to expel the émigrés, which he did. Louis and the agitators left the Jacobins, Girondists and loyalists without a cause for war, but they still had their reasons. Jacobin and loyalist causes were clear though mutually opposed. Girondists expected war would bring all dissidents together in a common cause — with their favored group, the bourgeosie, rising to the top. But the Jacobins' growing numbers swamped the Girondists.

On March 1, Leopold, forty-four, a fair-minded emperor but exhausted from visiting leaders to urge their support, lay dead in his bedroom, aphrodisiac at hand.[10] His son, Francis II, twenty-four, was all his father was not: combative, stubborn and cruel. Also on hand was Louis Joseph, Prince de Condé, Louis XVI's cousin who, fleeing France after the Bastille fell, organized an army of 20,000 noble émigrés in Koblenz, one of several such groups. On its expulsion, the Army of Condé regrouped in Austria, prepared to invade France to restore the monarchy. Also known as "the Princes' Army," it received many noble French officers, upgrading their ranks — Napoleon would invite its best officers to join *his* army — but Condé, after winning funds from Britain, Austria and others, ran out of money and the army disbanded in 1801. Francis of Austria, following his advisers, refused to declare war on France because if she started the conflict and lost, Austria would claim indemnities.

THIRTY-FOUR: DISASTERS AT THE FRONT

Poor harvests, regulatory fluctuations and government corruption brought food riots to France in the winter of 1792. Grain shortages challenged public trust in Louis XVI, called sarcastically "the baker king." In early March, war minister Louis, Comte de Narbonne-Lara, a military man who grew up at Versailles, summoned Lafayette, Rochambeau and Lückner to Paris.[1] With the king attending, they prepared a campaign. Lafayette would invade Austrian-held Flanders (now southern Belgium), Rochambeau would support him and Lückner would repel enemies at the Rhine. Louis gave this news to Marie Antoinette, who immediately reported to her nephew, Francis, by courier.

Lafayette, remaining in Paris for several weeks during the government's troubles, was violently criticized in the Jacobin Club. Robespierre demanded his army dismissal, calling him a hypocrite, deceiving citizens into avoiding Jacobins. Club members falsely claimed Lafayette had not returned to the army, as reported, but was secretly advising the king in the Tuileries. Robespierre misjudged Lafayette, believing he lusted for military dictatorship. Robespierre predicted for Lafayette conditions leading to Napoleon Bonaparte.[2]

On April 20, Louis XVI urged an enthusiastic Assembly to declare war on Austria. Only ten members voted no. Learning this, Prussia joined Austria and, after mustering troops, easily defeated the ill-prepared French armies.

Despite his poor and rankerous soldiers, Lafayette advanced into Austrian-held Belgium in late April 1792. On May 1 his army neared Namur, a French-speaking city. With his cajoling, Lafayette's army pushed back the enemy. But callow troops under General Robert Dillon, his feisty Irish-French friend who had served with Rochambeau in America, failed to protect Lafayette's army and ran from the Austrians. His troops then mutinied and murdered Dillon, dismembering him and burning his remains. Lafayette's longtime comrade, the engineer Gouvion, was also killed in battle.

Austrians in Belgium overwhelmed the raw troops of Duc de Lauzun, who through inheritance had become Duc de Biron. He had led a legion of 1,000 volunteers in America.[3] With these disasters, Rochambeau, the old regime's last *maréchal,* resigned, disgusted with his army's reverses and Assembly blunders. Discouraged, Lafayette, realizing his army's advances could not be held, retreated from Belgium. The foreign allies, enjoying their victories, stayed put, waiting to see what the French would do. They could easily have marched on Paris but took their time. The French public was greatly disappointed with its armies' defeats and losses but changes were coming.

Exasperated, Lafayette stepped away from military protocol. With no right to do so, he wrote the Assembly to complain about Jacobins' usurping the people's rights "by subjugating its representatives and its agents." They were turning reality upside down, "calling [followers of] the law aristocracy, and [Jacobins'] infractious patriotism."[4]

It was true. But the Jacobins had Pétion heading the Commune and they would soon control the National Guard and provincial governments. Lafayette's surprising outburst, brought on by frustration, was read to deputies and promptly forgotten. Again he spoke for himself, not from power within the enfeebled Feuillants. Jacobins marked him for removal. His enemy Danton claimed Lafayette had joined the tyrants trying to conquer France. The incendiary Desmoulins stuttered, "I knew it all along. For two years I have said Lafayette is a great scoundrel."[5]

At the queen's prodding, Louis XVI, although knowing Narbonne was a friend of Lafayette, Rochambeau and Lückner, dismissed him. Narbonne had shown people a letter Lafayette had sent him with Rochambeau and Lückner's approval. It described what "pernicious effects" would occur if Narbonne left the war office. The letter reached print, offended the king and delighted the Jacobins, who pointed out what occurs when generals intrude into politics. Narbonne had irritated the ultra-sensitive Jacobins when he appealed to the Assembly's "most distinguished members," which the Jacobins knew they were not.

Louis replaced his Feuillant cabinet with pro-royal Girondists, detested by the Jacobins. Louis made the deceptive General Charles François Dumouriez minister of foreign affairs. He needed the Girondists' support and they wanted a general in the field they could trust. Lafayette disliked Dumauriez, who could be on both sides of an issue. Louis, in his first year as king in 1774, had freed Dumouriez, jailed as a secret agent of foreign affairs minister Choiseul, who himself had been dismissed four years earlier for banishing the unpopular Jesuits.

Dumouriez, who for ten years was commandant of Cherbourg, had admired Mirabeau. Stunned by his death, Dumouriez became a Jacobin, then Girondist. As foreign affairs minister, he wrote the war declaration against Austria and ordered French invasion of the Austrian-held Low Countries.[6]

Wanting Biron to seize Mons and Brussels, Dumouriez plotted to ruin Lafayette, sending him orders completely altering the campaign. Lafayette was told to move his shoeless and horseless troops (shades of Valley Forge) in five days to Givet, Belgium, far from where they were in Metz. The order was designed to make Lafayette fail and be faulted. Rallying his men, Lafayette scoured the region for horses, worked all night dictating orders and shifted his army to Givet in three days. Biron, whom the Austrians would badly defeat, let Alexandre Berthier, Lafayette's adjutant general, see Dumouriez's private letter to Biron. It said Lafayette could not possibly meet his order.[7]

Louis XVI made Dumouriez war minister. But he resigned two days later to join Lückner's army because the king up to then had refused to accept the Assembly's decrees. Dumouriez's future would become extremely episodic…

THIRTY-FIVE: ACTS OF FUTILITY

On June 20, 1792, about 1,000 citizens from the city's roughest faubourgs, egged on by the Jacobins, entered the iron gates of the Tuileries Palace without resistance. They demanded the king withdraw his suspensive veto forcing émigré nobles' to return and expelling nonjuring clergy from France. Running through the palace, they insulted the queen and insisted Louis wear the red cap of freedom. He did so affably and even drank wine with them, hiding his anger. But Louis said he would not change his veto: the palace was not the place for this, nor was it the time to agree with them.

Where were his protectors the National Guards, whose numbers had recently been increased from 1,800 to 6,000? On May 29, a Girondist decree had disbanded them. But after several hours the crowd, totally out of place in the palace, left peacefully, believing the king would make the changes they wanted. Girondist Mayor Pétion, who hated the royal family, arrived shortly afterward. The agitated king criticized him for allowing the mass invasion of his privacy and ordered him to leave.

Lafayette, indignant over this breach of the king's protection, wrote to Lückner: "Ever since I have drawn breath it has been for the cause of liberty. I will defend it to my last sigh against every sort of tyranny, and I cannot submit in silence to that which the factions are exercising on the National Assembly and the King... But everybody is afraid of them, and I, who do not know that weakness, I will tell them the truth."[1]

He rushed from his northern camp alone in a carriage to Paris, stopped briefly at his house — his family was safely in Chavaniac — and denounced the Jacobins to their faces in the Assembly on June 28. He begged the deputies to punish the instigators of the palace invasion as criminals and outlaw the Jacobin Club that "invades the national sovereignty, tyrannizes over citizens and whose public debates leave no doubt of the atrocious sentiments of those who direct it."

The Jacobins and their minions remained silent, fearing a rumor Lafayette was about to bring in the army to expel them and take over the government. But the Assembly's right and center hailed his words, although all who did were hissed at immediately and later harassed in their homes. Lafayette's brief but fiery speech had no lasting effect since he offered no plan of action and there were few to support him. His indictment came too late. The king and queen wanted to be done with him, although Louis seemed pleased to see him soon after the motley invasion. But the queen's blue eyes remained cold. "It would be better to perish," she quipped, "than to be saved by M. de Lafayette." But Madame Ēlisabeth (1764-1794), Louis' loving absolutist sister, thanked him on his Tuileries visit for helping the royal family. If only the queen were not depending on Danton. Lafayette knew her paying him 50,000 crowns meant she expected he would save them.

But was that possible? Lafayette had come to the Assembly to vent his outrage with the hope of eradicating the Jacobins — but again not by his own hand. He wanted to believe Assembly moderates like the Comte de Vaublanc, royalist writer and artist, and Vincent Quatremère de Quincy, archeologist and art writer, both of whom had voted for his acquittal, still had power to inspire others. In speeding to Paris, Lafayette had left his vulnerable army near the Belgian border just as Charles William Ferdinand, Duke of Brunswick, was gathering his troops to invade France. For that breach, Lafayette could have been court-martialed or worse. Disgusted with the Assembly, he returned to his army. Nothing was done to stop the Jacobins.

Looking forward to a second *Fête de la Fédération*, Lafayette wanted to be in Paris for the event on July 14. But the Assembly declared only

Lückner, seventy, the ranking general, would attend. The constitutional bishop Gobet invited Lückner to dinner with a number of Jacobins, who plied the wine-addled Lückner with questions. The next day, six Jacobins reported to the Assembly the general had declared nobleman and army engineer Jean Xavier Bureaux de Puzy, serving under Lafayette, had come to Lückner's encampment with Lafayette's proposal to join armies and march on Paris. Lafayette heard the story and wrote to Lückner to free himself of the lying Jacobins. Lückner swore loyalty to Lafayette, saying the statements were "as false as they are impossible."

Dumouriez asked Lafayette for an explanation. He received this response: "Did I propose to *Monsieur le Maréchal* Lückner to march with our armies on Paris? To that I reply in four short words: That is not true." Ordered to appear before the Assembly, Puzy in July defended both generals. When he showed their correspondence and blamed the story on Jacobins and their howling partisans, the subject was tabled.[2]

Still wanting to help, Lafayette in early July secretly proposed to the royal couple through his aide-de-camp La Colombe that Lafayette and the National Guard would escort them to the royal Chateau de Compiègne, fifty miles northeast of Paris. In this new capital, he hoped, they and governmental bureaus would be free of harassment. He urged Louis to proclaim to his brothers and émigrés they should advance no farther. Louis was to announce, with Assembly agreement, his readiness to march at the head of his armies against the foreigners and to affirm his position, he would inform them he stood behind the constitution. Lafayette obviously did not know the royals' collusion. The queen told La Colombe, "We are very grateful to your general, but it would be better for us to be shut up in a tower for two months." They were soon to be imprisoned much longer.

Louis XVI, having rejected Axel von Fersen's second escape proposal, told La Colombe, "Tell [Lafayette] I am touched by the proof of attachment he has given me in proposing to run great risks on my behalf; but it would be imprudent to set so many wheels turning at the same time. The surest way in which he can serve me is by continuing to be the terror of the factionists while ably doing his duty as a general." Louis feared being Lafayette's hostage again. The plan did not remain secret and found its way to Jacobins and Girondists, joined to dethrone the king. Morris wrote to Jefferson, "I verily believe that if M. de Lafayette were to appear just now in Paris unattended by his army he would be torn to pieces."

Louis also rejected La Rochefoucauld's offer to accompany the royal family to Le Havre and escape to England. The sovereigns, knowing their imperiled status, were frightened but would not leave, expecting the invaders to rescue them. The queen would have nothing to do with Lafayette. He had harmed her more than anyone, she said. But when the Girondists urged Louis to dismiss him to better resist the invaders, he refused and reshuffled his cabinet.

Adopting a still tougher stance on June 8, the Girondists pushed through a third decree: on July 14 a camp of 20,000 federal troops with firearms and pikes would be called to protect Paris from invaders. The king balked at banishing the nonjuring priests but accepted the encampment. The queen called it "an army of 20,000 brigands to govern Paris."

The Legislative Assembly was growing more radical. On July 15, Jean Debry, a fanatic who wanted 1,200 "tyrranicides" to slay all of Europe's kings, demanded that Lafayette, the rebels' greatest enemy, be tried for treason. The vote, carried by the independents, was rejected 406 to 224.

Brunswick in a pompous July 25 proclamation ordered Parisians to give the king "full and entire liberty, and to insure to him and all of the royal family that inviolability and respect to which the laws of nature, and of nations, entitle sovereigns from their subjects." And should "the least violence, the least assault, be perpetrated against the royal family, the city would experience military execution and the guilty [receive] the death they have deserved." The duke's words produced an effect opposite to what he expected and later wished he had not written. Throughout France republicans began working together to end the monarchy.

THIRTY-SIX: STORMING THE TUILERIES

Rumors of impending attack on the Tuileries had been heard for weeks everywhere, including the commune, Assembly and palace. Two-thirds of the Assembly's delegates hated taking Jacobin orders and felt captured. But like the weakened Constitutionalists, they did nothing.

The king summoned Pétion on August 9 to report on what was occurring in the city and to get his authorization to repel any attack on the palace. Some members of the Assembly, assuming the king was forcefully holding him, called Pétion to hear his report. A group of Jacobins from the commune, also assuming the mayor was being held against his will at the Tuileries, came to the Assembly and convinced Pétion to leave with them, in effect becoming temporarily the commune's prisoner under guard of 300 men.

Antoine Galiot Mandat, Marquis de Grancey, sixty-one, who had a solid military record in the royal guard, succeeded Lafayette at the Paris National Guard. A nobleman who had lived at Versailles, Mandat favored a constitutional monarchy. He said he was dedicated to protecting the Tuileries and hôtel de ville with his last breath and would never voluntarily give up his post. But National Guardsmen, coming from the rougher Parisian faubourgs and no longer middle class, favored the Jacobins and Orléanists.

Mandat posted 950 Swiss Guards, the king's staunch defenders despite coming from a republic, and Mandat's troops in and around the Tuileries. To curb rioters he stationed eleven cannons in front of the palace, on nearby Pont Neuf (later removed) and behind the hôtel de ville in Arcade Saint Jean.

Jacobins enlisted volunteers and *fédérés* (provincials expecting to join the National Guard) to enter Paris. They and 500 toughs from Marseille planned a poorly devised insurrection for July 26 but Mayor Pétion halted it. A second effort joining faubourgeois and men from Marseille also failed but led to a new attack on August 10. In one of the era's many ironies, Claude Rouget de Lisle wrote a war chant for the Army of the Rhine and dedicated it to Lückner. But when the toughs from the south sang it fervently in Paris, it became *La Marseillaise,* the national anthem.

Mandat had enjoyed the commune's support but was unaware of its new revolutionary status. The Jacobin plan, with the *fédérés,* was to dissolve the *Département* of Paris, dismiss Pétion and assault the Tuileries. Danton called Mandat from the palace to the council hall at 3:45 a.m. on August 10 and accused him of authorizing guards to fire on the public in defence of the palace. Danton stripped Mandat of his command and ordered him to Abbaye prison, a former Paris convent. Danton, a thirty-two-year-old lawyer, had not sat in either of the Assemblies but was a Cordeliers leader. He with allies Robespierre, Desmoulins, Marat, Philippe Fabre d'Ēglantine and others gained power from the public's growing fear of invasion.[1]

As Mandat left the hôtel de ville with his son, a pistol shot from the mob outside hit him. He fell on the steps as his son cried, "My father! My father!" Killers with pikes stabbed Mandat twenty times. They severed his head, paraded it on a pike and threw his body into the Seine. The commune immediately named Santerre, the rebel who had caused trouble at Vincennes, commandant general of the National Guard. Lafayette's marble bust in the hôtel de ville was smashed.[2] Concerned for the king and hoping once more to raise the morale of the National Guard, Lafayette asked if he could ride with Louis in his carriage and speak as the king reviewed his guardians early one morning, hoping to buttress the loyalty of his presumed protectors. Louis agreed but the queen sent a note to Pétion and Santerre about it, firm enough for the mayor to cancel the review.

Pierre Louis Roederer, recorder of the Paris *Département*, spent the night at the palace. In his account, the queen summoned him at 4 a.m., concerned about defense preparations the Jacobins had ordered. He urged the royal family for their protection to retreat at once to the Legislative Assembly. "You propose," Vicomte Dubouchage, the marine minister, said, "taking the king to his foes." But only two days earlier, Roederer reminded him, two-thirds of the Assembly had supported Lafayette, and going to the Assembly would be the safest course.[3]

The queen wanted to resist any insurrection with force, claiming the court nobles and the royal guards could resist an attack. But the king's troop review at 5 a.m. on August 10 indicated he could not rely on many of them. The pike battalions were openly angry, shouting, "Down with the veto! Down with the traitor!" When Louis returned to the palace, these men moved near the Pont Royal and pointed cannons at the Tuileries. Two other battalions in the palace courtyards stationed themselves in the Place du Carrousel ready to attack.

About 6 a.m., insurgents broke into the arsenal, armed themselves and advanced on the palace in several columns. With *Marseillais* and Breton *fédérés* in the vanguard, rebels from Faubourg Saint Antoine totaled 15,000. Those from Faubourg Saint Marceau, Left Bank, were 5,000 but more gathered marching to the palace. Artillerymen were on the Pont Neuf to keep the marching columns apart. But city manager Manuel ordered them withdrawn, easing the rebels' way. Roederer, heading several *département* members, confronted thousands of angry men in front of the palace. So many men could not see the king or the Assembly, he said, urging them to choose twenty spokesmen. They noisily refused. Seeing the rebels commanding the square, Roederer reminded the Guardsmen who were fraternizing with the rebels the law required them to repel a force when attacked. He and departmental leaders returned to the palace.

A few insurgents advanced amicably. The Swiss Guard as a peace token threw down some cartridges. Suddenly gunfire began — who started it is unknown — and the Swiss Guards advanced from the palace's front courtyard into the square. Caught in side gunfire from the Louvre, they fell back to the palace's main entrance. Hoping to end the bloodshed, the king sent a note ordering the Swiss to cease firing and go to barracks. But it was not possible to stop in the face of heavy firing and they did not immediately retreat.

With ammunition running out, the Swiss retreated through the palace to the gardens behind. There near the central fountain the rebels surrounded them, separated them into smaller groups and slaughtered them. The rebels killed those in the palace, including courtiers and servants. Six hundred Swiss Guards were slain for advancing on the insurgents. Sixty were taken to the Place de Grève where they were massacred. Only about 100 survived. Other royal soldiers, numbering about 200, changed to civilian clothes and vanished in the crowd.

The king and queen were humiliated by hearing deputies debate what should be done with them and they were locked in an Assembly room overnight and next day. They were then sent in a carriage under guard, a journey of a mile or so, but taking hours as the masses pushed and shouted epithets. The royals were imprisoned in the Temple, an old fortress of the banished Knights Templar. They would not see the Tuileries again.

Lafayette called his friend, Duc de LaRochefoucauld, president of the Paris *Département*, and several other Assembly leaders to his house. His former admiring guards patrolled the mansion nightly for his safety and set up a welcoming maypole with tricolored streamers in the garden.[4] Lafayette tried to breathe new resistance into the deputies. They listened but were not initiators. He fired off another letter to the Assembly denouncing the Jacobins. It altered nothing. Feeling his failure, he left his guardian friends at a barrier erected against invasion at Saint Denis and returned to his army.

Assembly deputies accused Lafayette of deserting his troops and it was said he gave the king new escape plans. He was suspected of communicating with his cousin Bouillé and it was rumored he would be a high constable in a new royal government.[5]

Before August 10, Jacobins had discussed replacing Louis XVI with Frederick, Duke of York and Albany. George III's second son was chief of the Horse Guards. Even the Duke of Brunswick was considered, then the founding of a republic. After strong patriotic reaction to Brunswick's proclamation, the Assembly made Dumouriez a commander and sent him to head the army of the north. An angry Lafayette wrote the war minister: "A piece of news that I do not believe, and that I think must be a mere pleasantry… you are [sending] Dumouriez to the army that I command. I have accused him openly of madness, or of treason to the public good, and to me." Lafayette declared, if Dumouriez arrived, he would order him to leave. But his enemy joined Lückner.

THIRTY-SEVEN: ESCAPE AND CAPTURE

Lafayette learned on August 12 from a guard who had escaped the massacre what had occurred at the Tuileries. The political situation in Paris was now beyond his power. On that day Moselle deputy François Paul Anthoine called for Lafayette's condemnation. On August 17, the Assembly's executive council ordered him to hand over his command to Dumouriez before Lafayette's trial two days later. He considered going to Paris alone to fight the case. But deciding this would be a fatal mistake, Lafayette concluded his "sacred resistance to oppression" was futile. He was indicted for treason on August 19 after an all-night session during which a letter was produced as evidence. He was supposed to have written the queen urging her to arrange for the king to be insulted, giving Lafayette an opportunity to attack the capital.[1]

How far he had fallen! In not seeking power he had too few admirers in the Assembly to support him, although he still had many friends in the nobility and commons. He knew who his enemies were. To his liberal deputy friend, Duc de La Rochefoucauld d'Enville, forty-nine, he wrote: "If I regain my liberty, I shall become once more purely American, and finding again in that happy land an enlightened people, friends of liberty, observers of the law, grateful for the happiness that I had to be useful to them. I shall relate to my great friend Washington and all my other companions from the American Revolution, how, despite my efforts, the French revolution was defiled by criminals, thwarted by plotters and destroyed by the vilest of men using corruption and ignorance as instruments of destruction."[2] The duc never saw the letter. Jacobins in Normandy, excited by the Prussian invasion and on their way to volunteer at the front, dragged the duc from his carriage and, as his wife and mother watched in horror, decapitated him. They in turn went to the guillotine.

As Lafayette wrote in his third-person *Mémoires*, "Nothing remained to him but to seek asylum in a neutral country in order to remove his proscribed head from the executioner's grasp and in the hope that he might one day again serve liberty and France." He ordered his troops to fall back to Bouillon, Belgium, assuring their safety. France would not lose defenders because of his next action.

It was still summer but cold and rainy. Pretending to make a reconnaissance on August 19 after dark in civilian clothes, Lafayette rode away with twenty-two officers and aides. The closest to him were César de La Tour-Maubourg, Jean Xavier Bureaux de Puzy and Alexandre de Lameth. There were also the general's valet, Félix Pontonnier, servant Jules Chavaniac and the others' servants, Auguste Masson and René Pittlet.

The Jacobins suspected all were the king's defenders. Twenty-one miles from Bouillon, they crossed on exhausted horses into Austrian-held Belgium en route to neutral Holland.[3] It was so dark they could not see the road. Confused and fearing Jacobins were in pursuit, they took a fateful chance. They would ask the Austrians for permission to pass but would not reveal their names.

Speaking German, Puzy learned in order to continue they would need a passport from the commander of Namur in southern Belgium. Thrilled to have Lafayette in hand, the Austrians denied the request and Austrian cavalrymen escorted them to Namur, where, not thinking themselves prisoners, the captives refused to swear allegiance to France: for seeking freedom to act on their own they rejected their army status. Local authorities, not knowing how to deal with the problem, wrote to Vienna, 500 miles away, meaning days of delay.

Lafayette spent his time penning letters. He wrote Adrienne, "I am going to England where I wish all my family to join me. Let us settle down in America: there we shall find that freedom which no longer exists in France."[4] Claiming American citizenship, he asked William Short, American minister at The Hague, to intervene. But he contended Lafayette had been arrested as a Frenchman, not an American. His letter was referred to Paris and Gouverneur Morris, who, pontificating, urged nothing be done but "prayer and solicitation." Morris had meddled so much in Louis XVI's problems that after the king's death the revolutionary government asked for Morris' recall. Monroe succeeded him.

Finally word came from Vienna. Captives were divided into three groups. Since Lafayette, Pusy and Alexandre de Lameth — who had asked to join them because he had been indicted in Paris and Lafayette reluctantly agreed — had been National Assembly members, they would be held as Louis XVI's hostages. Line officers and common soldiers were expelled from Belgium but could not return to France, while other officers went to Antwerp as war prisoners.

Austrian logic was faulty: it was inaccurate to charge Lafayette as a revolutionary opposed to the king. No matter. Vienna decreed the four would become prisoners of Prussia. Duke Albert of Saxe-Teschen, uncle of Emperor Francis, wrote to Lafayette claiming he was not only responsible for the revolution but had also imprisoned the king, taken away his rights and powers and was the "principal instrument of all the disgraces overwhelming this unhappy monarch." The duke also charged that, although not émigrés, Lafayette and his group still held to anti-royalist ideas and should be imprisoned until the king re-established himself. But it was too late for that.

Filled with frustration on his thirty-fifth birthday, Lafayette was moved with the others away from the Netherlands to Luxembourg. At its fortress, French refugees immediately recognized them and contemptuously accused Lafayette of being an early agent of the revolution. One *émigré*, the Prince de Lambes, violently assailed him in front of the others. Lafayette may be the hero of two worlds, he was told, but he had infected Europe with the ideas of independence and personal freedom, imperiling the French monarchy's rule by divine right. Lafayette, accustomed to royalist views, let the prince rant since there was no reasoning with him.

The governor of Luxembourg sequestered the men in separate rooms at an inn with a sentinel at each door. They protested loudly and asked for passports from Saxe-Teschen. They were refused and threatened with public execution. They remained there until the Vienna court requested the governor deliver them to Frederick William II, King of Prussia, who had succeeded his uncle Frederick the Great.

Seven months earlier at Pillnitz, Frederick William had agreed with Emperor Leopold, Marie Antoinette's brother, to save the captive Louis and his queen and had appealed to other crowned heads to intervene with them if necessary. The captives were then transported at night in a rude cart under cavalry guard to Wesel, a Brandenburg-Prussian garrison town on the lower Rhine, where more crowds insulted them. They were put in irons, kept in separate cells in the castle and denied all conversation and exercise.

The Austrians sold their horses and weapons, keeping the money. "The king intends to have you all hanged for wretches who deserve no favor," they were told daily. The king was a tyrant dissipating Frederick's immense treasure. Leopold went along with him on the captives' poor treatment. This news galvanized the French. Generals rallied to government orders to expel these cruel enemies who had increased their fighting in France. Hordes of angry Frenchmen joined the army.

Dumouriez was ordered to take Lafayette's command. In Belgium, he helped to repulse the Prussians at Valmy and defeated the Austrians at Jemappes while hoping to spread the revolution there. In Paris he received ovations, but the rebels faulted his old-fashioned methodical style of warfare. Unsure of his own loyalties, Dumouriez tried to save Louis XVI during his trial and criticized the government for poorly supplying his army. Paris encouraged French troops to loot won territories while Dumouriez wanted Belgians to join the revolution.

In March 1793, Dumouriez turned over to the enemy French officials coming to investigate him. He then tried to incite his army to overthrow the revolutionary government. He failed and with Louis-Philippe, the Duc de Chartres, fled to Austria. Dumouriez later plotted with Louis XVIII to help both his and Louis-Philippe's reigns, but Louis XVIII never gave

Dumauriez the marshal's baton he craved. Settling in England in 1804, Dumouriez advised the British on Napoleon's defeat. Like many others, Dumauriez teemed with inconsistencies and died in England in 1823.

Lafayette in prison suddenly became gravely ill from lack of fresh air. La Tour-Maubourg was forbidden to see him. The illness abated and Lafayette slowly recovered. The Prussian king, hoping to take advantage of his weakness, offered to ease his imprisonment if he would join with Prussia and Austria. Lafayette refused to betray his country and his confinement was increased. The prisoners where herded into another cart and moved to Magdeburg on the Elbe River in Germany. On their slow sojourn east through enemy territories, the prisoners everywhere met citizens' admiration and even love for the hero of liberty whose story was well-known. Lives were at risk if guards saw anyone being friendly with him.

Lafayette managed to write from Magdeburg to American Ambassador Charles Pinckney in London on July 4, 1793:

> *My dear Sir,*
>
> *Whilst on this anniversary my American fellow citizens are having their joy, I join in a solitary bumper [wine toast] with the happy remembrances, the patriotic wishes which are crowding upon us — encircled as I am with ditches, ramparts, guards, double entries and palilladors [jailers], shut up in a quadruple gated, barred, chained, locked, grated, narrow, moisty, subterraneous dungeon and doomed to the moral and bodily hardships which revengeful tyranny is heaping on me... Owing to your kind interference, my dear Sir, the crowned gaolers have consented after eight months to let me know that my wife and children were alive — be pleased to acquaint them that my health is tolerably good — my affectionate respects to my venerated General and paternal friend — remember me to our friends in America...*

During the height of the Terror the prisoners were denied any information about their loved ones. They were kept for a year in a damp subterranean dungeon worse than their cells at Wezel. But they were together and sometimes allowed to walk the prison's bastions. In addition, Maubourg's sister, Madame Maisonneuve, arrived to voluntarily share her brother's fate. It was a good omen.

The fitful king ordered the prisoners moved to Glatz, a Silesian town on the Neisse River southwest of Breslau. Glatz had been a Prussian province since Frederick seized it in 1742. The town was spiked with a hilltop citadel and fortresses. Maubourg and Pusy accompanied Lafayette but, dangerously ill, Alexandre Lameth could not be moved. After many pleas, his mother won permission for him to remain in Magdeburg. The other allies invading France saw no reason to detain him.

The king moved the prisoners again, this time to Neisse, another Silesian city Frederick had captured. Later, when the Prussians and French declared peace, Frederick William freed Lameth. This self-serving and erratic king broke his agreement with Austria's exasperated Leopold. But after Louis XVI's execution, Frederick William lost interest in defeating France. Profligate expenditures kept him from wanting to pay an army.

THIRTY-EIGHT: THE HELL OF PRISON

Instead of freeing Lafayette and his friends as he should have, the king turned them over to Austria. The Austrians stripped them of what the Prussians had not taken: their watches and shoe buckles — and two of Lafayette's books because the word freedom appeared often in them. "Are they contraband?" he quipped. But humor was in short supply. The captives soon found themselves at their final dungeon, the dreaded prison of Olmütz, a town in remote Moravia. Because of Lafayette's imprisonment, the prison would become infamous in the West. Austria controlled the region and in 1840 absorbed it into its empire.[1]

Jesuits, invited to re-establish Catholicism there in 1566, built a monastery with twelve-foot-thick walls. It became a prison four years before the Frenchmen arrived. Their stone cells had a two-foot-square window opening set with iron bars. Rainwater turned an outside trench into a stinking marsh. Each cell, eight or ten paces deep, six or eight paces wide, had two doors, one of iron, one of wood, each more than a foot thick with bolts, bars and double padlocks. Walls kept breezes away during the almost intolerable summers while winter cold easily entered prisoners' bones. Four guards stood at the doors by day. At night, eight more, carrying loaded muskets with orders to kill, manned the outer walls. They watched the prisoners constantly, and would have received a hundred lashes if they spoke, sang or whistled to captives.

The warden and twenty-five others occupied a cellar guardroom. A corporal and four soldiers kept watch alternately and spied on the prisoners through ceiling grates. When an inspector entered a cell, four guards stood at both sides of the doors. A guard with drawn sword remained outside as an officer with drawn sword entered. Guards crossed bayonets as the inspector closely searched for weapons

Each captive was told he would never see anything but his cell walls or hear a voice. The men's door numbers — 2, 4, 6 — replaced their names. Cutlery and anything that could kill were forbidden. When the jailer brought the terrible food twice a day, guards examined it, crushing the bread while looking for messages. The captives, military men, lived on slops but survived on hope of eventual release.

Each cell had a bed of rotten straw filled with vermin, a broken chair and a worm-eaten table. Rain poured through air holes, down the walls and the men often awoke soaked to the skin. A dim lamp could be lit at night but dark weather meant gloom all day. The guards sneered at Lafayette's loyal servants sharing his fate but occasionally let them visit him. Always held at his cell doors, they had to abide by the routine.

Among Lafayette's many admirers who wondered where he was held was Justus-Erich Bollmann, twenty-three, native of Hoya, a town in lower Saxony. Eldest son of a vinegar manufacturer, Bollmann had just received his medical degree from Gottingen University but loved adventure more than medicine. Angered by Lafayette's disappearance, Bollmann had few illusions about the French Revolution, having witnessed the Swiss Guards' massacre in Paris. That year Bollmann, who spoke German, French and English, helped the Comte de Narbonne defect to London and join his lover, De Staël.[2]

She, with other émigrés and several Americans, including the Pinckneys and Alexander Hamilton's sister-in-law Angelica Schuyler Church, married to a Parliament member, were thrilled by Bollmann's success with Narbonne and hired him to find Lafayette. Bollmann failed to gain the general's release in Berlin in early 1794. He bought a fine carriage, crossed the Prussian and Austrian borders without suspicion, finally reaching Olmütz in Austrian-held Moravia. Bollmann did not keep a journal but Lafayette wrote him later, recalling the experience.[3]

At Olmütz's Golden Swan Hotel, Bollmann learned the prison had just increased security for important prisoners. They entered near midnight on May 18, 1794 and were given numbers to conceal their identities. Bollmann was sure it was Lafayette — State Prisoner No. 2 — and his comrades. The hotelier, however, reported the young man's questions to the police. But Bollmann's banker, a Lafayette admirer, told them Bollmann was a Hanoverian, a British subject and that the banker had done business with Bollmann's father who had sent his son to settle accounts. The police accepted that Bollmann's questions came from curiosity.

Bollmann then went to Vienna where he stayed at a hotel with Americans. After some weeks Bollmann took Francis Kinloch Huger, a medical student, into his confidence. In a rare coincidence, Huger's late father had welcomed Lafayette and other officers to his plantation in 1777. Huger grew up following Lafayette's life in print and vowed to help. "I saw an opportunity," he wrote, "to restore liberty to the man who at my own age had risked everything for me."

Bollmann, returning to Olmütz with Huger, hired a laborer, Johann Schramowsky, to deliver messages to Lafayette, but he was found inadequate to help in the escape. Bollmann purchased horses and he and Huger visited hot springs in Bohemia and Silesia. Huger posed as an English lord looking with his doctor for a suitable spa. They studied Moravia's borders, the prison road and renewed their travel permits. On November 5, 1794, they took rooms at the Golden Swan, noting espionage had increased because of the foreign prisoners.

Bollmann explained to the curious that Huger was his well-to-do patient and they moved about unquestioned. His banker introduced Bollmann to Karl Haberlein, a Bohemian staff surgeon at the hospital next door. Bollmann joined Haberlein on his prison rounds, played up to him while deploring the prisoners' condition, and the surgeon told him their names. Unknowingly, Haberlein passed books and messages to Lafayette, including the escape plans. Notes written in lemon juice on page margins could be read faintly when warmed by a lamp or sunlight. Haberlein handed similar books to Maubourg and Puzy.

For his rescue, Lafayette was to fein illness. Haberlein with prison commandant General Franz Anton Arco visited Lafayette next day. Haberlein wrote to Vienna explaining why Lafayette's health needed excursions in an open carriage. This was granted, provided an armed guard would prevent his escape. Lafayette enjoyed the rides several times a week in late afternoon. Excitement rose as the rides continued for three weeks.

Bollmann and Huger on two horses planned to reach the carriage and carry Lafayette away. "We are in a phaeton," Lafayette wrote in a margin, "No one with me but the corporal who, by the way, is afflicted with a rupture — and a clumsy driver. Have a trusty man with you. Stop the driver. I [will] frighten the little cowardly corporal with his own sword." If the rescuers had a third horse, he wrote, "I will not have the least difficulty to jump on..."[4]

There was no backup plan and the rescuers and Lafayette had never seen each other. They decided as Lafayette neared Bollmann, the general wearing a round hat would touch his forehead with a white handkerchief as identification. The carriage was identified with a guard walking behind. The rescuers had previously sent a hired man to the town of Hof, twenty-five miles from the prison and three miles inside Bavaria, where they had a carriage with two strong horses waiting. The rescuers would leave their mounts there, join Lafayette in the carriage and head west to Saxony and safety.

On Saturday, November 8, the two rescuers checked out of the hotel. They rejected a third horse to avoid attention. Huger's horse could carry two riders. Lafayette would ride alone on Bollmann's horse and the rescuers would follow on Huger's mount. But having Huger and Lafayette follow Bollmann would have made more sense. The young men knew the roads but Lafayette did not. The prison's ramparts had views of roads for three miles. But about a mile beyond the planned carriage stop was an intersection with trees to screen them.

The young men did not see the carriage at first but, on heading to Olmütz, they spied it. Lafayette was in a blue coat, wore a round black hat and was seated with the corporal. The driver was in front, the guard behind. The young men trotted past, then turned to follow the carriage. It halted; so did they. Lafayette and the corporal got out, strolled into a field and stopped to talk. Bollmann and Huger galloped up as Lafayette pulled on the corporal's sword. But instead of yielding, the corporal grabbed the blade, blood rushing from his cut hands, and shouted for help. Peasants in nearby fields looked up but, like the driver, just watched the struggle. But the rear guardsman ran shouting and waving to sentinels on the ramparts.

Lafayette, struggling to take the sword, misjudged the corporal's strength. Bollmann dismounted, throwing the reins to Huger. But Bollmann's horse, frightened by the clamor, ran off. Now dismounted, Huger watched helplessly. As Bollmann seized the corporal's sword, he grabbed Lafayette's cravat. The general cried, "He is strangling me!" Huger, passing an arm through his horse's bridle, pointed a pistol at the corporal who refused to release Lafayette. Jamming the pistol in his coat, Huger pulled the corporal's bloody hands off the general's throat. Lafayette fell as Huger pinned the corporal down, gagging him with a handkerchief. Bollmann helped Lafayette stand. Huger handed Lafayette his horse's reins and a money packet, shouting, "Get to Hof!" Lafayette mounted, started off but, not wanting to abandon his saviors, halted. Huger waved him on, repeating, "Get to Hof!" Lafayette, not knowing Hof, sped off. The men freed the feisty corporal who tried to run after Lafayette galloping away.

A peasant boy helped Huger recover Bollmann's horse and Bollmann climbed behind Huger. They could still see Lafayette ahead. Their horse, untrained for two riders, threw Bollmann. He remounted with the boy's help, but the horse reared again, throwing both men. Huger insisted Bollmann ride on alone. Huger would run and walk, hoping to reach freedom in Silesia. Bollmann rode away. Huger, an excellent runner, sped along until a peasant on horseback and three farmers, alerted by the prison alarm, seized him. They took him to the prison and Arco, who was aware of the significance of his famous prisoner's escape. He repeatedly questioned Huger, who felt justified in telling the truth.

"I did not think of harming anyone," he said, "I was assured it was the purpose of Monsieur Lafayette to cross immediately to America and not to mix himself any more in the affairs of the Empire." Arco, his future in the balance, wrote of Huger in his report: "The culprit was turned over to the military authorities for the ordinary Olmütz court, put in irons, as a criminal, and held in the strictest custody." Heavy rings were clamped on Huger's wrist and ankle and he was chained to the wall above his bed, a rough wooden bench.[5]

Lafayette, now in unfamiliar country, knew little German. Bollmann had not given him a map. Lafayette thought Huger had cried, "Get off," meaning get going.[6] At a fork, Lafayette turned in the direction opposite to the waiting carriage. Reaching Sternberg, a village fifteen miles away, on an exhausted horse, he offered 2,000 crowns for a fresh one. His accent, bloody clothes and the money raised suspicion. Before the mayor, Lafayette remained calm and told a believable story but when recognized, he denied his identity. When the mayor ordered him to Olmütz to make certain, Lafayette gave his name. Double-locked in his old cell, he was denied books and exercise and kept in isolation for a year as his health declined seriously.

Bollmann meanwhile searched for Lafayette in Hof and Silesia. His questions brought his arrest and he was remanded to Olmütz during Huger's civil court examination. Since Huger did not speak German, a lyceum professor, Christoph von Passy, tutor to the family of Moldavian Count Nepomuk von Mitrovsky, was Huger's interpreter.[7] Both prisoners were questioned separately for three months. The conclusion was they were not in an Austrian plot and worked only to free Lafayette. Charges were reduced to forcing a military post. This allowed them some freedom and better food, but questioning continued.

Huger smuggled out letters to Thomas Pinckney. The former governor of South Carolina, now ambassador to Great Britain, had known Lafayette in America. Huger's letter urged that his mother be informed about him, ending with, "Don't forget us."[8] Washington and other Americans were grief-stricken by Lafayette's capture. The United States government and members of the opposition in Parliament — Fitzpatrick, Fox, Sheridan, Wilberforce, Bedford and others — loudly defended the prisoners.[9] Prime Minister William Pitt, however, who could have set the prisoner free with a word because of alliances with Prussia and Austria, remained silent. The reason, his friends believed, was Lafayette's fighting Britain in the American Revolution. Huger's family asked Washington to intervene but the United States had no diplomatic ties with Austria. Huger's translator, Passy, talked so movingly to Mitrowsky of the two men that he provided unlimited funds to help them, including bribing judges.[10]

Bollmann and Huger were found guilty but their sentences, after time served, were a month's labor in irons. With more bribes, the judges reduced their sentences to two weeks and banishment from Austria. The two were imprisoned a total of eight months. Passy introduced them to Mitrowsky and helped them find freedom. When the crown's lawyers reported their findings to Vienna, the Olmütz court received an order denouncing the judges and demanding a new trial. Arco received a written reprimand but soon died of personally-felt disgrace. Haberlein, whom witnesses said knew nothing of the plot, nevertheless spent weeks in irons and later resurfaced as a surgeon general in Budapest, a mild demotion. The corporal was demoted and died in poverty. Hailed in London for their rescue attempt, Bollmann and Huger sailed together to the United States in 1796.[11]

Returning to South Carolina, Huger wed Ambassador Pinckney's daughter and became a rice planter like his father.[12] A character in the popular play, *Lafayette, or the Castle of Olmütz,* was based on Huger. Was he its hero? "Oh, no, indeed," he said. "Heroes are always married at the end of the play and I am not so fortunate. I am represented, however, as desperately in love with the daughter of the governor of the castle, and I am left in the same unhappy situation at the end of the play."[13]

Bollmann also gave up medicine for an adventurous life in the years ahead.

THIRTY-NINE: DESPAIR AND SALVATION

In prison Lafayette worried about his wife and children but was denied mail. He learned of Louis XVI's decapitation and the Terror but knew nothing of family members. Adrienne, at first forcefully held in Chavaniac and the nearby town of Brioude, was later imprisoned in Paris. The revolutionary government confiscated Lafayette and De Noailles properties.

At Washington's request, Adrienne sent him Georges, fifteen. The president had his godson stay at Harvard for six months to prevent a threat to American neutrality or international incident. As soon as Washington left the presidency, he welcomed his namesake to Mount Vernon where Georges slept in the mansion's garret. Enjoying Washington's other wards, he returned to Europe almost four years later at nineteen.

In Paris, James Monroe and his wife Elizabeth drove in their state carriage to Adrienne, who, an aristocrat, faced certain decapitation. The Monroes gave her food and let officials know her safety mattered to the United States. Adrienne, jailed for sixteen months in various Paris prisons, was released on January 22, 1795 — six months after her mother, sister and grandmother were decapitated and their bodies thrown into unmarked pits.

Using the little used family name Motier, Adrienne traveled with her daughters on American passports Monroe had given them to Dunkirk and by ship to Hamburg, reaching the Austrian capital in seven days. "I am on my way to you. That hope alone gave me a renewed sense of life when I was almost at the foot of the scaffold," she wrote her husband in invisible ink in a letter hidden in the cover of a volume of Buffon's *Histoire Naturelle.* Pulling aristocratic strings in Vienna, she obtained an audience with young Francis II, son of Leopold II. She found him "nothing but a petty crowned head; neither good nor bad" but soon thought otherwise.

Francis gave Adrienne a glowing picture of Lafayette's health, his care and said if she had problems to write to him personally. She believed him, later writing Mme. De Tessé after learning the truth she had seen everything "through rose-colored spectacles." Francis permitted the women to live in the prison. But, claiming he was unable to free Lafayette, the emperor warned if they left Olmütz they could not return. Adrienne knew Britain and Prussia were also partners in Lafayette's incarceration, another reason Pitt the Younger had done nothing for him who helped end British America.

Emaciated and weak from solitary confinement, Lafayette was overwhelmed with joy when Adrienne and teenagers Anastasie and Virginie threw themselves into his arms on October 15, 1795. They were shocked to see how much older than thirty-eight he looked. His lungs, never strong, were much worse. His hair had vanished on top and his clothes were rags. Adrienne, appalled, had also aged. Her face was lined under graying hair. That evening, she painfully told him of their loved ones' executions — aged family members *Maréchal* de Mouchy and his wife, Adrienne's mother, Henriette, her older sister, Vicomtesse Louise de Noailles (Louis's wife) and her infirm grandmother *Maréschale* Catherine de Cosse-Brissac. He wept with her.

The doomed were taken to La Conciergie. Their crime was being aristocrats. Some of their judges were former galley slaves. Placed in tumbrels with arms tied behind, they were driven slowly to the guillotine. The reek of blood had forced the scaffold from Place de la Concorde to Place de La Bastille, then eastward to Place du Trône. The women's priest, following on foot, gave them absolution from a street corner. The tottering grandmother, in mourning for her husband, climbed the scaffold first. Henriette followed. Their hats were torn off but they remained calm in their faith as the blade fell in dechristianized France. Louise, youthful in white, lowered her head in the yoke. A swift downward rumble and her blood gushed over the platform. Adrienne did not know where their bodies were but vowed to find them.

Lafayette in prison had heard of the Terror but knew of none who had perished. The king, the queen, Madame Ēlisabeth and Orléans had been executed. Santerre had ordered the drummers to drown out Louis XVI's words as he swore his innocence, although treasonously seeking invasion. Choosing for the new regime the sycophantic name "Philippe Ēgalité," Orléans voted for his cousin's death and could not save himself. Charlotte Corday, a young Girondist, fatally stabbed scrofulous Marat in his tub and was swiftly guillotined.

Also Bailly, Lavoisier and so many more were executed. Girondists, Hébertists and Dantonists went to premature deaths. Robespierre and twenty-one of his followers were guillotined the same day, ending the Reign of Terror. It claimed 41,000 lives in all classes. Some 250,000 insurgents and about 30,000 republicans perished in the scorched-earth destruction of Vendée, the diehard loyalist region in coastal France. Lafayette cursed the villains who had debased the revolution and swore to maintain his principles. Adrienne made his life seem better, but her health, weakened in prisons, grew worse. Her discolored limbs swelled with fluid and itching skin plagued her.

In prison, Lafayette's wife and daughters met him at evening under guard and later were locked in separate cells to sleep on vermin-filled straw. Guards took their three silver forks, forcing them to eat with their fingers. With her health growing worse, Adrienne asked to attend mass in prison. Told she could go but was forbidden to return to her cell, she chose to remain. She was allowed to send unsealed letters to her youngest sister, Pauline, married to the *Avergnat* Marquis de Montagu, and to the banker who forwarded money from an account to pay their prison keep, but she was forbidden to write to Georges. Bribing guards, she smuggled out letters describing their privations, published widely in newspapers. Learning his fate, public opinion again favored Lafayette.

Washington wrote a private letter to the emperor describing his adoptive son's virtues and asking that he be allowed to come to the United States.

His request was ignored. Lafayette's daughters, adapting to prison, remained cheerful. But Anastasie experienced a chronic cough from the foul damp air while Virginie developed a stoop she later overcame. To stay focused, Adrienne wrote her mother's biography with ink and toothpick in the margins of her volume of Buffon's *Histoire Naturelle*.[1]

FORTY: TAKING ON BONAPARTE

In Paris, the republic's upper house, 250 monarchic members, chose the Directory (*Directoire*), five men who weakly ran France from 1795 to 1799. The Lafayettes with each French victory over invaders found their guards softening from fear. Prussia, Spain and the Netherlands withdrew from the war. Signing the Treaty of Campo Formio of 1797, Bonaparte established his victory in Italy and the collapse of the First Coalition of foreign enemies. The treaty, ending the first phase of the French Revolutionary wars, forced Austria to cede Lombardy and Austrian Netherlands (Belgium) to France in exchange for Venice. Bonaparte also insisted on a clause freeing Lafayette, still considered a traitor under French law.

Because of French decrees against émigrés, Lafayette was not permitted to return. After lengthy negotiation, Emperor Francis agreed to let the Lafayettes go to the United States, provided they did not re-enter an Austrian state, return to France or complain of their prison treatment. Expecting to return one day to France, the Lafayettes agreed. Leaving prison on September 17, 1797, sickly shades of themselves, the Lafayettes, Maubourg, Puzy and their three servants received thunderous cheers traveling through Dresden, Leipzig and Halle, Germany. They reached Hamburg on October 5.

Lafayette wore his cockade to prove he was not an émigré. In Utrecht, the Netherlands, after discussing with Adrienne how effusive he should be, Lafayette wrote to Napoleon Bonaparte, whom he distrusted. Reading his first newspaper after prison, Lafayette was disturbed by the coup d'etat of 18 Fructidor (September 4, 1797). Deputies favoring the constitution were purged and elections cancelled in forty-nine departments. Officers were expelled or jailed and many journalists were deported. Barbé-Marbois and other leaders were exiled to French Guiana. So Lafayette wrote:

Citizen General,

The prisoners of Olmütz, happy to owe their deliverance to your irresistible arms, rejoiced during their captivity in the thought that their liberty and their life were associated with the Republic's triumphs and your personal glory.

Lafayette added his family was "even more attached because of the service you have done the cause of liberty and our fatherland." The choppy note displayed Lafayette's post-prison stress and contained a barb aimed at the coup. The Directory confiscated what remained of his property in Brittany.

After meeting with the former American consul in Hamburg, the family decided Adrienne's health was too poor for her to sail to the United States. And the Netherlands, perhaps still not a haven, might be caught in hostilities. The Lafayettes joined Comtesse, now Madame, de Tessé, Adrienne's aunt, who welcomed them to her estate in Wittmoldt on Lake Ploën in Danish Holstein. There they happily reunited with Adrienne's sister, Pauline de Montagu, who although loving them, did not share their republicanism. Lafayette liked the region and its liberty-loving citizens. After five weeks, he rented the Chateau of Lemkühlen, an hour and a half away, where he ecstatically welcomed Georges back from Mount Vernon. Lafayette received loans from American friends and others, but the family returned to Wittmoldt to save money.

They were overjoyed when Anastasie, their eldest child, married Charles de Latour-Maubourg, Victor's younger brother, at Wittmoldt. The couple would have twin girls but only the elder, Celestine, survived. Ten days later, Pauline gave birth to a daughter. Visitors included Simiane, Lafayette and Tessé's friend, who was now the companion of a

Jacobin, and Théodore Lameth with his aides-de-camp. Pauline wrote that Lafayette's mind was still in the days of the *Declaration of the Rights of Man* and early revolution. He saw later events, she wrote, as a great misfortune but no more discouraging to him than how sailors learn of past shipwrecks. She found him without rancor or hatred for the past and noted he had not changed his opinions.[1]

With return of his health, Lafayette resumed correspondence. He wrote the Directory urging amnesty for officers he had commanded. With Verginie, Adrienne, seriously ill from Olmütz, returned to France since she was not a proscribed person. She delivered Lafayette's letter to a director, Larevellière-Lepeaux, in Paris without effect. After visiting Aunt Charlotte in Chavaniac, she rejoined her family in Vienen, near Utrecht. Georges Lafayette, a passionate young militarist, enlisted in the Dutch Army in 1799. Although money was scarce and the Duchesse d'Ayen's estate was not yet distributed, fifteen or more people often joined their table as the Lafayettes lived in genteel privation in a free country. The threat of war arose: Britain and Russia, opposing French and Dutch Republics and Napoleon's moves on Egypt and Syria, invaded northern Holland. Fearful, Adrienne returned to Paris to speed family settlements. Lafayette decided to write a book comparing national economies and asked her to find a publisher. Exhausted from imploring bureaus to return their lands, she insisted he should find one himself. He did not write the book but dabbled with his memoirs. The threat to peace in the Netherlands ended when the Duke of York surrendered to the French on October 18, 1799.

Adrienne had informed Emmanuel Sieyès, member of the ineffectual and unpopular Directory, that should war come to the Netherlands, Lafayette would seek French asylum. Sieyès replied it would be better if he went to Prussia, now neutral. She retorted, Lafayette, formerly imprisoned in Prussia, would rather be jailed in his own country where he had a chance at a better future. Back in 1789, Sieyès' liberal essay had been a revolutionary manifesto. But on November 9, 1799 (18 Brumaire in the revolutionary calendar), Sieyès working with Bonaparte, began a coup overturning the Directory and bringing the Corsican to power. Lafayette while in Vienen approved of Bonaparte's Egyptian campaign since it spread French influence. But Bonaparte, twenty-nine, returning hurriedly from his abortive Syrian effort, ordered police to disperse the upper Chamber of Ancients with remaining royalists and seized supreme power as first consul of France.

Adrienne had a positive audience with Bonaparte. She thanked him for their release and asked that Lafayette be allowed to return home. This was not a favor, she reasoned — she knew Lafayette was too proud to ask for himself — but an action "with no more authorization than the liberal intentions which were then being proclaimed" in the government. She urged Lafayette to follow up with a note and he complied. She hoped there would be time for him to farm; she was ready for country life.

Receiving a passport through Monroe and reaching Paris, Lafayette immediately wrote Bonaparte and Sieyès that he had returned. The first consul, infuriated, saw Lafayette as a potential enemy leader or rallying point of opposition. He had Lafayette watched and repeatedly tried to win him over. Adrienne reclaimed her mother's Chateau de La Grange-Bléneau, a turreted and moated thirteenth-century castle amid 800 acres about forty miles southeast of Paris. After looking at nearby Chateau de Fontenay Trésigny, also inherited from Duchesse d'Ayen, the Lafayettes made La Grange their refuge, turning Fontenay over to Pauline.

Lithograph of La Grange's entrance by Deroy after Alvan Fisher landscape.
Courtesy Marquis de Lafayette Collection, Lafayette College.

La Grange was close enough to Paris for occasional visits but far enough away to avoid confrontation with a government they came to despise. With little agricultural knowledge but admiring Washington and Jefferson's abilities, Lafayette slowly became a gentleman farmer in the Brie countryside with the help of an overseer and neighbors. He developed a large vegetable garden to feed his growing family, brought in fruit trees, chickens and livestock. He bred merino sheep, producing the region's finest wool. He also razed the chateau's west wing, opening it to a park he filled with imported American trees and plants.

But mostly he kept to himself, resuming his omnivous reading, letter-writing and enjoying being a father and grandfather. In spring 1802, Georges married Emilie Destutt de Tracy, daughter of famed liberal philosopher and peer Antoine Destutt de Tracy. He had been a Constituent Assemblyman with Lafayette and, under him, a cavalry commander before he fled in 1792. Georges sired two sons and three daughters. Virginie wed Louis, Marquis de Lasteyrie du Saillant. A young army officer, Lasteyrie had been invited to visit the Lafayette and Tracy families at Chavaniac where elderly Aunt Charlotte retained all of her faculties, Virginie wrote. (Lasteyrie died in 1826 but established a continuing dynasty. In France descendants related to the general by marriage may add "Lafayette" to their family names.) The Lafayettes were happy to welcome James Monroe, in Paris negotiating the Louisiana Purchase, to La Grange in April 1803. Adrienne's embrace pleased the kind emissary; he had not seen her in nine years or the general in twenty. Adrienne asked whether the 10,500 acres Lafayette had been awarded as an American veteran could be converted into money. Monroe secured a low-interest loan from Baring Brothers Bank permitting the Lafayettes to pay off earlier debts, including 100,000 livres loaned from Gouverneur Morris in 1793. Adrienne wrote Morris she would pay him 53,000 livres. She cited a French law offering conversion rates favorable to the Lafayettes for debts acquired during revolutionary inflation Annoyed, Morris ended their friendship.[2]

Shortly after the United States purchased the Louisiana Territory in 1803, Lafayette received a letter from President Thomas Jefferson offering him the governorship. Citing family disabilities, particularly his ill wife, Lafayette turned it down. The next year, he must have been startled to learn his would-be rescuer Bollmann had been vice president Aaron Burr's second in his fatal duel with Alexander Hamilton. Bollmann gave the longtime antagonists the order to fire at each other on a dueling ground in Weehawkin Heights, New Jersey. There, Hamilton's eldest son Philip had similarly died three years earlier defending his father's honor. The latest event was the United States' most famous duel. Lafayette was much saddened by Hamilton's untimely death. Society shunned Burr but he escaped murder charges.

Gouverneur Morris gave Hamilton's eulogy and financial help to his large family. Burr hid in quiet New Hope, Pennsylvania, for a week to avoid capture. He resurfaced in 1807 when he was tried for conspiracy for attempting to join the Lousiana Territory with Mexico.[3] Bollmann, shortening his name to Bollman, was Burr's undercover agent in the alleged conspiracy. First embedded in Cincinnati's German community, Bollman later awaited Burr's orders in New Orleans. The stakes were large.

Spain, avoiding trouble with the United States over Mississippi River traffic and pressured by Bonaparte, had secretly given its Louisiana Territory to France in the Treaty of San Ildefonso in 1796. The unmapped region of 828,000 square miles stretched from the Gulf of Mexico to Canada and the Mississippi River to the Rockies. Bonaparte dreamed of linking France's island of Saint-Domingue with French farmers in Mississippi River towns by trading sugar, rum, rice and produce.

But Toussaint L'Ouverture, leading a black rebellion in Saint-Domingue, where yellow fever had already killed 15,000 French soldiers, forced Bonaparte's brother-in-law, General Leclerc, and 25,000 troops to quit the island. Jefferson, appalled by the rebellion but even more wary of France on America's western border, had indirectly offered Napoleon help with Saint-Domingue in 1801 but never gave any. "Those gilded Africans," as Bonaparte described the Haitians, ended slavery and established the world's first black republic in 1804, ending Bonaparte's interest.[4]

He then offered the Louisiana Territory to the United States for $15 million, or three cents an acre. The purchasing power of $15 million in 1803 was $276 million. Treasury secretary Albert Gallatin and Ambassador Monroe in Paris brokered the deal. Lafayette's friend

Barbé-Marbois, senator and former treasury director, represented France. Doubling itself, the United States bought the territory with government bonds accepted by Baring Brothers. Although at war with Britain, Bonaparte demanded the stable bank handle the sale. Paying Baring a huge commission, he cashed the bonds. Aaron Burr saw his chance.

Once a New Jersey patrician and hero under Arnold in Canada and at Valley Forge, Burr hated being an outcast. Despising Jefferson, he dreamed of creating a nation from Mexico, the Louisiana Territory and 350,000 acres in Louisiana he held near Mexican Texas. At his sensational Richmond trial in 1807, Burr was charged with raising an illegal army to seize Mexico from Spain. He allegedly planned to be a king, emperor or perhaps would give the region to the United States, since he could not persuade Americans living in the Louisiana Purchase area to leave the Union. He never declared what his plans were.

Jefferson wrote Lafayette that Bollman had "haughtily refused" federal immunity for his testimony against Burr, implying his own guilt. Bollman had also rejected Jefferson's earlier job offers, made because Bollman was the general's friend. Jefferson chided Lafayette:

"...Certainly had you been as I wished, at the head of the government of Orleans, Burr would never have given me one moment's uneasiness. His conspiracy has been one of the most flagitious of which history will ever furnish an example. He meant to separate the Western states from us, to add Mexico to them, place himself at their head, establish what he would deem an energetic [rule], & thus provide an example & an instrument for the subversion of our freedom. The man who could expect to [do] this with American materials must be a fit subject for Bedlam. The seriousness of the crime however demands more serious punishment yet; altho' there is not a man in the U.S. who doubts his guilt, such are the jealous provisions of our laws in favor of the accused against the accuser, that I question if he is convicted...

"I am sorry to tell you that Bollman was Burr's right hand man in all his guilty schemes. On being brought to prison here, he communicated to Mr. Madison & myself the whole of the plans, always however apologetically for Burr as far as they would bear. But his subsequent tergiversations have proved him conspicuously base. I gave him a pardon which covers him from everything but infamy. I was the more astonished at his engaging in this business from the peculiar motives he should have felt for fidelity. When I came into the government, I sought him out on account of the services he had rendered you, cherished him, offered him two different appointments of value, which, after keeping them long under consideration, he declined for commercial views, and would have given him anything for which he was fit. Be assured he is unworthy of ever occupying again the case of any honest man…"[5]

Jefferson, knowing Burr had tried to steal the presidency in 1800, wanted him convicted. But the jury, guided by Supreme Court chief justice John Marshall, Jefferson's distant cousin and political foe, found no evidence Burr had committed treason. He made no overt act and was not present at what the prosecution said was the embarkation point: Blennerhasset Island in the Ohio River near Marietta. There men in many longboats were to launch a conquest that never occurred. Seeking evidence, federal troops virtually destroyed Harman Blennerhasset's farm, forcing him to move to Louisiana. The only evidence was Burr's encrypted letter to his partner, General James Wilkinson, who in the American Revolution had passed along Thomas Conway's insubordinate phrasing.

Wilkinson had also sworn a secret allegiance to Spain in 1787, seeking to detach Kentucky, where he was a successful merchant, and Western settlements from the Union. He also yearned to seize Spain's Mexican provinces. A double traitor, Wilkinson with Spain's help had briefly controlled Kentucky's shipping to New Orleans. He hid his duplicities from Jefferson in Washington. When Lafayette declined Louisiana's governorship, Jefferson selected the army's commanding general for it: Wilkinson, who informed Jefferson of the conspiracy, saying Burr concocted it. At Jefferson's orders, Wilkinson declared martial law in New Orleans and sent soldiers up the Mississippi to capture and jail Burr and a few accomplices.

In Richmond's August heat, Burr's prosecutors proved nothing in his sensational trial and he was aquitted. But Burr, judged morally bankrupt, fled to Europe and lived off friends' handouts. Burr returned to New York in 1812 to learn his daughter Theodosia, wife of South Carolina Governor Joseph Alston, in sailing to greet him was lost at sea off Cape Hatteras. Grieving Burr resumed his law practice, wed and divorced a wealthy widow and lived on Staten Island until dying at eighty in 1836. After Richmond, Wilkinson faced several courts-martial and congressional investigations. He was removed from office for power abuses in New Orleans. Hiding his treachery, Wilkinson was returned to his New Orleans command in 1812 and promoted to major general. In the War of 1812, he seized Mobile from Spain but botched an invasion of Montreal, ending his career dishonorably.[6] Bollman, however, went on to further adventures.[7]

FORTY-ONE: GRAVES OF THE MARTYRS

At La Grange, Adrienne had a designer create for her husband a small Louis XVI-style library with a star-patterned parquet floor in a turret space next to his second floor bedroom. Here he gathered his favorite books on curving shelves. Mementos included framed copies of the *Declaration of Independence* and the *Declaration of the Rights of Man and Citizen*. From his window Lafayette called daily instructions through a horn to his farm manager who was for many years his former army secretary and servant at Olmütz, Félix Pontonnier, later tax collector of nearby Fontenay.

Lafayette's library at La Grange. Photograph, 1929.
Courtesy Marquis de Lafayette Collection, Lafayette College.

Lafayette invited many celebrities in politics and culture to La Grange where he entertained lavishly and criticized — laughing with his family — at journal accounts of Bonaparte's governmental changes and aggressions. Lafayette also followed rural politics in Courpalay, the closest town, and Rozay-en-Brie, where his kindness to workers and the poor became legendary. Georges discovered the blade of his father's congressional sword, buried during his absence, had rusted. In 1791 the National Guard had presented him with a sword with a blade forged from Bastille bolts. Since both weapons were equally "eloquent of liberty," he had the second blade attached to the first's gold hilt.

Adrienne and Pauline had searched for their dear ones' graves for some time. They found the site through a young lacemaker who had followed the wagons after seeing her father and brother guillotined. Fifty-five people a day went to the scaffold in June and July of 1794. Following public complaints about the gore and stench in Place de la Concorde, the guillotine was moved east to Place de la Bastille, then to Place du Trône, renamed "Throne Overturned" during the revolution.[1]

At night the corpses were hauled in bloody wagons to two large pits in confiscated land behind the nearby Convent of St. Michel de Picpus. Workmen removed victims' clothing for their use or resale. They covered the remains with lime as the pits awaited more bodies, eventually holding 1,306. The name Picpus, it is said, originated in the fifteenth century; monks may have lanced lesions resembling flea bites (*pique puces*), or may have worn puce cassocks.[2]

Since the martyrs were denied a burial ceremony, Adrienne, Pauline, Poix and others purchased plots near the site for their graves and built a convent chapel in 1803. It was agreed to unite the properties as the Picpus Cemetery in 1806. The convent's nuns reared girls and took in women boarders. With a sizable donation from Adrienne and others, the nuns made their daily prayers a perpetual service for the martyrs, their executioners and all victims of totalitarianism. Martyrs' names are listed behind the altar. Adrienne spent many hours praying and grieving in this somber chapel.[3]

As *Femme* (Wife) Lafayette, Adrienne had sat endless hours in government offices to regain family properties and won most back. She welcomed Lafayette's many illustrious visitors to La Grange and oversaw the family's needs and expenses. She also continued to suffer from rashes, eruptions, baldness, swollen and infected limbs. Her worried daughters first moved her to her Aunt Adrienne de Tessé's country house in Aulnay, Charente-Maritimes, then to her Paris townhouse. Adrienne's helpless doctor, Lobhines, called in Corvisart, Napoleon's physician. Lafayette was summoned from Chavaniac. Adrienne, given a medicine containing lead, was likely dying of it.[4]

Despite intense headaches, she fervently kept her faith and loved her husband to the end. The family gathered around her. Barely conscious on her last day, she said, "Tell Madame de Simiane I love her." And "Today I shall see my mother," she said sweetly as she overcame delirium. Lafayette kissed her and held her hand. Whispering to him, "*Je suis tout à vous* (I am all yours)," she passed away at forty-eight on Christmas Eve 1807.

Jefferson responded, one widower to another:

"...This...has been a sincere affliction to me. My knowledge of the extraordinary worth of our deceased friend, her amiable & excellent character, her value to yourself, her family & friends, and the void it would make at the house of La Grange, sufficiently appraise me of the immensity of this loss. But on this subject I will say no more, for experience in the same school has taught me that time & silence are the only medicines…"[5]

Now fifty, Lafayette had loved his wife in his special way and had prayed for her health. He closed her bedroom to everyone but would enter through a hidden door, spending special times there alone. A small portrait there shows a wan Adrienne. She wears a tall black toque covering her head and a black robe concealing her misery. Never remarrying, Lafayette always carried a note folded in four with his wife's last words in Anastasie's hand. He and Pauline buried Adrienne by the martyrs' wall. In 1821, Lafayette in succession shared all of his properties between his three children while retaining their usage and enjoying their profits. His will has not been found, being unnecessary.

In 1814, Adrienne de Tessé bequeathed to Lafayette her townhouse with courtyard, 8 Rue d'Anjou and around the corner from the Ēlysée Palace, Rue du Faubourg St. Honoré. There Lafayette had a first floor apartment, a German-born valet — former soldier Sebastien Wagner, called Bastien — a driver and carriage. Preferring simplicity, Lafayette did not dress the servants in livery. He opened Tuesday evenings to Americans and other visitors, invited or not, and took in stride government flunkies spying on them.

Having ignored the National Guard for years, Napoleon in 1813 called up 190,000 men to maintain domestic peace as his army retreated into France from allied attack. The emperor wore the Imperial Guard uniform and later favored it on Saint Helena. Paris surrendered in March 1814. The Senate voted the emperor out on April 3 and he abdicated three days later.

FORTY-TWO: NOT THE BEST OF WORLDS

Louis, Comte de Provence, had spent twenty years in exile orbiting Europe, Russia and Latvia. Artois had lived in London and Holyrood Castle in Edinborough. In Koblenz, Louis had a lavish émigré court of 150,000 nobles, clergy and commoners who had fled the guillotine; and he had built a standing army with his cousin, the Prince de Condé. In 1799, without issue, Louis forced his niece Marie-Thérèse, surviving child of Louis XVI and Marie Antoinette, to marry her cousin and his nephew: Louis Antoine, Duc d'Angoulême, Artois' eldest son, unadmired by his uncle but a potential king. The couple was not in love and remained childless. Louis XVIII had earlier tried to buy his way to the throne from Napoleon, who, though always needing cash, ignored him. Louis now drew satisfaction from the turning of tables.

On April 12, 1814, Artois, whom his brother Provence in exile had made lieutenant general in charge of police, entered Paris with the victorious allies and formed a secret force without telling his brother. Louis XVIII returned to the capitol in May with more allied troops and officers of the realm. He despised being reminded he came back "in the vanguard of the enemy." Arriving to much public acclaim in a coach drawn by six white horses, Louis nevertheless failed to persuade the allies to restore absolute rule. Accepting a constitutional monarchy, as Lafayette wished, the king reluctantly signed the Charter of 1814, establishing a two-house Parlement, 90,000-member electorate and religious freedom. The public received the Bourbons, Lafayette wrote, "with general goodwill." Although his desire to aid France by rejoining the National Guard was rebuffed, he found himself welcoming the Bourbons. "...Forgiving the wrongs they had done...I wished and hoped with all my heart that liberty might associate itself with the reign of Louis XVI's brother and daughter."[1]

Dressed in his Guards uniform, Lafayette resigned himself to pinning a white cockade to his hat, hoping it would somehow advance freedom, and attended Louis XVIII's first public audience. The king, pleasant on the surface, said the only way he and Artois could return to Paris in the most seemly costume for the occasion was to wear their Guards uniforms. Although gluttonous, Louis dressed with some style. Gentlemen's breeches over the next twenty years would evolve, with many variations, into trousers. Lafayette welcomed the more comfortable mode derived from working men.

The general, in conferring at the same audience with Prussian king Frederick William III, son of Lafayette's former captor, won swift freedom for his son-in-law, Maubourg, a war prisoner. Lafayette also met with Louis-Philippe, forty-one, who had succeeded Orléans, his guillotined father, in 1793. Tainted by being a colonel under the traitor Dumouriez, the new Duc d'Orléans favored restoration but he disliked Louis XVIII for his contempt of the Orléans branch of the royal family. Louis-Philippe while in exile had wondered Europe, fathered two illegitimate children and spent four years touring in the United States. Impressed with his understanding of the American political system, Lafayette called Louis-Philippe "the only Bourbon compatible with a real constitution."

At Germaine de Staël's apartment, Lafayette met Czar Alexander I, who was promoting a peace treaty with France. The severe Russian winter of 1812 had reduced Napoleon's army, the largest in Europe, from 422,000 men to 10,000. Lafayette liked the czar's liberal attitudes. Alexander warned him the Bourbons had not altered their beliefs but he saw Louis-Philippe as open to change. Lafayette asked the czar why he accepted Louis XVIII. Because, he replied, the French legislative committee in charge was ready to have him without conditions. Furious royalists and returned émigrés, back in power, attacked Lafayette, blaming him for causing the revolution. Stung by their claims, he retreated to La Grange.

But on March 1, 1815, Napoleon entered Cannes from Elba, mustering 1,000 eager soldiers. Brigades not purged from the Bourbon army defected to him. Suffering from gout, the king sent D'Orléans, his disliked cousin, and D'Angoulême to stop Napoleon without success. Louis quit the Tuileries on March 20. Napoleon returned that evening to command for his famed One Hundred Days. He who had established a civil rights code in 1804 — banning birth privileges, granting religious freedom and offering government jobs only to the most qualified — now promised to build liberty "on a constitution in conformity with the people's will and interest."

Joseph Bonaparte implored Lafayette, ever skeptical of Napoleon's motives, to join his brother. Lafayette wrote, "He again became the army's man, and even the revolution's man, to the misfortune of France."[2] Lafayette had remained quiet during the epoch of the man he despised, thinking Napoleon's time would be brief. But he lasted more than sixteen years, finally forcing Lafayette to take on a new role, but still one without followers.

He remained at La Grange. A plebiscite spottily approved the new constitition. Lafayette had abstained from voting but on May 10 the Department of *Seine et Marne* elected him a member of the Chamber of Deputies with fifty-six of seventy-nine votes, the first of four terms. He sat on the liberal or left side of the Chamber. Wounded at Tilsit, Prussia, while in Napoleon's army, Georges was elected deputy from Haute-Loire, Chavaniac's department, and sat beside his father. The conservative majority prevented Lafayette's becoming Chamber president but he was elected one of five vice presidents. Meeting in committee with the emperor, Lafayette found him "an old despot angered by the part his position forces him to play."[3]

En route to army command, Napoleon followed the National Guard out of Paris. The allies defeated Napoleon disastrously at Waterloo, Belgium, on June 18. France lost more than 25,000 troops. Near physical collapse, he rushed to Paris two days later, intent on restoring his power and dissolving Parlement. Rising in the Chamber, Lafayette then denounced him, calling on France to return to the displaced standards of liberty, equality and public order. He filed motions declaring the nation under threat and any attempt to dissolve the Chamber would be high treason. On June 22, Lafayette told the minister of state to inform Napoleon he had one hour to abdicate. When Lucian Bonaparte addressed the Chamber, urging the nation to follow his brother, Lafayette answered:

"It followed him to the sands of Egypt and in the deserts of Russia, onto fifty battlefields, in defeat as well as victory...and for having followed him we now must mourn the blood of three million Frenchmen... I only see one man standing between us and peace; we have done enough for him. Our duty is to save the fatherland." He was in the delegation that saw a calm and dignified Napoleon accept his fate. Lafayette said, "You may well believe that I did not put myself forward!" for that role. The emperor abdicated in favor of his three-year-old son, Napoleon II, whom he called the king of Rome. As Alexander I had advised, the Chamber did not consider the child's succession. His mother, Austrian Princess Marie Louise, hurried with him to Vienna. Called Franz, he died there at twenty-one of tuberculosis in Schönbrunn Palace.

The occupying allies entered Paris on July 6.[4] Two days later the provisional government welcomed Louis XVIII, who was waiting in Ghent, Belgium. Lafayette, as he had planned to do in 1792, urged Napoleon to find freedom in the United States. But Britain may have been his intention. Unable to breach a British naval blockade off coastal Rochefort, he surrendered in his green, red and white uniform and tall black hat on the frigate *H.M.S. Bellerophon*. The British secretly wished to avoid *habeas corpus* restrictions and an unpredictable trial. The furious former emperor was held on *Bellerophon* off Plymouth for months before being sent on the frigate *H.M.S. Northumberland* to life imprisonment on Saint Helena in the south Atlantic.[5]

The French court refused to let Lafayette lead the National Guard again but named him to a delegation to negotiate peace with the allies near Strasbourg.[6] But it was too early. The allies chose to occupy France and force her to pay reparations. In Paris, Lafayette remained in his apartment. "I should like to go to La Grange with my children," he wrote, "but I cannot bear the idea of doing the honors (saluting) to a German, English or Russian garrison. So I stay in my little room and cannot leave it without undergoing the most painful feelings." Prussians briefly occupied La Grange but did little damage.

FORTY-THREE: THE WHITE TERROR

Obese, devious and complex, Louis XVIII knew how to accept changes and remain a sovereign. He loved literature, the Enlightenment and even Voltaire. Numbering his reign, not from 1814 but from the death in prison of his nephew, the dauphin, nineteen years earlier, Louis XVIII tried to reverse the new charter that recognized citizens' rights. He switched moderate ministers for conservatives. Repressive conditions were far from what Lafayette wished — liberty under Louis seemed as lost as under Napoleon — but he had an advantage over the king.

Both knew that Lafayette, as National Guard commander, had had access to the hanged Marquis de Favras' secret memorandum proving that Louis XVIII, then Provence, had plotted to place Louis XVI under restraint, or have Provence replace him. A widower, Louis XVIII had a liaison, probably platonic, with the widow of the magistrate who first received the Favras report. She was called "Snuffbox." The king was said to sniff tobacco from her breasts. Louis had destroyed the report, but its knowledge gave Lafayette, a ready center for protests against Louis, the edge over an old enemy. Despising how Louis twisted the charter, Lafayette wrote Jefferson, "The sovereignty of the people is flatly denied."[1]

At La Grange, the family called Louis XVIII's action "royalist Jacobinism." Among visitors were Victor, third Duc de Broglie, a liberal Chamber member, and his wife. Victor's grandfather had been the royalists' would-be leader against the revolution. He had lost a son in America in 1782 and was elected to the Society of the Cincinnati. He was the father of Victor, son-in-law of the late Germaine de Staël. Victor found that Lafayette loved to entertain his large family and friends with bountiful dinners and wine.

"If he was to be loved," Broglie wrote, "M. de Lafayette had to be loved for himself alone, which, however, was easy since there was no advantage in being one of his real friends. He made no distinctions, excepting between those who repeated, and those who did not repeat, whatever he said himself. He was a prince surrounded by people who flattered him and robbed him. All that splendid fortune was frittered away through the hands of adventurers and spies." French historians De La Fuye and Babeau noted Broglie exaggerated some. Yet Lafayette gave his provisions to the poor in the 1817 farm crisis.[2] Another visitor was Dutch-born French romantic artist Ary Scheffer, who arrived with his political brothers. He painted several portraits of Lafayette, including one on his deathbed, looking asleep in a black skullcap. Scheffer donated a full-length portrait, Lafayette's favorite, to the U.S. House of Representatives.[3]

One of Louis XVIII's first acts was hiring architect Pierre Fontaine to design a lavish stone memorial dedicated to his brother, sister-in-law and other martyrs in a cemetery of the Madeleine Church. It had already had innumerable interments when Louis XVI and Marie Antoinette's headless bodies were dumped there in 1793. A nobleman had marked the spot and Louis XVIII had their scant remains removed to St. Denis. The Chapel of Forgiveness *(Chapelle d'Expiatoire)* rose somberly at the north end of Rue d'Anjou, a short walk from Lafayette's townhouse.

At the chapel one opens a door, climbs twelve steps, passes through another door and walks into a strange garden. Arched granite tomb fronts carved with winged hourglasses, symbols of time's passage, line both sides. They mark the burial site of 1,000 Swiss Guards slain at the Tuileries as well as Philippe Ēgalité, Charlotte Corday and Jean-Paul Marat. The eighteen tomb fronts recall Louis XVIII, who erected the memorial with state funds. At its south end, a Grecian temple has lifesize stone sculptures depicting angels attending the king and queen. A marble altar and an inlaid cross mark where the royals were interred. The chapel was completed two years after Louis XVIII's death in 1824.[4]

Engraving after Ary Scheffer's full-length portrait, *Lafayette*, 1824.
U.S. House of Representatives, Washington, D.C.
Courtesy Marquis de Lafayette Collection, Lafayette College.

Just as political reaction occurred when the Jacobins fell, the White Terror, named for the white Bourbon flag, was an ultra-conservative response in rural and southern France that shook France from July 1815 to September 1816. During this time, 80,000 Bonapartist officials were removed from power and some, including *Maréchals* Ney and Brune, were killed. (Victor de Broglie was the only peer to vote against Ney's execution; Brune was savagely murdered.) The terror increased as the king set policy for elected deputies from differing political parties. With Artois' help, Louis XVIII threw out moderates for a totally reactionary ministry. New laws helped increase the influence of the wealthy and curbed civil liberties, including press freedom. Under the law, candidates could run in other than their home departments. The king was infuriated with Lafayette's 1818 re-election. It was from the Sarthe Department west of Paris, where he won 569 votes of 1,055.

Lafayette spoke freely on many subjects in the Chamber of Deputies. For one liberal cause, he said, "I shall ask for the abolition of the death penalty until I have the infallibility of human judgment demonstrated to me." His Parisian salon saw meetings on improving press freedom and many other issues. He was a witness in one of several trials of men charged with conspiracy against the safety of the state. The situation worsened with the Duc de Berry's assassination in 1820: Artois' second son, an army officer of forty-two, was stabbed outside the Paris Opera by a saddler, Louvel. He said his chief reading matter was *The Declaration of the Rights of Man*, bringing the ultras' stranglehold on government and press freedom. Students in Grenoble also attacked Artois' elder son, D'Angoulême. Lafayette's militancy against suppressions of freedom greatly increased the warlike nature of those years.[5] Even with his secret Favras advantage over the king, Lafayette was at risk in a virulent time, yet his contempt for danger remained strong.

He enjoyed fomenting opposition. As an elderly advisor and supporter, Lafayette was at the core of the Carbonari (in French, *Charbonnerie*): young liberal and anti-clerical Italians and Frenchmen who wanted an Italian to replace Joachim Murat. He was the brilliant general and brother-in-law of Napoleon, who made him king of Naples and Sicily. After first putting his easy-going brother, Joseph, on that throne, Napoleon forced him to become king of Spain in 1808. Joseph, a former lawyer in a foreign environment, spoke little Spanish and, as José I, was called *Pepe Botella,* Joe Bottle, for tippling. He abolished the Inquisition but he could not control Spain amid French battles for supremacy and guerrilla counterattacks. Joseph wished to return to Naples, but Napoleon, seeing this as weakness, waged and lost the Iberian Peninsular War to Spain, Portugal and Britain. Defeated at the Battle of Vittoria, Joseph abdicated. He and Napoleon's army returned to France in 1813. (Joseph hid and later retrieved, with the help of his great Philadephia friend Stephen Girard, the Spanish crown jewels he had hidden in Switzerland.) Austrians, controlling Italy, wanted Murat gone and defeated him in battle. Losing a final attempt to regain the throne, he bravely met a firing squad in 1815.

Like Freemasons with stone-cutters, Carbonari patterned their secret society on a trade, charcoal-burning, and dotted Europe with cells. Masons could join them as masters; others served a brief apprenticeship. Lafayette found common cause with them and the Bonapartists, disgruntled with Louis XVIII's repressions. Excited by Lafayette's old libertarianism and financial support, Carbonari interrupted government meetings with loud demonstrations.

Successful banker Jacques Laffitte, liberal deputy and Charbonnarist, told Lafayette, who constantly reasserted his unchanging views: "You are a statue in search of a pedestal. It would not much matter to you if it were on a scaffold." Lafayette's answered, "Perhaps." But later, at sixty-four, he reflected, "I have lived a long time. It seems to me I should end my career worthily, even if on the scaffold, a martyr for liberty."

In the Manuel Affair of 1823, rightists expelled a deputy for his speech proclaiming revolutionary France's right to forcefully defend itself. Despite being banished, he continued to sit surrounded by leftist delegates. When the National Guard came to remove Manuel, Lafayette shouted, "What, the National Guard used to carry out such an order? This dishonors them!" The guardsmen withdrew.[6] Former Bonapartist officers, meeting in the *Bazar Français*, a store on Rue Cadet near the Opera, planned attacks in Paris and elsewhere to topple the government. But talks collapsed over whom would replace the king. Lafayette was nearly compromised.

Invited to join a conspiracy in the Alsatian city of Belfort, he chose not to go perhaps because of the distance or intuition. There were arrests but he avoided incrimination. His Chamber speeches against Louis XVIII helped strengthen military and liberal resistance. Deputies loudly criticized Lafayette's Carbonarist activities but his friend Victor de Broglie deflected these accusations.

The general was outspoken and closer to former Bonapartist enemies. He boldly offered 70,000 francs to the head of Bicêtre Prison to let Carbonarist prisoners escape. Police entered just as Lafayette's agent was about to give 10,000 francs as a first payment. Lafayette, although out the money, was not found to be the briber for a long time.[7] In the end, the Carbonari accomplished little beyond stimulating Italy's later unification. But from these meetings, Lafayette hired a young colonel whom the army had cashiered for such activity.

Lafayette knew his political expenditures, a large family and visitors ("Spongers," Broglie called them) had drained his fortune. Louis XVIII's henchmen probably engineered his 1824 Chamber defeat: 152 votes to the Bourbon candidate's 184. But fortune was calling again from across the ocean.

PART FOUR: THE NATION'S GUEST

FORTY-FOUR: TOUR OF TRIUMPH

No one could have known the impact Lafayette's visit to the United States would have forty years after its revolution. By 1824, the nation of twenty-four states had lost the euphoria of independence. The federal government was adolescent and citizens mostly identified themselves with their states. Americans were interested in getting ahead, through small industry, commerce and continental exploitation, not the country's international significance. Educational standards were low and political corruption common. Travel was by horseback, carriages and wagons over rutted mud and plank roads.

Americans stayed on farms, tended urban vegetable gardens and traveled little. Money was scarce. Days were filled with hard labor at home while new factories grew without safety standards. Child labor flourished. Railroads did not exist. Merchants and immigrants moving inland depended on river and canal transportation while wooden sailing ships carried American commerce around the world. Canals, supported by rivers, lakes and portages, were the era's greatest improvement: men shoveled trenches four feet deep and mules hauled away earth and stone.

Canals swiftly turned hamlets into trade centers. Because of their hard lives, people aged rapidly. Anyone at seventy was thought to be quite elderly. Without mass amusements, there was time to listen to and prepare long orations. The industrial revolution was welcomed as a social improvement, but with it time became as important as labor and materials.

At La Grange days after losing the election, Lafayette opened a second letter dated February 24, 1824 from President James Monroe inviting him with the consent of Congress to visit the United States as the nation's guest.

Lafayette had put aside an earlier letter from Monroe until he realized the journey could coincide with laying the cornerstone of the Bunker Hill Monument. This aspect of the trip would be internationally significant and, for the Masons, the event of the century. The tour would have a profound effect on Lafayette's life and welfare. Although thrilled by the invitation, he rejected having a warship come for him, as Monroe offered, and instead Lafayette sold some cattle and borrowed money for the journey. His effect on the United States would be profound, waking the still young nation to its victorious past.

As the "Nation's Guest," Lafayette received free room and board for himself and three companions plus free franking privileges, given only to members of Congress and former presidents, a boon because of his heavy correspondence. Lafayette wanted Frances Wright to join him, but his children who were not fond of her protested. So she followed him, traveling with her sister, Camilla. Lafayette introduced Wright to Jefferson, Madison and many other notables. More enamored with the United States than on her first visit, Wright made a strong impression and eventually became a citizen.

Lafayette traveled with his son Georges, forty-five; a male secretary, the former colonel Auguste Levasseur, twenty-nine, who regularly mailed news reports and American clippings to French journals on the general's experiences[1] — and a German-born valet. Levasseur published *Lafayette in America* in France in 1828 and the next year in the United States. He mentioned the general's "faithful servant" Bastien once in his account but never Fanny Wright.

Lafayette did not know his scribe well, writing home in his first letter on board, "We congratulate ourselves more every day for our association with Le Vasseur [sic], who is truly excellent and full of merit with a very pleasant personality." The general surely approved of his credentials. Levasseur had been a junior army officer in the twenty-ninth regiment at Neuf-Brisach, Alsace. But because of his likely involvement in Charbonnerist plots of 1821-1822, Levasseur was forced to resign. The plotters failed to drive Bonapartists from their thrones but were precursors of Italian independence. This account is from Levasseur's book.

Lafayette sailed from Le Havre at noon on July 13, 1824 aboard *Cadmus*, a three-masted American merchant ship named for the mythical brother of Europa. The day was fine and the ocean calm. The general did not linger with a large crowd of well-wishers on the wharf, since police, gendarmes and soldiers, opposing his popularity during the Bourbon restoration, tried to suppress the crowd's "noble ardor." His fans gave way rather than cause disorder and bloodshed. As Lafayette passed beneath the American flag on board, the crew cheered him three times, echoed on shore and from sailors on other ships. A squall the next morning claimed two top gallant masts, but produced, Levasseur wrote, "no other effect than that of furnishing us with an opportunity of admiring the calmness of our excellent Captain [Francis] Allyn in giving, and the vigor of the crew in executing, his orders."

Later, as *Cadmus* lay becalmed in mid-ocean, seven British officers with nothing better to do — their ship, bound for a Halifax garrison, also dead in the water — came aboard rather arrogantly, recalling to the crew the British mood when burning Washington City in the War of 1812. The Britons' attitude changed on meeting Lafayette, who shook their hands. They soon left with some Madeira and claret Allyn had stowed in their boat. Without further incident, *Cadmus* reached Staten Island on August 15. 1824. Thundering artillery from diamond-shaped Fort Lafayette in New York harbor announced the returning hero. Since it was Sunday and the city observed the Sabbath, a huge welcome was set for next day. The Lafayette party, cheered by welcomers bobbing in many boats around *Cadmus*, stayed the night with vice president Daniel Tomkins, the general's old friend, at his house on Staten Island.

Next day, Lafayette reached the city in a magnificent armada paving the water with elegantly decorated boats of every description. He was greeted by 200,000 people at The Battery at 2 p.m. The Lafayette Guards, with the general's portrait emblazoned on their chests, escorted him before a long line of militia. As he walked by, each corps presented arms and saluted with its colors. All wore a "Welcome Lafayette" ribbon. Shouts and cannons thundered from forts and warships. "Ah!" a young officer said to Lafayette, "Could this thundering welcome but resound to Europe, that it might inspire the powers which govern you with the love of virtue — and the people with the love of liberty!"

Francis K. Huger, who with Bollmann had spent eight months in prison at Olmütz, was a welcomer and Lafayette embraced him. Huger, fifty-one, was now a South Carolina legislator and rice farmer. Bollmann had died in Jamaica three years earlier. Novelist James Fenimore Cooper, thirty-five, also saw Lafayette's arrival and would become his friend in Paris in 1831.

At City Hall, Lafayette gave himself to the crowds pressing through the doors. Mothers with children asked his blessing. Feeble men who had served in the war were reanimated, speaking to him of their battles. Black men reminded him of his efforts for people of color. Young laborers said, "We also belong to the ten millions who are indebted to you for liberty and happiness!" Tears prevented many from speaking. Others hugged Georges while describing their admiration for his father. Lafayette heard himself called "Marquis" everywhere which is how the Americans remembered him. He reminded them he had long ago rejected that title. But later in Philadelphia, an elderly woman pushed through the crowd. "Let me pass," she said, "that I may again see that good young marquis!"

At five o'clock the party went to the City Hotel, where the American flag was draped over the door with the banner "The Nation's Guest" visible from a distance, a favorite title during the general's eleven-month, eight-day visit.

A sumptuous feast with political and military leaders capped Lafayette's second day in New York. For the next four days he spent two hours in City Hall where as many attended as the first day. He also visited learned societies, met members of both the bar and the Society of the Cincinnati. Through Washington's family, the Society presented Lafayette with a wreath-encircled golden eagle medal that Washington had commissioned for himself from Pierre Charles L'Enfant. Lafayette enjoyed this gift immensely and exhibited it at La Grange.[2]

A French girl in her father's arms placed a garland of immortelles on his head. There would be many such wreathes. If Lafayette saw one coming, he would snatch it away. As for his speeches, he sometimes wrote responses beforehand but mostly spoke without notes. His remarks were long and in the era's orotund style. He often said with truth his battles helped save America from tyranny. Americans were overwhelmingly pleased with him while the country's development amazed him. He was wined and dined everywhere, so much so that *to be lafayetted* was a catchphrase of the period.

Lafayette's tour consisted of trips to Boston and beyond, then Trenton, Bordentown, Philadelphia and arrival in Washington, D.C. From there it was up to Harrisburg in the winter and in spring when roads were passable a long journey into the South as far as New Orleans, then north on the Mississippi and Cumberland Rivers to St. Louis, Nashville and on to Ohio River towns, Washington, Brownsville and Uniontown, Pennsylvania, on to Braddock's Field and Pittsburgh, on to Butler and Erie, then across western New York partly via the new Erie Canal and a rush to Boston to lay the cornerstone of the Bunker Hill Monument. He then traveled north again as far as Maine before returning to the capital for a stay at the White House as President John Quincy Adams's guest plus last visits to former presidents in Virginia. From the White House, dignitaries escorted Lafayette down the Potomac to Mount Vernon where, after a lingering look, he boarded the *U.S.S. Brandywine* for France.

Here is a collection of especially moving events that Levasseur recorded in his journal. "Every village had its triumphal arch, upon which were almost always inscribed the names of Washington and Lafayette, or the dates of the battles of Brandywine and Yorktown," he wrote. "These large impressive structures were made of wood, covered in canvas and painted to resemble cut stone. Everywhere [we were] announced by the sound of cannon, everywhere received and complimented by the magistrates of the people and everywhere obliged to alight to receive testimonials of the love of the entire population." People traveled twenty miles and more to see the hero.

It took five days and nights to reach Boston, two hundred miles from New York. The party traveled till midnight and started out at five o'clock next morning. Throughout, the journey's charms helped prevent fatigue.

At nearly sixty-seven, Lafayette favored his stiff leg with a walking stick and carried a black top hat. He thought of himself an old man. Fortunately, he could nap at any time and anywhere. Heavy banqueting added to his girth. To conceal his baldness Lafayette wore a curly hairpiece called a short wig. Fame and vanity being often related, he dyed his hair dark brown. Georges, forty-five, exposed his bare pate.

In early morning on arrival at an arch outside the city, the mayor of Boston standing in an open carriage animatedly addressed Lafayette, who rose in his carriage. Both spoke as many thousands silently listened. Levasseur wrote, "[It] offered to my astonished vision the *beau idéal* of a popular festival, a republican triumph." Lafayette was deeply affected on seeing the troops' blue and white uniforms like those he designed. He exclaimed repeatedly, "My brave light infantry! Such was their uniform! What courage! What resignation! How much I loved them!"

A young officer presented a sword to the general. "Do you know this sword?" he was asked. "I find, at least," he said, "that it strongly resembles those which I brought from France to arm the sub-officers of my light infantry." "It is one of them," the youth replied. "My father received it from your hands; it served him gloriously in gaining our independence. He religiously preserved it in memory of his general and would have been happy to present it to you himself. The day before yesterday he still hoped to do so, and this hope softened his last moments — on that day he died. He has not bequeathed me wealth, but has left me this sword which will be the most precious of legacies if you sanction his gift."

"Take it," Lafayette replied, "guard it carefully, so that in your hands it may preserve the rights it did so gloriously in the hands of your father."

FORTY-FIVE: EMOTIONS ON HIGH

After a large reception in the State House came many visits in and around Boston. The most important was seeing the site of the future Bunker Hill Monument on Breed's Hill, actual site of the battle, where a committee of Freemasons, including Massachusetts Congressman Daniel Webster, was raising money for it. The granite obelisk would commemorate the valiantly fought battle, nevertheless lost to General Lord William Howe and would contain Masonic symbolism. The Masons asked their longtime brother to lay the cornerstone the following year and he eagerly accepted.

Governor William Eustis invited the party to the military camp at Savin Hill, near the ocean. Lafayette, observing firing practice, was invited to shoot at a target floating on the water at some distance. His shot shattered it, unexpected from an elderly man. Young soldiers and their ladies come to see him applauded. A "brilliant ball" — Levasseur often used these words — concluded the happy day at Eustis' country house.

In Quincy, the Frenchmen dined with a gentleman whose one-story house seemed too humble for his presidential eminence "We found the venerable John Adams," Levasseur wrote, "in the midst of his family. He received and welcomed us with touching kindness: the sight of his friend imparted a pleasure and satisfaction which appeared to renew his youth. During dinner, he kept up the conversation with an ease and readiness of memory which made us forget his eighty-nine years." Confined to his room, Adams could barely rise from his chair and "his hands were unable to convey the food to his mouth without the pious assistance of his children or grandchildren. …We left him filled with admiration…"

Long in the past was Adams' scathing letter to anti-Washington Representative Benjamin Rush, of Philadelphia. Adams had quoted Mirabeau's saying Lafayette always "advertised his disinterest [in power] — this never fails." As though quoting Lafayette, Adams had added sarcastically, "All manner of persons may have the benefit of my services, gratis, provided all ways and only that they will yield me their unlimited and unsuspecting confidence and make me commander in chief of 500,000 men, and after I shall have gained a few victories make me a king or an emperor, when I shall take a fancy to be either."[1] Adams in this letter conceded Washington was an exception to this rule. Lafayette, emulating him, was also. But Napoleon had more than fulfilled this expectation.

Before leaving Boston, the party watched a three-hour reenactment of the battle of Bunker Hill. Afterwards in a large tent where Lafayette met 1,200 people, the men stood before a large silver bowl holding "fragments of arms or projectiles, military buttons, etc." from the battlefield. Eustis offered them their choice of mementoes.[2] On August 31 on their way to New Hampshire, they stopped in Lexington, Concord, Salem, Marblehead and Newburyport, Massachusetts.

In Lexington, a young man brought forward a long rusty musket, saying, "My father bore it on the nineteenth of April 1775. In his hands it commenced the work that Washington and you so gloriously achieved. I am happy to make it known to you." Lafayette, examining it, advised the lad to have it inscribed "with the date of April nineteen, the name of the brave citizen who carried it, and keep it in a box secured from the ravages of time." The young man promised he would. In coastal Marblehead, where the general could stop only for breakfast, unsubstantiated legend says the corner of a clapboard house still at Hooper and Union Streets was cut away to allow his carriage to pass.

In Newburyport, the quartet stayed at Tracy Tavern where Washington had slept in 1789, with the room kept as it was for thirty-five years. Lafayette was pleased to sleep in his paternal friend's bed. Next day in Portsmouth, New Hampshire, the governor greeted him with some of Lafayette's old military friends. His party saw several Indians who had come from Canada to meet him. "Their dresses had no other character than that of misery," wrote his secretary. "Crosses and chaplets (beaded strings) had taken the place of their beautiful head-dresses of plumes, their furs and their arms; their drunk [sic.] visages had nothing of that noble expression which is said so particularly to distinguish the savage man… When asked if they were happy in the vicinity of the English, [the chief] replied that they loved the French very much; and immediately he and his companions shook hands very cordially with us…"

The general that evening met 400 women at a ball and left at midnight in carriages headed to Boston. Arriving at two a.m., they started out again at four p.m., reversing the tour south to include Worcester, Massachusetts, and Tolland, Connecticut. Many troops met Lafayette when he entered Hartford, leading him with pomp to the governor in the state house, where Lafayette responded to his address. General William Wadsworth, who had been at Yorktown, presented Lafayette with his epaulettes and scarf with traces of his blood he had worn at Brandywine. Emotions ran high and it was difficult to contain them.

Outside, 800 children gave Lafayette a gold medal inscribed with the date, September 4, 1824. The party walked through flower-strewn streets to a school for the deaf. Sixty children with hands on their hearts pointed to a sign: "What the nation expresses we feel." After reviewing troops and surrounded by many well-wishers, they boarded the steamboat *Oliver Ellsworth*. Stopping in Middletown for acclaim, at 7 p.m., they continued down the Connecticut River to Long Island Sound and New York.

Lafayette wanted to enter quietly. But ship of the line *U.S.S Franklin* fired a thirteen-gun salute on sighting *Ellsworth's* flags and streamers, signaling Manhattan. On landing at the Fulton Market there were as many people to accompany Lafayette to his hotel as on his first arrival.

Two days later on his birthday, Lafayette dined with the Society of the Cincinnati. Veteran army and navy officers formed the nation's oldest patriotic group in 1783 to promote values fought for in the Revolution. Preceded by a military band, elderly heroes of forty years past stepped or tottered, holding each other's arms for support. The golden eagle medal that Washington had owned was pinned to Lafayette's jacket.

Spectators watched silently out of respect as the old soldiers all marched off to the banquet to recount war experiences during dinner. Near its end, a curtain opened revealing a large transparency, a painting on thin fabric lit from behind: Washington and Lafayette were seen holding each other's hand before an altar of Liberty as America presented them with a civic wreath. A general read Washington's order of the day at Yorktown for October 11, 1781, describing how Lafayette's division was to "mount the trenches tomorrow." Applause and three cheers shook the hall. Another general then sang *The Captive of Olmütz,* a ballad Americans had grieved over thirty-two years before.

During the next days Lafayette examined public works and forts. Most noteworthy was Fort Lafayette in The Narrows near Long Island's point. Considered bomb-proof, its cannons' range could cross those at the Staten Island fort. A Fort Lafayette feast on September 8 had this bill of fare:

Chickens, turkeys, hams, tongues, pigeons, ducks, turkeys *à la Francaise*, snipe, woodcock, plover, wild ducks, veal and beef *à la mode*, lobsters, lambs' tongues in jelly, anchovies, crabs, tartlets, cheese cakes, puffs, jellies, blanc-mange, oranges, peaches, pineapples, melons, grapes, etc., etc. Wines: claret, White Hermitage, Madeira and Champagne.

The party visited orphanages, poorhouses and hospitals. It was most impressed with the Abolition Society's free school for young black children, coinciding with Lafayette's opposition to slavery. He was excited to be unanimously elected a society member. A boy spoke, "You see, general, these hundreds of poor African children before you. They participate with the white children in the blessings of education. Like them, they learn to cherish the recollection of the services you have rendered to America, and moreover they revere in you an ardent friend in the emancipation of our race and a worthy member of the society to which we owe so much gratitude." He gave his speech perfectly.

In all of these organizations the visitors noted the neatness of rooms, white linen, good food, and especially superintendents' kind treatment of their charges. There were more than forty such institutions in the city in 1824. The party toured the Academy of Arts with its collection of John Trumbull paintings and the Public Library with 20,000 volumes. At City Hall, they watched more than 1,000 firemen with forty-six pumping engines hose down a burning house in two minutes. Their banners held portraits of Washington and Lafayette on horseback. The visitors were unimpressed with the city's two shabby theaters. That would soon improve with a *Lafayette Theatre* and several others, many destined to burn down.

The grand event of this New York stay was a magnificent festival at Castle Garden, a former circular fort 600 feet in circumference. It rose on a mound in front of the Battery and by then used for public events. The party crossed a carpeted bridge flanked by beautiful green trees. The middle of the bridge shone with an illuminated pyramid with a large bright star at its center reading *Lafayette*. Over the entrance a flowered arch held a massive statue of Washington standing on two cannons. America held a shield saying, "To the Nation's Guest." Inside 6,000 people honored the hero of two worlds and also danced. When the general entered, white sheets fell to reveal the event to crowds watching from vessels in the harbor. Above Lafayette's seat was a transparency of La Grange with changing lights showing it from dawn to dusk with the caption, "This is his house."

Several times, when Lafayette walked on the floor, dancers rushed to meet him, stopping the dance. The Lafayettes left at two a.m. The event committee and a large number of women joined them as they embarked on the steamboat *James Kent* for Albany. They said goodbye to *Cadmus'* Captain Allyn, who carried their letters to France.

FORTY-SIX: HUDSON JOURNEY

Kent's engines drowned out Castle Garden's music and there was no sleep for the visitors. Women on board took more than eighty beds. Most of the men spent the night on the upper deck. They heard crewmen shout as they worked to push the boat off an oyster bank. As the steamer chugged north at ten miles per hour, cannon salutes every few minutes exploded from villages on both Hudson shores.

Veterans clustered around the general as they passed Tarrytown, recalling André's capture. Old men raged against Benedict Arnold as they passed his former house where his treason was learned. *Kent* finally docked at West Point. Cannon thunder caroming off the hills announced their arrival. As two guns continued to fire over the valley, Lafayette rode with Elizabeth Schuyler Hamilton, his comrade's widow, in an open carriage as others, including a column of women who had come with Mrs. Hamilton, climbed the steep road to the United States Military Academy. On reaching its plain, Lafayette immediately reviewed 200 cadets' maneuvers. He noted three Frenchmen among professors. The party left West Point at 6 p.m. The women returned to New York. *Kent* was four hours late reaching Newburgh.

A crowd of 30,000 waited impatiently in the dark. Magistrates calmed them as the visitors rushed in an open carriage on torch-lit streets to the Orange Hotel to meet the mayor and have supper. Loud groups gathered outside and were not to be denied seeing the hero. From a balcony the mayor explained reasons for the delay and presented the general, who thanked the cheering throng for their support. He went to a hall full of women and children who had given up hope of seeing him. They showered him with wreathes and flowers. On leaving the town of Hudson, the party found a double row of men standing all the way to the boat, many expressing their esteem.

In the morning at Poughkeepsie, and later in Clermont, the scenes were repeated. In Greenbush they were whisked in a barouche to a triumphal arch in town with magistrates, entertainment and women prepared to dance; but put aside so Lafayette could reach Albany by nightfall. In towns and villages, he spoke with ease and appropriateness at least four or five times a day, to the surprise and admiration of listeners. But *Kent* drew too much water. Nearing Albany, the party changed to a shallower ferry hauling horse teams. The four men sat in two carriages, each with four horses. Also on board were thirty light horsemen, in Lafayette's escort to the state capitol, and more than 100 pedestrians. In the dark, horses shied at welcoming booms and flashes and could have leaped a chain into the river. Fearing for his father, Georges left his carriage and, with attendants, held the horses' bridal reins until docking before another huge gathering.

Albany's reception was dramatic. A band led the procession to the capitol along streets lighted with blazing bonfires. A live bald eagle, perched on an arch, flapped its wings as Lafayette passed on the way to the State House. Senate galleries were filled with many women. The mayor addressed him: "Those who have shared with you the tolls of our revolution and who still live hail you as a friend and brother... In each of the hearts which beat around you, you hold the place of friendship and your eulogy is in all mouths." Lafayette, moved, noted how the city had grown:

"It is not a half-century since the town, then ancient, it is true, but still very small, served me for headquarters upon the frontier of a vast wilderness," he told the assembly. "I received here, as the commandant of the northern departments, the renunciation of the royal power and the acknowledgment of the more legitimate sovereignty of the people of the United States...The present generation is already distinguished by two glorious wars, and still more by its sincere attachment to the institutions whose excellence assures it an incontestable superiority over the haughty power which wished to arrogate over it the right of control." As the governor presented him to the public from a balcony, an eagle, this time artificial, dropped a laurel and an evergreen crown on his head, which the spectators loudly applauded. The day ended with a supper and ball, which the nation's guests left at midnight.

Six miles from Albany lay Troy, across the river from the Erie Canal's eastern end. The canal was early nineteenth century America's greatest feat. New York governor DeWitt Clinton had banked his career on what critics called "Clinton's Ditch." A former state legislator, U.S. senator and three-time mayor of New York City, Clinton built his dream on $7.1 million of state money. President Jefferson approved of his idea but thought its time lay in the future. The canal, four feet deep, forty feet wide, 360 miles long, was an immediate success and was soon called eighth wonder of the world. Goods moving in mule-towed boats at four miles an hour made New York City America's shipping capital and turned upstate hamlets into boomtowns. The canal became the country's most important migration route west for Europeans and proved the nation could occupy the continent.[1]

The canal originally had eighty-three locks, later much reduced. Begun in its middle and finished eight years later in 1826, it boasted five locks at its western end lifting boats sixty feet to Lake Erie. Lafayette had to visit it. He was impressed with Clinton on his first ride in 1824. They traveled west to a federal arsenal in Gibbonsville, New York, with its large store of weapons from the Revolution. The party consisted of Clinton and dignitaries who filled five boats. Clinton was re-elected in time to open the canal, pouring water from Lake Erie into the Atlantic, but he died suddenly at age fifty-eight two years later.

Lafayette had another experience in Troy: an emotional visit to the Troy Female Seminary, later the Emma Willard School, where young women were, and still are, taught to be equal to men. This was in accord with the general's ideas of equality for all. He saw over the doorway an arch of evergreens and flowers and the motto: "We Owe Our Schools to Freedom; Freedom to Lafayette." Introduced to founder Emma Hart Willard, he was led alone into the school. A female chorus sang, "To visit us thou hast left thy beloved family in a distant land, but be not afflicted; art thou not here in thy country? Behold how many of the daughters of Columbia are proud and happy to salute thee by the tender name of father." Willard, who wrote the song, gave him her *Plan for Improving Female Education*, which impressed him.

On leaving, Lafayette, profoundly moved, had tears in his eyes. The school's teachers surrounded him and 200 young women, dressed in white and singing, followed him to the gate. As they said goodbye, several thousand spectators watched in reverential silence. It was the beginning of a friendship between the general and a pioneer of women's education. A recent widow, Willard became a prolific writer of textbooks and other works. She remarried and later divorced. Her son John Hart Willard succeeded her at the school. On September 11, 1830, she wrote the hero:

> *"This month it is six years since on this very spot for the first time I grasped the hand of my country's benefactor, now my own friend. I say it unhesitatingly for has not Lafayette said it, in those precious letters which I have read so many times? When you were first here you promised me that you would come again and you came; and I then promised you to visit France and La Grange, that little Paradise, where the beings best beloved by you reside, and where all the social virtues cluster around you. The period which I had fixed (my son being now old enough to accompany me, and profit by traveling) has at length arrived, and I trust in God's Providence to have shortly the happiness of redeeming my promise..."*

She sailed with her son, twenty, on October 1 aboard *Charlemagne*, a fast three-masted square-rigged New York packet ship built in 1828. Lafayette, ever gracious, invited Willard to his family's box at the Paris Opera, and she sailed to France to visit several times. Willard in an 1831 letter strongly urged him to return to America but his age interfered.[2] Another woman, a Mrs. Taylor, presented Lafayette, who had known her family during the revolution, with a mounted collection of some 200 plants "as a reminder of Troy." Late that evening, with the cheers of the populace in their ears, the Lafayettes boarded *Kent* where they had left her in Albany. After three days redescending the river they were back in New York City.

FORTY-SEVEN: SOUTHERN WELCOMES

Leaving Manhattan for the third time on September 22, Lafayette walked to the dock. People gathered at his hotel and, saying their farewells, slowed his pace on the streets. The large group who accompanied him to the *Edward Kent* was unusually quiet, knowing the visitors would be away for some time. Lafayette began this journey by crossing the Hudson to Jersey City. New Jersey was full of memories of his battles and thrusts against the British and Hessians. He anticipated the experience and was not disappointed. Citizens of Bergen presented him with a cane carved from the apple tree under which he and Washington breakfasted. A storm felled the tree in 1821. To his pleasure, an engraving on the cane's gold head recounted its past.

Over two days the travelers moved through Newark; Elizabethtown and Princeton. The College finally awarded the honorary doctor of letters it awarded him *in absentia* in 1790. There was a "very beautiful breakfast in the college refectory, the largest room in town." The ceremony was under a circular canopy, Peale's portrait of Washington prominently displayed. Then on to the capital, Trenton, where before "a great concourse of people" the magistrate expressed "the sentiments of love and gratitude by which every citizen was animated towards him."

An arch and twenty-four maidens, each bearing the name of a state on her belt, welcomed him with a chorus. He exclaimed he had never seen the American states more beautifully represented.

The travelers had a welcome touch of Europe at Point Breeze, 1,000-acre estate of Joseph Bonaparte, elder brother and pawn of Napoleon I, in Bordentown, south of Trenton. Bonaparte, fifty-five, was a former lawyer and a good diplomat whose brother made him king of Naples and Spain. Joseph spoke little Spanish and in Iberia was known as *Peppe Botella* (Joe Bottle) for tippling. His Jersey neighbors called him "the good Bonaparte." Lafayette had always liked him. They were similar: liberal, well intentioned and ineffective in wielding power.[1]

Bonaparte added a lake a half mile long to his property and his regal mansion and elegant gardens enhanced a bluff over the Delaware River. He lived with a superb collection of European paintings, bronzes and a mistress who bore him a child. His wife, Julie Clary, lived in Brussels; they never saw each other in twenty-five years. Clary's sister was Desirée Bernadotte; that is, Queen Desidera of Sweden. To honor Lafayette, Bonaparte opened his estate to all who wished to meet the hero of two worlds. This was not unusual, he said. Although not a citizen, he invited the public to celebrate American independence each Fourth of July. He and Lafayette talked for an hour alone in his study over fine wine. Bonaparte lived quietly in Bordentown seventeen years before returning to Europe. Seen as a potential Bonapartist leader, France forbade his return and he died in Florence in 1844. He was placed near the emperor in the Invalides.[2]

Entering Pennsylvania over a covered bridge at Morrisville, the Frenchmen met the governor at the head of troops and spent the night at a federal arsenal in Frankford before joining civic and military officers in procession to Philadelphia. Some 6,000 militiamen defiled before them, led by distinguished General John Cadwalader, commander of an elite Philadelphia squadron early in the war.

"Never could it be more truly said," Levasseur wrote, "that a whole population came out to meet Lafayette; none remained at home but those whom age and feebleness detained." Bleachers for spectators rose to houses' eaves. Several trade groups crafted workshop displays along the street. Banners with portraits of Washington and Lafayette read,

"To their wisdom and courage we owe the free exercise of our industry." Levasseur found the printers remarkable: they printed and gave away an ode to the general. Their banner read: "Liberty of the Press Surest Guarantee of the Rights of Man."

A cavalry brigade led the procession, Lafayette following in a magnificent barouche pulled by six horses. Beside him sat a judge who had been "secretary and soul" of the revolutionary war office; then came elected officials, Georges and Levasseur and eight tented floats with forty veterans each and finally a column of infantry. All halted at Independence Hall. Senators, legislators, city council members, judiciary and military officers welcomed them. A thirteen-gun salute ushered them into the historic building. The site had been virtually unused for twenty-five years. The welcoming committee spruced it up for the occasion. Lafayette would meet the public there.

They strode down the corridor to a statue of Washington where the mayor spoke. Lafayette could scarcely conceal his emotions, remembering how he impatiently waited to serve the cause in 1777. He spoke of those feelings in his response, dwelling on the hall's historic importance. He so impressed his audience that the historic shrine and Liberty Bell became symbols of the nation's founding, It also heralded the American birth of historic preservation. His speech was one of the most important on the tour.

Lafayette spent hours greeting those present, followed by an elaborate dinner and toasting. One toaster wished for Greece's war of independence "a leader like Washington and a friend like Lafayette." Not many knew he was supporting Greek insurgents against the Turks. That evening, 160,000 people, 40,000 from across the country, strolled about the lighted area around the hall celebrating liberty's champion. On other days, Lafayette heard addresses by: the clergy (nearly eighty pastors of all denominations led by Congress' wartime chaplain); the American Philosophical Society; the Bible Society, the University of Pennsylvania; the Chamber of Commerce, the Bar Association, the Washington Light Infantry, Lafayette Benevolent Association, revolutionary soldiers, French residents and so on. To each he replied with his usual elegance and also visited public and charitable organizations.

At an unfinished penitentiary, Lafayette said that he regarded solitary confinement as a prelude to madness. Alluding to Olmütz, he said to understand such confinement one had to experience it. He opposed guards watching prisoners too closely. He told of his year in solitary and of being allowed to see a companion only an hour a day, finding neither privation reforming. He was in prison for wanting to revolutionize the public against aristocracy and despotism. He said he passed his solitude thinking about this but his confinement never changed his mind.

On October 5, after eight days in the city and many dinners, including one by Cadwalader, the visitors, with an arrangements committee, a battalion of volunteers and many staff officers, bade Philadelphia goodbye and sailed on the Delaware to Chester. They were met in the hall where Lafayette's leg was treated in 1777. Chester women made an excellent supper and the Frenchmen stayed at the home of a former companion in arms.

Next morning, they crossed the river into Delaware, as a new committee arrived. Lafayette was pleased to see General Allan McLane, seventy-eight, wearing a revolutionary hat and feather, leading the delegation. McLane had helped Lafayette elude the British at Barren Hill and, according to his memoirs, convinced De Grasse to delay rejoining the Franco-British war in the West Indies and instead sail to the Chesapeake to contain Cornwallis. Successful at Yorktown, McLane retired from the army and for thirty-two years was collector for the port of Wilmington.

Lafayette attended the wedding of a former French friend's son in New Castle, Delaware.[3] They sailed to Baltimore on the steamboat *United States*. A committee met them near Frenchtown, saying the Maryland governor would welcome them at Fort McHenry in Baltimore harbor. Lafayette recognized two friends, Colonel Paul Bentalou, an officer in Pulaski's legion, and François Duboismartin, now eighty-three, who procured *La Victoire*.

Lafayette invited an old friend, secretary of state John Quincy Adams, en route to Washington City, to join him crossing the Chesapeake during a storm at night. The Lafayette party had a stateroom with beds. Georges saw the dining room was converted into a dormitory with hard mattresses for the others, including Adams. Georges offered his bed but Adams politely refused, saying it was reserved for the general and his companions and, even if he had wished to accept, he respected the committee's wishes. Another bed was placed in the stateroom, but not because of Adams' status. The general requested his presence and Adams accepted.

At the fort, Continental veterans and many mutilated in the War of 1812 welcomed them. Crowds of soldiers and magistrates opened the way to him and he saw Washington's headquarters tent, brought from Mount Vernon. Governor Samuel Stevens received him there, and Lafayette replied to his address. Georges was happy to see George Washington Parke Custis, called "Wash" or "Tub," the president's adopted son as well as step-grandson, who had brought the tent.[4] Georges, two years Custis' senior, had spent three years with him at Mount Vernon when the general was imprisoned in Olmütz. The two embraced with tears, remembering the first president and their time as almost-brothers.

Lafayette and party moved to the city in an open carriage drawn by four horses for another reception and speech by Baltimore's mayor in a street covered in carpets for the occasion. The Maryland militia paraded, playing *Lafayette's March,* one of many melodies and dramas honoring him. A rifleman carried the flag under which a shell had killed General Pulaski in Savannah. Bentalou, the legion's oldest officer, found Lafayette's visit sufficiently glorious to unfurl it. At a splendid dinner Adams toasted to applause: "The tears of glory, gratitude and joy shed under the tent of Washington." The ball given by the city "was every thing [*sic*] that was perfect of the kind... and disposed with inimitable taste," Levasseur wrote, calling Baltimore one of the most handsome cities in the Union.

FORTY-EIGHT: A DOOMED SOCIETY

Baltimare was collecting donations for a 160-foot column, surmounted by a sixteen-foot marble of Washington in a toga, erected in Mount Vernon Place in 1829. In its shadow, a bronze equestrian statue of Lafayette was dedicated in 1924, symbol of American-French cooperation after World War I.[1]

In Baltimore, the general visited the grave of General David Poe Sr., the city's assistant deputy quartermaster general who gave $500 silver dollars to Lafayette to clothe his men. His wife helped make 500 pairs of "pantaloons," breeches joined to stockings. Poe donated $40,000 to the Revolution. In 1814 at age 71, he helped to defend Baltimore against the British. The Continental Congress, embarrassed at not repaying the debt, gave his destitute widow a yearly pension of $240.[2]

After a last sumptuous banquet the visitors boarded carriages for Washington. On October 12, a volunteer cavalry, mostly farmers, under Captain Samuel Sprigg, three years previously governor of Maryland, would escort them to the capital. The guests changed from carriages to open barouches, driving through the countryside of the new city for a half-hour before seeing a house, although the semblance of a city occupied land between the Capitol and the White House. Cannons marked their passage through a triumphal arch with streets filled with spectators.

Architect Charles Bulfinch, succeeding L'Enfant, completed the Capitol's low wooden dome in time for Lafayette's visit[3] The mayor addressed Lafayette before several thousand people who "rent[ed] the air with acclamations of joy and welcome." The procession moved slowly to the gates of the President's House, as it was called.

British soldiers in 1814 had burned the mansion and other federal buildings after Dolley Madison fled with Gilbert Stuart's full-length portrait of Washington. The Britons, after consuming an interrupted state dinner, threw long torches of "hellfire" through the windows, gutting the building. Canadian literary critic Northrope Frye gives a reason: Americans burned Toronto, called York, in the winter of 1813; half the population died of pneumonia.[4] Monroe moved into the mansion in 1817, opening it to the public on January 1, 1818. Spectators followed Lafayette to the President's House but stopped short of entering the unguarded grounds out of respect for the president and the nation's guests. A butler at the door led them to the oval audience room, later the Blue Room.

The fifth president came to Lafayette eagerly as everyone stood: four cabinet secretaries, army and navy officers, senators and a few public leaders. They sat in a semicircle with Monroe at center. All dressed in dark blue suits without lace, embroidery or decorations, to Levasseur strikingly unpretentious compared to European rulers. Monroe, protégé of Jefferson and friend of Madison, was a lawyer, former senator, governor of Virginia and ambassador to France, Great Britain and Spain. Jefferson had waxed of Monroe: "He is so honest that if you turned his soul inside out there would not be a spot on it."

But one of his ideas was doomed. With Madison, Henry Clay, Andrew Jackson, Daniel Webster and Francis Scott Key, Monroe had co-founded the American Colonization Society in 1816. Hoping to improve the lives of black Americans, they planned with other white people, slave-owners as well as abolitionists, to send free blacks to Liberia in West Africa, where it was thought they would have better lives than in the South. The society printed scrip to speed black emigration. Liberia's capital, Monrovia, was named in honor of the president the year

Lafayette attended a society meeting on February 19, 1824. Levasseur noted slavery's heinous history and that Lafayette was made a society vice president for life. Formed under Supreme Court justice Bushrod Washington, the quasi-religious organization misjudged not only the cost but also blacks' reluctance to move. Despite Liberia's English-speaking, democratically elected black leaders, it was an undeveloped disease-prone foreign country. The society in a decade exported just 2,500 people.

"You are aware from my last letter," Monroe said to Lafayette, "how much I desired to have you in my house along with your two companions during your stay in this city; but I am obliged to renounce this pleasure. The people of Washington claim you: they say that [since you are] the Nation's Guest, none but the nation has a right to lodge you. I must yield to the public will, and the municipality has prepared a hotel, provided a carriage and in short, anticipated all your wants. You must accept their invitation but I hope that this will not hinder you from considering my house as your own.

"You will always find your places ready at my table, and I wish whenever you have no engagement with the citizens that you will dine with me. This evening the municipality expects you at a public banquet. Tomorrow you will be present at a grand dinner that I give to the principal officers of government. But once these ceremonies are concluded, I will do everything I can that you may be as frequently as possible a part of my family." The general promptly accepted.

At the grand dinner, Lafayette, who knew how to be magnificently eloquent, toasted: "The City of Washington! The central star of the constellation which enlightens the whole world."

He pleaded for Greek independence with Adams at Gadsby's Tavern in Alexandria.[5] While he was dining with city leaders, Adams informed him of Louis XVIII's death. Lafayette expected that Charles X, the arrogant Artois, would be a poorer king. While in Alexandria, Lafayette paid his respects to Ann Hill Carter Lee, widow of General Henry ("Light Horse Harry") Lee (1756-1818) and mother of Robert E. Lee. Parke Custus had wed his wife, Mary Lee Fitzhugh, in the drawing room. Robert E. Lee would marry their daughter.[6] After spending time in Georgetown, on October 17, Lafayette traveled with several politicians, including secretary of war John C. Calhoun, on a two-hour steamboat trip to Mount Vernon.

For both Lafayettes, seeing the house again on its majestic site deeply touched them as they climbed the road from the dock. The estate was as Georges remembered it from twenty-eight years before. Washington's nephew, Bushrod Washington, owned it. The visitors saw the Bastille key where the president had placed it on the wall near the staircase in "the passage."A special place, it was the family's summer drawing room welcoming Potomac breezes.

As most visitors remained indoors, three of Washington's descendants led their guests to his tomb, about two hundred paces to the southwest, as cannons at nearby Fort Washington marked the occasion. Set among dark cypresses the tomb was a slightly raised red brick vault slaves had built. The wooden door had no inscription but held greens and withered garlands. Lafayette entered and reappeared a few minutes later, eyes full of tears. He led his son and secretary inside and the three knelt beside the coffins of the president and his loving wife. The younger men respectfully saluted and, rising, threw themselves into Lafayette's arms, mingling tears. Lafayette showed his emotions many times during the tour, but this visit was among his most touching moments. He took sprigs from a cypress and preserved them. He was given a ring with a bit of Washington's hair and a box from the oak under which William Penn signed a treaty with the Indians.[7]

Overnight the guests, with delegates and women, steamed on the *Potomac* down to Yorktown for its annual celebration, then as now, on October 19. Amid acclamations the general and companions were put up in the house Lord Cornwallis occupied in the siege forty-three years before. Lafayette had a bed; everyone else slept on mattresses or straw. A volunteer guard of sixty officers bivouacked around the house. In a field under Washington's tent that traveled with the visitors, Lafayette greeted officers from area regiments. Two elderly Continental soldiers were so overcome they fainted after shaking his hand. Lafayette was deeply shocked that only he and the American patriots were mentioned, not a word for Rochambeau and the French soldiers and sailors who had died for American liberty; it had become a purely American commemoration. (Formerly called the Alliance and Liberty Monument, the word "Alliance" is no longer appended.)

He was led to a triumphal arch built over the British redoubt he had overcome and heard an eloquent address on America's gratitude to him. A wreath appeared. "Take it,' he said to Hamilton Fish, who as a soldier had followed him into the redoubt. "This belongs to you also; preserve it as a deposit for which we must account to our comrades." Lafayette then spoke of "such honorable evidences of friendship from my ancient companions" in battle. The afternoon was a festival. Servants found a large chest, part of Cornwallis' stores, holding blackened candles. Lit in a circle, they became a perimeter for an outdoor ball with dancing until they expired. Night was half over as guests retired.

The general's Williamsburg friends, no longer prominent, welcomed him and the party stayed the day. They left nearby Jamestown by boat for Norfolk; along the way Lafayette recounted his reconnoiters. They entered Hampton Roads where two forts saluted as the boat reached the wharf. Norfolk citizens expressed gratitude with patriotic festivities. The guests visited Portsmouth's naval yard next day. A young woman dressed as the "Genius of Norfolk" received Lafayette under an arch. Expressing city sentiments, she made a grand impression while a ball crowned the day.

At 11 p.m., the visitors steamed north on the James River to Richmond, where the general met forty soldiers he had led. He astonished them by remembering names. Justice John Marshall welcomed him with civic and military officers and a vast concourse of citizens. Among them was Edgar Allan Poe, fifteen, an orphan living with foster parents. Legend says the general was honored with "The Lafayette Oak," a live oak still growing in what would become the lawn of the future White House of the Confederacy.

FORTY-NINE: DREAMS OF ABOLITION

The United States abolished slave trading in 1808, but slave smuggling continued until about 1862. Abolition came in 1866. The United Kingdom ended slavery in 1833, France in 1848. Lafayette said, "I would never have drawn my sword in the cause of America if I could have conceived that thereby I was founding a land of slavery."[1]

Eager to see Jefferson, the general nevertheless stopped on the way to visit Petersburg, twenty-five miles from Richmond, which had importuned him. It was a pleasant experience. He had burned the town fighting the British in 1781. He remarked how much it had gained by that action. A proud townsman replied, "At that time we had nothing but miserable wooden houses to receive you in, and now there are large well-built brick dwellings in which we can offer you all the comforts of life." After resting two days in Richmond, the visitors, joined by the city's volunteer cavalry, left for Monticello eighty miles away. They stopped that night in Milton, then on to Charlottesville.

The meeting at Monticello was memorable and long — ten days, November 5 to 15. In his carriage Lafayette rolled up the mountain to the famous house with 120 cavalrymen. Two hundred spectators along the drive silently saw the living legends embrace. "They flew into the arms of each other," a newspaper reported — and cried with happiness before entering the mansion.

The general found Jefferson, eighty-one, "feeble and much aged" but "in full possession of all the vigor of his mind and heart." Jefferson, gray, bent at the shoulders, using a cane, had long since given up his old-fashioned queue. He would step off a porch to mount his horse, Old Eagle, for daily rides in the afternoon. He sipped three or four glasses of wine a day.[2] Levasseur noted the president exhibited in his entrance hall a collection of Indian objects explorers Merriwether Lewis and William Clark had brought back, calling it "the most varied and complete that has ever been made." He found Shawnee Chief Tecumseh's battle weapons not remarkable in themselves but for whom had owned them.

Lafayette understood Jefferson's need to answer his correspondents in writing, what the president called his "epistolary *corvee*" (forced work), since he shared the same attitude.[3] The former president received more than 1,000 letters a year. The Sage of Monticello, surrounded by his daughter, Martha (called "Patsy"), his many grandchildren, and slave servants, suffered many years of intrusion from the invited and uninvited. The house sometimes seemed like a hotel with as many as fifty overnight guests, helping to drain his funds.[4] He was also being urged to become a spokesman for states' rights and upholding slavery in the South. Jefferson had written Lafayette on December 26, 1820 about the Missouri Territory issue:

"...All know that permitting the slaves of the South to spread into the West will not add one being to that unfortunate condition, that it will increase the happiness of those existing, and by spreading them over a larger surface, will dilute the evil everywhere, and facilitate the means of getting finally rid of it, an event more anxiously wished by those on whom it presses than by the noisy pretenders to exclusive humanity. In the meantime, it is a ladder for rivals climbing to power."

Lafayette responded from La Grange on July 1, 1821:

"Are you sure, my dear friend, that extending the principle of slavery to the new raised states is a method to facilitate the means of getting rid of it? I would have thought that by spreading the prejudices, habits and calculations of planters over a larger surface you rather increase the difficulties of final liberation. Was it not for that deplorable circumstance of Negro slavery in the Southern States not a word could be objected, when we present American doctrines and constitutions as an example to old Europe?"

And on June 1, 1822:

"While I feel an inexpressible delight in the progress of everything that is noble minded, honourable and useful throughout the United States, I find, in the Negro slavery, a great drawback upon my enjoyments. It raises a sigh, or a blush, according to the company, American or foreign, where I happen to be. Let me confess, my dear friend, I have not been convinced, and the less as I think more of it, by your argument in favor of dissemination.

One is I believe more struck with the evil when looking upon it from without. As to the remedies, they may be better ascertained from within... To see that plague cured, while I live, is next to impossibility, but I would like, before I die, to be assured that progressive and earnest measures have been adopted to attain, in due time, so desirable, so necessary an object. Prudence as well as honour seems to me to require it."

The general unleashed at Monticello his old "hobbyhorse" of letting slaves earn their freedom and his awareness of Washington's proposal for gradual emancipation. Admitting slavery to the Missouri Territory, much debated in Congress, horrified Lafayette. But Jefferson clung to his belief that extending slavery to the West, where it was out of place, would in time extinguish it. Both men could exhaust each other on the subject.

The visit was not all that opportune, Jefferson's granddaughter, Mary Jefferson Randolph, wrote her sister Ellen (Eleanora) Wayles Randolph Coolidge from Monticello on August 18,

...There's so little rain falling that I should not be very much surprised if the Marquis himself (of whom we are in hourly expectation) preferring this cloudy weather to our hot sun should be the cause of interruption. As much pleased as I shall be to see the old general again, I cannot help wishing that his visit had been made at a less inconvenient period. Grandpapa's health appears to depend so much on his being allowed to attend exclusively to his own comfort and inclinations, that I fear he will suffer from the sacrifice of both, that he will think it necessary to make, not only to his old friend, but to the crowd of visitors that will be attracted here by the presence of La Fayette...[5]

Lafayette, although tired, was buoyant about his tour's dazzling success. But Jefferson was depressed by his ill health and growing debts. The neck of his bladder was inflamed. He had diarrhea and prostate problems, possibly cancer.

He liked to ignore his problems because he could not see his way out of them. To escape the crowds, he could still take the two-day coach ride to his hideaway plantation, Popular Forest, near Lynchburg. He had designed this beautiful octagonal house recalling Monticello as both a personal pavilion and seasonal sundial, with the sun's rays entering fan windows on solstices and equinoxes.[6]

Lafayette and Jefferson discussed many topics, from politics to farming and beyond. So much history had passed between them! It also would have taken hours, if not days, to weigh how France had changed since Jefferson's years there, not to mention the two revolutions, Napoleon, Olmütz, exile in the Netherlands and the current American and French governments. Lafayette could chide his friend over slavery and the president could remind him he might have prevented Burr's treachery. Madison, a mellowing force and Jefferson supporter, came to invite the general and his party to his home, Montpelier.

Both presidents, at Lafayette's behest, invited Fanny Wright to join them. Jefferson had many hours discussing slavery and other topics with her. But she was generally appalled at the hypocrisy of Southern planters hailing the General, whom she called Father, as a champion of freedom when they kept humans in perpetual bondage.

Levasseur questioned Jefferson's slaves: "The good appearance and gaiety of the Negroes at Monticello attested the humanity of their master, if so noble a character had need of an attestation. All those with whom I conversed assured me they found themselves perfectly happy and were not subject to bad treatment; that their task was light, and that they cultivated the grounds of Monticello with greater satisfaction because they were nearly certain of not being torn from their homes to be sent elsewhere during Mr. Jefferson's life."

On a lighter note, Jefferson warned Lafayette of his adoring public: "I fear they will kill you with their kindness, so fatiguing and exhausting must be the ceremonies they force upon you. Be on your guard..." Jefferson knew what he was talking about but may not have seen the humor in a quip Adams wrote saying *he* had been prescient enough to avoid becoming popular.[7]

Despite his infirmities, Jefferson led the trio in his carriage, an elegant calash his slaves had built, on a tour of his "academic village," the University of Virginia and the library building Jefferson adapted after the Pantheon in Rome. Lafayette received a fine reception and banquet attended by Jefferson and Madison. Jefferson, a deist, had not only designed the campus (and miscalculated its cost) but also for years had controlled the curriculum — no religion courses were offered — even with two other presidents, Madison and Monroe, on the board. The students were enthusiastic about Lafayette. They did not want to let him leave and tried to join him in the carriage. A student presented an unusual gift.

"...Someone gave Lafayette a rattlesnake [Martha wrote Ellen on August 26] that threw Levasseur into raptures. The general is going to carry it to France, a bear also and some dozens of Indian moccasins which they were carrying to the ladies of their family...[8]

The Monticello visit was delightfully mellow. Jefferson's lavish entertaining of his French guests exhausted his red wine supply. His order of the year before arrived after they left. It included: 150 bottles of red Bergasse, 100 bottles of Ledanon, seventy-five bottles of Blanquette de Limoux, fifty bottles of Muscat de Rivesalte, and "for experiment," a thirty-gallon cask of *vin ordinaire*.[9] Jefferson, like Lafayette not a good budget manager, left debts of several million dollars in today's money. His will freed five members of the Hemings family, although not his concubine Sally Hemings, who died about 1835. Jefferson knew, Joseph J. Ellis writes, auctioneers would claim many, if not most, of his 130 slaves. They and Monticello were sold on January 15, 1827, still leaving the family a large debt.[10]

While staying at Montpelier four days, the general was the guest of honor at a dinner in the yellow dining room with the diminutive former president, seventy-four, his charismatic wife Dolley, seventeen years his junior, and farming gentry neighbors. Understanding the planters and the Madisons' dependence on slaves, Lafayette never missed an opportunity to defend the right of all men to be free. The guests discussed the problem frankly, confirming at least Levasseur's belief that slavery would soon end in Virginia. He was too optimistic; freedom for all would take forty-one more years. Dinner topics included "spiritual slavery" in Europe caused by nationally sponsored religions. This sin, the Virginians said thankfully, did not exist in their country. Yet Madison had been instrumental in legally denying Episcopalian claims to appointments or other largesse in Virginia. Madison also talked with Fanny Wright. Dolley wrote to her brother-in-law, John G. Jackson:

We have lately had a visit from Genl. LaFayette & family of a few days — the former, you know, was an old friend of Mr. M — s. I was charmed with his society — & never witnessed so much enthusiasm as his appearance occationed [occasioned] here and at our court house, where hundreds of both sexes collected together, to hail & welcome him. The General enjoyed himself so much he has promised to spend some time with us again, before he leaves this country.[11]

Inspired by plans for the Washington Monument, Dolley, as one of the last Federalists, attended its Masonic cornerstone-laying in 1848. She had sold Montpelier and moved to Lafayette Square in Washington, recalling the first president's friendship with Lafayette. She also circulated a poem she had written earlier in the classically allusive style of the time, calling Lafayette "Europe's noblest son!"[12]

There were off-color whispers about the general's friendship with Wright, a wealthy Scotswoman, thirty-eight years his junior. They shared the same birthday and both were orphans at a young age with sizeable inheritances. Southerners were shocked to learn the relationship was not sexual but based on Fanny's ardent abolitionism. To win them to the worthiness of founding a farm where blacks could be educated and earn their freedom, Wright informed the Madisons she much wanted the retired president's "testimony under his own hand" in a letter. She later wrote Dolley in an effort to win Madison's support but received nothing from either of them.[13]

Earlier, on March 19, 1825, Wright, then thirty, and her sister, while on their way to meet Lafayette in New Orleans, stopped to see Robert Owen's short-lived utopian community in New Harmony, Indiana. Owen's son, William, wrote on that day, "...Miss Wright is a very learned and a fine woman, and though her manners are free and unusual in a female, yet they are pleasing and graceful and she improves upon acquaintance." That year she urged Congress to accept *A Plan for the Gradual Abolition of Slavery in the United States Without Danger of Loss to the Citizens of the South.* She would co-edit an abolitionist newspaper with Owen's son, Robert Dale Owen. With New Harmony in her thoughts, Wright purchased eighteen slaves — with some financial support from Lafayette, whose thinking greatly influenced hers — and 640 acres on the mosquito-infested Wolf River (*Nashoba* in Chickasaw) east of Memphis. Here in the hostile South she founded her own hardscrabble utopia, Nashoba.

Still hopeful, Fanny wrote to Lafayette on steamboat stationery printed with the letterhead *On the Mississippi*, February 14, 1828:

Dear Father, regarding my deed of trust to Nashoba, we have now instituted a fund into which we each throw one hundred dollars per annum, begging of all future associates to do the same. In this manner the Nashoba property now stands free of all burden whatsoever to those funds which may accrue from the rent of lands, emancipating labor of the slaves (who now stand to us in the light of tenants), sales in the store, increase of stock, etc., will be devoted to the one object to which we stand pledged by my deed — a school which shall be especially open to children of color. Two years from this time we trust to be in a situation to open it. Fortunately, enough remains to me from my original capital to allow of my entering our present association in the manner & on the terms described.[14]

But stories of free love and other alleged activities emanating from the rustic compound hurt its development. Nashoba failed in three years.[15] Wright took her black friends to Haiti, now independent, and continued to proselytize. She became internationally famous for lectures and writings on abolition, feminism, atheism and other tinderbox issues. Fluent in French, she married a Frenchman in Paris, and after a few years they moved to Cincinnati, Ohio, where they divorced in 1850. Like Lafayette in 1807, Wright slipped and broke her leg in a fall on the ice; in her case, a stairway. After much suffering, she died at fifty-seven and was buried in Cincinnati in 1852, largely forgotten until the rise of the feminist movement.

Leaving Montpelier on November 19, 1824, the Lafayette party soon came to Orange, Virginia, and its county courthouse where they met two long lines of revolutionary veterans that age had kept from Yorktown. They were grateful to rekindle friendship with the general and his memories of them. Dessert followed a dinner with the local custom of thirteen toasts. Afterward, Madison, who had ridden with them to a wood, bade adieu and turned toward his estate. The travelers soon discovered a large crowd gathered about a triumphal arch and young women strewing flowers on a path. Lafayette had opened the road in 1781 for a forced march from the Rapidan River to Michunk Creek, where his troops prepared to resist Cornwallis' intention of seizing the middle states' magazines at Albemarle. He spoke to the young people of their fathers:

"It was here at the moment when I effected by this path a movement which would have been so fatal, if unsuccessful, that they abandoned their harvests to join my little army, and during that whole campaign, the separation from their families, fatigues of every description, the ruinous abandonment of agriculture and difficulty of procuring provisions did not prevent them from remaining with the army far beyond the time we had any right to ask of them."

Out of modesty, his secretary wrote, the general didn't add that when the volunteers complained and he had admitted he could not pay them, he permitted them to leave. But, he had added, he had no intention of abandoning his post and would remain with his small band of regulars. Like Washington at Valley Forge, he found the disgruntled remained. They asked, "Who is the wretch who could ever dream of abandoning the marquis?"

Traveling forty miles a day, the companions moved north to Fredericksburg. There young boys, called the Lafayette Cadets, delighted them. The town was a-glitter and after a mayoral welcome a splendid supper followed. Lafayette had once visited Washington's late mother at her house on Chestnut Street.[16] Masons in grand ceremony escorted the visitors to a Sunday service at the Episcopal Church where the minister was a Mason. Before returning to Washington, the afternoon was spent with Lawrence Lewis, Washington's nephew and private secretary who had married Washington's step-granddaughter Eleanor ("Nelly") Custis, in Fredericksburg. A militia escorted the visitors to the Potomac and an evening steamboat ride back to the capital.

There Lafayette found messages from Southern and Western states urging him to visit and received in his suite their congressmen, telling of welcoming plans. He accepted them all but not until spring. There was another visit to Baltimore. As a member of the Agricultural Society, Lafayette judged a livestock exhibition, during which many toasts were made to the nation's guest, and he admired a steam boiler that could have fed his sheep rapidly. He also accepted many gifts that could improve French agriculture. There was time to visit the Lewises at Woodlawn, then Judge Bushrod Washington at Mount Vernon and George Custis at Arlington House majestically overlooking the Federal City. Settling in for the winter because of roads' impassability, the nation's guests felt a quickening pace as a highly contested presidential election reached its zenith.

FIFTY: A SURPRISE GIFT

Lafayette was fascinated by one of the nation's most unusual contests. After two terms, "the Era of Good Feeling," Monroe was stepping down and the Federalist Party had dissolved. Four candidates were eager for the presidency: Secretary of State John Quincy Adams; Speaker of the House Henry Clay; General Andrew Jackson, hero of the 1812 war, and Treasury Secretary William Crawford. The public voted regionally but inconclusively for favorite sons. Adams, Clay, and Crawford were of the rural Republican-Jefferson Party that evolved into the Whig and Republican Parties. Jackson led what became the Democratic Party. He won the highest popular vote, the most electoral votes but not a required fifty percent of the total vote. By law the House of Representatives decided the outcome. Clay and Crawford supported Adams. Adams as president named Clay vice president and Crawford secretary of state to howls of "corrupt bargain." Not taking sides, Lafayette considered the first eight presidents his friends. His biggest surprise came at Monroe's insistence.

On December 6, 1824, Monroe called on Congress to compensate Lafayette for his expenses in the American Revolution, a rarity for the government. In December 1823, Monroe had warned world powers to stay out of the Western Hemisphere, called the Monroe Doctrine some twenty years after his death. His invitation to Lafayette to visit was designed to re-enforce for the world his role in establishing American sovereignty. Committees quickly arranged a reception for him. The House of Representatives adopted resolutions that the general should be congratulated for accepting Congress' invitation to tour the nation, to express its profound respect for his services during the revolution and his current return to the United States.

A joint committee on December 6 determined Lafayette should be invited to address both houses of Congress. On the morning of Dec. 9, he was conducted, at his request without pomp, into the Senate where each member greeted him. The next day, twenty-four House members accompanied him to the House floor where a huge crowd including leaders of government, ambassadors (but not the French one), and the Supreme Court came to honor him. Speaker Clay addressed Lafayette:

The vain wish has been sometimes indulged that Providence would allow the patriot, after death, to return to his country, and to contemplate the intermediate changes which had taken place — to view the forests felled, the cities built, the mountains leveled, the canals cut, the highways constructed, the progress of the arts, the advancement of learning and the increase of population. General, your present visit to the United States is a realization of the consoling object of that wish. You are in the midst of posterity.

Clay showed emotion in his delivery as his powerful sonorous tribute deeply affected listeners.

...In one respect, you behold us unaltered, and this is in the sentiment of continued devotion to liberty, and of ardent affection and profound gratitude to your departed friend, the father of his country, and to you, and to your illustrious associates in the field and in the cabinet, for the multiplied blessing which surround us, and for the very privilege of addressing you, which I now exercise. This sentiment, now fondly cherished by more than ten millions of people, will be transmitted, with unabated vigour, down the tide of time, through the countless millions who are destined to inhabit this continent, to the latest posterity.

Stepping to the podium, Lafayette, first foreigner to address a joint session of Congress, surprised many by replying extemporaneously:

Mr. Speaker and Gentlemen of the House of Representatives — While the people of the United States, and their honourable representatives in Congress, have deigned to make choice of me, one of the American veterans, to signify, in his person, their esteem for our joint services, and their attachment to the principles for which we have had the honour to fight and bleed, I am proud and happy to share those extraordinary favours with my dear revolutionary companions; yet it would be, on my part, uncandid and ungrateful not to acknowledge my personal share in those testimonies of kindness, as they excite in my breast emotions which no words are adequate to express...

Among the most touching remarks in his long reply:

The approbation of the American people, and their representatives, for my conduct during the vicissitudes of the European revolution is the highest reward I could receive. Well may I stand firm and erect, when, in their names, and by you, Mr. Speaker, I am declared to have been in every instance faithful to those American principles of liberty, equality and true social order, the devotion to which, as it has been from my earliest youth, so it shall continue to be to my latest breath...

Congress decided it needed to do more to express the nation's gratitude. On December 20 a Senate bill was reported out of committee proposing he should receive $200,000 payable at a percentage over ten years and 24,000 acres in a fertile township at Tallahassee, Florida. But as the bill was about to go to the House, Senator Nathaniel Macon, of North Carolina, said although he agreed Lafayette deserved the gift and had spent much money in service to the United States, so had many native-born Americans.

Senator Robert Hayne, of South Carolina, argued this was no reason not to compensate Lafayette. He figured since 1776 the general had spent $140,000 of his money in service of the country, which easily would have reached $200,000 with interest. (Comparable to several million dollars today.)

"He put shoes on the feet of your barefoot and suffering soldiery," Hayne declaimed. "He spent his fortune on you, he shed his blood for you and without acquiring anything but a claim upon your gratitude he impoverished himself." The bill passed the Senate 37-7, garnered a swift House majority vote and Monroe quickly signed it. Those who didn't vote for this grant were still Lafayette's friends and partisans. It was difficult then as now to oppose a national icon.[1]

Lafayette, who had been visiting the Maryland Legislature in Annapolis, knew nothing of the proceedings. When presented with the act, he felt considerable embarrassment and was at first tempted to refuse it because he thought what he had already received was enough. But, seeing how the bill was drawn, he felt he could not refuse the gift *America* was giving him through its representatives and immediately decided to accept it. He promptly assured Congress of the deep gratitude he felt as an American soldier and an adopted son of the United States. Newspapers spread the news and it proved to be very popular.

Virginia, New York, and Maryland wanted to "heap additional favors" on the General but he repressed further donations. Those who voted against the gift were vilified in the press. When told by some Congressmen that twenty-six of them voted against the bill despite positive feelings for him, Lafayette replied, "Well, I can assure you that if I had had the honor of being your colleague, we should have been twenty-seven, not only because I partake of the sentiments which determined your votes but also because I think that the American nation has done too much for me."

Widely reported, his words only increased his popularity. The nation's guests were pleased to learn at Monroe's post-election party in the White House that the winning and losing contenders, except for Crawford, who was ill, shook hands and congratulated each other in the best of form, so different from the changing of European dynasties.

FIFTY-ONE: HONORS FOR THE FALLEN

On New Year's Day, 1825, Lafayette was guest of honor at a grand dinner in Washington. The people's representatives — from Monroe, who avoided such large gatherings, on down — expressed admiration. Since there was "no reason to flatter those in power" they unleashed their sentiments. Many wished all Americans could have shared the evening. One of Monroe's last acts was to change the informally named Presidents' Park north of the White House to Lafayette Park. Elaborate bronze statues honoring the general and other revolutionary leaders came later.[1]

Despite a bitterly cold January, Lafayette made a point of visiting York and Harrisburg where militiamen's legs almost froze standing guard.

In Washington, Lafayette sat for several portraits. The most impressive was by Samuel F.B. Morse, commissioned by the City of New York for $1,000. The eight-foot tall, full-length painting remains in City Hall's council chambers. After the first sitting, Morse confessed to his wife, Lucretia: "This is the man now before me, the very man, thought I, who suffered in the dungeon of Olmütz, the very man who took the oaths of the new constitution for so many millions, while the eyes of thousands were upon him… the friend and companion of Washington, terror of tyrants, the firm and consistent supporter of liberty, the man whose beloved name has rung from one end of the continent to the other, whom all flock to see, whom all delight to honor. This is the man, the very identical man! My feelings were almost too powerful for me."[2]

Morse posed the general standing magnificently in a high white cravat, black frock coat and lemon stirrup trousers. The splash of a red-silk-lined black cape lights his left shoulder. His right hand rests on a stone railing holding busts of his heroes Washington and Franklin. The stylized rather than realistic face looks wide-eyed to the right. The sky is both radiant and dark. Morse in his veneration created one of the most powerful images of the 19th century. During the painting's course, Lucretia Morse died in New Haven. Morse was unable to reach her before burial. Lafayette expressed his profound sympathies. Unsuccessful as an artist, Morse later turned to experimenting, co-inventing the telegraph and Morse Code. He visited the general in Paris and had a lifelong correspondence.[3]

In early February, Georges, with the help of congressmen and postmaster general John McLean, plotted how the visitors could cover 5,000 miles of wilderness, meet appointments and reach Bunker Hill on June 17. A Washington family member lent a large coach. Saddle horses were purchased for the worst miles and luggage reduced to a minimum. On Washington's birthday, February 22, Lafayette, Monroe and president-elect Adams attended a grand ball. Next day the guests embarked on the Potomac for Norfolk, and Suffolk, Virginia. Murfreesboro, North Carolina, was so illuminated it looked ablaze. The horses sank to their knees in a muddy road. Despite drivers' shouts and curses, they refused to move, delaying guests an hour. The town's cordial welcome told Lafayette he was as much appreciated there as anywhere.

The next day they were in Halifax, North Carolina, and spent the night; Cornwallis was headquartered there when he made the mistake of invading Virginia. They reached Raleigh next day and admired the Capitol's marble sculpture of Washington by Italian master Antonio Canova. Volunteer dragoons traveled 150 miles to be Lafayette's guards. While he was near the head of a procession, horses pulling an open two-wheeled coach ran off, throwing the vehicle, two passengers and driver against a tree. A general was knocked unconscious. Another general, friend of the first, was about to bleed him with a lancet, common where surgeons were scarce. Georges persuaded him not to; the wounded man had recently eaten and phlebotomy in such cases had been fatal. Next day the recovered man warmly thanked Georges for intervening.

On March 4 they reached pretty Fayetteville, North Carolina, the only city named for Lafayette he visited. He had eluded Cornwallis there. Rain fell in torrents. His party before reaching town saw miles of men and boys on horseback awaiting him. Elegantly dressed women crowded watery streets to see the hero for whom the city had been renamed from Campbellton forty-two years before. He spoke on an elevated platform at the town hall.[4] Leaders extolled him for remaining faithful to liberty and being first to proclaim the rights of man in Europe. At a private house where he lodged, he was told by the head of a committee, "You are here in your own town, in your own house, surrounded by your children. Dispose of all — everything is yours." He attended several parties and took time to inspect a new Lafayette Hotel. He toasted: "Fayetteville! May it receive all the encouragements and attain all the prosperity anticipated by the fond and grateful wishes of its affectionate and respectful namesake."[5]

Despite the rain, militias maneuvered beneath the house's balcony and were there next morning as the party passed them on the way out of town. Lafayette alighted from his carriage and, passing through the ranks, took each soldier by the hand. This excited the spectators to follow their guests on the road many hours.[6] A day after North Carolina troops turned them over to their South Carolina counterparts, the guests became separated in a deep forest after a difficult day of crossing overflowing rivers, when their escorts lost their way in the dark. About 10 p.m. Georges and Levasseur, sensing the general and the others were far ahead, were suddenly violently jolted and heard a loud crash. Their carriage's wiffletree (the pole securing horses) had broken, leaving them stuck in a marsh until dragoons in the procession had them mount their horses. In several minutes they reached their house for the night. They ate and slept well, except for a trumpet blown to rally scattered riders.

The next day was clear. The party made its way to Camden, South Carolina. Lafayette was invited to lay the cornerstone for a new memorial to his friend Kalb. He had fought valiantly as second in command under inept General Gates, who delayed marching on Cornwallis despite his having fewer troops than Gates on August 16, 1780. The British beat the Continentals in what has been called the war's worst American defeat. The battle lasted an hour but claimed nearly 200 American lives and many wounded. Congress replaced Gates with General Nathanael Greene. Leading the Southern campaign, he soon drove Cornwallis north. Kalb, a vital fifty-nine, commanded Delaware and Maryland troops who had come south with him. With his horse killed beneath him, he fell from his eleventh wound and died three days later, depriving the patriots of one of their greatest generals.

On March 9, 1825, his remains were re-interred in the graveyard before Camden's classical revival Bethesda Presbyterian Church. Robert Mills, designer of the Washington Memorial, conceived the church and the fifteen-foot white marble shaft; its supporting twenty-four granite blocks represented the American states. After his friend's remains were placed in the tomb, Lafayette rested his hand on the shaft as it was lowered into place. His presence was recorded on the monument.[7] Lafayette spent the rest of the day with veteran companions who recalled battles together.

On the way to Charleston in the rainy night, Levasseur's carriage broke down in a forest. The horses with Georges' carriage, traveling behind Levasseur's, became frightened, ran between trees, wedging the vehicle. Dignitaries in another carriage picked up both men. Another time in the dark the guests became lost and sat for an hour in the rain before being rescued around 11 p.m. They laughed at supper about their latest predicament with Lafayette, who had reached safety ahead of them.

In the warm March weather, they found blossoming fruit trees and magnolia-perfumed air on entering Charleston "like a delicious garden." Lafayette had first stepped onto American soil twenty-five miles north. Residents recalled that first visit and lavishly entertained over three days with as fine a reception as any offered. Joining Charleston's militia as an honor guard were men from the state's farthest parts, marching fifty miles a day to show their patriotic gratitude. One unit wore the uniform Lafayette designed for the Paris National Guard. He was delighted to have Francis Huger ride beside him in several processions. Huger had fought in the War of 1812 under his father-in-law, General Thomas Pinckney, who had tried to have Lafayette released from prison. Huger married Pinckney's daughter, they had seven children and Huger bought Pinckney's estate, Altamont, calling it Long House. Charleston gave Lafayette a gold-framed miniature of Huger and a map of Charleston in a silver case.

In Savannah, Lafayette laid cornerstones for Generals Greene and Pulaski's monuments. General Greene left the army in 1780. For his heroism, Georgia gave him the run-down Mulberry Grove plantation on the Savannah River north of the city. It had belonged to John Graham, former British lieutenant governor. General Anthony Wayne, who led the battle of Savannah, was honored with an estate nearby, but Wayne, with money problems, lost it and returned to Pennsylvania. Greene, also debt-ridden, had fathered many children. One boy spent a year with the Lafayettes.

Deeply stressed, Greene tried to be a rice farmer but became ill. His eyes hurt as they had in battle, his forehead swelled mysteriously and he was bled to no avail. He died at forty-three of apparent sunstroke in 1786 and was buried in the Graham vault in Savannah's Colonial Park Cemetery. Noted architect William Strickland's fifty-foot-tall white marble obelisk to Greene was erected in Johnson Square in 1830. Greene's remains, unknown for many years, were found in the vault and reburied at the monument in 1902. Pulaski also had a post-mortem history. He died at thirty-four in the battle of Savannah in 1779 and laid to rest in Greenwood Plantation, near Thomasville, Georgia. His remains were moved to Savannah's Chippewa Square, where Lafayette placed the cornerstone in 1825. But a new monument was erected in nearby Monterey Square in 1855. When it was restored in 1996, the crypt revealed an iron box and a plate with Pulaski's name. The box held bones consistent with his height and dimensions and two cornerstones.

In Savannah, Lafayette met Achille Murat, son of Joachim Murat, deposed king of Naples executed in 1815, and Caroline Bonaparte, sister of Napoleon and his brothers. The four visitors were impressed Murat was not only a naturalized American but mayor of Tallahassee. The next year he would become city postmaster and marry Catherine Willis

Gray, Washington's great-grandniece. When Georges praised Joachim Murat's chivalric bravery as a French field marshal, his son moments later told Levasseur, "Mr. Georges has caused me a great happiness. He has spoken well of my father to me."

Boarding the steamboat *Alatamaha,* the party traveled more than sixty miles north though marsh country to Augusta, where the general received artillery discharge and three cheers from those on two steamboats. This was answered with *Yankee Doodle* and three rounds of gunfire. The boats raced, belching smoke so black passengers could not see each other. *Alatamaha* won. Lafayette wanted to stay a day but agreed to stay two. Townspeople added to his activities, fatiguing him and causing his companions momentary worry. They visited the village of Hamburg, South Carolina, on the river's other side. It already had a port filled with vessels. Leaving Augusta on March 25, they passed through Warrenton and Sparta to Milledgeville, Georgia's then capital, over the worst roads on the tour. The general's carriage resisted accidents but could have broken down twenty times. Lafayette vomited from the strong jolts but any alarm passed after a night's sleep in Warrenton. He was received in Milledgeville as a father and friend with ceremonies at the state house and Masonic lodge. Citizens' affection and kindness nearly brought him to tears.

On to Macon, they passed through primordial woods seeming to have been there forever. Macon, a log village, had been "grubbed" or cleared only eighteen months. They were handsomely entertained and saw well-mannered women dancing in fine clothes. Again in the forest, roads were difficult, making them too late to meet 100 Indians who had left after many hours, hoping to meet the white father. A heavy rainstorm unlike any seen in Europe besieged the travelers, but they found a cabin built by an American. They met a number of braves drying their clothes at a large fire on the hearth. Without being recognized, the visitors sat down with them and attracted little attention. It was the first time Levasseur could interview red men who answered questions in a kind of pantomime. After the storm, the Lafayettes reached more log cabins owned by a merchant who traded goods from the coast for Indian furs.

At the door waiting for the owner were two Creeks. The younger man, named Hamley, addressed the general in perfect English, saying he had attended college but, having white and Indian parents, had gone native. (Many white colonists did that.) He invited them to his nearby cabin. Levasseur and two governor's aides de camp accepted. This cabin had a pinewood fire, two beds, rude chairs, baskets, bows and arrows and a violin hanging on a wall, everything half-civilized. The older man took down the violin and heavily played Indian melodies. Hamley asked his guests to dance. The Americans demurred but Levasseur, being younger or less reserved, did some national steps. Immediately Hamley, holding a shawl, began dancing, at first slowly and then more boldly, faster and faster, giving cries the chronicler found had an inexpressibly striking effect on them as white men. Hamley's wives, two attractive Indian women, did not enter the cabin during the dancing. There were also a few black people around, fugitives given a home. Levasseur would have hunted with Hamley, but the journey resumed next morning, March 31.

Crossing a bend on the Chattahoochee River dividing Georgia and Alabama, they met the Creeks they had missed who wanted to honor the general. In beautiful native clothing, men, women and children danced and leaped around Georges, first ashore. They touched his clothing in astonishment, causing him almost as much embarrassment as pleasure. As the others moved back, Creek braves came forward for a ceremony. The chief gave a long cry, a signal for all to salute. As Lafayette stepped ashore, the strongest men asked him to remain in his small carriage. They carried it like a palanquin, not wanting their father to walk on wet ground. The chief said in English to Lafayette they were happy to be visited by one who had never made distinction of blood or color between Americans. He was the honored father of them all. The men clasped Lafayette's right arm in friendship. They pulled him in the carriage up a hilly embankment to their village where they entertained with a boisterous war game the general enjoyed.

The mixed-blood leader, Chilli McIntosh, twenty-eight with a fine physique, was college educated. He was the eldest son of criticized chief William McIntosh. Young McIntosh sadly foresaw his nation's swift destruction. Governor George Troup, Chief McIntosh's first cousin, wanted the Creek out of Georgia. With the federal government, Troup forced McIntosh, who lacked tribal authority, to sign the 1825 Treaty of Indian Springs, favored by Jefferson and Andrew Jackson. It sent the Creek to Louisiana Purchase lands west of the Mississippi. John Quincy Adams opposed the treaty but gave up trying to change it. McIntosh's reward for treachery was a rural log cabin farm called Indian Springs. The furious Creek burned his house and shot him to death as he tried to escape. But they were forced from Georgia in 1827. Cherokee and other tribes followed. Indian Springs became Georgia's first state park. The Lafayettes were among the last foreign whites to know Georgia's Indians as friends.

After more Indian experiences near Line Creek, Alabama, the party finally reached the village of Montgomery, Alabama. Chilli, accompanying them, joined them at a ball where he danced with several beautiful women who had no idea of his origins. Afterward, he bade farewell: "I hope [the general] will not forget us," and disappeared into the night. At 2 a.m., the Lafayettes boarded steamboat *Anderson* on the Alabama River. Lafayette's cabin was richly furnished and the Crescent City had sent ahead musicians playing patriotic airs. The travelers stopped for a day in Cahaba, the state capital, where the general received special entertainments.

They met dinner guests who had been driven from France and lived in reduced prosperity in a small town named fittingly Gallopolis but it would vanish. After three days and a brief stop in Claiborne, Alabama, the men reached Mobile. Alabama's oldest city, after difficult early days under the Spanish and French, was prosperous. It once exported 400 cotton bales but now shipped 60,000 bales. A New Orleans delegation arrived on *S.S. Natchez,* a two-year-old New York side-wheeler, to carry Lafayette there, but he remained in Mobile long enough to attend a public dinner, a ball and a Masonic celebration, sleeping on the boat after the day's emotional pleasantries.

FIFTY-TWO: SPECIAL DAYS IN NEW ORLEANS

Cannons roared Mobile's goodbye at daybreak as *Natchez* weighed anchor. The captain cut across the Gulf of Mexico to the Mississippi's mouth rather than a route more inland. It was a dangerous choice since severe storm sent seasick passengers to cabins in the loudly creaking vessel only to see waves enter portholes, inundating their beds and expecting to founder at any moment. The storm lingered with heavy rains. Next day on entering the wide river they saw enormous alligators basking on thousands of fallen cypresses seeming to defy the navigator. At midnight New Orleans' batteries fired a 100-gun salute as *Natchez* approached. They awoke on board next morning to cries of "*Vive la liberte, vive l'ami de l'Amerique! Vive Lafayette!*" They were surprised to see the shore covered with men wearing French uniforms.

Despite the rain, an immense crowd cheered on the levee as the general disembarked amid booming artillery. After a procession with sixteen marshals, the governor spoke of the liberty Frenchmen received in Louisiana while freedom under the Bourbon Restoration was problematical in France. The general replied with much feeling and toured the battlefield south of the city where General Jackson and his troops defeated a much larger British army in 1812, Britain's last attempt to regain the continent. The war helped to send Jackson to the presidency. Lafayette knew intimately how Americans loved war heroes.

The rain slowed the large procession into the city. In *Place d'Armes*, later Jackson Square Lafayette was impressed by a victory arch sixty feet high and fifty-eight feet wide decorated with colossal sculptures of Justice and Liberty and two trumpeting figures of Fame with banners emblazoned with Lafayette and Washington's names. A seven-foot-tall entablature read, "A grateful republic dedicates this monument to Lafayette." On top of it Wisdom rested an arm on Franklin's bust. Under the arch, Mayor Roffignac welcomed the general, who recalled the courage and loyalty in the Revolution of the mayor's father, an *Averngnat*, moving him to tears. Amid the cheering crowds the guests were conducted to city hall, the *Cabildo*, originally the palace of the Spanish governors, where he was praised by the city council's leader and given the use of a large reception hall for the visit.

The building would have been his headquarters had he accepted Jefferson's offer to govern the Louisiana Territory. The men were shown their rooms for five days at a hotel the people called "Lafayette House." After a rest, the general on a balcony reviewed the troops, all dressed in elegant uniforms and moving precisely. He enjoyed seeing grenadiers, light infantry, cavalry, federal guards, New Orleans guards, Lafayette guards and riflemen. He was particularly pleased with 100 Choctaws marching in accustomed single file. Allies of Americans in the Seminole war, they had camped a month near the city to see "the great warrior, the brother of their great father Washington." He also was delighted to meet a large group of black veterans of the Revolution.

Next day at the *Cabildo,* although heaped with praise from government representatives, Lafayette avoided mention of slavery and emphasized how Louisianans were greatly improving laws their former Spanish and French overlords left and so sound they could guide the rest of the country. Invited to American and French theaters, he drew lots: first the American, then the French. He was applauded at both. In the first he drew the audience's attention away from a performance of *The Prisoner of Olmütz* in his honor. At the second, the audience rose with cries of "*Vive Lafayette!*" as he entered his box for the last act of

The School of the Old People, followed by an ode to him. The audience applauded every allusion.

On Tuesday, April 12, with the opening of the Faubourg Lafayette suburb, Spanish emigrants and refugees thanked him for opposing in the Chamber of Deputies Napoleon's invasion of Spain and suppression of its liberal constitution. On his last two evenings he took part in a public ball, a Masonic dinner and a vaudeville show called *Lafayette in New Orleans.* The nation's guests were much impressed by the citizens' cordiality and richness of details equaling the best they knew. He visited the Marigny plantation of Antoine Jacques Philippe de Mandeville beside the Mississippi.[1] Louis-Philippe had dined there in 1798 on gold dishes, it was said, afterward thrown into the river as no one else would be worthy of them; if true, a miscalculation, in view of the Nation's Guest.[2]

Before leaving, Lafayette successfully mediated a disagreement between the city militia's officers and staff. Saying if he had known of their disagreement he would not have accepted the city's invitation, he had them shake hands in agreement. Meanwhile, he wrote Illinois Governor Edward Coles, "...I don't think but by rapid movements I can gratify my ardent desire to see every one of the Western states and yet fulfill a sacred duty as the representative of the Revolutionary Army on the half-secular jubilee of Bunker Hill..."[3]

Natchez churned upriver and the general attended banquets, balls, and militia parades in Baton Rouge, Natchez, Mississippi, Kaskaskia, Illinois, and entered St. Louis for another procession and ball on April 29. Along the way he shook children's hands and twice was startled to meet soldiers who had fought with him. Among odd sights on the wide southward flowing river where flatboats — Levasseur calls them arks — resembling large boxes carrying grain, cattle and poultry to New Orleans. To return the 1,700 miles north each summer, the boatmen, often Kentuckians, bought cheap steamboat passage, provided their own food and helped the crew with such chores as loading firewood and provisions.

The travelers saw some log cabins in the thick forests but none that could be called a village. Mosquito curtains provided the only relief from insects descending at night. They noted where tornadoes had toppled trees, creating numerous snags and sawyers. Held fast in the riverbed, these tree limbs could pierce boat bottoms, sending passengers to their graves. Thanks to city escorts bringing them food and drink, as well as dramatically changing landscapes, the visitors never had a boring moment on board.

FIFTY-THREE: SINKING IN THE OHIO RIVER

On the Mississippi they captured five young Canada geese unable to fly and were given gifts: Mexican curassows, wild turkeys, Devonshire cows, partridges and a grizzly bear. Fowl and cattle were sent to La Grange where Lafayette "exerted himself to multiply their numbers." William Clark, Missouri Territory governor and former explorer, shipped the grizzly to Paris. Lafayette donated it to the King's Garden and it was exhibited in the menagerie.

Reaching the Ohio River, the *Natchez* pilot turned back, having exhausted his knowledge. A delegation arrived on a smaller boat, *Mechanic,* adapted for narrower channels, to escort them to Nashville, on the Cumberland River, an Ohio tributary. They had been waiting a while, not knowing the general's plan to visit St. Louis. It was decided he should continue to St. Louis on *Natchez* with some of the delegation, the rest waiting for them on *Mechanic* in the Ohio. At sundown *Natchez* anchored off Carondelet, a village named for a French-born Spanish governor of the Louisiana Territory and five miles south of St. Louis. About sixty French Canadian farmers lived there. When they knew who was there they rushed out to visit the hero of two worlds, bringing gifts Lafayette felt he had to accept or else offend. These included tamed geese, a fawn, petrified wood and shells. Since they had no deeds, the farmers feared losing their lands and asked him to intercede. With his help verbal grants established land ownership. Later, the city government was in Lafayette Hall, that fire destroyed in 1949.

Next morning, Governors Clark and Coles of Missouri escorted the guests into St. Louis. The general, seated in a carriage drawn by four horses, received a huge welcome. He was shocked to greet in the crowd a son of Alexander Hamilton closely resembling his father. It may have been William Stephen Hamilton, Illinois surveyor and a scout in the state's Black Hawk War of 1832; Levasseur did not say. The visitors toured the city, marveling at Indian mounds where bones and artifacts were discovered, proving the new world was ancient, a startling concept for Europeans. They would see more of them on their journey. They viewed the governor's outstanding museum of Indian objects, and he gave Lafayette a buffalo coat. They dined at the home of Peter Choteau, son of St. Louis' first settler and town founder in 1763, present at "the feast of republican gratitude." There were many toasts on the edge of the western wilderness. The men climbed on *Natchez* at midnight and, about to leave in the morning, townspeople showered them with Indian curiosities. During an unplanned stop at Kaskaskia, Illinois, at Governor Cole's insistence, the voyagers learned how remote its people were. They knew little of Napoleon, who always acted as though news of his exploits spanned the world. The men visited some Indian villages. In one they met Mary, daughter of a late brave who had fought under Lafayette and bequeathed to her his most precious possession, the general's letter that she carried like a talisman.

Descending the Mississippi, they reached the Ohio and churned north to the Cumberland before nightfall. It was difficult leaving their new friends on *Natchez,* on which they had traveled for a month and covered 1,800 miles. They reluctantly boarded *Mechanic,* launched a few years before in Wheeling, on which they expected to soon have the same pangs on leaving new companions. General Andrew Jackson greeted Lafayette on Nashville's dock, joining him in a carriage as church bells pealed. They passed militiamen dressed in brilliant uniforms and rode under an arch on the way to an even larger one in the town square. Thousands of flags were draped from windows. The governor affectionately addressed Lafayette and his response was heartfelt. Forty veterans of the revolution, many aged, expressed feelings to him amid acclamations. One elderly German-born man named Hagy served under Lafayette. Throwing his arms around the hero, he cried, "I have enjoyed two happy days in my life: when I landed with you at Charleston in 1777 and the present. Now that I have seen you once again, I have nothing more to wish for. I have lived long enough." Listeners were moved to silence.

The Lafayette party stayed at the home of a Dr. McNairy. Later that evening Jackson presided at a dinner in the general's honor for 200 people. Among the toasts were: "To the present age — it encourages the reign of liberal principles. Kings are forced to unite against liberty, and despotism to act on the defensive." Lafayette answered: "The State of Tennessee and Nashville, its capital — may our heritage of revolutionary glory be forever united to the unfading laurels of the last war, and thus form a perpetual bond of union between all parts of the American confederation." The wish, offered directly, may have alluded to his condemnation of slavery which he did not normally express in the South, not wishing to offend his greeters. The nation's guests then attended a Masonic celebration with 300 brothers. Returning to their beds, they saw the town brilliantly illuminated with houses displaying transparencies of Lafayette and various emblems. Their sleep must have been blissful, away from pounding steam engines.

Next morning, the general reviewed militias that had camped south of town, some men coming fifty miles. He later walked among them to express his admiration for their discipline and gratitude for their affection, later visiting a young women's academy and Cumberland College. With citizens' voluntary subscriptions, the college would begin departments of languages and philosophy, in Lafayette and Jackson's names. At 1 p.m. the guests with an entourage joined Jackson for lunch. He would be elected president for two terms in 1829, His house and 1,000-acre farm, The Hermitage, a few miles outside Nashville, was stark and underfurnished by European standards. After he showed his slave-tended gardens and farm, some friends begged him to display arms he had received in honor of his victories in the War of 1812.

Besides a fine lustrous American sword and saber covered with inscriptions were the two saddle pistols Lafayette had given his adoptive father in 1778. Washington probably left them to his beloved cousin, William Augustine Washington, who bequeathed them to his son-in-law, William Robinson, who presented them to Jackson. Handling them to Lafayette, Jackson asked if he knew them. Examining them, he recalled he had given Washington and said he experienced genuine satisfaction finding them in the hands of "one so worthy of possessing them." Old Hickory blushed. "Yes! I believe myself to be worthy of them," he said, pressing the beautiful pistols and Lafayette's hands to his breast, "if not from what I have done, at least for what I wished to do for my country." Everyone applauded, saying the weapons could not be in better hands. Jackson returned Lafayette's gift, bequeathing the pistols to Georges, who received them in Paris in 1846. They remained in the family for several generations until sold in Paris in 1958 and again in 2002.

After dinner at the Jacksons' the party returned to Nashville to attend a sparkling ball and boarded the *Mechanic* with Tennessee Governor William Carroll and two of his aides-de-camp for the journey on the Cumberland to the Ohio, where Carroll turned back on the morning of May 8 and Coles rejoined them. The Lafayette party shared the largest cabin, usually occupied by women in the boat's lower stern and reached by descending stairs. After Coles left, Lafayette spent the day writing to La Grange's superintendent on what he wanted done before his return and to correspondents. Moving up the broad river, the Lafayettes, fearful of losing time, urged the captain to push the small boat as fast as possible. They stopped for an invited dinner at Shawneetown, Illinois, an important government center for the Northwest Territory.

Lafayette retired at 10 o'clock. Strolling on the lower deck, Georges thought it strange the pilot had not slackened pace in the dark. Going to sleep, he felt safe: no one had let the trip's travails trouble them. At 11 o'clock the only sound was the engine pounding. Only the pilot and two crewmen were awake. Suddenly a terrible crash shook the boat, stopping it short. Lafayette awoke with a start. Georges and Levasseur ran half-dressed on deck to learn what had happened. Passengers said they had probably hit a sand bank and there was no danger. Levasseur grabbed a lamp and rushed to the captain. They ran to the hold and found it half-filled with water. "A snag, a snag!" the captain shouted above the passengers' cries of alarm, "Bring Lafayette to my boat!" They had struck a large boulder, later called "*Mechanic's* Rock," near the mouth of Deer Creek, Indiana.

The pandemonium was not heard in the large cabin, but the general's valet, Bastien, and Georges had him half-dressed. Levasseur told Lafayette, "We shall go to the bottom, General, if we cannot extricate ourselves and we have not a moment to spare." Georges scooped up what he thought his father needed and Levasseur quickly gathered his papers pell-mell. Since Lafayette was not yet completely dressed and his hair not combed, he said they should go ahead and he would join them when they had an escape route. "What!" Georges shouted, "Do you think that in such circumstances we will leave you for a moment?" And they each seized a hand and dragged him to the door. Smiling at their haste he moved along until stopping on the middle of the stairs — he had forgotten a gold snuffbox with an enameled portrait of Washington. Levasseur fetched it. At that moment the vessel began to list. It appeared they might not escape before she sank.

On the upper deck, all was in confusion with passengers looking for rescue, some with their trunks, and calling for Lafayette. He was with them but in the dark no one recognized him. The boat heeled more and more to starboard. The captain from his rescue craft called to Lafayette to enter but the confusion on deck kept the party from reaching him. Levasseur shouted, "Here is General Lafayette!" and the clamor turned instantly to silence as the passengers made way for him, some pulling back from wanting to leave first. Then the problem was the general, ever gallant, wanting others to escape first. He was soon forced to acquiesce since the tender could hold only up to ten people. The listing steamboat forced the matter. Its lower deck was already four feet under the black surface.

Levasseur jumped in the boat first and two men with their arms under the general's shoulders lowered him, stiff leg and all, as the tender dipped precariously. The former president of the Louisiana Senate helped keep Levasseur from pitching into the cold water. There were soon nine people aboard but how far away was land and which shore? The captain at the rudder chose the left bank, ordered his two crewmen to row gently and all reached safety in minutes. Suddenly Lafayette realized Georges was not with them. His usual sangfroid vanished as he called out, "Georges! Georges!" His shouts were lost in the cries of passengers still on board and loud steam explosions.

Lafayette was distraught and nothing could calm him as he walked the shoreline, asking others if they had seen his son, a good swimmer. Levasseur and the captain returned for more passengers until they found Georges and Bastien on the boat. She had reached bottom but was not submerged. Georges recovered about sixty of 200 letters they had addressed — the rest were lost — and found some baggage, including his father's trunk. Completely at ease, Georges had planned to stay until the others were safe. Unlike a fearful man who nearly drowned in three feet of water, Tennessee's Governor Carroll, with little on board, calmly removed his shoes, stockings and hat to assist in the rescue. No one died but the rain didn't help. A fire was built and Lafayette lay on a mattress dry on one side. Besides the trunk with the general's most valuable papers, a leg of smoked venison, a cookie tin, a case of claret and a keg of Madeira surfaced. With no fatalities, the rescuees reacted as if at a party.

The rain stopped as two large boats paddled down the Ohio loaded with freight for New Orleans. A rescued passenger, Nielson, owned one of the vessels, the *Paragon.* He generously ordered her turned around to keep the Lafayettes on schedule. A half-hour's rowing and they were on board and in two days set foot in Louisville. Toasts that evening at a public dinner saluted Lafayette and Nielson, who received a piece of engraved silver plate. The next day, after visiting Jeffersonville, Indiana, on the river's other side, the general returned to Louisville for more festivities before setting out for Cincinnati, passing through many towns in Kentucky and under a triumphal arch in Frankfort, the capitol, where the governor welcomed him to wild applause. The general reluctantly found he had to travel on Sunday to meet his schedule.

FIFTY-FOUR: NAMED FOR MARIE ANTOINETTE

After attending a public dinner in the pretty town of Versailles they were on to Lexington, Kentucky, and Ashland, Henry Clay's estate. The secretary of state was away but his wife, Lucretia Hart Clay, mother of their eight children and tended by a few slaves, welcomed them. The travelers spent two days of "uninterrupted entertainments" in town. In the unfinished Grand Masonic Hall, Lafayette sat down to dinner in front of a large white castellated cake containing individually hand-grated blanched almonds. The caterer, Giron, created it in honor of his fellow Frenchman. American and French flags of sugar topped the confection and Masonic symbols covered it.[1] On May 17, the general breakfasted with Masons in the hall and sat for his portrait by Matthew Jouett, who added trees to his copy of Ary Scheffer's 1822 portrait. A group from Lafayette County accompanied the travelers next to Louisville as the rain came and went.

They arrived at the Ohio River with their Kentucky friends on May 19 and looked across the half-mile-wide water to Cincinnati rising on its hills. That city's delegation met them in boats carrying them and the Kentuckians across to a thirteen-gun salute and thousands shouting repeatedly, "Welcome, Lafayette!" Governor Jeremiah Morrow received the general on the riverbank with a verbal tribute and escorted him in an open carriage to a hotel.

Revolutionary General William Henry Harrison, now an Ohio senator, received Lafayette at his office and expressed gratitude for America's freedom. Lafayette returned his thanks as everyone in the crowded quarters listened excitedly. (Former Northwest and Louisiana Territories governor, Harrison took Indian lands by treaty and defeated Chief Tecumseh at Tippecanoe, Indiana, in 1811. He would become ambassador to Colombia, dealing with Bolivar. As ninth president in 1841, Harrison, sixty-eight, gave a long inaugural address as snow fell and, after a month in office, died of pneumonia.)

Lafayette knew of the death of Presley Neville, his dashing aide-de-camp in the war, who had had his political job in Pittsburgh taken away and had died in debt two years earlier. Lafayette asked immediately about his son, Cincinnati resident, Morgan Neville, author and former editor of the *Pittsburgh Gazette.* Told he was ill with fever, Lafayette, whose name descended in the Neville family, rushed to Neville, who told him he had spent all he had to pay his father's debts. Lafayette wrote a check for $4,000 drawn on the United States Bank and slipped it under Neville's pillow.[2]

The general left with Masons for their hall where members of many lodges welcomed him. A public dinner and fireworks followed with more excitements next day. He met in the morning with 600 school children who scattered flowers under his feet and surrounded him with happy cries. Harrison and other officers led a grand military parade for him. The arrival boat placed on wheels was part of the procession. An orator gave a moving address in the public square. Swiss immigrants from the Indiana town of Vevey, that the travelers missed while in Kentucky, came to pay tribute to the hero they had admired before coming to America. They said persecutions in their former home forced them to leave. They embraced Lafayette and presented wine of their vintage resembling light claret. That evening, a ball preceded a sumptuous patriotic banquet attended by more than 500 people, three state governors and others of rank. At midnight on May 22, at a signal from Vevey's artillery, the travelers boarded the steamboat *S.S. Herald.*

They briefly visited river towns Portsmouth and Galliopolis, Ohio.

Lafayette stopped at the home of a congressman who had voted against his federal grant. Representative Vinson was in Washington but his wife convinced the general the nay vote was because the bill varied from regular form and no other reason. Fifteen miles west of Marietta, Lafayette passed Blennerhasset's Island. He surely recalled how Aaron Burr, living in Marietta, had sought funds from wealthy English-born Harmon Blennerhasset for Burr's abortive 1803 misadventure. Federal troops burned Blennerhasset's mansion but he escaped charges of treason and moved to Natchez. Failing there because of British incursions in the War of 1812, he returned to England and died in poverty, leaving his wife to die similarly in New York.

Anticipating "Mariette," as he called it, Lafayette stepped into cheering crowds on the sloping embankment. At Marietta, the Muskingum River, flowing past Indian burial mounds, joins the Ohio. Gazing from the prospect across the street from the Lafayette Hotel, the second one on the site, one can imagine people and tooting riverboats welcoming the general. A state marker calls Lafayette, who stayed overnight in a private house, "the nation's first tourist." Levasseur barely mentions Marietta, now known for its riverboat museum and early history, but he noted few French-speaking settlers lived in the region. Yet French explorers, possibly Robert Cavelier, Sieur de La Salle, named the Ohio "*la Belle Rivière*" in 1669. Marietta, first permanent settlement in the Northwest Territory, was growing rich on river traffic. It lies on the north shore near the state's southeastern border which in Lafayette's time separated Ohio from northern Virginia, now West Virginia.

Marietta was named for Marie Antoinette, "who gave aid," town folk said, "during the darkest days of the American Revolution," in 1788. This surely recalled for Lafayette memories of the queen and his role in her life. While in Pennsylvania, Lafayette had no reason to visit Azilum ("Asylum") that his brother-in-law Noailles planned in 1793. The hamlet was on the Susquehanna River ten miles south of Towanda in the commonwealth's northeast corner. Liberal royalist émigrés, fleeing France and rebellious Haiti, built the rustic spot. Louis-Philippe d'Orléans and his brother stayed there during their American exile, beginning in 1796. Talleyrand also visited. Dauphin County, seat of Pennsylvania's capital Harrisburg, was named for Louis XVI and

Marie Antoinette's first son, Louis-Charles, in his birth month of March 1785. The county seal bears a fleur-de-lis.[3]

After a banquet and overnight in Wheeling, the travelers re-entered Pennsylvania, banqueting in the town of Washington. As was customary, people everywhere crowded the hero's path and gave him their greatest honors. "Little Washington" held brilliant festivals. At Brownsville the guests crossed the Monongahela River in a boat with twenty-four white-clad girls who crowned Lafayette with flowers as he entered town. Behind schedule next day, he hurriedly left lunch for a delegation from Uniontown, Fayette County, named for him in 1783. They arrived there at six o'clock, hours later than expected.

FIFTY-FIVE: FRIENDSHIP HILL

The welcome was special. Albert Gallatin, who had come at 11 a.m., orated. Swiss-born, he was Lafayette's friend in Paris and United States minister to France (1816-1823). As Jefferson's Treasury secretary, he helped find $15 million for the Louisiana Purchase. Four elegant bays took Lafayette in a barouche under two decorated arches. Blue-sashed postilions in white uniforms sat on each horse. The cheering populace filled the streets as church bells rang. In a pavilion at the courthouse, Lafayette met Gallatin and took a seat with others. Gallatin's speech, one of the tour's best, reviewed the hero's life and love of liberty. The remarks took an hour. Gallatin said in part:

The name which this county bears, an early evidence of public gratitude, that name, whilst it perpetually reminded us of your virtues and of your services, has also given us a more than common interest in all your fortunes. Let this be our apology for detaining you, even at the risk of wounding your modesty a few minutes longer than is usual on occasions like this.

In the first Assembly of Notables it was on your motion that the report of one of its bureaus recommended the restoration of the Protestants of France to their civil rights, a report on which was founded the decree to that effect issued the year before the commencement of the French revolution.

When this last event took place although belonging to a distinguished family of the privileged class, you instantaneously appeared as one of the most zealous and ablest defenders of the people. The part you played, on all the momentous questions agitated at that time, is known to the world. But it has perhaps been a common error to believe that France had reaped no other fruits from her revolution than wretchedness and blood shed, that no material benefits had ultimately accrued to the nation from that portentous event. If, however, the magnitude of the obstacles to be overcome in every quarter shall be duly considered, and if we compare what France was at the epoch of our revolution with what it now is, there will be found less cause of astonishment that no more was effected, than of regret that it should have been purchased at so dear a price...

A banquet with illuminations and speeches followed at Spottsylvania House where Lafayette stayed. He left at 6 a.m. with Gallatin to tour New Geneva, a village Gallatin founded on the Monongahela, hoping it would be an important link between Washington and the Ohio. Wishing to give the general respite from the crowds, Gallatin led the party up a steep drive to Friendship Hill, his estate overlooking the river. They found the lawn filled with people waiting to meet Lafayette. Gallatin welcomed them. "Mr. Gallatin's best liquors were strewn in profusion on the tables," the *Uniontown Genius of Liberty* reported next day. Lafayette spoke from a balcony to the crowd and stayed the night.[1]

He returned next day to another hotel and "the evening was spent in gaiety and hilarity."[2] Later that year, Gallatin judged his new town was a failure and his wife felt isolated in the wilderness. So with his family Gallatin departed forever. In New York, he joined what became the Gallatin Bank. In 1848, Uniontown topped its courthouse with an eight-foot finial sculpture of Lafayette as he appeared there in 1825 with top hat and cane. Artist David Gilmour Blythe made it of painted two-inch poplar planks and tin.[3]

On May 29, the travelers rode north by carriage through Perryopolis to the Monongahela town of Elizabeth, then Elizabethtown, where they had luncheon. It was Sunday and no parade was allowed. The general spoke in front of the Walker Hotel and expressed condolences to Erich Bollman's brother Lewis. Lafayette also visited another brother and Erich's daughters in Philadelphia. A barge carried the party up the

Monongahela to where the French and Indians defeated Braddock in July 1755. Grain farmers resisting taxation had gathered there during the 1794 Whiskey Rebellion, but Washington's federal troops turned them away. Nearly seventy years after the battle, a plow could not turn a furrow without exposing bones and weapon fragments, Levasseur wrote. They stayed at Pittsburgh lawyer George Wallace's mansion built on the 328-acre field in 1804. The 1755 battle was a major defeat for Britain and the colonists. Although the latter won the French and Indian War, the battlefield escaped early commemoration as a park.[4]

At daylight, cavalry volunteers from Pittsburgh escorted the travelers as a crowd covered the road for miles. Lafayette visited a federal arsenal halfway to the city where he received a twenty-four-gun salute and an invitation to breakfast. He inspected the armory and workshops, finding everything of manufacturing excellence for which Pittsburgh was already renowned. Reaching the city through the Lawrenceville district, he reviewed the militia and met veterans. Asked if he remembered the young soldier who first offered to carry him on a litter at Brandywine, Lafayette threw himself into the senior's arms. "No, I have not forgotten, Wilson, and it is a great happiness to be permitted to embrace him today!" Wilson and many spectators were thrilled. The general also knew the Reverend Joseph Patterson, who visited him with leaders of different faiths. Patterson fired his musket in two terrible campaigns and at Germantown.

The party which now included a young Frenchman, M. de Syon, from Washington, whom the general had invited to travel with him, stayed at the Mansion House Hotel, Fifth Avenue and Wood Street, in the heart of the city.[5] It was a few blocks from where Fort Fayette, at Penn Avenue and Ninth Street, had replaced old Fort Pitt from 1792 to 1794 and was General Wayne's chief supply base.[6] Lafayette visited factories, especially ones making flint glass, then the city's largest industry. Manufacturer Benjamin Bakewell presented him with a set of cut-glass tumblers with his sulphide profile on their bottoms.[7] When Monroe visited in 1817 Bakewell had given him two decanters. The White House then ordered glassware worth $1,032. Monroe may have alerted Lafayette to the factory. Levasseur compared the quality to Baccarat, French *cristallerie* founded in 1764.[8] The Boston and Sandwich

Glass Company also produced a small pressed glass salt: a steamboat with "Lafayet" impressed on the sidewheel housing. But these were minute instances of the country's Lafayette mania. His visit created a booming demand for commemorative objects: badges, waist ribbons, gloves, plates, cups, saucers, and vest buttons with his image as well as paintings, wood carvings, sculptures and furniture.[9]

FIFTY-SIX: SPEEDING ON THE ERIE CANAL

In Pittsburgh, Lafayette stayed at the Mansion House on the northwest corner of Wood Street and Fifth Avenue, an annex of the Masonic Hall. His second floor room, painted with sun, moon and stars, was the Masons' lodge room and held a mahogany four-poster bed. Four revolutionary generals' names, Greene, Lincoln, Mercer, Wayne, were carved in the posts. Atop the canopy, a large gilt eagle grasped in its beak long silken Washington and Lafayette streamers. At a luncheon, Harriet Preble, aquainted with Lafayette in Paris, wrote: "The simple details of his salutations, and of his hat, which he touched even in his sleep, is almost worth a place in history… That hesitating step, which was so peculiar to him at Draveil (Paris suburb); seating himself, slowly rising, then rising quickly to salute all whom you introduced to him."

On Tuesday, May 31, he stood as sponsor of a baby, Gilbert Lafayette Beelen Fetterman, at St. Patrick Roman Catholic Church.[1] Lafayette visited Félix Brunot (1752-1838), a French Huguenot doctor who had served in the American Revolution. Neither Levasseur nor *The Pittsburgh Gazette* reported the visit. Like Blennerhasset, Brunot, born in Morey, Burgundy, had lived on an island in the Ohio River still named for him, but flooding had forced Brunot to live downtown on Penn Avenue, where Lafayette and he "ran to greet each other, embraced and wept for joy."[2] As Lafayette thought of Washington as his father, Brunot family lore says he called Brunot his foster brother. After receptions and dinners, the party left Pittsburgh May 1 on the Butler Plank Road.[3]

Reaching Butler, thirty-five miles north of Pittsburgh, they lunched at Mechling's Inn and stayed at the Old Stone House, a wayside hotel. They ate at a plank table and climbed a steep staircase to a barracks-style room.[4] Lafayette said to the region's veterans, "Farewell, my friends. This is the last time you shall see me." The party toured Allegheny College in Meadville and Waterford, site of Fort LeBoeuf, there Washington had delivered Dinwiddie's 1753 demand that French troops quit the region.

On June 3, a cavalcade escorted Lafayette into Erie, where he banqueted beneath sails of British vessels that Commodore Oliver Hazard Perry captured in 1813. After a three-hour combat against a much larger force, Perry had scrawled on the back of an old envelope to William Henry Harrison, "Dear General, we have met the enemy and they are ours. Two ships, two brigs, one schooner and one sloop."[5] The party left Erie at 3 p.m. for a steamer in Dunkirk, New York, waiting to take them to Buffalo. Not wanting to delay the boat, they traveled ten hours east without stopping. In many villages they saw citizens by large bonfires waiting "to salute the national guest with patriotic acclamations."

Jolted on a tree-trunk road, they awoke at 1 a.m. in Fredonia to a cannon's roar and were dazzled by a thousand lights suspended from trees and houses. Men and boys stood on one side of the road, women and girls on the other. All had waited hours in the cool air. An orator on a platform greeted them. Burning rosin fires surrounded the stage as citizens filed past to speak and shake hands. After a collation, the nation's guests left at 3 a.m., boarding the boat in early morning. In Dunkirk, a town with an attractive bay and French name, as music played a committee and many women met the party on board. By noon they had neared Buffalo but a storm delayed mooring until 2 p.m.

The British had nearly destroyed Buffalo in the War of 1812, but the visitors were impressed with its air of prosperity. They rested at the Eagle Tavern, where many citizens wanting to meet the hero. One was elderly Red Jacket, chief of the Senecas, who had been with Lafayette at the great Oneida council at Fort Schuyler in 1784. Lafayette asked what had happened to the young brave who had eloquently opposed burying the hatchet. "He is before you," Red Jacket replied. Proud of his native tongue, he refused to answer Lafayette in English, although knowing it, until his interpreter translated into Seneca. The general spoke his few remembered Seneca words and pleased the chief.[6]

After a night in Buffalo,[7] the guests went by carriage to Niagara Falls. Crossing a wooden bridge near the cataract, Lafayette then toured Goat Island with its owner Augustus Porter and was enchanted. The site seemed otherworldly: 100 verdant acres flanked by water rushing into the abyss, enshrouding clouds and endless roar. Lingering for two hours, Lafayette was tempted to buy the island for $1,000 but decided that, living in France, he would rarely see it. They all slept that night in Lewiston and arose at 5 a.m. for breakfast at Fort Niagara, where the river enters Lake Ontario. The garrison greeted them with a twenty-four-gun salute.

The travelers left for Lockport, New York, with some eighty citizens on horseback escorting them to the village. Workmen in the quarry of the nearly completed Erie Canal — it would open fully on October 26, 1825 — suddenly set off hundreds of small explosions, shooting small stones into the air and also at many welcomers. The guests admired the workers digging the remaining channel and saw it was already bringing "comfort and abundance" to the wilderness. A reception and banquet followed. The party boarded a light packet boat that rose in one of the five double sets of locks: one set lifted traffic to the canal, the other lowered boats to Lockport and the Niagara River.

On the long descent to Albany, they found comfortable cabins at 7 p.m. on the *Rochester,* an engineless canal boat, and slept during the sixty-five miles to Rochester. They admired the boat's speed (a steady five miles an hour), the excellent draft horses and towpath. The boat carried forty tons and had a draft of two and a half feet, with the crew changing horses every six hours. The replacement horse had a stall on board, and there was a portable bridge for it to step to the towpath.

Before leaving, they heard a great cheer: "*Lafayette!*" They were astonished to see they were suspended on a stone aqueduct seventy feet high, one of several taking the canal over rivers. An immense crowd below surrounded them. Several waterfalls rumbled beneath them as the Genesee River rolled below for a distance of fifty feet. In carriages the guests joined a reception in Rochester that "in affection and elegance" equaled any they experienced. They moved on land through villages — Canandaigua, Geneva, Auburn, Ithaca and others, stopping briefly to enjoy receptions, traveling 130 miles day and night to rejoin the canal in Syracuse at 6 a.m. Syracusans had been up all night waiting for them. Their prepared dinner made a fine breakfast.

They left at 9 a.m. amid booming artillery and many wishes for the tour's happy conclusion. There were similar remarks and welcomes in Rome, Utica, Schenectady and elsewhere. Lafayette was amazed the land he was passing through so rapidly was where he had had so much difficulty saving Fort Stanwix from Britain's tomahawk-wielding Indian allies. He could scarcely believe the great changes. Three Indian chiefs asked for an interview, recalling their helping him in the campaigns of 1777-1778. He recognized them and was surprised two who were old earlier were still living. They said they had to give up hunting for farming and were thankful the government helped when harvests failed. They had fought the British with Americans and were willing to help again if necessary.

Lafayette praised their sentiments, asked them to regard Americans as good brothers and pleased them with French gold coins. Because of the grueling schedule he refused an Oneida County group. They wanted him to lay the first stone for a monument to De Steuben, who had died at sixty near Steubenville, New York, in 1794. The baron was his friend and "no one was more worthy," he said, of a memorial than he who had shared the dangers of the Virginia campaign. But Lafayette could not risk the hard journey and possibly miss his appointment.

On the packet boat *Governor Clinton*, a red man, an Onandagan, startled them. When the captain refused to stop for him, the brave ran ahead and jumped off a low bridge onto the boat deck. "Where is Kayewla?" he asked and was shown the general. Stretching out a hand he said, "I am the son of Wekchekaeta," of him who loved you so well that he followed you to your country when you returned there after the great war. My father has often spoken to me of you and I am happy to see you." Lafayette knew his father had died and was glad to meet his son who was about twenty-four. They talked for several minutes and Lafayette gave him several dollars. Then the brave, as spontaneously as before, leaped like a deer ten feet to shore and disappeared into the forest. The general explained how in 1778 he had taken Wekchekaeta to Paris, but he became disgusted with society and sailed home to his tribe.

FIFTY-SEVEN: THE SUPREME CEREMONY

The sojourners reached Albany before sunrise on June 12 and the next day crossed the Hudson en route to Massachusetts. With 150 miles of good roads to go, Lafayette was sure they would reach Boston on June 15 well in time for the ceremony. There were brief visits in Pittsfield, Worthington, Chesterfield and Northampton. On the stagecoach from Brookfield, they arrived at 2 a.m. in Worcester, where they slept and breakfasted at the Exchange Hotel. They arrived in Boston at noon on June 15 and stayed at the mansion of merchant turned Federalist Senator James Lloyd. Levasseur found few believed Lafayette could return to Boston on the precise day he planned for the ceremony, many viewing his difficult journey as almost a miracle. "And our astonishment," he wrote, "is increased when it is recollected that this extraordinary journey (of upwards of 5,000 miles in less than four months) was performed by a man of sixty-seven years of age!" Lafayette's elation was tempered on learning Governors Brooks and Eustis, whom he regarded as friends, had died.

He had not underestimated the importance and impact of the Bunker Hill cornerstone laying, a great American event of 1825; even likening it to 1790's *Fête de la Fédération*.[1] On June 16, he was again welcomed at the state capitol. New governor Levi Lincoln Jr. congratulated him on his successful journey. After Lafayette's response, many members of the House and Senate, as well as other friends who had come for the Bunker Hill event next day, warmly greeted him. John Quincy Adams, respected but aloof, had become president in March. He strongly opposed the Masons, rejecting their brotherly bonds of friendship and secrecy. He not only shunned leading the Bunker Hill ceremony but helped found the Anti-Masonic Party that supported his return to the House of Representatives in 1831.[2] At age seven Adams with his mother, Abigail, had witnessed the historic battle from Braintree, a Boston suburb. Americans lost this battle but gained glory for their courageous defense.

Lafayette headed the procession. He left the Lloyd mansion at 7 a.m. with the sun shining amid ringing bells and artillery reports. He went to the Grand Masonic Lodge of Massachusetts, receiving welcomes and compliments from officers and delegates of six states' grand lodges. At 10 a.m., 2,000 Masons, sixteen volunteer cavalry corps, civil and military authorities gathered at the gold-domed state capitol. A half-hour later, the procession of about 7,000 started for the historic site. Marching at the head were 200 officers and soldiers of the Revolution.

Forty veterans of Bunker Hill, wearing large ribbons inscribed with the historic date, June 17th, 1775, followed in eight open carriages. One man carried the drum he had played that day to rally battalions. Next, a phalanx of monument subscribers walking six abreast, 2,000 Masons in full regalia and Lafayette in a superb calash drawn by six white horses. After them came a long file of carriages with Governor Lincoln, his staff and a great many others of distinction. With the sounds of music and bells, cannon thunder and cheering crowds, 200,000 people from all the states and foreign countries gathered at 12:30 p.m. in a natural amphitheater on the hill where the future memorial would rise.

The original wooden memorial, fifteen feet tall with a gilt urn on top, had been removed. Masons of Boston's Charlestown district, future home of the granite obelisk commemorating the first major battle of the war, presented Lafayette with a gold-headed cane carved from a former timber and engraved with the day's significance. Lafayette assisted as the first stone was placed. Another stone covered an iron box filled with medals, coins and an engraved silver plate telling of the monument's founding. The grand master of the Grand Lodge of Massachusetts then poured symbolic corn, wine and oil on the stone as a chaplain gave a benediction.

The gathering moved to the hill's northeast side where Daniel Webster, president and co-founder of the committee, stood on a platform to address more than 10,000 listeners seated on benches. More than 30,000 spectators farther up the hill watched but could not hear the proceedings. A great chorus of musicians filled the air before the pastor who had fought in the battle implored the Almighty in prayer to bless the labors of this day. Webster, forty-three, noble looking and a well-known orator, took the platform to swelling applause from "the cloud on the hill," as he called the audience, lasting several minutes. Well into his address in which he paid homage to George Washington, assembled veterans and representatives of government, Webster reached a crescendo:

> *We wish that this column, rising towards heaven among the pointed spires of so many temples dedicated to God, may contribute also to produce in all minds a pious feeling of dependence and gratitude. We wish, finally, that the last object to the sight of him who leaves his native shore, and the first to gladden him who revisits it, may be something which shall remind him of the liberty and the glory of his country. Let it rise! Let it rise, till it meet the sun in his coming, let the earliest light of the morning gild it, and the parting day linger and play on its summit!*

Addressing bareheaded Lafayette, Webster intoned: "Fortunate, fortunate man! With what measure of devotion will you not thank God for the circumstances of your extraordinary life. Heaven saw fit to ordain that the electric spark of liberty should be conducted through you, from the new world to the old; and we have long ago received it in charge from our fathers, to cherish your name and your virtues." Whenever Webster invoked the general's name, aged veterans removed their hats and the multitude's roars were deafening. The whole assemblage chanted a hymn ending the second part of the ceremony.[3]

A procession marched to a gentlemen-only banquet on the summit. Under an immense wooden building 4,000 sat down to lunch. Speeches and toasts followed. Lafayette thanked the association for the future monument. In a toast he cried: To "Bunker Hill and that holy resistance to oppression which has already disenthralled the American hemisphere. The anniversary toast at the jubilee of the next half-century will be — to Europe freed!"

The monument was erected between 1827 and 1842 as funds were raised. The nation's first railroad, horse-drawn cars carrying gray granite from a Quincy quarry twelve miles away, became a reality, leaving vaunted canals to die.[4]

The evening of Bunker Hill, Lafayette saw a performance of *Charles II* at the Boston Theater. Actors staged a tableau of La Grange and a sentimental scene of the general at Washington's tomb. Staying in Boston five days, he said he would choose it if he ever were to live in the United States. On June 18, he and Mayor Josiah Quincy made a last trip to President John Adams. He would die on July 4, 1826, as would Jefferson — and Monroe in 1831. On June 20, the Massachusetts Mechanics Association gave Lafayette a splendid dinner at the Marlboro Hotel. Important public officials and the commonwealth's most distinguished figures attended

Lafayette accepted invitations to Maine, New Hampshire and Vermont while New York City asked his presence for its Fourth of July celebrations. The months of the tour were growing short, but he agreed to the requests because leaders made the stops agreeable and rapid. He spent June 21 on Boston farewells. With an arrangements committee and volunteer cavalry, the quartet made a hasty visit to upper New England, traveling at eleven miles an hour.

In the border town of Pembroke, Massachusetts, they met a New Hampshire delegation headed by Webster's older lawyer brother, Ezekiel. After David L. Morrill, governor of New Hampshire, welcomed the general to the state house in Concord, he was pleased to meet a large number of old fellow soldiers there. Dinner followed in a public square with 600 guests. He sat among 200 toasting revolutionary officers and soldiers. That evening the musical society had an excellent oratorio and reception at Morrill's house where crowds of women met Lafayette and discussed politics. Next day he traveled with the cavalry through Dover, New Hampshire, to meet the Maine delegates who directed them to Portland, the capital. Visiting Kennebunkport, Lafayette accepted a public dinner and left at 4 p.m. for Saco to spend the night.

Portland's grand welcome with arches equaling the best seen dazzled them. One arch carried a model of *La Victoire* and the banner, "I will purchase and equip a vessel at my own expense!" Other arches listed his American battles. Governor Albion K. Parris addressed him at the state house, recalling the era that gave Lafayette his American reputation. Masonic officers received him and he received a doctorate of letters from the academy and a public dinner. Since Portland was as far as he could go to make commitments, he reluctantly turned south. It was Sunday and the governor would not accompany him, setting off a controversy in Portland, Concord and Boston newspapers. His schedule left no choice.

On June 28, the travelers reached Burlington, Vermont, where Governor Cornelius P. Van Ness introduced Lafayette to the public. He had passed through Windsor, Woodstock, Montpelier and other towns in the Green Mountain State, its name and sobriquet from the French: *vert* (green) and *mont* (mountain). Burlingtonians had paid for the University of Vermont's first structure which burned in 1824. They were now paying for the second. Lafayette laid its cornerstone and went to a Van Ness reception.[5]

Around midnight they boarded *Phoenix*, one of two awning-covered steamboats that plowed south all night through Lake Champlain. At noon on June 30, they reached the village of Whitehall, New York, on the Vermont border, where Arnold built ships to deter the British from Canada. The guests took a carriage with several horse relays, stopped at Schuyler's mansion and slept in Waterford, New York.

FIFTY-EIGHT: LAST TRAVELS ON TOUR

After his exhausting journey, Lafayette may have wished his remaining time to be spent at leisure in New York or Washington. But he moved about as before. From July to September 1825, he returned to places he had promised to revisit. After a breakfast in Troy and banquet in Albany on July 1, the guests took the *S.S. Bolivar* for New York with Friedrich List, the German economist (1789-1846) the general invited. List, favoring protectionism over free trade for America, wrote of the tour in German newspapers.[1]

On July 4, Lafayette received a great welcome in New York's City Hall, where he was the embodiment of the country's forty-ninth anniversary and laid the cornerstone for a mechanics' library in Brooklyn Heights that day. Before a large gathering and assisted by Long Island Masons, he assisted at the ceremony. Greeting the crowd, Lafayette held the young Walt Whitman, an event the poet recalled as being "touched by the hand and taken a moment to the breast of the immortal old Frenchman."[2]

Working men, waving trade banners, followed the general to a Manhattan church where, after the homily, he listened to a reading of the *Declaration of Independence*. Levasseur was impressed by children who could recite it. Lafayette returned to City Hall to continue the reception with a lavish dinner and toasts. He went to a theater and Castle Garden for gala performances. In following days, he met with old war officers and saw a balloon ascend at Castle Garden. On July 9, he was rowed across the Hudson to dine with his Continental Army friend Colonel Richard Varick, member of King's College's board of directors. His house looked on the charming village green of Hackensack, New Jersey.

Rowing to Manhattan from Jersey City, oarsmen on the ferry offered Lafayette *American Star,* a twenty-seven foot racing rowboat, tan outside and blue inside. Built in Brooklyn in 1819, it had beaten a British crew from the frigate *Hussar* on December 9, 1824 in a friendly race in New York harbor, the crew winning a $1,000 prize. Fifteen-year-old coxswain John Magnus said, "We hope that you will take the boat back to France where it may remind you of your grateful friends you have left behind, the ingenuity of the mechanics of a country which you assisted to liberate and also our great naval motto, 'Free trade and sailors' rights.'"

The smiling general replied, "No keepsake could be more welcome; the more gratifying indeed, when offered from the hands of the five victors. It shall be carefully and fondly preserved. I beg you, gentlemen, to accept and transmit to your companions the congratulations, the thanks and the good wishes of a veteran heartily devoted to the great naval motto, 'Free trade and sailors' rights.'"[3]

The following Monday, the general attended a performance at the Lafayette Circus, Laurens Street near Canal Street. The big top tent was invented in 1825. Exiting the Mansion House on Broadway, the guests left New York for the last time on July 14. Wharves held an immense crowd of sad faces, witnessing his sailing in silence, except for a last farewell. The tour would end in less than two months. Lafayette planned to revisit American presidents and spend time in Philadelphia and Washington.

He swept through Hackensack and Paterson and was guest of honor at a reception and banquet in Morristown. On July 15, he rode through Chatham and Springfield to Newark and Elizabeth to a banquet at Craig's Hotel. In Elizabeth, Lafayette visited the grave of the Reverend James Caldwell, rebel Presbyterian army chaplain killed in an argument with an American sentry who was tried and hanged. British soldiers previously had fatally shot Mrs. Caldwell. Lafayette sent their son, John Edwards Caldwell, to upscale Pension Lemoyne in Paris, excused from Catholic classes. He returned to America, became editor of *The Christian Herald* and was a prominent philanthropist.

The travelers continued to New Brunswick for dinner and arrived at Princeton at 10 p.m. for a faculty-student reception. In Trenton next day, Lafayette breakfasted with the governor and his staff, revisited Joseph Bonaparte and Achille Murat before boarding *S.S.Delaware* for Philadelphia, remaining eight days. The Philadelphia Athaneum elected him an honorary member and he addressed the William Penn Society. The party visited Germantown and Barren Hill.[4] He breakfasted with Benjamin Chew, owner of the mansion whose wall carried cannon and musket balls, and made two trips to review Fairmount Park's new waterworks.

Again the general attended receptions in Independence Hall with civic matrons, the Society of the Cincinnati and watched a fireworks display. Back on the *Delaware*, the visitors sailed down to Wilmington for a Masonic dinner and visited Éleuthère Irenée du Pont at his home on the Brandywine. The Du Ponts fled France in 1799. E.I. had studied explosives with Lavoisier, guillotined father of modern chemistry, and brought that knowledge to the United States. With French capital in 1802, he founded E.I. du Pont de Nemours to manufacture black gunpowder.

On July 25, the guests and many veterans walked the Brandywine battlefield in blistering heat. Lafayette recalled troop placements, materiel and names of those who supported him. He stopped by the house of farmer Gideon Gilpin. Dying in bed, Gilpin recognized him, shedding tears of gratitude for his visit. West Chester citizens offered dinner after which the party joined a delegation from Lancaster, where they were pleased to see how so many adherents of various religions could live and work in harmony.

They journeyed down the Susquehanna to Baltimore, reaching the wharf at midnight where friends surrounded the general. Suddenly, a large fire lit the dark as a store burned in the port. Lafayette was ushered to his hotel. Georges and Levasseur ran to help stop the blaze but found firemen with four engines quenching it. After two days in Baltimore and many goodbyes, they started for Washington on August 1. President Adams' second son, John, twenty-two, driving an elegant carriage, met them a few miles from the capital. He asked them to go with him to the White House where the president insisted they stay for their last visit.

The mansion had not changed with new occupants, remaining unadorned. Adams invited the party to dinner with two friends who accompanied them from Baltimore. Levasseur found that Adams' intelligence and manners freed him of any claim he behaved like an aristocrat. On August 2, Lafayette toured the frigate, *U.S.S. Brandywine,* fourth and last of forty-four-gun warships beginning with *U.S.S. Constitution,* carrying 467 officers and men. She weighed 1,708 tons, was 175 feet long, had a forty-five foot beam, a twenty-two foot draft and moved at thirteen knots. She would transport the general, his party and a large cache of American gifts to France.

It has often been written that *Brandywine* held soil from Bunker Hill for Lafayette's grave. Historian Robert Crout has found Lafayette ordered the soil four years later, through his New York agent, a hogshead of Bunker Hill earth from Charlestown selectmen "to be placed over his body at his decease."[5] American frigates were named for American rivers. Adams insisted the ship bear the name of the creek that the battle and the nation's guest made famous. The general accepted Adams' offer. The sailing date would be September 7. The news set off a new wave of White House invitations. Lafayette spent his last days in the United States with friends. On August 6, Adams drove Lafayette, Georges and his friend in the president's carriage south without an escort. Adams' son and Levasseur followed in a two-wheeled tilbury.

Lafayette expected it would be his last visit to Virginia, where he was remembered for his 1781 campaign. Adams drove to Monroe at his new house, Oak Hill, a farm worked by slaves thirty-seven miles from the nation's capital near Leesburg. At the Potomac Bridge, Adams underpaid the gatekeeper who ran after him shouting, "Mr. President! Mr. President! You have paid eleven cents too little!" As Adams took out his purse the keeper spied Lafayette and wanted to return the toll, knowing Lafayette could cross bridges and ride roads free. Adams explained the general was traveling privately as a friend and insisted on paying. The man accepted this, the only toll asked during Lafayette's stay. Adams recorded in his *Memoirs* the carriage broke down before reaching Monroe.[6] Adams wrote of his guest, "There is fire beneath the cinders."[7]

The Monroes seemed content at Oak Hill. But lacking money they would soon sell their first estate, Ashlawn-Highland, near Monticello, a site Jefferson had chosen. The Lafayette party was surprised that Monroe, besides being president and having held other high offices, had been elected a justice of the peace. The title of president, Monroe said, didn't keep him from being useful. The party stayed three enjoyable days. Oak Hill, from August 6 to 10, was filled with visitors seeking Lafayette. The party then went with Adams, Madison and Monroe to Monticello and Montpelier August 13 to 25. Jefferson because of his pains spoke and moved little, living but eleven more months.

As for Monroe, his wife, Elizabeth Kortright Monroe, died in 1830. Selling Oak Hill, he moved to New York to live with a married daughter, dying at seventy-three in 1831. Madison, after selling off land at Montpelier to stay solvent, died at eighty-five in 1836. Dolley Madison left Montpelier for Lafayette Square, where she entertained. Suffering from rheumatoid arthritis, she scrimped by wearing her old clothes, hid her distorted fingers in gloves and died at eighty-one in 1849. Like Lafayette, the three unpensioned presidents were better politicians than managers of their own fortunes.

FIFTY-NINE: AMERICAN FAREWELLS

Before returning to Washington, Lafayette was invited to a festival in his honor in Leesburg, joined by Adams, Monroe and Chief Justice John Marshall. The travelers were lavishly entertained and spent the night at Belmont, a plantation of the 1790s built by Assemblyman Ludwell Lee and his wife who was his first cousin. Lee was Lafayette's aide-de-camp in 1781 and a nephew of Richard Henry Lee, a signer of the *Declaration of Independence*. The general stood as godfather for Lee's elder baby daughter who died that evening. Monroe, for whom Belmont was a presidential refuge in the War of 1812, stood with Adams as godfathers of a younger daughter.[1]

Saying goodbye to Monroe, the Lafayettes and Adamses left Leesburg at 10 a.m. the next day, hoping to reach Washington quickly. But August heat claimed a horse that collapsed in a roadside ditch. Everyone tried to save the expiring animal and sat on the grass awaiting a horse. They were stared at but no one recognized them. They reached the White House after sunset.

Lafayette visited Woodlawn and Mount Vernon, dining with a "large company." At Arlington, George Custis, Washington's stepson and ardent patriot, was much impressed, as were many other

Americans, with Simon Bolivar's republican battles for South American independence from Spain. Custis wished to salute Bolivar with a miniature of Washington and a gold medal the nation had given the president at a July Fourth festival. He asked Lafayette, as the hero of two worlds, to present the gifts with a covering letter to *El Liberador.* The general performed the ceremony at a White House reception for the Colombian legation on September 2. Bolivar thanked him in a letter: "Washington given by the hand of Lafayette is the crown of human awards."[2]

To celebrate Lafayette's sixty-eighth birthday, Adams hosted a grand state dinner at the White House on September 6. It was a time for many sad goodbyes. Stately columned Arlington House was illuminated and Lafayette presented with a miniature of Colonel Francis Huger. Lafayette wrote Jefferson on the seventh, "My heart is too full to write more. A thousand blessings on you and family…"[3]

Washington City proclaimed a general holiday as Lafayette said farewell to America the next day at a White House reception around noon. Civic, military and naval leaders came with Washington, Georgetown and Alexandria authorities, multitudes of citizens and strangers. Leaving his White House rooms, Lafayette entered the main hall in silence, leaning on the district marshal and the president's son. Adams orated:

> *At the painful moment of parting from you, we take comfort in the thought that wherever you may be, to the last pulsation of your heart, our country will ever be present to your affections; and a cheering consolation assures us that we are not called to sorrow, most of all, that we shall see your face no more. We shall indulge the pleasing anticipation of beholding our friend again. In the meantime, speaking in the name of the whole people of the United States, and at a loss only for language to give utterance to that feeling of attachment with which the heart of the nation beats, as the heart of one man, I bid you a reluctant and affectionate farewell!*

An approving roar drowned his last words. Lafayette, deeply affected, took moments before replying. "Amidst all my obligations to the general government, and particularly you, sir, its respected chief magistrate, I have most thankfully to acknowledge the opportunity given me, at this solemn and painful moment, to present the people of the United States with a parting tribute of profound, inexpressible gratitude..."

He spoke fifteen minutes. In tender leave-taking, he burst out, "God bless you, sir, and all who surround us. God bless the American people, each of their states and the federal government. Accept this patriotic farewell of an overflowing heart; such will be the last throb when it ceases to beat." He stepped forward and threw himself into Adams' arms, both crying, "Adieu, adieu!" Moving back a few steps, Lafayette's feelings overcame him and, again falling on Adams' neck, said, "God bless you!" Spectators also cried as they surrounded him, shaking his hand a last time. It was as highly emotional a moment as it was solemn.

To compose himself Lafayette retreated to his rooms. Louisa Adams, her daughters and nieces came to express their good wishes and regrets at his leaving. Mrs. Adams, born in London to an American father and English mother, was a fine hostess and the only foreign-born First Lady. For his birthday, she and the girls gave Lafayette a bust of her husband and a copy of French verses. The first salvo of a twenty-four-gun salute boomed outside. He had momentary thoughts of remaining. But the nation's guests entered carriages with the secretaries of state, treasury and navy as the president waved and called his last goodbye from the portico. At that signal, troops there for the occasion bowed their flags.

The procession moved slowly to the Potomac where *Mount Vernon* took them down river. The militias of Alexandria, Georgetown and Washington marched in columns to receive his last farewell. He boarded with the secretary of the navy and government officers accompanying him to the *Brandywine.* The huge crowd of spectators on shore kept a profound silence, becoming a mournful wail that mingled with Fort Washington's artillery fire as the steamboat pushed off. They heard a similar sound as they passed Alexandria. Waving farewell to Mount Vernon, Lafayette deeply realized the sacrifice he was making to France in leaving America's appreciation.

He did not depart unscathed. *Mount Vernon* ran around on an oyster bank and was, as on the Hudson, refloated during the night. At 10 a.m. they reached the *Brandywine* at the Potomac's mouth. The general was to enter the first tender when nausea struck him.[4]

He boarded a while later with one official, navy secretary Samuel Southard, a former senator, who presented the general to Commodore Charles Morris for safekeeping. Lafayette stepped back from the railing. Friends in bobbing boats on the bay saw the last of him. Full honors were offered as the ship prepared to sail. Crew manned yard arms, gunners were at their stations, sailors stood at attention on deck... But as Morris was about to cast off, the *U.S.S. Constitution* came near with a large group of Baltimoreans wishing to say farewell. By the time they left it was too late to sail. *Brandywine* weighed anchor in the morning for her first major voyage.

Entering the Chesapeake, she sailed under a rainbow like the one Lafayette had seen on first arriving at Staten Island. The last arch they would experience in America. Morris said Adams ordered him to take Lafayette wherever he wished in Europe and in the meantime he was absolute master of the ship. The general chose Le Havre because his family would be waiting there, and he wished to return to people who had sent him over with such affection.

Two days out a terrible storm in the gulfstream sent the frigate rolling and pitching. Besides almost all aboard becoming seasick, she leaked. Pumps could not clear the salt water. Morris decided they were too deep in the water and ordered part of the ballast, 32,000 pounds of iron, jettisoned, solving the problem. Riding higher in the ocean, sailors found the leak just under the loading limit and quickly repaired it. The rest of the twenty-four-day crossing was without incident but winds made it unpleasant. Another occurrence eased discomfort. When parents heard Lafayette was to sail on *Brandywine*, they beseeched Adams to let their sons sail with him. Since that was not possible, he decided each state should have a midshipman aboard.

Lafayette was pleased so many of the sailors were sons of revolutionary soldiers. He was like a father to them and their eyes filled with tears as the journey ended. They asked to present a gift. Shortly in Paris, Lafayette received an exquisite silver urn. Made there, it depicted in colored enamel the United States Capitol, Lafayette's visit to Washington's tomb, *Brandywine* at Le Havre and the sailors' tribute.[5]

It was night. Morris did not trust the high waves and winds. He sent an officer into port to fetch a pilot. The Lafayette party learned from letters dropped off by a fishing boat around midnight that family and friends, including Levasseur's father, had been awaiting them several days. The pilot came early to guide *Brandywine* to port, but her size forced anchoring out in the harbor. About 3 p.m. the captain fired a salute of twenty-four guns which the fort returned. A steamboat brought out Lafayette's family and friends at 11 p.m. *Brandywine's* officers and men surrounded him, presenting him with *The Stars and Stripes* from the stern. There were many emotional farewells as the general entered the boat amid cheers from the warship and crowds on the wharf.

Morris had orders to accompany Lafayette to Paris while the ship sailed to the Mediterranean to reinforce a squadron. This time, there were no problems from the police. The party stayed with a prominent citizen who offered his house for as long as the general wished. He left next day for La Grange by carriage. Georges and his family traveled on the Seine by way of Rouen. The general stopped there at the home of a wealthy merchant and old friend from the Chamber of Deputies who insisted on entertaining the guest of America and invited Rouen's most distinguished citizens. They too wanted to meet him. French newspapers had carried many articles on his American adventures and honors, bringing him a fresh burst of national attention.

Near dinner's end, Lafayette learned a large crowd had gathered in the street. As he went to a balcony to speak royal guards and police began to disperse spectators. The guards' reserve showed their reluctance to obey the command, possibly from Charles X. Police horses knocked down mothers, children and wounded several people. Many were harshly arrested. The police waited for Lafayette to enter a carriage and escorted him to his hotel while young men at the door kept the gendarmes outside.

Well-wishers fleeing the melee came inside where Lafayette received them. He was delighted to hear how his tour had increased France's glory. But the despotic police embarrassed and saddened everyone in Lafayette's party. Captain Morris and his officers accompanying him to Paris witnessed the attack, noting how a public that had fought for liberty submitted to bayonets. Young men said they had not protested more to spare the general the anguish of greater resistance, and the Americans commended them.

Next morning, October 8, young men on horseback filled the hotel courtyard and escorted Lafayette without incident while receiving citizens' good wishes. Horsemen relieved the earlier group which placed a crown of immortelles on his New York Militia sword in the carriage. The party slept that night at St. Germaine-en-Laye and reached La Grange next day. Near the chateau Lafayette joined a large gathering from nearby districts. His greeters acted as if he were their father. They had planned for three days to salute his return with a festival, filling the old chateau and courtyard until evening. Guests led the Lafayettes amid music and illuminations under another triumphal arch inscribed: "Friend of the People." Lafayette was thrilled to be welcomed by those who knew him best. Dancing lasted all night with cries of, "Long live the people's friend!" He was happy to be with his family again.

PART FIVE: THE OLD AGITATOR

SIXTY: A THIRD REVOLUTION

Dismissed unceremoniously as head of the National Guard, Lafayette, seventy-three and an old man, now lived mostly in his first floor suite at 8 Rue d'Anjou. De Tessé had left him her *hôtel particulier* with a large courtyard. In his ground floor suite, he entertained on Tuesdays when anyone, but especially Americans, could visit him. The street was steps from Rue du Faubourg St. Honoré and the Ēlysée Palace. Going north, it was a few blocks to the Chapel of Friendship, belonging literally to an earlier age.

Fenimore Cooper often visited Lafayette, finding his lodgings "neat but simple," sufficient for one but not the most elegant *pied de terre.* "Here I have seen princes, marshals and dignitaries of all degrees ringing for admission," he wrote, "not one appearing to think of [anything] but the great man within." There were a large entrance hall, two salons and a smaller room where he wrote and later had his bed. The rooms were *en suite,* connected laterally with one or two rooms and offices. His attendants were his German-born valet Bastien Wagner, a footman to help with his carriage and a coachman. Fenimore Cooper never saw a cook or female. The servants did not wear livery but "all of his appointments, carriages, horses and furniture are those of a gentleman." Despite Lafayette's love of American fashion, the novelist never saw a carpet, "getting to be common in Paris," there or at La Grange.

"His meals are quite frugal though good — a *poulet rôti* — invariably making one dish. There are two or three removes a dish at a time, and the dinner usually concludes with some preserves or dried fruits, especially dates of which he is extremely fond." Having already eaten, the writer would join him "for one or two of the latter." Their talk was of what occurred that day in the Chambers: European politics, nullification in America [South Carolina forbade collecting tariff duties it deemed discriminatory and unconstitutional, precursor to secession] or "the latest gossip of the chateau [La Grange] of which he is singularly well informed though he has ceased to go there."

Fenimore Cooper asked about the late royal family. Lafayette described Louis XVI as well-meaning but addicted a little too much to the pleasures of the table and would have done well enough if he had not listened to poor advisors. The writer was surprised to hear Lafayette say, "Louis XVI owed his death as much to the bad advice of Gouverneur Morris as to any one other thing." He explained that Morris, coming from America, was listened to with great respect and always gave opinions against democracy. He advised resistance when it was not only too late but dangerous. The general did not question Morris' motives but merely affirmed his bad judgment. "Morris' aristocratic sentiments were no secret," Lafayette said without malice.[1] Morris wrote, "My friend Lafayette has his head so high in the clouds that he is not able to see the realities at his feet."

In *Gentleman Revolutionary*, Morris biographer Richard Brookhiser claims Louis XVI lost credibility and Lafayette effective leadership when the king and his family tried to escape France and the general forced their return. Morris played a role in the king's life, as he did in Washington's, writing Louis witty letters and even a first draft of a royal address to the National Assembly that was not given. Morris urged the king not to bribe legislators as they were not "worth corrupting" but to give bread to the poor as a grand gesture, observing that the French "seldom concern themselves with the good but rhapsodize over the beautiful."

Lafayette told Fenimore Cooper that Louis XVIII was the falsest man — his expression was *l'homme de plus faux* — he had ever met. He gave the obese king credit for having a great deal of talent but his duplicity was innate and did not stem from his position. The general of course knew him from youth, and even as young men Lafayette and his friends would say it was unsafe to confide in the Comte de Provence. Lafayette, however, spoke kindly of Charles X, saying he was the most honest of the three brothers but quite unequal to the crisis of his reign. The general thought Charles was sincere in his religious sincerity and it was by no means improbable he was a professed Jesuit. As for Marie Antoinette, Lafayette called her an injured woman and exonerated her from all of the coarse charges made against her. But he found her partiality — the novelist's word — for Axel von Fersen, indiscreet, considering her position. Regarding trouble over slavery in the United States, Lafayette said that separating the Union would break his heart. "I hope they will at least let me die before they commit this *suicide* on *our* institutions," he said. "He particularly deprecated the practice of talking about such an event, which he thought would accustom men's minds to it."[2]

Stendhal also appreciated Lafayette, who the novelist saw in the classical mode, although finding Levasseur "uncouth." As the top guest at the home Madame De Tracy, his daughter-in-law's mother, Lafayette would limp in with "his badly made clothes" and short wig, "giving away nothing, like an old family portrait," to sit surrounded by admiring, even sycophantic sympathizers. "Polite in the manner of royalty," he would abruptly leave them to "admire the pretty shoulders of a new arrival" and his eyes lit up as soon as they chanced upon the base of a pretty bust; "all of this enabled him to spend his last years pleasurably."[3]

Ascending the throne, Charles X swore to defend the charter, giving the impression he would follow his brother's policies, including on religion, Charles' great interest: "All Frenchmen are equal in my sight; all have the right to my love, my protection and my benevolence."[4]

He immediately restored the titles "royal highnesses" to his Orléans cousins whom his brother had denied because Philippe Ēgalité voted for Louis XVI's death. Prime minister Jean Baptiste de Villèle helped Charles X obtain laws favoring the nobility, clergy and granting indemnities to owners of estates seized in the revolution. Stabilizing the economy, Villèle won bonds for those renouncing ownership, costing France some 988 million francs. Early in his reign, Charles' sons were insulted in the streets. Devout Charles, atoning for early amatory indiscretions, it was said, secured a law forbidding blasphemy and sacrilege. He ordered death for profaning the Catholic Mass, thus giving more power to Jesuits and supporters of papal authority over civil law.

Charles saw these ordinances as necessary to maintain the monarchy. He next tried to re-establish primogeniture which was rejected by the Chamber of Deputies. Some of Charles' changes occurred before he was crowned in splendor at Reims Cathedral in May 1825. He would attempt to rule by divine right, and said, "I would rather hew wood than live under the conditions of the king of England." Charles' unpopularity surfaced in April 1827 during his review of the Guard Royale in the Champ de Mars. Shouts of "Down with the ministers!" were heard, and Charles saw the crowd's sullen faces. The next day he disbanded the citizen militia but this growing enemy did not surrender its arms. Lafayette was re-elected to the Chamber of Deputies in June 1827 from Seine et Marne, his home district was Meaux, with 264 votes to 72.

Appalled by Charles' actions, he again resisted with liberal and Bonapartist help. In 1829, Charles unwillingly agreed to compromise but replaced Villèle with a haughty ultra-royalist, Vicomte de Martignac. Charles lost patience when the Chamber's liberal opposition blocked measures that his ministers, who were not in the majority, presented. He fired Martignac, whom he disliked, replacing him with Prince Jules de Polignac, an even more extreme royalist. Polignac lost his party majority in August 1829, and to hold on to power, he dissolved Parlement. In January 1830, he sent a military expedition to Algeria to defeat pirates plundering Mediterranean shipping and win a popular victory. (Algeria remained a French colony until 1962.)

Charles' speech to reconvened Chambers of Deputies and Peers on March 2 received many negative responses insisting the royal government should act with the Chambers' approval. Despite the bill's thirty-vote majority, Charles called for new general elections. In his *Ordonnaces de Saint-Cloud,* published July 26, he dismissed the newly-elected Chamber of Deputies, censored the press, rewrote the electoral system and requested new elections in September. Influential journalist Adolphe Thiers, writing in the liberal newspaper *Le National,* called for open revolt. Forty-three journalists added their signatures. That evening in the Palais Royale gardens, crowds shouted, "Down with the Bourbons! "*Vive la Charte!*" When police closed the area, protesters moved to the street and smashed street lamps. On July 27, first of the Three Glorious Days of the July Revolution, soldiers in the streets were struck from roofs with paving stones, tiles and flower pots. Troops fired into the air but the battle continued with twenty-one citizens killed by nightfall. When police closed newspapers the next day, citizens threw stones and the police fired back. Paris was in a war state and gun shops were looted by evening. Charles called *Maréchal* Marmont to stablize the revolt turned revolution. He moved against the rioting citizens. But some of his soldiers defected and he was forced to retreat to the Tuileries. Lafayette and four other deputies asked him to urge Charles to revoke his ordinances. At Marmont's request, Martignac spoke to the king who refused, deeming them necessary for his rule. Seeing the serious situation, Charles dismissed all of his ministers and shut down the government.

Lafayette and Chamber members met that evening at Jacques Laffitte's house and discussed asking Louis-Philippe, Duc d'Orléans, to become a constitutional monarch. They produced posters favoring him and toppling the government. Deputy Casimir Périer, who would become Chamber president, replacing ineffective Laffitte, who had turned rightist, insisted there should be no more violence and there was surprisingly little. Members of the terminated Chamber, seeking to maintain their lawful roles, spoke in favor of the king but opposed his action preventing them from advising him as elected representatives. Lafayette, spokesman for the Chamber's republicans, was indignant. He declared the king had broken the public's trust with his illegal ordinances, had caused his soldiers to massacre the public and therefore should be replaced.

He and fellow deputies decided the public's insurrection was warranted, the tricolor should again become France's flag and Charles and his ministers should be declared the people's enemies. On the way to this meeting with Jules de Lasteyrie, the general had difficulty with his bad leg climbing over several barricades. Returning to his apartment, he was recognized. His way was eased. The crowd, expecting he would form a republic, cheered him. Reaching home, he did not know he had been named commander of the newly revived National Guard. On July 29, he spoke to a large number of liberal leaders about accepting his former command: "A veteran of 1789 may be of some service in our present grave circumstances. Attacked on all sides, we are bound to defend ourselves."[5]

He assured friends, "My conduct at seventy-three years of age shall be what it was at thirty-two. It is important, I feel, that the Chamber should reserve its decision as to my appointment, but my own duty as a citizen prescribes I should respond to public confidence and devote myself to the common defense." How July 1830 reminded him of 1789!

From city hall he wrote a shower of brief orders on July 29 and 30. Returning from Saint-Cloud, three deputies reported they had persuaded Charles to rescind the ordinances. Lafayette was briefly absent but his spokesman responded, "Too late! The throne of Charles X has collapsed in blood." To which the leftists shouted, "No more Bourbons!" An emissary from Charles told Lafayette the king would withdraw the ordinances. "Too late," he said, "You will have to resign yourself to the facts. The Bourbons are through."

Lafayette, who could have determined the nation's future, who could have become its dictator, even though it would be totally out of character and against his long-proclaimed principles, again insisted it was not he but the government that should decide. Even Washington had been selected by Congress. Lafayette had not changed his view: France after twenty-five years was still not sufficiently educated to become a republic. He did not believe he could lead it there. To avoid attack, minutes after midnight on July 31, Charles, his family and most of the court left Saint-Cloud, expecting to find safety at Versailles. In Paris, Louis-Philippe accepted Charles' offer of his former post, lieutenant general of France.

The road to Versailles was filled with wandering troops and deserters. The palace governor met Charles outside of town to report it was unsafe. National Guards wearing the tricolor occupied *Place d'Armes*. Charles veered to Trianon. Later that day, with his son, Angoulême, and his troops, the king rode to Chateau de Rambouillet, arriving before midnight. He had more than enough power — 12,000 soldiers, three top cavalry regiments and forty cannons — to overwhelm the National Guard, of which Georges Lafayette was its commander's aide-de-camp.

When on July 30 Lafayette had sent an advance group to observe Charles' army and demand return of the crown jewels, Swiss Guards fired on them, wounding a colonel in the foot and killing his horse. Hoping to be rid of the king, Lafayette called up a large band of armed citizens and inspected them on the Champs Ēlysées before they rode off to Rambouillet in a startling array of unlikely conveyances, from omnibuses to fiacres and carts. Amused, Lafayette called this ramshackle spectacle "the most singular and interesting of armies."[6]

The situation in Paris quickly grew worse, culminating in the July Revolution of 1830, known in France as the Three Glorious Days. On July 27, the public, furious at Charles' ordinances, went to high windows and rained paving stones, roof tiles and flower pots on soldiers in the streets. Troops fired into the air and by evening twenty-one citizens were killed. There would be a total dead of about 2,000. On July 28, about 4,000 barricades, consisting of almost every tree in Paris, rose in streets around the city. Citizens captured the Tuileries, Louvre and battered the hôtel de ville which the liberals quickly reclaimed. That evening there, Charles de Rémusat, a young journalist opposing Charles' ordinances, asked Lafayette if he would lead a provisional government. The general remained silent — his family dissented but friends urged him on. Did he want to be president of a new republic? "No, certainly not," he replied. He had no need of higher office. "Well then," said Rémusat, "You must help us put the Duc d'Orléans on the throne."

A suddenly mute Lafayette believed France after twenty-five years was still not ready to be a true republic. The provinces, where his status was high, wanted him as president but many deputies, recalling the blood bath of the First Republic, were horrified of a second. Also many citizens were still loyal to Charles. To Lafayette, voters, numbering only 110,000 out of 25 million Frenchmen, were not sufficiently educated to elect a second republic, his view since 1789. As a politician, he believed the nation should decide the question through the Chamber of Deputies. Others thought differently. Joseph Bonaparte wrote him to urge that his nephew, the king of Rome in Vienna, more Austrian than French, be summoned to the throne while Legitimists urged Lafayette to become regent for the child they envisaged as Henri V. He waited until November to refuse them all.

Long favoring Orléans, Jacques Laffitte now led a number of deputies, with a lame drummer beating a broken drum, to the Palais Royal. The duke, sleeping the previous night not in his bed but the building's attics to be ready for anything, kept calm, hoping to be called to the throne but not sure that would occur. He embraced Laffitte and appeared with him on a Palais Royal balcony. Ēgalité's son then led the procession on foot eastward to Lafayette at the hôtel de ville. Parisians, more Fayettist than Orléanist, shouted, *"Vive Lafayette!"* more than"*Vive le Duc d'Orléans!* Surrounded by students of the Polytechnic School, Lafayette met them at the front steps. The Chamber's nomination of Louis-Philippe as citizen king of the French, a contractual monarchy, not as absolutist Philippe VII of France, which Lafayette strongly opposed, was read aloud to those gathered and received coolly. The king-elect responded, "I promise to dedicate myself to France's happiness."

Extending his hand, Lafayette led Louis-Philippe to the meeting hall upstairs. Presenting him before like-minded delegates with a large tasseled tricolor flag he helped resurrect after an absence of fifteen years, Lafayette drew Louis-Philippe onto another balcony in view of the crowd below and embraced him. "Lafayette's republican kiss made him a king," said right-wing writer and Lafayette critic François René Chateaubriand. Orléans' enemies stood silently. On August 2, amid the cheering for him and Lafayette, Charles X abdicated, not in favor of his son, the dauphin (Angoulême), but a grandson, Henri, Duc de Bordeaux, who was nine. Angoulême at first resisted his father. Their loud words were overheard in the chateau. But after twenty minutes the dauphin countersigned the document. Both expected that Louis-Philippe, as lieutentant general, would acclaim the boy King Henri V. But Louis-Philippe ignored the directive. On August 9, Chamber members proclaimed him king.

Charles requested twelve *maréchals* accompany him to Cherbourg en route to London. Louis-Philippe sent three. Charles bitterly resisted leaving Rambouillet with so small an escort. A *maréchal* said, referring to Lafayette's volunteer Guards, "There are 80,000 armed men approaching us!" When Charles questioned this, he was told, "Sire, I have not counted them, but it is a large and very annoyed body." There were not more than 12,000 to 20,000 Guards, soldiers in name only.[7]

Charles asked a courtier's advice. He was told, although it would be easy to disperse the Guards with his troops and weapons, it only would help the next government, republic or Orléanist, politically. Learning his cousin had accepted the crown, Charles left Rambouillet with 1,200 men. Crowds cheered him as he passed en route to Cherbourg. He and his family boarded a steamship Louis-Philippe ordered and sailed to England. The British public, waving small tricolors, mocked Charles, who adopted the name "Comte de Ponthieu," after a Norman county. As guests of British royalty, Charles and his entourage, including the Angoulêmes, returned to Holyrood House. Creditors, still trying to collect vast sums from his last exile, followed. His wife had banked money in London. The Bourbons then moved to Prague and Hradschin Palace, as guests of Francis I of Austria, in 1832-1833.

When Charles' widowed Italian-born daughter-in-law, Caroline, Duchesse de Berry, wed a minor Neapolitan noble, the ex-king banned her from seeing her children. Failing to raise a royalist army in the Vendée, Caroline was imprisoned but released when she bore a daughter to her new husband. Charles' other daughter-in-law, Duchesse d'Angoulême, protested his treatment of De Berry. He relented in 1834. On Emperor Francis' death in 1835, the Bourbons moved to Gorizia, northeast of Venice, for its mild climate. Charles died there of cholera in 1836. He and his family, including the Angoulêmes — his son, Louis Antoine, is identified as Louis XIX — were entombed in the Franciscan monastery.[8]

SIXTY-ONE: BITTER CAUSES, FINAL ACTIONS

Lafayette has been criticized for not asking Louis-Philippe for a written pledge to lead France toward democracy. Wanting to believe the best of him despite his being a Bourbon, Lafayette decided the fifty-seven-year-old citizen king was the best man to lead the nation. A letter would have been of little purpose and the general was on his guard. Although there were many pleased letters from the United States and elsewhere — even from novelist Mary Shelley for the "hero of three revolutions" — praising the new government, the July Monarchy also had critics calling it a "bastard solution."[1]

The turmoil had been a strain on Lafayette. He was further disappointed when the king no longer asked for his presence at court or refused to permit, at Lafayette's urging, the return of political prisoners, particularly Joseph Bonaparte.

Tiring of his savior, Louis-Philippe found ways to diminish him as the old hero suddenly enjoyed new compliments from abroad on the swiftness of the July Revolution and his elevation to the heights of French Masonry with many banquets in his honor. The king ordered that National Guard commanders' authority be limited to their cities, eliminating need for a commander in chief, as Lafayette again was.

Stung, he immediately resigned his commission. But he was quietly assuaged when asked to become the first king of the Belgians, a new constituent monarchy independent of the Netherlands. But that he also refused.[2]

Leopold I, forty-one, prince of Saxe-Coburg and Gotha, was then selected. Louis-Philippe, fearing war with the Netherlands, refused the Belgian kingship for his son, Louis, Duc de Nemours, which gained Great Britain's friendship, but married several of his children into a number of royal families. His daughter, Louise Marie, wed Leopold I in 1832.

Some parts of Louis-Philippe's life (1773-1850) overlapped Lafayette's. Like his father, Louis-Philippe professed liberal ideas. After service at nineteen as a colonel, then lieutenant general in the Army of the North under Dumouriez, Louis-Philippe escaped the Terror as a widely-traveled exile in the United States for four years. He met Washington, Hamilton and Jay. Returning to Europe in 1800, he had many undercover adventures. He taught geography, mathematics and languages in a Swiss boy's academy, avoided Condé's army in exile and sired two illegitimate sons. He lived out of France twenty-one years, fifteen of them in England. In Palermo, Louis-Philippe wed Princess Marie Amalie of the Two Sicilies, daughter of Ferdinand IV, in 1809. They had ten children; two died young. Orléans remained in Sicily until Napoleon fell. Louis XVIII, welcoming his cousin back to France, had restored his lands and vast wealth.

As citizen-king, Louis-Philippe played down royal pomp, carried an umbrella, supported the arts and greeted the public at the Palais Royal before moving his family into the Tuileries. Legitimists supported the Duc de Bordeaux, who became Comte de Chambord, who as pretender to the throne owned one French property, Chateau de Chambord. Louis-Philippe invited wealthy businessmen rather than nobles to his court and altered laws to help them as working-class conditions worsened. But under his education minister, François Guizot, public schools were established for the first time. The king approved Napoleon's remains being placed in the Invalides in 1840. As Louis-Philippe slowly tightened his Bourbonesque grip on power, his popularity waned. He became the butt of liberal cartoonists, including Honoré Daumier, who turned the king's jowls and head into a pear, with "The Pear" becoming a popular nickname. Daumier pictured Lafayette on a sofa having a nightmare with a pear riding on his paunch. Another cartoon pictured Lafayette handing Louis-Philippe his crown and saying, "Sire, you may put on your hat."

Having a penchant for hugging people and being sometimes called "Father Kisser," Lafayette saw his own actions as questionable. "I seek to make reparation for my public faults by all sorts of motions of personal friendship."[3]

When Charles X's ministers were on trial in the Luxembourg, Lafayette watched the proceedings and chose to orate on the value of humanity and respect for justice. The king thanked him in writing since it saved him from seeking bloody revenge which he abhorred. Instead, the king busied himself with embellishing the family necropolis, a neo-Gothic wedding cake in Dreux, Eure-et-Loir. He also doted on Chateau d'Eu, his summer palace in Normandy. The restrained but elegant furniture of the period was named after him. But Louis-Philippe, seeking his own strength, ignored Lafayette-influenced pronouncements from city hall. Remaining cordial to the royal family, Lafayette refused to become honorary commander of the National Guard. He also saw through the king's falseness in inviting him to seek in the Chamber of Deputies a clearer determination of his abolished commandership. He also refused membership in the *Académie Française*, finding it as ill-fitting "as a ring on a cat."[4]

Lafayette, no friend of the Congress of Vienna's Treaty of 1815 that ignored various oppressive conditions in Europe, immersed himself in European and South American freedom movements which the July Revolution helped set off — matters Louis-Philippe opposed as possibly leading France to war. In February 1831, a Polish delegation invited Lafayette to become First Grenadier of the Warsaw National Guard, to which French premier Casimir Perier, now conservative and anti-interventionist, addressing Lafayette in the Chamber, said, "French blood belongs only to France," with Guizot saying the same to the Poles' French defender. Lafayette comforted himself with the Monroe Doctrine's warning against Spanish intervention in Latin America. In June, he gave a manifesto to the voters of Meaux, telling how "The tricolor daydreams of a July veteran have become the law of France since 1830." He was re-elected a deputy of Seine-et-Marne in July 1831 and deputy mayor of the town Courpalay near La Grange in October.

Returning to his familiar gadfly role in the Bourbon Restoration, Lafayette, nearing seventy-five and a living legend, agitated the king as he championed the rights of suppressed nations. He argued on behalf of Polish insurgents. He never forgot how Kosciuszko's 1794 uprising as supreme commander of the Polish National Armed Force had failed to liberate Poland and Lithuania from imperial Russia and the kingdom of Prussia after Poland's second partition. He remembered reclusive Kosciuszko tending his rose garden in Paris and remained a close friend until the Polish hero's death in 1817.

In the 1830s Lafayette hid insurgents fleeing persecution in La Grange's attic, an area the family called "the Polish corridor," knowing the government was spying on them. He also invited other Poles, probably including pianist and Polish activist Frédéric Chopin, to meet and dine with French leaders in his apartment. Lafayette formed a plan with Fenimore Cooper. The novelist agreed to help escaping Poles who came to his door. At least one did: Joseph Troskolaski, who fought the Russians, arrived penniless and spoke no English. Wanting work, he beseeched Fenimore Cooper in New York and Cooperstown, New York, to little avail. After much stress he became a surveyor in Natchez and disappeared from record.

Still riding his anti-slavery hobbyhorse in 1831, Lafayette sent three friends and forty Norman peasants to begin a free labor colony in the thirty-five square mile township in Tallahassee that Congress gave him in 1825. Grape arbors were built, lime and mulberry trees planted. But crops failed, farmers sickened and the project died within months. Two years later, Lafayette, who never visited it, sold his land to speculators for $46,520. Private properties already on the land caused him headaches; Georges settled them after his father's death. Tallahassee named Lafayette Lake for him and his name appears on its streets and in neighborhoods.[5]

Meanwhile, Lafayette fought successfully to keep Chamber of Peers members from inheriting their seats. He also favored French intervention against Dom Miguel, who claimed the throne of Portugal.

Several Frenchmen were thrown into prison over it. He was pleased his grandson joined the expedition. Lafayette appeared when Louis-Philippe pardoned jailed enemies of the Bourbon Restoration. But the king was heard to say the general was a scourge who ought to be eliminated.

Alvan Fisher: *View of La Grange's Park with the Hero of Two Worlds, 1820-1830.* Courtesy Marquis de Lafayette Collection, Lafayette College.

As much as Lafayette harangued and continued to agitate the government, he remained committed to law, order and fairness. His friend, Bonapartist deputy Jean Lamarque, a popular and fierce foe of the Restoration, and Casimir Perier died in June 1832 in a cholera outbreak. Bonapartists and republicans, using Lamarque's large funeral to attract more dissidents, turned the event into a rebellion. Lafayette, a pall-bearer, was caught in the riot. He failed to find his carriage and joined Georges in his. Young rebels, removing the horse and seizing the shafts, tried to pull Lafayette to the hôtel de ville to lead the insurrection. When he refused, several men, waving a red flag emblazoned with "Liberty or Death," threatened to kill him and throw him into the river. He would write, "I am sorry for them with all my heart," later laughing,

"It was not a bad idea: a death that was a call to arms." The army and National Guard, with the king attending on horseback, suppressed the rebellion, leaving 800 killed or wounded. (Victor Hugo would use the revolt in *Les Miserables.)*[6]

Despite cholera in Seine et Marne, Lafayette returned to La Grange and continued to sequester Polish refugees. In disgust he ended his governmental post in Courpalay but retained his Chamber seat, respecting that voters had elected him to it. The Chamber's tribunal was his favorite bully pit where he chastised the government for new laws opposing Polish refugees, comparing these restrictions to those of the despotic Russians. His anger grew hot with the arrest at La Grange of Joachim Lelewel, an important Polish historian and officer under Prince Adam Czartoryski, exiled for participating in 1830's Polish rebellion. Lelewel had official permission to stay at La Grange if he did not leave, but, as police reported, he made clandestine visits to Paris. At Hôtel Lambert, a grand mansion on Ile de St. Louis in the city's heart, he met with Polish émigrés who gathered so regularly "Hotel Lambert" became synonymous with them.

The interior minister, citing "a misunderstanding," dismissed the report. But Polish poet and patriot Julian Niemcewicz, addressing a banquet for 200 Poles at Lafayette's house, declared that age had dimmed their host's "intelligence" but not his need for an audience.

Undaunted, Lafayette spent spring and summer at La Grange but often visited the city, heading or sitting in at meetings. He created an agricultural society, tended to correspondence and claimed he received 250 letters a day. He turned the chateau into a museum of his American memorabilia, including Scheffer's copies of portraits of Washington, Franklin, Kosciuzko and Lafayette's favorite image of himself: Scheffer pictured him holding his hat and cane with his left hand reaching into his coat pocket, done on his last return from the United States. Lafayette joked he had his hand in his own pocket, not someone else's like some politicians.

Entrance to Chateau de La Grange. Author photograph, 2002.

The old warrior now battled another enemy, possibly prostatitis blocking urination, or bladder disease. Shortly after his triumphal tour, he suffered so badly in his left ankle he claimed it would take eight or nine days of complete bed rest to erase it. Dr. Jules Cloquet, who he had appointed the National Guards' surgeon, was a close friend and advisor to several other physicians attending the general. Cloquet, witnessing Lafayette's last months, prescribed hot baths and massages that helped some. Cloquet, devoted to the general, wrote *Recollections of the Private Life of General Lafayette,* a series of letters prompted by an American admirer following the general's death. It was serialized in the *New York Evening Star.* But Cloquet could not bring himself to name the source of the patient's problem, writing only of "this organ." Although Lafayette suffered much he was sanguine and trusted his doctors. When Jefferson had a similar problem, Lafayette asked Cloquet for a box of surgical instruments for his friend, wishing he could send the surgeon too.

Cloquet attended a duel between two Chamber deputies. General Thomas Bugeaud, fifty, of a noble Périgord family, supported Louis-Philippe. Liberal deputy François Dulong, forty-one, from the northern department of the Eure, criticized Bugeaud's action as jailer of Duchesse de Berry following her role in the abortive legitimist Vendée uprising of 1833; in jail she had a daughter to her secret Italian husband. Dulong asked Bugeaud if the military should have submitted to being her jailer. Although not violently hostile to Dulong, Bugeaud felt he had to protect his honor. The duel, expected to be a routine, occurred in the Bois de Boulogne on January 28, 1834. Georges Lafayette was a Dulong second. Beaugaud, stepping forward, shot the left side of Dulong's head open, drawing blood and brain matter before Dulong could fire. Unconscious and convulsive, he was bled copiously into a salad bowl while being rushed by carriage to his hotel room on Rue de Castiglione. Lafayette visited him often while Georges and a Lafayette doctor remained with him. Dulong died the next morning. Bugeaud later became a *maréchal* and conqueror of Algeria.

Lafayette urged a deputy friend of Dulong not to despair or resign but wait for better times: "They will arrive, be certain of that, and it would be distressing for the future of our country to let ourselves be carried away by a perfectly natural feeling of disgust."[7] His serenity at seventy-six recalled that of Washington. Lafayette also said, "My long life has taught me that in important personal questions the best thing is to decide against one's own interests."[8]

In pain and grieving Dulong's death, Lafayette insisted on walking in the funeral procession from the hotel to Père Lachaise and standing through long speeches in cold rain. He was weak on reaching home, unable to void and experienced paralysis. Doctors gave him the usual treatments: stimulating massage and sulfurous douches. He felt improvement when "the organ" contracted. But gout attacked his lower limbs, lungs, stomach and eyelids. He recovered enough to resume working at his small desk, reading in a favorite leather chair or in his single bed set parallel to the wall. It had elegance, in the Polish style, javelins holding aloft a yellow canopy. He had no wrinkles, his vision was excellent but his hearing had faded some and his hip pain remained.

Bastien attended him and, exhausted, would fall asleep in a chair. His master would not have him disturbed and he served to the end. Lafayette delighted in frequent visits from Princess Cristina di Belgiojoso, twenty-five, wealthy Italian writer and journalist. Separated from a libertine husband, she sought Italian independence from Austria. She had entertained Lafayette and many others in her Paris salon. The relationship was like Lafayette's with Fanny Wright. Belgiojoso's father died when she was a baby. She too saw Lafayette as a father figure and he admired her intelligence. Cloquet often found her by his bedside. Georges visited daily. His father's dear friend, General Carbonel, of the National Guard, also came often. Lafayette told stories, recalling the time Louis XV was embarrassed when Comtesse du Barry exclaimed, "Oh, I am fried," from drink. The king, flushing with shame at her remark, remained mortified that evening. He also saw the king collapse with fatal smallpox at his last supper with her.

Lafayette's other delights were his pets: a small white female dog that followed him everywhere and a white cockatoo on a stand. He often caressed it and the parrot always showed excitment on seeing him. He read his newspapers and kept up with Andrew Jackson's battles with the United States Senate, that nation always in his thoughts. He grieved at the death of Madame Louise Joubert, who had painted him sitting on a mossy bank in La Grange's park around 1830.[9] Cloquet noted the general had no idea he would soon follow her. One day Lafayette said to him, "The *Swiss Gazette* has just killed me, and yet you know nothing of the matter!"

He was able to take carriage rides, usually to the Blois de Boulogne and the Beauséjour house where he enjoyed visiting his granddaughter, Natalie de Latour-Maubourg, now Madame Adolphe Perrier, with his latest great granddaughter. Lafayette's last letter, of May 1, 1834, was to the president of the Society for the Abolition of African Slavery. It expressed his confidence in the ultimate success of the cause.[10] One afternoon in early May, a cold wind blew, the temperature fell and he was caught in a heavy rain. Later feeling pain in his limbs, he began shivering and lapsed into a coma. His surgeon noted painful swelling near "the organ." Reviving, though weaker, he heard Dr. Guersent say, "We wish to restore you as soon as possible to health. We are responsible for your situation toward your family, your friends and the French nation of which you are the father."

"Yes, their father." Lafayette said, "...On condition they never follow a syllable of my advice." As the doctor encouraged him, Lafayette said,

"You can do nothing for me. Life is going now. It is like the flame of a lamp. When the oil is used up, when there is no more oil, then the flame is out." On May 20, 1834, he asked to have the locket with a wisp of Adrienne's hair taken from around his neck for him to hold and shortly, at seventy-six, he died in Cloquet's arms, with Georges and family members present. A flame surely had been extinguished.

David M. Blythe: *Lafayette*, finial sculpture, 1848. Fayette County Courthouse, Uniontown, Pa. Author photograph.

Louis-Philippe denied Lafayette an official funeral and ordered that the long procession, arranged by the Chamber of Deputies, be flanked with guardsmen on either side of streets to prevent outbursts. His probable feelings were captured by Daumier's lithograph of the king pretending to weep behind his praying hands as Lafayette's black catafalque moves through a huge crowd to Picpus Cemetery. He was buried beside Adrienne and their descendants would follow him there.

But was Lafayette buried under a blanket of American soil as often said? His rightist foe, writer and politician René Chateaubriand, who attended the funeral, claimed in a posthumous book there was insufficient time to find the earth of liberty at La Grange. Would Georges have defaulted on his father's wish? Lafayette intended the soil to be with him. Sometimes intention can be more meaningful than reality.[11]

The Second French Republic arrived fourteen years later with the Revolution of 1848. Deposed Louis-Philippe, fearing for his life, escaped as "Mr. Smith" with his wife to England, guests of Queen Victoria at Claremont, a Surrey estate. He died there two years later in a gardener's cottage. His and his wife's remains were moved to the Orléans mausoleum in 1876.

SIXTY-TWO: A LIVING LEGACY

News of Lafayette's death reached New York on the American packet ship *Silas Richard* on June 19, almost a month after the fact. President Jackson ordered the same honors for him that Washington received thirty-five years earlier. Flags flew at half-mast, both houses of Congress were draped in black and memorial services were held around the nation. At Congress' request on December 31, 1834, John QuincyAdams, now a congressman, gave a long eulogy on his friend's character and accomplishments before senators and representatives in the House, a last goodbye to a friend and patriot.

In France, Lafayette's memory remains alive in many ways and hearts, from the names of streets, statues and high schools to a department store chain. But nowhere has he received such widespread regard as in the United States. In France it is sometimes thought Lafayette had several opportunities to lead the country as president. Memory of him was strong during World War I when the United States came to France's aid as France had once helped America. That intensity has dimmed. My informal polling indicates many Americans do not know his name. Yet French, Americans and others who cherish liberty join each Fourth of July to honor Lafayette at his grave. The American ambassador speaks in tribute, as do French dignitaries, both hailing their nations' mutual cooperation while American and French military musical groups salute the general. This *ceremonie* has occurred for more than a century.

There on July 4, 1917, General John J. Pershing, commander of the American Expeditionary Force, and others assembled heard Colonel Charles E. Stanton say memorably: "It is with loving pride we drop the colors in tribute of respect to this citizen of your great republic. And here and now in the presence of the illustrious dead we pledge our hearts and honor to carrying this war to a successful issue. Lafayette, we are here."

An American flag has flown over Lafayette's grave for many years, even during the Nazi era. Each year, flower sprays cover the grave and the American flag is renewed before the public and representatives of the Daughters of the American Revolution, Sons of the American Revolution, the American Friends of Lafayette and others. They also honor him on October 19, anniversary of the Battle of Yorktown and he is also memorialized with World War I generals in a stained-glass window of the American Methodist Memorial Church, Chateau-Thierry, France. Ary Scheffer's deathbed portrait of Lafayette is in the collection of the National Museum of Franco-American Friendship and Cooperation, Chateau de Blérancourt, Aisne, Picardy.

An ironic series of events began in 1935 when Comte René de Chambrun (1906-2002), a direct descendant of Virginie Lafayette de Lasteyrie, married Josée Marie Laval (1911-1992), socialite daughter of businessman and politician Pierre Laval. Humbly born on June 28, 1883, in the village of Châteldon, northeast of Clermont-Ferrand, Auvergne, Laval was elected to the Chamber of Deputies in 1914, became a senator in 1926, then prime minister and foreign minister. He was four times premier of France during a turbulent time. As a young socialist lawyer in Paris, Laval represented trade unions and the General Confederation of Labor, but after service in World War I he became a conservative.

During the 1930s, he negotiated the Italo-Ethiopian pact appeasing Benito Mussolini's conquest in Africa. During the Nazi occupation of France in World War II, Laval was premier in the puppet government of General Henri Philippe Pétain, the eighty-five-year-old hero of World

War I. Holding northern France in thrall, the Nazis relegated the French government to the resort town of Vichy, northern Auvergne, where hotels housed government workers.

Laval, shrewd and tough, was nicknamed "the horse-trader." Short and natty, he always wore a white tie, favored homburgs and carried a walking stick. Since his wife, Jeanne, a Châteldon native, disliked state affairs, slender Josée de Chambrun, chic in Parisian gowns, was her father's escort and hostess. Her notebooks describe evenings at Maxime's, winning Longchamp horseraces and socializing with Nazi officials who said they enjoyed speaking French in Paris.

Laval, a millionaire owner of newspapers, Radio-Lyon and a well-known sparkling water company, lived in a medieval chateau in the village of Châteldon, twenty miles southeast of Vichy in the volcanic Puy-de-Dôme region.

Laval had a Jewish personal secretary but bonded with the Nazis.[1] Although he was accused of being an anti-Semite and an enemy of Freemasons, his son-in-law loyally defended Laval. De Chambrun insisted in several books that Laval often opposed and stalled the Nazis on removing and executing Jews and Masons.[2] Laval and his ministers met in Berlin with Adolf Hitler and allowed deportation of French workers to Germany. But Laval and Pétain distrusted each other. When Pétain heard Laval was rumored to be after his job, he dismissed him in 1940.

Probably with Chambrun interceding, Laval returned as premier in 1942. He devised a program detested in France: for every three French people agreeing to work in Germany, one French skilled worker in a Nazi prison would be returned. Laval accepted the Nazis, he said, because France without them would have been overrun with "Bolsheviks and their followers." He often claimed Nazi collaboration saved France from destruction.

Facing defeat in 1944, the Nazis flew Laval and Pétain to safety in Germany, later moving Laval to sanctuary in Spain. Dictator Francisco Franco, who had met with Laval in better days, immediately informed the Americans. Seizing Laval in Austria, they turned him over to the Free French in Paris. At his badly handled trial, Laval pugnaciously defended himself before a less than impartial High Court of Justice.

French commander Charles De Gaulle refused to intervene. Laval was an embarrassment. Josée squirreled his diary page by page out of Fresnes Prison near Paris. Laval believed if his trial were fair he could prove his actions were honorable; otherwise he would be executed.

Found guilty of treason, Laval on the morning of execution swallowed potassium cyanide from a defective vial long sewn into his jacket. Found nearly unconcious in his cell, he had left a note saying he would not die by French bullets. His stomach was pumped out and he was barely able to walk. But at sixty-two, wretchedly ill from poison, Laval placed a white tie and a tricolor scarf around his neck, saying he pitied the chief prosecutor and firing squad. At his request his eyes were not covered. He cried, "*Vive la France!*" as he was shot near the prison on October 15, 1945. De Gaulle wrote in his diary Laval died bravely. Pétain, his death sentence commuted because of age, died in prison at ninety-five in 1951. Chambrun was tried and acquitted.[3]

Shortly after the Chambruns' marriage on August 20, 1935, Laval and his wife Jeanne gave Josée and René money to purchase the champion of liberty's dilapidated castle.[4] This gift made possible the Chambruns' preservation of the chateau as well as their discovery of Lafayette's long-lost letters, documents and books in fourteen walled-up attic rooms in 1956. René de Chambrun spent forty years collating them. With a $300,000 federal grant, a Library of Congress team microfilmed the collection in La Grange's kitchen, the only room with electricity, in 1995-1996. Federal funds for copying foreign texts came from two private donors in the 1920s: Vermont banker James B. Wilbur and John D. Rockefeller Jr. The sixty-four reels of 6,400 feet of microfilm are viewable in reading rooms of the Library of Congress, Cleveland State University Library and the National Society of the Sons of the American Revolution, Louisville, Kentucky. The originals remain at La Grange.

Josée, Laval and friends called short, sharp-minded René de Chambrun "Bunny." The son of Ohio-born Clara Longworth, distinguished translator of Shakespeare into French, Chambrun was a nephew of Nicholas Longworth, speaker of the House of Representatives, and Pétain's godson. Longworth married Alice Roosevelt, becoming Theodore Roosevelt's son-in-law.

Chambrun's father, Aldebert, was descended from a noble family from the Lozere region south of Chavaniac-Lafayette. Chambrun was a successful international lawyer with Paris and New York offices. His clients included designer Coco Chanel and Spanish architect José Maria Sert. Through family connections, Chambrun was the longtime president of crystal-maker Baccarat. The Chambruns joined Laval in 1931 on the first visit of a French prime minister to the United States. As world war loomed, Chambrun, a French army captain, was sent to Washington in summer of 1940 but failed to influence President Franklin D. Roosevelt, who opposed Laval's pro-German position. In his book *I Saw France Fall. Will She Rise Again?* Chambrun informed Americans of the war threat. He also helped Europeans, including historian Golo Mann, Thomas Mann's son; novelist Franz Werfel, his wife, Alma Mahler-Werfel; and filmmaker René Clair to escape to the United States.[5]

After the war, Chambrun wrote three books attacking Laval's trial and what he called false charges against his father-in-law, never losing his loyalty to Laval or France.[6] The Chambruns invited biographer André Maurois to write a biography, *Adrienne*, published in the United States in 1961, using La Grange's documents. Often speaking at the Picpus ceremony, Chambrun wrote a 1977 book of the Lafayettes' prison experiences and collated La Grange's documents before welcoming the Library of Congress. Earlier, Chambrun failed to achieve United States citizenship, based on Maryland, Virginia, Massachusetts and Connecticut's granting Lafayette and male heirs that privilege. In August 2002, Congress granted citizenship to Lafayette but not his descendants, an honor given to only five others.

At La Grange, the Chambruns had unknowingly bought a time capsule and a labor of love. Adrienne had reclaimed the property from her mother's estate near the end of the French Revolution and gave it to Lafayette. Laval adored Josée, his only child. When she and René told Laval they wished to buy and restore the property, he visited the decrepit estate with its irregular stone walls, five turrets and moat. Lafayette had partially filled in its western moat to reach its park, designed by artist

Hubert Robert (1733-1808), stocked with American trees and plants. Altered in the seventeenth century, the chateau had remained virtually untouched since Lafayette's time.

La Grange-Bléneau descended from the ancient De Courtenay family, which at the end of the Middle Ages owned the town and chateau of Bléneau, Burgundy.[7] Guillaume, seigneur de La Grange, wed Marie de Courtenay. The two names descended in the families of Courtenay-Ligniéres, D'Aubusson-De la Feuillade and D'Aguesseau. François d'Aubusson, duc de La Feuillade, was a *maréchal* de France (1634-1675). His heirs sold the estate to Louis-François du Pré, Parlement counselor. His daughter, Anne du Pré, Adrienne Lafayette's grandmother, wed Jean-Baptiste d'Aguesseau.[8] Laval found the property in such poor condition he assumed it would not fetch much. And he was predisposed since he also lived in a chateau. The couple bought La Grange and its rich farmland from René's cousin, Louis Lasteyrie, also descended from Virginie.

But like his British mother, Lasteyrie was a royalist, living his long life, including the Nazi occupation, at La Grange. After his wife died, he and a servant barely held the place together, letting it sink into decrepitude, including the chapel, housing family carriages. Lasteyrie loved the place because it had been his mother and grandmother's home, not because of Lafayette, whose ideas he detested. Lasteyrie's grandmother was a lady-in-waiting to Louis-Philippe's queen, Marie Emilie. To Lasteyrie the chateau was a legacy for René and Josée.

They allowed him to stay for life. Still owning the usufruct of the estate, he occupied a ground floor room and hall in the mansion's oldest part. A virtual hermit, he died twenty years later in the winter of 1955. The Chambruns lavished repairs on the property but slept there only three nights in twenty-five years, attending church services in Lasteyrie's honor, ending when his friend, the village priest, moved away. They created the *Fondation de Josée et René de Chambrun* in 1959. Josée, tough-minded like her father and a smoker, died of lung cancer at eighty-one in 1992. Chambrun passed away in May 2002 at ninety-six. The foundation, wealthy from converted Baccarat stock, owns and oversees La Grange, Chateau de Châteldon and a medieval house and pharmacy in the village. La Grange, homelike with historic treasures, is restricted to scholars and historians. The foundation operates from the De Chambruns' former Right Bank apartment.[9] They and the Lavals are entombed at Châteldon, which is closed to the public. A stone bust of Pierre Laval surmounts a garden wall.

The late Cleveland businessman John Horton befriended "half-Ohioan" René de Chambrun and arranged with him and the Library of Congress to purchase and donate a set of La Grange microfilms to the Cleveland State University Library. There Horton, a member of the American Friends of Lafayette, translated French history for pleasure late in his life.

The later history of Lafayette's birthplace, Chateau de Chavaniac, divides into several eras. An English-born Scot, John Moffat, acting for the French Heroes and Lafayette Memorial Fund in World War I, was president of the National Allied Relief Committee that raised more than $50 million for war victims. On behalf of the organization, renamed the Lafayette Memorial Committee, Moffat purchased the chateau and 175 acres from a later Marquis de Lafayette: Gilbert V's great grandson — Gaston Pourcet de Sahune-Dumottier de Lafayette — in 1916. The committee's purpose: to restore and preserve Lafayette's birthplace as a memorial and archive of French-American friendship.[10]

The group knew from its earlier solicitations in the United States that invoking Lafayette's name was extremely helpful in raising funds. For two dollars the public could buy "Lafayette Kits" — toiletries and "all that two dollars could buy" for soldiers in the war. Chavaniac's salons and library became warm and cheerful as Moffat and his second wife made them their residence. Moffat installed electricity and bathrooms with running water. With foundation money, he erected buildings for 200 Parisian children exposed to tuberculosis and an orphanage for children left parentless in World War I. Then he added a school, dormitory and dairy farm. The village of Chavaniac made Moffat a citizen and changed its name to Chavaniac-Lafayette in 1957. Moffat died at eighty-one in 1966 and is buried in a tomb at the foot of the chateau's front terrace.[11]

In 1964, Americana collectors Arthur H. Dean, prominent New York lawyer and a diplomat in the Eisenhower era, and his wife, Mary Marden Dean, donated 10,000 Lafayette items, including family paintings, to Dean's alma mater, Cornell University, in Ithaca, New York. The collection came from Chateau de Chavaniac-Lafayette as well as Lafayette's heirs and the collections of French antiquarian Dieudonné Fabius (d. 1942), who gathered them from 1912 to 1940. Books from Parisian dealer Marcel Blancheteau, donated in 1964, also added to Cornell's holdings. A French committee, Friends of Lafayette, managed Chavaniac for years, keeping it open to the public. A sound and light program on Lafayette's times and a short film on the American Revolution run in rooms mostly empty of furniture. The Department of Haute-Loire in 2009 repaired the chateau's roofs and took over control of the chateau as a monument and memorial. In addition, villagers in colorful period clothing celebrate their hero and namesake each Fourth of July.

Lafayette College, founded in 1826 in Easton, Pennsylvania, holds in its Marquis de Lafayette Collection at Skillman Library 5,000 items of memorabilia, including Lafayette letters to Washington, books, banquet menus, objects owned by Lafayette and, from his United States tour, newspaper articles, posters, broadsheets, sheet music, clothing and pottery. The collection began in 1926 when the college's New York Alumni Association acquired portrait engravings and seventeen letters from a private New Jersey collector. In 1932, fifty-two American and French members established the American Friends of Lafayette that yearly visits sites Lafayette knew and gives to Lafayette causes. The group encourages collecting memorabilia, manuscripts, letters, prints, books and promotes new books, research articles, television programs and web sites. Lafayette College has been the repository of the Friends' collections and annual *Gazette* archive since 1940.

The Lilly Library at Indiana University, Bloomington, besides being home to a sizable number of letters and printed materials, owns a La Grange household account book (1814-1818 with appended dates to 1824) prepared by manager Pontonnier with approving signatures of Lafayette and Georges. Walter Pennett Gardner, a Jersey City banker, collected this Lafayetteana. Glass manufacturing scion George Alexander Ball, on behalf of the Ball Brothers Foundation, acquired the collection for the university in 1977.

The Library of Congress team in 1995-1996 copied 25,000 Lafayette letters and documents relating primarily to the 1780s to 1830s. The Library holds: a secret code Washington and Lafayette used during the American Revolution, Lafayette's hand-written corrections to the *Declaration of the Rights of Man* and Adrienne Lafayette's copy of a volume of Comte de Buffon's *Histoire Naturelle*, containing in its cover the letter she smuggled to her husband about her coming arrival at Olmütz. Included in this collection are many family letters as well as Capitaine du Chenoy's original maps of Lafayette's American battles.

SIXTY-THREE: THE GOLDEN EAGLE RETURNS

On December 11, 2007, the De Chambrun Foundation purchased a unique one-and-a-half-inch-long golden eagle medal. George Washington, as president of the Society of the Cincinnati, commissioned it from Pierre Charles L'Enfant. Lafayette's great-great granddaughter, Baronne Genevieve Meunier du Houssoy of Paris, consigned it to Sotheby's New York during Lafayette's 250th anniversary year in 2007, a time of many Lafayette celebrations. The medal had three bidders and sold in eleven minutes for $5.3 million — $4.3 million plus Sotheby's premium — ten times the price of any medal sold at auction.

Arnaud Meunier du Houssoy, the baronne's son, did not believe originally that the De Chambrun Foundation would buy the medal and did not approach it but said afterward he thought La Grange was one of the three best homes for it, the others being Mount Vernon and the Society of the Cincinnati, a bidder.[1] The baronne's father, Guy d'Aucourt, was the son of Marthe de Pourcet de Sahune, daughter of Nathalie du Motier de Lafayette, Georges Lafayette's eldest child. The son of the baronne's elder sister, Solange de Beaumont d'Autichamp, Humbert de Beaumont d'Autichamp, has followed his ancestors as a member of *la Société des Cincinnati de France.*

Pierre C. L'Enfant: Society of the Cincinnati golden eagle medal returned to La Grange after record-setting auction. Courtesy Sotheby's, 2007.

Other items more recently purchased at auction and returned to the chateau are: Ary Scheffer's copy of Gilbert Stuart's portrait of Washington; an oval pastel of Lafayette in his National Guard uniform by Jean-Baptiste Weyler (Strasbourg, 1747-1791); two Jean Pierre Houel watercolors of the blessing of National Guard flags at Notre Dame, September 26, 1789. (At this memorial service in the Church of the Sepulcre, Paris, the Lafayettes honored citizens who died in the Bastille attack, August 18, 1789); a drawing, *The Olmütz Jailer*, by Anastasie; miniatures of Adrienne, Georges Lafayette, Franklin, Huger and Washington by Nicholas M. Hentz after Gilbert Stuart; pastel portraits of Adrienne and Clémentine by Scheffer; and a gold cross hairpin with strands of Adrienne's hair. The sale included Washington's cotton equestrian umbrella and four Lafayette walking sticks.[2]

Lafayette's indelible impression on Americans led to invoking his name wherever quality was desired for honorable sites and up-scale objects. His name has been invoked in many places from his actions in the Continental Army and later.

Fayetteville, North Carolina, was the first city to be named for him and Fayette County, Pennsylvania, the first county, both in 1783. New York City's Lafayette Street and venerable La Grange Terrace were built in 1830 in the East Village. Although *The New York Times* has described the aged party-wall houses' Corinthian columns as "looking like three-week-old celery," real estate tycoon William Astor, John Jacob Astor's son, built the elegant marble row for Cornelius Vanderbilt and other wealthy residents. Five remain. Lafayette sold the 24,000 acres Congress gave him in Tallahassee in 1831 but they remain part of the city's history.

About 600 American counties, cities, towns, districts, parks, schools, neighborhoods, theaters, inns and other buildings bear the name of Lafayette or La Grange. The most famous site is Lafayette Square, a seven-acre park with five heroic bronze sculptures of revolutionary generals and Andrew Jackson across from the White House. There are Lafayette Squares in Buffalo, Cambridge, Indianapolis, Los Angeles, New Orleans, Saint Louis and Savannah. Most have associations with the general. There is an Avenue de Lafayette in Boston. Fayette County, Kentucky, originally part of Virginia's Kentucky Territory, chose its name in 1780, two years and eight months after the general first landed in America.

Lafayette is honored in Paris with an Avenue de Lafayette and Rue de Lafayette, on the Right Bank, *Galéries Lafayette*, the famous department store chain founded in 1893, and historical monuments. Although many visit the Arc de Triomphe and the Arc du Carrousel honoring Napoleon's battles, Lafayette is probably best remembered in Paris by Paul Wayland Bartlett's 1908 bronze equestrian statue five million American school children paid for in 1908. Originally in the courtyard of the Louvre, it was replaced by architect I.M. Pei's pyramid entrance to the museum. Since 1985 it is mounted on a site along the Cours Albert Ier on the Right Bank of the Seine between Pont de l'Alma and Pont des Invalides.

The hero is also superbly commemorated in the Lafayette Escadrille

Memorial, a large art moderne mausoleum in Paris' Parc de St.-Cloud. Sixty-seven volunteer American fighter pilots — six members of the original thirty-eight Americans under four French officers forming the squadron — are entombed there. They flew for France before the United States entered World War I and absorbed the corps. The mausoleum, dedicated on July 4, 1928, bears in its central arch Lafayette's profile in a circular relief. When the original French command became an American command, the only black pilot, Eugene J. Bullard (1894-1961), was dropped from the squadron since blacks were not permitted to fly then in American military service. The United States Air Force readmitted Bullard posthumously in 1961.

The French Memorial's arch resembles that of Valley Forge's 1917 National Memorial Arch, where Lafayette is listed among the American Revolution's eight major generals. Both majestic structures resemble Rome's ancient Arch of Titus. Lafayette is also remembered wherever the oppressed know his ideas of personal freedom. The South Sudanese made this a point while seeking independence in 2010.[3] As it was forecast in 1790, Lafayette in the collective memory will continue to gallop down the centuries wherever people thirst for freedom.

ADDENDA

There is room in Lafayette's history for the unusual. When the United States Navy seized the magnificent French ocean liner *S.S. Normandie* to keep her from the Nazis, she was renamed *U.S.S. Lafayette.* (The liner at her pier is framed in a taxi's rear window in Alfred Hitchcock's *The Thirty-Nine Steps,* 1935.) A workman's acetylene torch accidentally set her afire as she was being converted to troop service in 1939. Settling to the bottom of the Hudson River at Pier 88 in New York, she was scrapped after the war. The Metropolitan Museum of Art, New York City, and the Carnegie Museum of Art, Pittsburgh, hold outstanding examples of her grand interior panels.

The Lafayette, an automobile of quality, once carried the general's cameo on its grille. Begun in Indianapolis in 1920, the boxy sedan was manufactured in Milwaukee until 1937 when Nash Motors took it over, downgrading it to its lowest-priced Lafayette Nash model and ending production in 1940.

The 2,000-seat Lafayette Theater, 123rd Street and Seventh Avenue, in New York's Harlem, was the first theater to welcome blacks down from balconies to orchestra seating. It presented Broadway shows and many other fine cultural events. It was the center of important black jazz musicians of the era and great stars performed there. Orson Welles presented a *Voodoo Macbeth* as part of the Works Project Administration's Federal Theater Project. Later the Lafayette was a vaudeville house, movie theater and church.

In 1830, Paris named a boulevard for Lafayette. The upmarket Galéries Lafayette began in 1893 on Rue de Lafayette, first of many branches in French cities that have honored Lafayette with boulevards, avenues, squares, schools and sculptures. They include Bordeaux, Brest, Grenoble, Lille, Lyon, Marseille, Nancy, Nantes, Metz, Poitiers, Rennes, Strasbourg, Toulon, Toulouse, Tours and Versailles.

The United States Navy named three ships for the general. The last was *U.S.S. Lafayette*, a 425-foot-long Polaris A-2 missile-bearing submarine. General Dynamics Corporation launched her at its electric boat division in Groton, Connecticut, on April 23, 1963. Powered by a nuclear reactor, she cruised at 22-25 knots with two crews of thirteen officers and 130 enlisted men. After protecting American interests around the world, she was decommissioned and dismantled in Bremmerton, Washington, in 1992.

There are also landmarks of a lasting nature. Mount Lafayette, a summit in the Franconia Range of New Hampshire's White Mountains, rises 5,249 feet and is a popular climb. In outer space, *23244 Lafayette* spins as a minor planet in the main asteroid belt, discovered at the Lowell Observatory's Near-Earth Object Search at Anderson Meza, near Flagstaff, Arizona, on November 20, 2000.

In historic Rochefort, France, construction of a replica of French Navy frigate *Hermione* began in 1997. The original took Lafayette on his second voyage to the American Revolution. He sailed from Rochefort on March 11, 1780 carrying secret news from the king that French reinforcements would join the war. Sources vary on whether *Hermione* carried twenty-six, thirty-two or thirty-six twelve-pound-ball cannons, but she and her replica are and were made of French oak and have three decks. Built in eleven months in 1779, the original ran aground and sank in high seas thirteen years later. The new *Hermione,* sailing to the United States in 2015, will remind the world of her special heritage. It is the lasting spirit of Lafayette.

Lafayette Sites in the United States

Eighteen American counties are named Lafayette, or Fayette, and thirty-five cities are called Lafayette, Fayetteville or La Grange. Twenty-one states have at least one city or town so designated. (Asterisks indicate county seats.)

STATE	COUNTY DATE	CITY/TOWN
Alabama	Fayette (12/20/1824)	Lafayette*
Arkansas	Lafayette (10/15/1827)	Fayetteville*
California		Lafayette
Colorado		Lafayette
Florida	Lafayette (12/23/1856)	
Georgia	La Fayette* (5/15/1821)	Fayetteville*, LaGrange*
Illinois	Fayette* (2/14/1821)	La Grange, La Grange Highlands,
Indiana	Lafayette* (12/28/1818)	La Grange Park
	La Grange* (2/2/1832)	West Lafayette
Iowa	Fayette (12/21/1837)	
Kentucky	Fayette (5/1/1780)	La Grange*
Louisiana	Lafayette Parish (1/17/1823)	Lafayette*
Minnesota		Lafayette
Mississippi	Lafayette (2/9/1836)	Fayette*
Missouri		Fayette,* La Grange, Lake Lafayette
New Jersey		Lafayette
New York		LaFayette (1825), Fayetteville, La Grange

North Carolina		(4/18/1783)	Fayetteville,* La Grange
Ohio	Fayette	(2/19/1810)	Lafayette, Allen County; Lafayette, Madison County, West Lafayette, Coshocton County, Lagrange
Oregon			Lafayette
Pennsylvania	Fayette	(9/26/1783)	Fayette City, Lafayette Hill
Rhode Island			Lafayette
Tennessee	Fayette	(9/29/1824)	Lafayetteville,* Lafayette
Texas	Fayette	(12/14/1837)	La Grange*
West Virginia	Fayette	(1831)	Fayetteville*
Wisconsin	Lafayette	(1847)	Lafayette (town).

In Wisconsin: Lafayette is a township in Chippewa and Walworth Counties and La Grange a town in Monroe County. In Indiana, Lafayette is a town and county seat in Wayne Township, Tippecanoe County.

Primary Sources

LF: Lafayette's monogram, as seen at La Grange, is used in references.

Memoirs: *Memoirs, Correspondence and Manuscripts of General Lafayette.* The first volume is in English, five later volumes are in French online at the Darlington Collection, University of Pittsburgh Library.

Idzerda I: *Lafayette in the Age of the American Revolution: Selected Letters and Papers, 1776-1790, Volume 1.*

LG: *Lafayette in America* by Louis Gottschalk. L'Esprit de La Fayette Society, publisher. Three volumes in one with discontinuous pagination.

Apostle: The Apostle of Liberty: A Life of La Fayette by Maurice de La Fuye and Ēmile Babeau.

Buckman: *Lafayette, a Biography* by Peter Buckman.

Lafayette, Usurpateur du Vaisseau La Victoire by Bernard de Larquier.

Lafayette and the Liberal Ideal, 1814-1824 by Sylvia Neely

Lafayette in America in 1824 and 1825 by Auguste Levasseur. Translated by John D. Goodman, M.D., 1829.

Endnotes

PART ONE: The Adventure

One: Promise of Fame

1. Pons Motier, seigneur de La Fayette, owner of an estate in Aix-la-Fayette, Puy-de-Dome, married Alix Brun de Champetières in 1240. He fought at Acre, now in Israel, dying about 1300. From this union sprang two family branches. Their eldest son Gilbert Motier de la Fayette inherited his family's holdings and title.

    In 1250, La Fayette knights joined Louis IX, Saint Louis, on the Sixth Crusade. In 1356 at Poitiers, Jean Motier de La Fayette died trying to defeat Edward, Prince of Wales in the foremost battle of the Hundred Years War. Gilbert Motier de La Fayette III (1380-1462), marshal of France, fighting beside Joan of Arc, repelled the British in 1429. There was also illicit romance: Louise de La Fayette (1616-1665), maid of honor to Anne of Austria, wife of Louis XIII and mother of Louis XIV, was the king's lover. She entered a nunnery where he often visited her. Another noblewoman, Marie-Madeleine Pioche de la Vergne (1634-1693) wed François Motier, Comte de La Fayette, in 1655. They lived in his Auvergne chateau but separated in 1659 and she returned to Paris. After his death she was called Madame de La Fayette. Her 1678 masterpiece *The Princess of Cleves* is called the first historical novel.

    Until the late fifteenth century, the Motiers de La Fayette lived in the province of Forez in central Auvergne. Around 1600, Gilbert Motier IV married Isabeau de Polignac and they moved south to Velay and Saint-Romains castle. Today these ruins of the powerful Polignac family remain near Le Puy-en-Velay, closest city to Chavaniac, our Lafayette's birthplace. After many generations the original line died out. In a secondary or cadet line during the late 1700s, descendants of Pons' second son, Roch Motier de Champetières, Gilbert Motier I's younger brother, inheriting estates and titles, took the name Motier de La Fayette. Mostly through marriage, the new Motiers de La Fayette gained more domains and titles: Chevalier and Baron de Vissac, seigneur de Vedières, Fargettes, Jax, Le Bouchet and others.

2. Today the rambling structure is Château Musée Lafayette. The village was renamed Chavaniac-Lafayette for its most famous citizen in 1957.
3. The village has 333 inhabitants.
4. Memoirs.
5. Silesia, southeast of Berlin, is now in Poland.
6. Maurois, *Adrienne*, 25.
7. Charlotte (1729-1811) was widow of Jacques Guérin de Chavaniac, baron de Montialoux.

Two: Independent Spirit

1. Bouillé's paternal grandmother, Madeleine, married Antoine de Bouillé in 1694. She was the sister of Ēdouard Motier de Champetières, husband of Catherine de Chavaniac and LF's paternal grandfather.
2. *Maréchal* was a national honor, not a specific title; today it means field marshal.
3. The revolution forced D'Ayen to flee to Switzerland in 1792. He returned in 1814, became a Restoration peer and died in 1824.
4. Buried in the Church of St. Roch, Chavaniac-Lafayette, Julie left her son beautiful Chateau de Reignac with its fine chapel, near Tours. LF and Adrienne often stayed there.
5. In the old regime, a livre was about equal to a franc, or twenty copper sous.
6. Wikipedia, *Louis XVI; Family Life.*
7. See John Hardman and Munroe Price (Voltaire Foundation, Oxford, U.K.); Jean-Christophe Petitfils' *Louis XVI*, Perrin Editions, 2005; or Bernard Vincent, Gallimard Editions, 2006.

Three: Young Love

1. The Noailles' mansion today is deluxe Hotel St. James & Albany. It fronts on Rue de Rivoli, nonexistent in LF's time.
2. The palace was burned in 1871.
3. Louis Noailles served brilliantly under LF, his brother-in-law, in America and helped to conclude surrender terms at Yorktown. In 1790, he proposed abolition of noble titles and privileges to the Assembly. As the revolution grew, he moved to the United States and became a partner at Bigham's Bank, Philadelphia. In 1793, expecting Marie Antoinette's escape from France, he founded *Azilum* (Asylum), a futile refuge for her in northeastern Pennsylvania.
4. Maurois, 39.
5. More than seventy-five American Masonic bodies are named for Lafayette. W.R. Denslow, *10,000 Famous Freemasons.*

Four: Call of America

1. Kalb was from Huttendorf, near Erlangen, Bavaria.
2. Idzerda I, 31.
3. *Archives Diplomatiques* MD, p 37. Louis XV banished Choiseul to Chanteloup, his estate, after he nearly started a war with Britain over the Falklands.
4. Braddock gave Washington his bloodied scarlet sash; New-York Historical Society collection.
5. R. Chernow, *George Washington.* Pennsylvanian Daniel Boone was a teamster in Braddock's train.
6. Famous writer and British Parliament member.
7. LG, *Lafayette in America*, 1975.
8. Caron took the name "Beaumarchais" from the first of his three wives' property.
9. It still exists. Congress settled Beaumarchais' claims with his heirs in 1835. During the war he wrote *The Barber of Seville* and *The Marriage of Figaro.* Rossini and Mozart respectively made them into operas.
10. S. Johnson, *The Invention of the Air*, 128.

Five: Visit to George III

1. Scone displays the desk in Stormont's bedroom. See Internet.
2. See Sparks, Chapt. X.
3. B. de Larquier, *Lafayette, Usurpateur du Vaisseau La Victoire*, 1987. Based on Broglie's documents released by his descendant Odon de Quinsonas Oudinot and letters in De Kalb family archives. See: *Revue d'Etudes Anglophones*, No. 16, Printemps 2004, *Introduites et Présentées par Bernard Vincent: Lafayette et la Guerre d'Independance: Neuf Lettres Inédites: Dossier 1, Université d'Orléans, France: www.paradigme.com/sources/sources-PDF/sources16-1.pd*.
4. French historian Jacques de Trentinian's estimate of value of armaments in the hold.
5. His title was Comte de Noailles, Prince-Duc de Poix. Trained as a soldier, he became a politician and was elected to the Estates-General as a noble from Amiens and Ham. After a duel with a Versailles guard commander, he left France. Joining the August 1792 riots, he again fled when his parents were guillotined in 1794 but returned in 1800. He lived at his Oise estate and died a Restoration peer in 1819.
6. Theater Royal, Drury Lane; Buckman, 35.
7. I am grateful to Bernard de Larquier for this list of officers and his book. Larquier, 67, etc.
8. Brice (1751-1784), son of a Maryland criminal court judge, became a brigadier general. He married, fathered a son and died the same year. Son James Edmund Brice (1784-1827) was a U.S. consular agent at Cap Haitien, Haiti. See R.H. McIntire, *Annapolis, MD., Families*, Gateway Press, Baltimore, 1979. See Brice miniature, Idzerda I, 50.
9. Maurois, 50.

Six: Journey to the Unknown

1. C. Tower, 172.
2. Idzerda I, **75.**
3. Ibid., 76.
4. Maurois, 58-59. The South Carolina Historical Society, Charleston, has no record of *La Victoire* or crew, perhaps because they were foreign.

5. Idzerda I, 76. Du Buysson, honored in France by the king, died at thirty-four in 1786 from wounds suffered while trying to help Kalb in Camden, S.C., battle.
6. Augur, 41.
7. Idzerda I, 79.
8. Eric Pominville, National Park Service, located Du Coudray's initialed gravestone, Old Saint Mary's Churchyard, Philadelphia.
9. Connecticut today honors Deane as a patriot.
10. Idzerda I, 88.
11. De Larquier, 145-147.

Seven: Joining a Revolution

1. R. Chernow: Washington's corpse was measured to toe ends, accounting for his presumed height later of six feet, three inches.
2. Gist, of Dunbar, Westmoreland County, Pa., was the first white scout in southeastern Ohio. His son, Lt. Nathaniel Gist, sired Sequoia, creator of the Cherokee syllabary.
3. The University of Mary Washington, Fredericksburg, Va., honors her, as does the City of Fredericksburg with a limestone obelisk.
4. R. Chernow, *Alexander Hamilton*, 95-96.
5. Educated in England, John Laurens (1754-1782) was a lawyer and statesman. In a short life he wed and fathered a daughter in London he never saw. Influenced by LF, Laurens recruited a Continental regiment of 3,000 slaves and promised them freedom for fighting. Laurens' father freed his slaves after his son's death as he had wished.
6. Alexandre Dumas' source was Courtilz de Sandras' 1700 novel published twenty-seven years after the real D'Artagnan's death. A Bastille warden and friend of the real D'Artagnan told Courtilz about him while Courtilz was a prisoner there.
7. LF to A.H., 11/10/1780, Gilder Lehrman Institute of American History, New-York Historical Society, doc. no. GLC03323.
8. LF probably met L'Enfant at Valley Forge. He joined the army as a volunteer in 1776. An architect, L'Enfant attended Paris' Royal Academy of Painting and Sculpture. He drew officers' portraits, including Washington's, at Valley Forge.

9. A heroic bronze *Hercules* still stands on a pinnacle atop the eight-sided folly. Its reservoir feeds a huge stepped waterfall.
10. Now Elkton, Md.
11. Now Route 1.
12. Master gunsmith Jacob Walster of Saarbrucken, France [now Germany], fifty miles from Metz, made the pistols, signed and dated 1775-1776. The Richard King Mellon Foundation, Pittsburgh, donated them to Fort Ligonier, Westmoreland County, Pa., in 2005. They were purchased at Christie's New York January 18-19, 2002 for $1,986,000, setting auction record for firearms. See Christie's catalog, *Important American Furniture, Silver and Folk Art*, 289-301.
13. Both, of 1778-1780, are in collection of Washington and Lee University, Lexington, Va.
14. William Alexander (1726-1783), popularly known as Lord Sterling, was a brave high-ranking army officer whom Washington valued. Born in British New York City, Sterling, the name he favored, claimed a contested Scottish earldom. He died of alcoholism before the war ended.
15. T. Fleming, 118.

PART TWO: Success and Failure

Eight: Recovery and Duplicity

1. Idzerda I, 121.
2. In Montgomery County, eastern Pennsylvania.
3. B.J. Nolan, p 137, *Lafayette in Pennsylvania, Pennsylvania History magazine*, 1934.
4. See Internet: *Bermuda-online.org/France.*
5. L'Enfant created jewelry (medals) and designed the Federal City. Washington later urged L'Enfant, who lived 10 years with a man in Philadelphia, to end the relationship. See first note in next chapter.
6. See T. Fleming, *Washington's Secret War.*
7. Buckman, 69.

Nine: The Effective Baron

1. See B. Arnebeck essay, "*To Tease and Torment: Two Presidents Confront Suspicion of Sodomy,*" *geocities.com/bobarnebeck/L'Enfant.*
2. Fleming, 208.
3. LG, 180.
4. Ibid., 194.
5. Ibid., 181.
6. Recent accounts give them credit for acting bravely under fire from superior enemy numbers.
7. T. Fleming, 332. The portrait was returned and is in the White House.
8. R. Leckie, *George Washington's War,* 471-489.
9. June 1778.
10. Ibid., 475.
11. See J. J. Ellis, *His Excellency: George Washington.*
12. See R. Leckie.

Ten: Depending on Rochambeau

1. Capes Henlopen and May.
2. Buckman, 78.
3. Karapalides, 119.
4. Courtyard plaque, Hotel St. James and Albany, Paris, marks the event.
5. LF to Comte de Maurepas, March 14, 1779, Idzerda II, p 244. LF met with Franklin, who suggested he organize this operation with Jones, March 23, 1779.
6. Trentinian to author: "LF wrote the legend his way, having outlived the others."
7. Vergennes to LF, Sept. 16, 1779, Cornell University exhibition, *Lafayette: Citizen of Two Worlds,* 2007-2008. He also wrote: "I am not marvelously pleased with the country you have just left. I find it barely active and demanding." (S. Shiff, *Benjamin Franklin and the Pursuit of America,* Bloomsburg, 2006.)

Eleven: Second Return to War

1. Buckman, 92.
2. See S. Dunn, *Sister Revolutions.*
3. B.F. to LF, August 24, 1779. LG, 44.
4. Ibid., 51.
5. Buckman, 93.
6. LG, 69.
7. G.W. to LF, May 1780.
8. Karapalides, 149.

Twelve: A Terrible Treason

1. His bedchamber is intact in Webb-Deane-Stevens Museum.
2. Buckman, 97.
3. B. Whitlock, 220.
4. M. Haiman, *Kosciuszko, Leader and Exile, Library of Polish Studies No. 5*, 1977. West Point's first bronze statue hailed Kosciuszko and Poland greatly honors him. See M. Haiman, *Kosciuszko in the American Revolution, Library of Polish Studies No. 4*, 1975.
5. For LF's Virginia campaign chronology: *xenophongroup.com/mcjoynt/laf.va.*

Thirteen: The Virginia Campaign

1. Battle toll: 72 French killed, 112 wounded; 30 British killed, 73 wounded. See A.T. Mahan, *Major Operations of the Navies in the War of American Independence,* London, 1913, 173-174.
2. LG, ed., *The Letters of Lafayette to Washington, 1777-1799,* New York, 1944, 159.
3. LF to La Luzerne, April 10, 1781, LG, *LF in America*, 213-14.
4. LF to Greene, April 17, 1781, loc. cit.
5. C.W. Abrams, *The Campaign*, see Internet.
6. M. Goodwin, *A Brief & True Report Concerning Williamsburg in Virginia*, 75-81, 282-287. Colonial Williamsburg Foundation, unpublished paper by M.R.M. Goodwin, Sept. 1956.

7. Tory losses: 48 killed, 145 wounded. *Monticello Newsletter*, Vol. 17, No. 2, Winter 2006.
8. ***www.patriotresource.com/people/clinton.html***.
9. B.F. Stevens, ed., *The Campaign in Virginia, 1781.* London, 1888, 65-70.
10. Because of highway construction, The Virginia Society and the National Society of the Colonial Dames of America moved this exquisite brick manor to Richmond in 1933, making it a house museum on the same river.
11. Gilder Lehrman Institute of American History, doc. No. GLC04775. John Armstrong, Madison's secretary of war, once owned this note.
12. LG found the closest version in Clinton to Lord Germain: "La Fayette could not escape him." Lafayette wrote in his *Mémoirs*' "Manuscript No. 1," 1800-1814, he intercepted a Cornwallis letter with the words.

Fourteen: Victory at Yorktown

1. The dark brick colonial shows bombardment scars. Yorktown is active but never regained its former importance. In 1862 during the Civil War, Winslow Homer drew scenes there for *Harper's Weekly.*
2. See **www.hudsonrivervalley.net/books/battleoffVAcapes.htl.**
3. LG note, 306; also 236.
4. Ibid., 232. Bernard Faÿ, French historian, Nazi collaborator, discovered Provence wrote the song.
5. Talley: Americans: 11,133; French: 7,800. (D. N. Moran, *Casualties during the American Revolution,* Liberty Tree Newsletter, March 2006, Sons of Liberty Chapter, Sons of the American Revolution.
6. C.B. Williams, *Biography of Revolutionary Heroes,* Wiley & Putnam, 1839, 275-278.
7. It is still visited.
8. See **www.nps.gov**.
9. Figures reflect some exaggeration of killed and wounded on both sides.
10. Eleven regiments were represented, including: *Bourbonnais, Gatinais/Auvergne, Legion de Lauzun, Royal Deux-Ponts, Santonge, Soissonais, Auxonne Artillerie.* They are honored annually on Oct.

19. The Daughters of the American Revolution helped identify many French dead and in 1931 placed bronze tablets listing 133 French war dead in Square de Yorktown, Paris, near Benjamin Franklin statue.
11. His chateau is visitable in Thoré-la-Rochette.

Fifteen: War in the Caribbean and Elsewhere

1. Nov. 15, 1781. LG, 337.
2. See New Jersey Archives and History Bureau, Trenton. LG, *Lafayette in America*, 337.
3. LG, 342-345.
4. *Newport Mercury*, Dec. 29, 1781. Nolan, 212-13.
5. Dec. 22, J.P. Jones papers; De Koven II, 219.
6. These Saint-Simons were related to Louis, Duc de Saint-Simon (1675-1755), diarist of Louis XIV's Versailles. His younger brother continued the family line to present.
7. Thirty-one of fifty-six nobles not officers came from the law.
8. See G. Bodinier, lieutenant-general retired, French Army Historical Service, others, *Les Officiers de L'Armee Royale,* 80. From *La France de la Révolution et les Ētats-Unis d'Amerique, Fondation Singer-Polignac.*

Sixteen: Charged with a Purpose

1. Born Oct. 22, 1781, Louis Joseph died June 4, 1789 of tuberculosis. A second son, Louis Charles (March 27, 1785-June 8, 1795), Prince Royal, "Louis XVII," died in prison, also of tuberculosis.
2. Buckman, 123.
3. Ē. Taillemite, *Louis XVI, or the Immobile Navigator,* **Ēditions Payot**, Paris, France, 2002.
4. Louis XVI to C. Malesherbes. J. Hardman, *Louis XVI,* vii, Yale, 1993.
5. See French historian J.-C. Petitfils. George III also began a collection of 65,000 books and 22,000 pamphlets.
6. LG, 350.
7. Buckman, 114.
8. G.W. to LF, Mount Vernon, August 15, 1786.

9. Buckman, 123.
10. See LG biography, *Lady-in-Waiting.*
11. Cornell University Library exhibition, 2007-2008.
12. Charles Alexandre d'Alsace de Chimay d'Hénin Liétard, Prince du Saint-Empire, 1748-1794.
13. B.F. to Morris, Jan. 28, 1782, Smyth, VIII, 374; LG, 353.
14. The Netherlands recognized U.S. independence in 1782, Spain in 1783.

Seventeen: The Elusive Peace

1. According to the EB, Mesmer is regarded as the father of hypnotism.
2. For Lansdowne's support, Americans gave him Gilbert Stuart's painting of *George Washington*, called the *Lansdowne Portrait,* Smithsonian National Portrait Gallery. At Lansdowne's estate Bowood House (now a hotel and arboretum) near Bath, his librarian Joseph Priestly identified oxygen in 1775.
3. LG., 384. Franklin, Adams and Jay wrote praising LF for his efforts.
4. W. Stahr, 156. *R. Oswald Notes*, August 7, 1782. R. B. Morris, ed., *John Jay: The Winning of the Peace*, unpublished papers, 1780-1784.
5. French Army and Navy Archives, Chateau de Vincennes, Paris, hold detailed embarcation plans.
6. De Grasse had captured *H.M.S.S. Richmond* and *Iris* in the Chesapeake on Sept. 11, 1781. France added *Richmond* to its navy and kept her name.
7. LG, 395.

Eighteen: Dealing with Madrid

1. LG, 404.
2. Ibid., 405.
3. See *Organo Oficial de la Sociedad Economica de Amigos de Pais, www.amigospais-guaracabuya.org.*
4. LF to Livingston, March 2, 1783.
5. Historical Society of Pennsylvania, *Windows on the Collection: Franklin in France*, May 2006.

6. *Bibliotheque Nationale de France* report to author. Also in a letter of June 7, 1785, Kroch Library, Cornell University, LF hired a notary to find and buy a plantation comprising "land, habitations, Negroes and tools" at a maximum price of 300,000 livres, to be run and managed by Daniel Lescallier, French Guianan colonial administrator.
7. La Grange documents, Library of Congress, *et al.*

Nineteen: A Heartfelt Visit

1. *APS Minutes of 1784*, collated 1882, 126-127.
2. But in *Cosi Fan Tutti, 1790,* Mozart spoofed Mesmer.
3. LF to AL, August 20, 1784, Idzerda, V 403-04.
4. The birds soon died. Washington sent them to Peale, who wanted them for his museum; now in Museum of Comparative Zoology, Harvard.
5. It remains in the White House with taxidermied pets.
6. Barbé-Marbois later surprised Lafayette by recreating in his elegant house Washington's Hudson dining room.
7. See **www.henrybolduc.com.**
8. French soldier Victor Riquet, 22, became diplomat Duc de Caraman. He was a relative of Princess D'Hénin. His chateau was in Chimay, Belgium.
9. H.G. Unger, 199.
10. Chester County, Pa., records, Dec. 13, 1784.
11. Buckman, 121.

Twenty: Quarrelsome Estates

1. The Society of the Cincinnati, Washington, D.C., has 1,000 members and is dedicated to American Revolutionary history. The City of Cincinnati is named after it.
2. Conway became governor of France's Indian colonies, later joining an unsuccessful royalist force in southern France. Returning to Ireland, he led a brigade and died in June 1795.
3. It is not known if LF was fully reimbursed. The Society paid him $894. *Society Proceedings*, May 7-19, 1787. M. Myers Jr., *The Insignia*

of the Society of the Cincinnati, The Society of the Cincinnati, 1998, 21.

4. B. Whitlock, 281.
5. The United States granted him, one of six foreigners so honored, that status in 2002.
6. Buckman, 124-125.
7. The Regent (diamond), now in the Louvre.
8. B.C. Davenport, *A Diary of the French Revolution by G. Morris* (1789-1793), 1939, VI, 221, 223.
9. Colonne moved to London, remaining almost to his death in 1804.
10. Davenport, 190-191.
11. A laboring family ate 1.2 tons of grain a year, 80 percent of it grown around Paris.
12. Orléans' great-great-grandfather was Louis XIV's brother; his grandfather was young Louis XV's regent.

Twenty-One: Time for Expertise

1. The chateau was destroyed in 1870. Its park holds the Lafayette Escadrille Monument.
2. It still houses government offices and private stores.
3. Witness Mahatma Gandhi and Dr. Martin Luther King. LF to G.W., M. de la Fuye, E.A. Babeau, *The Apostle of Liberty*, 81.
4. Brienne became a cardinal in Rome. He returned to France during the revolution. Pius VI repudiated him for taking the oath of the civil constitution. Revolutionaries arrested Brienne and he died in prison in 1794.

Twenty-Two: The Tennis Court Vow

1. Whitlock, 306.
2. Ibid., 310. The Edict of Toleration was enacted in November 1787.
3. Ibid., 188.
4. G.W. to LF, Mount Vernon, June 19, 1788. *The Outline of Liberty, G. Washington: A Collection*, compiled, edited by W.B. Allen, Indianapolis Liberty Fund, 1988.

5. Dissolved on September 30, 1791. Legislative Assembly and constitution of 1791 succeeded it. F. Mignet, *History of the French Revolution, 1789-1814*, 1824.
6. Whitlock, 326.
7. LG, *Lafayette in the French Revolution*, 91.

Twenty-Three: Declaring Citizens' Rights

1. Bouchez and Roux, 368; Bailly *Mémoires*, ii, 326, 341.
2. In 1958, General Charles de Gaulle created the Fifth Republic, maintaining those rights.
3. See P.A. Kropotkin, *The Great French Revolution, 1789-1793,* 1909. On Internet or Vanguard Printings, New York, 1927
4. Breteuil negotiated royal purchase of Chateau de St.-Cloud.
5. Kropotkin, Chapter 13.

Twenty-Four: Fall of the Bastille

1. The museum was called Certius, Boulevard du Temple, Marais District.
2. Sade was moved to Charenton, an asylum offering gentle care. He died there at 74 in 1814.
3. Possible source of the "cake" admonition.
4. Whitlock, 339.
5. Virginia commissioned two Lafayette busts. One, preceding Houdon's standing marble of George Washington, is in the State House, Richmond. The other, broken, long lost and restored, is in the Louvre.
6. Whitlock, 333.
7. LF *Mémoires;* but not in Bailly's *Mémoires* or other accounts.

PART THREE: Trials and Disappointments

Twenty-Five: The Great Fear

1. Whitlock, 334.
2. Chefs, forced to leave chateaus, improved French cuisine.

3. Lafayette borrowed the Phrygian cap, or *bonnet rouge,* from an ancient Roman custom of honoring recently freed slaves with a red cap. A tile with this image is mounted over Chateau de Chavaniac's north entrance.
4. The United States National Guard and others are based on the French militia.

Twenty-Six: A Second Revolution

1. Maillard died of tuberculosis in 1794.

Twenty-Seven: Bread, Blood and Tears

1. The seller was vastly wealthy Duc de Penthièvre, who died of natural causes in 1793. Orléans was his son-in-law. Today the chateau, with its dairy, is the French president's summer residence.
2. Whitlock, 366.
3. Their daughter, Marie Thérèse Charlotte, the reactionary Duchesse d'Angoulême (1778-1851), revisited the palace as an adult.
4. Orléans' sons were: Louis-Philippe, Duc de Chartres, 16, Duc de Montpensier and Comte de Beaujolais, who was absent with a cold. Madame Genlis, a famous educator, was their governess-teacher. C.F. Montjoie, *Histoire de la Conjuration de L.PJ. d'Orléans Surnommé Ēgalité*, V 4, 40-41.
5. Plaques on the Tuileries Garden's fence, Rue de Rivoli, mark the Assembly's site.
6. *Assignats* were first printed in 1791 in an issue of 400 million francs ($4 billion today). Eventually 45,500 million in face value were printed before being abandoned as useless. The plates were destroyed in 1797.

Twenty-Eight: The Great Festival

1. In France this remains the formal name of the July 14 event, not "Bastille Day."
2. The Eiffel Tower rises at its northern end.

3. The mounded earth remained until the Second Empire, 1852-1870.
4. The large painting, *Fête de la Fêdêration, July 14, 1790*, 1792, by Charles Thévenin (1764-1838), Musée de Carnavalet, Paris, recaptures this stirring LF event.

Twenty-Nine: Dealing with Mirabeau

1. Whitlock, 379.
2. Jean Antoine Nicolas de Caritat (1743-1794): *Fragments of Justification, Oeuvres de Condorcet*, Vol. 1, 1847; Fromann Verlag reprint, Stuttgart, 1968, 583.
3. Mirabeau to LF, Dec. 1, 1789, Whitlock, 380.
4. Ibid., 383.

Thirty: Day of the Daggers

1. Noelle Destremau, *Un Jardin Historique à Paris: Picpus,* pamphlet, 1994.
2. Now home of the French Military Archives and Museum.
3. M. De la Fuye, E.A. Babeau, *The Apostle of Liberty*, 144.
4. Ibid., 145.
5. Ibid., 143.

Thirty-One: The King's Betrayal

1. Built by Louis XIV, the gate still stands.
2. Beauharnais, a nobleman, fought in America, becoming a general. He was guillotined in 1794. His widow, Josephine de Beauharnais, married Napoleon I.
3. *La Marseillaise's* sixth stanza: "...But not these bloody despots/these accomplices of Bouillé/all these tigers who piteously/ripped out their mothers' wombs..."
4. *Apostle*, 150.
5. Refusing a reward of 30,000 francs for his information, Drouet was elected to the National Assembly and voted to execute the king.
6. He died in London in 1800.

Thirty-Two: Champ de Mars Horror

1. After criticizing the "rebel constitution," Condorcet (1743-1794) hid for months in Paris and later commited suicide in prison. His remains disappeared. In 1998, France placed an empty coffin in the Panthéon, honoring him.
2. Du Pont was the father of Ēleuthère Irenée du Pont, founder of E.I. Du Pont de Nemours Corp., Wilmington, Delaware.
3. *Apostle*, 174-176.

Thirty-Three: A New Political Club

1. The order was founded in Feuillans, near Toulouse, in 1577.
2. F.A. Aulard, *La Société des Jacobins, Recueil de Documents,* 6 v. Paris, 1889, V. 531.
3. Ibid., 290.
4. Ibid., 294.
5. French revolutionaries, angry with émigrés, seized the region in 1794, making it a French department, later returning it to Germany.
6. Carnot voted for the king's death. As a Directory member he supported Napoleon, who ennobled him.
7. He referred to France and the United States. LF's first autobiography, *Mémoires de Ma Main*, V. III, 121.
8. Nov. 1791 election: Pétion, 6,728 votes; Lafayette, 3,126. Turnout was less than 10 percent of 80,000 "active" voters. Voter ignorance was a factor.
9. *Apostle*, 178.

Thirty-Four: Disaster at the Front

1. De Staël, Narbonne's mistress, helped him gain his post. Narbonne was likely Louis XV's son.
2. *Apostle,* 183-184.
3. LF overshadowed him. Biron, although favoring the revolution, was guillotined in 1793.
4. *Apostle,* 304.

5. Ibid.
6. Austria controlled Southern Netherlands, the future Belgium, 1713-1794. France captured and held it, 1794-1815.
7. Whitlock, 450.

Thirty-Five: Acts of Futility

1. Whitlock., 457.
2. Ibid., 466.
3. *Apostle*, 198.
4. *Mémoires*, V. III, 345.
5. Bertrand de Molleville, *Mémoires*, V. II, 294.

Thirty-Six: Storming the Tuileries

1. Fabre added "d'Ēglantine," dog rose in French, for a silver rose he won for academic excellence. Dramatist, poet, Cordeliers president and secretary, Fabre named the revolutionary calendar's months. Falsely tried, he was guillotined in 1794, seriously weakening the radicals.
2. The bust was recovered, repaired and is in the Louvre.
3. *Chronique des Cinquantes Jours,* 1832.
4. Whitlock, 461.
5. *Apostle*, 199.

Thirty-Seven: Escape and Capture

1. *Correspondance Secrète*, August 18, 1792, V. II, 617.
2. Mémoires.
3. At Rochefort, Province of Liège, Belgium.
4. LF to A.F, August 21, 1792.
5. Woodward, 316-317.

Thirty-Eight: The Hell of Prison

1. Moravia — *Morava* — is today a province of the Czech Republic. Olmütz, *Olomouc* in Czech, lies in the mountains northeast of Brno. The prison is now a Czech army headquarters. The city has a Lafayette Street and Lafayette Hotel.
2. She also had a liaison with Talleyrand.
3. Details: see P. Spalding, *Lafayette: Prisoner of State*, University of South Carolina Press, 2010; also J.W. Baker, "The Imprisonment of Lafayette," *American Heritage Magazine*, June 1977.
4. Ibid.
5. Ibid.
6. Ibid.
7. Spalding, 134.
8. F.K. Huger to Thomas Pinckney, Jan. 5, 1795, South Carolina Historical Society, Charleston. 9. House of Commons debate, December 16, 1796.
10. Spalding, 134.
11. Huger was graduated from the School of Medicine, University of Pennsylvania, in 1797. A 1907 plaque in Medical Hall salutes his bravery.
12. Huger was in the War of 1812 and served two terms in the state legislature.
13. He said of the rescue, "I simply considered myself the representative of the young men of America and acted accordingly." He died at eighty-one in 1855.

Thirty-Nine: Despair and Salvation

1. Susan Fenimore Cooper, the novelist's eldest daughter, praised Adrienne's account and her daughter Virginie de Lasteyrie's biography of Adrienne published by the Lafayette family. S. Fenimore Cooper, "Mme. De Lafayette and Her Mother," *Putnam's Magazine*, August 1870; 202-213.

Forty: Taking on Bonaparte

1. From *Life of the Marquise de Montagu.*
2. R. Brookhiser, *Gentleman Revolutionary: Gouverneur Morris.*
3. See N. Isenberg's Burr biography, *Fallen Founder.*
4. T. Fleming, *The Real Story Behind Napoleon's Sale of Louisiana,* American Revolution Roundtable, History News Network, May 28, 2004. Library of Congress: Louisiana: European Explorations and the Lousiana Purchase, **http://memory.loc.gov**. From the 1820s, France extracted huge war indemnities from Haiti for many decades.
5. T.J. to LF, Washington, D.C., July 14, 1807. Box 23, folder 22, Kroch Library, Cornell University; Monticello. T.J. offered Bollman the U.S. Rotterdam consulate, the commercial agency at Santo Domingo and the Indian agency, Natchitoches, La.
6. While finagling, Wilkinson died and was buried in Mexico City in 1825.
7. Bollman began a vinegar factory with two brothers in Philadelphia and London. In Europe in 1814, he worked for Baring Brothers, unsuccessfully writing Bolivar to deal with Baring. Bollman witnessed the 1815 Vienna peace conference returning Europe to pre-Napoleonic status and Talleyrand's diplomacy preventing reprisals against France. Bollman backed an abortive monetary standard based on platinum, discovered in 1820's Russia. He thought platinum, more valuable than gold, could stop inflation by holding its value. He was first to find practical uses for platinum: plating boilers for sulfuric acid and minting coinage. He wed Elizabeth Nixon in Philadelphia and they had two daughters. Unable to promote platinum in the United States, he moved to London with his daughters. In Colombia, he negotiated shipment of forty tons of platinum ore to a London chemist. Returning from Colombia, Bollman, fifty-two, died of yellow fever in Kingston, Jamaica, December 10, 1821. His Saxon town named a street for him. Lafayette was ever grateful to his would-be rescuers. See: J.A. Chaldecott, *Platinum Metals Review,* Vol. 27, April 1983, 81-90; *"Nehmt das Pferd, Ihr Seid Frei!"* B. Bei der Wieden, *www.ppr-hamburg.de/de/reportagen/Bollmann.html*.

Forty-One: Graves of the Martyrs

1. Now *Place de la Nation.*
2. M. M. Crawford, *Mme. De Lafayette and Her Family,* James Pott & Co., 1907, 309-314.

   With peace, Princesse Amélie de Salm-Kyrbourg de Hohenzollern-Sigmaringen purchased the site. She added a stone cross and monument to honor her brother, Prince Frédéric III de Salm-Kyrbourg, buried there. She enclosed the graves with a rubblestone wall in November 1796. Frédéric had built the beautiful Palace de Salm near the Lafayettes' hôtel. A male hairdresser won the palace in a revolutionary lottery. Napoleon made it the home of the French Legion of Honor in 1802. The rebel tribunal that had dispersed the convent's nuns reopened Picpus as "a house of health and detention" in 1792. There the wealthy, including De Sade, eluded execution in the Terror. But others, their money gone, were removed to the Conciergerie and executed in the Place du Trône.
3. June K. Burton essay, Lafayette Collection, Cleveland State University Library, 2001.
4. Today Sisters of the Sacred Hearts of Mary and Jesus and the Adoration reside in the convent.
5. T.J. to LF, Washington, D.C., July 14, 1807. Box 23, folder 22, Kroch Library, Cornell University; Monticello.

Forty-Two: Not the Best of Worlds

1. *Mémoires,* V. 356.
2. Ibid., 311.
3. Ibid., 237.
4. Allies at Waterloo: Britain, Russia, Prussia, Sweden, Austria, the Netherlands and several German states.
5. F.L. Maitland, *The Surrender of Napoleon, www.Gutenberg.net.*
6. In Haguenau, Alsace, France.

Forty-Three: The White Terror

1. S. Neely, *Lafayette and the Liberal Ideal*, 17.
2. *Apostle*, 243.
3. It hangs in the House of Representatives to this day. Ary Scheffer (1795-1858) was an important romantic artist of neoclassic and religious subjects. His Paris house is the *Musée de la Vie Romantique.* He painted portraits of Louis-Philippe and family. Many Scheffer paintings are in the Dordrecht Museum, Netherlands, where he was born and is the subject of a memorial bronze in a square.
4. Site: *Parc Louis XVI*, Boulevard Haussmann, several blocks west of the Madeleine.
5. *Apostle*, 245.
6. Buckman, 261.
7. *Apostle*, 259.

PART FOUR: The Nation's Guest

Forty-Four: Tour of Triumph

1. Andre-Nicolas, called Auguste, Levasseur, 1795-1878. See LG's inventory, *LF Letters in America.*
2. LF's great-great-grandaughter, Baronne Meunier du Houssoy, consigned the medal to Sotheby's New York, announced on LF's 250th anniversary. It fetched a record $5.3 million on Dec. 11, 2007.
3. Kroch Library, Cornell, box 47, folder 21.

Forty-Five: Emotions on High

1. Signed letter, circa 1807-09, GLC08023, Gilder Lehrman Institute of American History.
2. The Bunker Hill Museum, which opened in 2007 across from the monument, contains the small trowel LF used in the ceremony.

Forty-Six: Hudson Journey

1. "*The Erie Rising*," Cait Murphy, Rosanne Haggerty, *American Heritage*, April 2001, 62-71.
2. In 1986, Marquis Gilbert de Lafayette, a descendant, renewed the friendship by visiting the school.

Forty-Seven: Southern Welcomes

1. Buckman, 251.
2. The mansion no longer exists.
3. New Castle celebrates its past annually.
4. Custis became Gen. Robert E. Lee's father-in-law in 1831.

Forty-Eight: A Doomed Society

1. LF descendant René de Chambrun was a dedicator.
2. Poe was Edgar Allan Poe's grandfather. Both rest in Westminster Burying Ground, Fayette and Greene Streets, west Baltimore.
3. The capitol's cast-iron dome was erected in the 1850s.
4. B. Moyers, *A World of Ideas*, 497.
5. Still in operation.
6. The house is a museum today.
7. S.J. Idzerda, A.C. Loveland, M.H. Miller, *Lafayette, Hero of Two Worlds*, Queens Museum catalog, 1989, 134.

Forty-Nine: Dreams of Abolition

1. Quoted in William Lloyd Garrison's letter to Louis Kossuth, *Concerning Freedom and Slavery in the United States*, 39-40, Samuel J. May Anti-Slavery Collection, Division of Rare and Manuscript Collections, Cornell University Library. Also see website of Skillman Library, Lafayette College, *Lafayette and Slavery*.
2. J. J. Ellis, *American Sphinx: The Character of Thomas Jefferson*, 275, 279.
3. Ibid., 277.

4. Ibid., 276.
5. Family Letters Project, Small Special Collections Library, University of Virginia, Thomas Jefferson Foundation, 2006. http://familypapers.dataformat.com.
6. Poplar Forest is restored.
7. Ellis, 277.
8. Family Letters Project, University of Virginia.
9. See *Jefferson's Memorandum Books*, Princeton, 1997, note, 1408.
10. Ibid., 345, 347.
11. C. Allgor, *A Perfect Union*, 364, 386.
12. Autograph, June 25, 1842, Princeton University Library.
13. Allgor, 365.
14. LF letters, Kroch Library, Cornell University.
15. Nashoba's site was in Germantown, Shelby County, Tenn.
16. It still exists. Washington and Monroe were born in the region. The University of Mary Washington oversees the James Monroe Museum and Memorial Library, containing his law office, Chestnut Street. An unsigned painting, *Gathering of Well-Wishers*, n.d., depicts the Lafayettes and Monroe at the White House portico; attributed to Pietro Bonanni, Italian who worked on the Capitol.

Fifty: A Surprise Gift

1. Congress paid with two checks of $120,000 and $80,000. LF deposited them in the Bank of the United States. The first check is in the Valley Forge Historical Society collection. *See* www.USHistory.org.

Fifty-One: The Supreme Ceremony

1. Jean Falguiere and Marius Mercie's bronze and stone sculpture with Lafayette and others was placed at Pennsylvania Avenue and 16th Street in 1891.
2. February 8, 1825, *Samuel F.B. Morse: His Letters and Journals*, I: 262.
3. Morse, who met Fenimore Cooper at Lafayette's home, died wealthy in 1872. Morse's house, Hyde Park, N.Y., is a museum.
4. The current historic Market House replaced it in 1832.

5. S. Idzerda, *Marquis de Lafayette, V. 13, American National Biography, 1999.*
6. The Fayetteville Independent Light Infantry Armory and Museum, 210 Burgess St., exhibits Lafayette's carriage with tonneau.
7. De Kalb's bravery is not forgotten. Six American counties bear his name.

Fifty-Two: Special Days in New Orleans

1. Now Faubourg Marigny.
2. *Ideas on Liberty:* J. Powell, *Lafayette: Hero of Two Worlds*, V. 47, No. 9.
3. Chicago Historical Society archives.

Fifty-Three: Sinking in the Ohio River

PART FIVE: The Old Agitator

Fifty-Four: Named for Marie Antoinette

1. See Grand Lodge of Kentucky web site: *http:grandlodgeofkentucky.org/history.html,* or Sons of Union Veterans of the Civil War, *http://suvcw.org/pr/art030.htm*. Mary Todd Lincoln's family had the recipe and Abraham Lincoln called it the best cake he ever ate.
2. W.H.Venable, *Beginnings of Literary Culture in the Ohio Valley,* 1891.
3. The dauphin died of tuberculosis at ten in 1795. The next dauphin, Louis-Joseph-Xavier-François, tutored to revile his parents, died in prison at ten in 1798. His heart, linked by DNA tests to Marie Antoinette, was interred at the Cathedral of Saint Denis in 2002.

Fifty-Five: Friendship Hill

1. The National Park Service maintains the unfurnished mansion museum.
2. F. Ellis, *History of Fayette County*, Philadelphia, Pa., 1882.
3. The sculpture is in the Fayette County Courthouse, Uniontown, Pa.

4. The landscape Lafayette saw is gone. Part of Braddock and North Braddock Boroughs, it was urbanized and industrialized. The mansion became a women's seminary, later site of General Braddock High School's football field. State markers and a fifteen-mile hiking trail honor Braddock's Field.
5. A bronze marker on PNC Bank's skyscraper marks the visit. The Daughters of the American Revolution headquarters, Washington, D.C., has the crystal chandelier from Lafayette's room.
6. Reactived during the War of 1812, the fort was abandoned in 1813 and sold. Capt. Meriwether Lewis launched the three-year expedition of the American West there in 1803.
7. See the National Museum of American History.
8. The Franklin Institute awarded Bakewell, Page & Bakewell a silver medal that year for producing the finest cut glass in America.
9. See S.J. Idzerda, et al., catalog, *Lafayette, Hero of Two Worlds.*

Fifty-Six: Speeding on the Erie Canal

1. *Pittsburgh Gazette*, June 3, 1825; *Western Pennsylvania History*, V. VII, No. 5, 143-146.
2. C.W. Dahlinger, "*General Lafayette's Visit to Pittsburgh in 1825*," excerpt *W. Pa. Historical Magazine*, July 1925. V. 6, No. 5.
3. Today Perry Highway/Route 19.
4. Built in 1822, it is now a museum of the period.
5. National Park Service web site, "Battle of Lake Erie," *nps.gov.* Since 1915, Perry's Victory and International Peace Memorial, a 317-foot tower and observation gallery, has marked the friendship of the United States, Britain and Canada.
6. The Seneca Nation in western New York today has more than 7,300 tribal members with casinos providing services and programs to members. It hosts a city, Salamanca, within its aboriginal territory.
7. The city later honored the hero with Lafayette Square.

Fifty-Seven: The Supreme Ceremony

1. *Mémoires*, V. 5.
2. Adams incorrectly believed Masons were anti-American. J. Wheelan in *Mr. Adams's Last Crusade*, 87, notes Adams objected to Masons' use of the Bible to justify themselves.
3. See M. Klamkin, *The Return of Lafayette.*
4. Webster returned to welcome the completed monument in 1843.
5. Called Old Mill, it still stands.

Fifty-Eight: Last Travels on Tour

1. J. List, *Schriften of Friedrich List,* band II, 77.
2. *The Uncollected Poetry & Prose of Walt Whitman*, P. Smith, 1932, 2:286.
3. The boat is at La Grange. A replica, *The Lafayette*, was built at Mystic Seaport Museum, 1976. J. Gardner, *The Log of Mystic Seaport*, Mystic, Conn., 1972.
4. An unincorporated community nearby in Whitemarsh Township, Montgomery County, Pa., where LF stayed, is called Lafayette Hill.
5. Bunker Hill newspaper report, May 16, 1829. Hogshead: a barrel holding a quarter ton, or 63 gallons.
6. V.VII, 41.
7. Ibid., 49.

Fifty-Nine: American Farewells

1. Now Belmont Country Club clubhouse, Ashburn, Va.
2. J. Hutson, *Library of Congress Information Bulletin*, Sept. 18, 1995.
3. *Letters of Lafayette and Jefferson*, Chinard, 435.
4. *National Journal of Washington*, Sept. 10, 1825.
5. The vase is a showpiece at Chateau de Vollore, Volloreville, Auvergne, home of Michel and Genevieve Aubert de La Fayette. Madame descends from Lafayette and Rochambeau.

Part Five: The Old Agitator

Sixty: A Third Revolution

1. J.F. Cooper, *Gleanings in Europe: The Rhine*, T. Philbrick, M. Geracht, 3-4.
2. Ibid., 256.
3. Buckman, 258-259.
4. *Apostle*, 281.
5. Ibid., 295.
6. Ibid., 307.
7. Ibid.
8. Now Nova Gorica, Slovenia.

Sixty-One: Bitter Causes, Final Actions

1. *Apostle*, 308.
2. Queen Paola of the Belgians, born in 1937, descends from Lafayette through Anastasie.
3. Ibid., 315.
4. Ibid., 316.
5. *Tallahassee Democrat*, Oct. 6, 2002.
6. *Apostle*, 325.
7. Buckman, 278.
8. A. Katzko, *Lafayette: A Life*, 1936. Title page quotation possibly in *Mémoires*.
9. Portrait, *Musée de l'Armée*, Paris.
10. *Mémoires*, V. VI, 763-767.
11. F.R. de Chateaubriand, *Mémoires d'Outre-Tombe, 1848-1850,* Bk. XLII Chap. 3, Sec. 1.

Sixty-Two: A Living Legacy

1. R. de Chambrun, *Pierre Laval: Traitor or Patriot?*, 264.
2. Ibid., 80-86.
3. *The Guardian*, Oct. 16, 1946.

4. Y. Pourcher, *Pierre Laval Vu par Sa Fille*, 123.
5. W. Morrow & Co., 1940.
6. Obituary: René de Chambrun, The (London) Independent, August 17, 2002.
7. Now in the Department of Yonne.
8. See J.-A. Dulaure, *Histoire des Environs de Paris*, Paris, 1838.
9. Six bis, Place du Palais Bourbon, Paris 75007.
10. See H. Donnet, *Chavaniac-Lafayette: Le Manoir des Deux Mondes*, Le Cherche Midi Ēditeur, 1990.
11. M.C. Smith, R. Eaton, "*The Real John Moffat*," Eugene O'Neill Review, V. 31, 2009.

Sixty-Three: The Golden Eagle Returns

1. A. Meunier du Houssoy, e-mail to author, Nov. 1, 2008.
2. See "Sale 5601, Collection de Veil-Picard: *Tableaux et Dessins Anciens et du XIXe Siècle,*" *Christie's,* Paris, June 23, 2010.
3. "They wanted an American-style revolution and they saw [Roger] Winter [executive director, United States Committee on Refugees] as their Marquis de Lafayette." M. Teague, *National Geographic*, Nov. 2010. South Sudan became independent in July 2011.

Sixty-Four: Addenda

Bibliography

Helen Augur, *The Secret War of Independence*, Duell, Sloan and Pierce, New York, N.Y./Little Brown, Boston, Mass., 1955.

Bodinier, Gilbert, *Les Officiers de l'Armée Royale, Combattants de la Guerre d'Independence des Etats-Unis de Yorktown a l'An II [1794]. Service Historique de l'Armée de la Terre, Chateau de Vincennes, Vincennes, France, 1983.*

Brandon, Edgar Ewing, *A Pilgrimage of Liberty, A Contemporary Account of the Triumphal Tour of Gen. Lafayette.* Lawhead Press, Athens, Ohio, 1944.

Brookhiser, Richard, *Gentleman Revolutionary, Gouverneur Morris.* Free Press, New York, N.Y., 2003.

Campan, Jeannette Louis Henriette Genet, *Memoirs of the Court of Marie Antoinette.* Paris, 1823. Online: www.fullbooks.com/memoirsofthecourtofmarieantoinette.html.

Chadwick, Bruce, *George Washington's War.* Sourcebooks Inc., Naperville, Ill., 2004.

Chambrun, René de, *Les Prisons des Lafayette: Dix Ans de Courage et d'Amour.* Librairie Academique Perrin, Paris, France, 1977.

Cloquet, Jules, *Recollections of the Private Life of General Lafayette*, Baldwen & Cradock, London, U.K., 1835.

Cooper, James Fenimore, *Gleanings in Europe: The Rhine*, text established with notes, Thomas Philbrick, Maurice Geracht, State University of New York Press, Albany, N.Y., 1986.

Chernow, Ron, *Washington: A Life*, The Penguin Press, New York, London, 2010.

Alexander Hamilton, The Penguin Press, 2004.

De La Fuye, Maurice, Ēmile A. Babeau, *The Apostle of Liberty: A Life of La Fayette*, Thomas Yoseloff Inc., New York, N.Y., 1956.

Doniol, Henri, *Histoire de la Participation de la France en l'Ētablissement des Ētats-Unies d'Amerique. Imprimerie Nationale*, 1886-1902, 5 vols. Reprinted 1967 by B. Franklin.

Donnet, Hadelin, *Chavaniac Lafayette: Le Manoir des Deux Mondes*, Le Cherche Midi, Paris, 1957.

Dunn, Susan, *Sister Revolutions.* Faber and Faber, New York, N.Y., 1999.

Ellis, Joseph J., *American Sphinx; The Character of Thomas Jefferson.* Vintage Books. New York, N.Y., 1998.

Fontanon, Paul, *Lafayette et la Brivadois, L'Almanch de Brioude*, Brioude, France, 2007. Fruchtman, Jack Jr., *Atlantic Cousins: Benjamin Franklin and His Visionary Friends*, Thunder's Mouth Press, New York, N.Y., 2005.

Gershoy, Leo, *The French Revolution and Napoleon.* Prentice-Hall, Inc., Englewood Cliffs, New Jersey, 1964.

Gottschalk, Louis, *Lafayette in America*, First Bicentennial Edition, L'Esprit de Lafayette Society, University of Chicago, three volumes in one, 1975.

— Gottschalk, Maddox, Margaret, *Lafayette in the French Revolution through the October Days.* University of Chicago Press, Chicago, Ill., 1969.

Herold, J. Christopher, *The Age of Napoleon.* American Heritage Publishing Company, New York, 1963.

Hardman, John, *Louis XVI*, Yale University Press, New Haven, Conn., London, 1993.

Hibbert, Christopher, *Redcoats and Rebels: The American Revolution through British Eyes.* W.W. Norton & Co., New York, N.Y., 1990.

Idzerda, Stanley J., Loveland, Anne C., Miller, Marc H., *Lafayette, Hero of Two Worlds.* The Queens Museum, Queens, N.Y. University Press of New England, Hanover, N.H., 1989.

Idzerda, Stanley J., editor, *Lafayette in the Age of the American Revolution: Selected Letters and Papers, 1776-1790.* 5 vols. Cornell University Press, Ithaca, N.Y., 1977.

Jefferson, Thomas, *The Life and Writings of Thomas Jefferson.* The Bobbs-Merrill Company, Indianapolis, Ind., no date.

Johnson, Steven, *The Invention of Air,* The Penguin Group, New York, N.Y., 2008.

Jouve, Daniel & Alice; Grossman, Alvin, *Paris: Birthplace of the U.S.A.*, Grund, Paris, 75996, France, 1997.

Kramer, Lloyd, *Lafayette in Two Worlds.* The University of North Carolina Press, Chapel Hill, N.C., 1996.

Kropotkin, Peter, *The Great French Revolution, 1789-1793*, 1909. G.P. Putnam's Sons, N.Y.; online Vanguard Printings, N.Y.

Lafayette family, *Mémoires, Correspondance et Manuscrits du Général Lafayette.* Six vols. Vol. I in English. Sanders and Otley, New York, London, 1837. See online: Darlington Digital Library, University of Pittsburgh: six vols. in French, H. Fournier, Paris, 1837-1838.

Larquier, Bernard de, *La Fayette, Usurpateur du Vaisseau La Victoire.* Imprimeries Maury, Millau, France, 1987.

Latzko, Andreas, *Lafayette, A Life.* The Literary Guild, New York, N.Y., 1936.

Leckie, Robert, *George Washington's War.* HarperCollins, New York, N.Y., 1992.

Levasseur, Auguste, *Lafayette in America in 1824-1825.* Carey and Lea, Philadelphia, Pa., 1829.

Lewis, W.H., *The Splendid Century: Life in the France of Louis XIV.* William Morrow & Co., New York, N.Y., 1953.

Loveland, Anne C., *Emblem of Liberty, The Image of Lafayette in the American Mind.* Louisiana State University, Baton Rouge, La., 1971,

Manceron, Claude, *Blood of the Bastille; from Colonne's Dismissal to the Uprising in Paris.* Simon and Schuster, New York, N.Y., 1989.

Maurois, Andre, *Adrienne, The Life of the Marquise de La Fayette.* McGraw-Hill, New York, N.Y., 1961.

Paul, Joel Richard, *Unlikely Allies, How a Merchant, a Playwright and a Spy Saved the American Revolution.* Riverhead Books, 2009.

Parmet, Herbert S., Hecht, Marie B., *Aaron Burr: Portrait of an Ambitious Man*, Macmillan, New York, N.Y., 1967.

Poulet, Anne L., *Jean-Antoine Houdon, Sculptor of the Enlightenment.* National Gallery of Art/University of Chicago Press, Chicago, Ill., 2003.

Pourcher, Yves, *Pierre Laval Vu par Sa Fille.* Le Cherche Midi, Paris, France, 2002.

Rhodehamel, John, ed., *The American Revolution: Writings from the War of Independence.* The Library of America, New York, N.Y., 2001.

Selig, Robert, *March to Victory*, United States Center for Military History, Publication No. 70-104-1, April 2007. Available online.

Stahr, Walter, *John Jay, Founding Father.* Hambleton and London, New York and London, 2005.

Taillemite, Ētienne, *Louis XVI, Ou le Navigateur Immobile.* Payot, Paris, France, 2002.

Taine, Hippolyte A., *Origines de la France Contemporaine*, six vols. Online in English.

Tebbel, John, *Turning the World Upside Down: Inside the American Revolution.* Orion Books, New York, N.Y., 1993.

Tower, Charlemagne, *The Marquis de Lafayette in the American Revolution.* DaCapo Press, New York, N.Y., second edition reprint, 1970.

Unger, Harlow G., *Lafayette.* John Wiley & Sons, New York, N.Y., 2002.

Articles

"The Lafayette-Washington Pistols," *Important American Furniture, Silver and Folk Art, Christie's New York, N.Y.*, auction catalog, Jan. 18-19, 2002, *289-301.*

Sale 5601, online auction catalog, *Collection de Veil-Picard: Tableaux et Dessins Anciens et du XIXe Siecle,* Christie's, Paris, June 23, 2010.

M. Teague, "Southern Sudan's Shaky Peace," *National Geographic*, Nov 2010.

E.L. Schulz, booklet with exhibition *France in the American Revolution,* Oct. 19, 2011-April 14, 2012, The Society of the Cincinnati, Anderson House, Washington, D.C.

INDEX

Page numbers in *italics* indicate illustrations.

Printed in the United States
By Bookmasters